Emotions and Culpability

The LAW AND PUBLIC POLICY: PSYCHOLOGY AND THE SOCIAL
SCIENCES series includes books in three domains:

Legal Studies—writings by legal scholars about issues of relevance to
psychology and the other social sciences, or that employ social science
information to advance the legal analysis;

Social Science Studies—writings by scientists from psychology and the other
social sciences about issues of relevance to law and public policy; and

Forensic Studies—writings by psychologists and other mental health scientists
and professionals about issues relevant to forensic mental health science and
practice.

The series is guided by its editor, Bruce D. Sales, PhD, JD, University of Arizona;
and coeditors, Bruce J. Winick, JD, University of Miami; Norman J. Finkel, PhD,
Georgetown University; and Valerie P. Hans, PhD, University of Delaware.

* * *

Emotions and Culpability

HOW THE LAW IS AT ODDS WITH PSYCHOLOGY, JURORS, AND ITSELF

Norman J. Finkel
W. Gerrod Parrott

AMERICAN PSYCHOLOGICAL ASSOCIATION
WASHINGTON, DC

Portions of this volume are reprinted with permission from "Two Conceptions of Emotion in Criminal Law," by D. M. Kahan and M. C. Nussbaum, 1996, *Columbia Law Review*, 96, pp. 269–374, copyright 1996 by The Columbia Review Association; from *Justice, Liability & Blame: Community Views and the Criminal Law*, by P. H. Robinson and J. M. Darley, 1995, Boulder, CO: Westview Press, copyright 1995 by authors; and from *Judging Evil: Rethinking the Law of Murder and Manslaughter*, by S. H. Pillsbury, 1998, New York: New York University Press, copyright 1998 by author.

Published by
American Psychological Association
750 First Street, NE
Washington, DC 20002
www.apa.org

To order
APA Order Department
P.O. Box 92984
Washington, DC 20090-2984
Tel: (800) 374-2721; Direct: (202) 336-5510
Fax: (202) 336-5502; TDD/TTY: (202) 336-6123
Online: www.apa.org/books/
E-mail: order@apa.org

In the U.K., Europe, Africa, and the Middle East, copies may be ordered from
American Psychological Association
3 Henrietta Street
Covent Garden, London
WC2E 8LU England

Typeset in Goudy by Stephen McDougal, Mechanicsville, MD

Printer: Hamilton Printing, Castleton, NY
Cover Designer: Berg Design, Albany, NY
Technical/Production Editor: Devon Bourexis

The opinions and statements published are the responsibility of the authors, and such opinions and statements do not necessarily represent the policies of the American Psychological Association.

Library of Congress Cataloging-in-Publication Data

Emotions and culpability : how the law is at odds with psychology, jurors, and itself / Norman J. Finkel and W. Gerrod Parrott.
    p. cm. — (Law and public policy)
    Includes bibliographical references.
    ISBN 1-59147-416-7
    1. Guilt (Law) 2. Law—Psychological aspects. 3. Emotions (Philosophy) I. Finkel, Norman J. II. Parrott, W. Gerrod. III. Series.

    K5065.E49 2006
    347.73'75019—dc22   2005037627

British Library Cataloguing-in-Publication Data
A CIP record is available from the British Library.

Printed in the United States of America
First Edition

To our wives, Marilyn and Marian

Plura . . . multo homines iudicant odio aut amore aut cupiditate aut iracundia aut dolore aut laetitia aut spe aut timore aut errore aut aliqua permotione mentis, quam veritate aut prescripto aut iuris norma aliqua aut iudicii formula aut legibus.

Marcus Tullius Cicero, *De Oratore*, II, 178

[Men decide far more problems by hate, love, lust, rage, sorrow, joy, hope, fear, illusion, or some other inward emotion, than by reality, authority, any legal standard, judicial precedent, or statute.]

CONTENTS

PREFACE

Poor Lodovico! That Shakespearean character has witnessed an act—Othello striking Desdemona—that his mind cannot comprehend, for his constructs do not admit the possibility. To Lodovico, this assault no doubt results from heat of passion, but not for good reason; yet a conundrum arises because this Moor is a man whose reason is always in control, who is never shaken by emotion. Confused, Lodovico asks,

> Is this the noble Moor whom our full senate
> Call all-in-all sufficient?—Is this the nature
> Whom passion could not shake? Whose solid virtue
> The shot of accident, nor dart of chance,
> Could neither graze nor pierce? (IV, I, 261–265)

Lodovico is like the Law, we submit, which reluctantly acknowledges that emotions can distort thinking, disable control, fuel motive, and drive action—but nonetheless gives it scant standing in the Law's account of culpability. Rather, the Law's story has been dominated by two determining elements, the so-called objective act (*actus reus*) and the so-called subjective intention (*mens rea*), which must conjoin at the moment-of-the-act for a judgment of culpability to result. With the *dramatis personae* reduced to two, with an evolving psychological motion picture reduced to a still-life snapshot, and with the entwined objective and subjective perspectives reduced to simplistic antagonists, the Law's story ends up looking nothing like what Shakespeare presents on the stage. Moreover, it does not match with the jurors' notions of commonsense justice, nor does it accord with the facts and theories of Psychology.

These disconnects are what prompted two psychologists—one with interests in commonsense justice and culpability, the other with an interest in emotion theory, and both with deep respect for that great psychologist of emotions, William Shakespeare—to come together and write this book. When we began to examine the Law's theories of emotion and its broader "psychology" across crimes, defenses, and doctrines, we, like Lodovico, were perplexed. But unlike Lodovico, we were perplexed because the Law's theories neither fit the facts nor were internally consistent; in fact, in many places, the theories contradicted one another.

For example, when the Law tries to account for emotion in the crime category of manslaughter, we find the Law embracing inconsistent and incoherent theories in the common law and Model Penal Code (American Law Institute, 1962). Specifically, the common law's focus on certain objective provocations that occur "of a sudden" leads to mechanistic and invariant conclusions that such provocations produce the necessary degree of "heat of passion" such that "reason cannot reassert control"—which lead to the normative conclusion that manslaughter's mitigation is warranted; but the mechanistic conclusions result not from factual determinations, but by legal fiat.

The Code's doctrine of "extreme emotional disturbance," to the contrary, presents us with disembodied emotions roiling within the subjective psyche, disconnected from external provocations, with willful minds of their own; this portrayal is no theory at all, and it certainly does not comport with psychological facts regarding the complex interrelations between emotions and objective and subjective factors. The common law seems to mirror Othello's account of himself—as an individual "not easily jealous, but who, being wrought/Perplext in the extreme" (V, ii, 345–347) by Iago's provocations, loses control over his emotions and kills his faithful wife. The Code, to the contrary, seems to reflect Emilia's view that jealousy is internal to the man, as "a monster/Begot upon itself, born on itself" (III, iv, 159–160). Yet external versus internal or objective versus subjective views turn out to be simplistic dichotomies, particularly when compared with the complex theory of emotion and culpability that Shakespeare developed through the play, which his Elizabethan audience embraced, we submit, because it resonated with their understanding of human nature.

In this work, we examine the Law's theories of emotions across some of the criminal law's crimes, defenses, and doctrines and demonstrate that these turn out to be psychological theories, for they advance explanatory claims about the emotional nature of our human nature. We also show that these psychological folk theories are neither consistent nor comprehensive, failing, for example, to account for why emotions sometimes aggravate, mitigate, excuse, or justify when it comes to culpability. Through these "within-subject" analyses of the Law's various theories, we show how and why the Law is at odds with itself, as our subtitle conveys.

But theories, even consistent and comprehensive theories, can be wrong. This is why we do two "between-subject" (or between-perspectives) analyses, comparing the Law's theories with those offered by academic Psychology and by commonsense justice (those theories held by ordinary citizens who serve on juries). Through these comparisons, our broad aim is to inform the Law, suggesting where, when, and how the Law may right its theories of emotion and culpability (as well as its understanding of psychology). This aim should not be confused with usurping the Law or proffering psychological surrogates that would undermine the Law's normative judgments of culpability: in fact, nothing we recommend would replace normative judgments with psychological surrogates. Rather, to paraphrase law professor George Fletcher (1988, p. 154), our aim is not to defeat the law but to improve the law, to realize the law's inherent values. We do bring the empirical *is* to the normative *ought*, because these two realms come together in the Law and in criminal trials. Our view is that the Law's normative *ought* must rest on a human nature that is sound, and this can be done by taking men and women as they are, to paraphrase both Rousseau's words from *The Social Contract* (1762/1950) and Rawls's words from *The Law of Peoples* (1999).

This book has benefitted from our wonderful colleagues here at Georgetown University. Our thanks go out to David Crystal, Rom Harré, Ali Moghaddam, Ray Reno, Steve Sabat, Nancy Sherman, and Jen Woolard for numerous conversations, collaborations, and writings. We also benefitted from the generous assistance and research efforts of our former students John Burke, Liticia Chavez, Keven Duff, Jen Groscup, Shari Handel, Kevin Hughes, Marie Hurabiell, Stephanie Smith, and Matt Spackman. Our thanks also go out to colleagues elsewhere—Sol Fulero, Marsha Liss, and Chris Slobogin— for their research collaborations. A special thanks to Sam Pillsbury, John Darley and Paul Robinson, and Martha Nussbaum and Dan Kahan (Columbia University Press) for permission to quote their works, and to Jim Averill, Thomas Dixon, Joshua Dressler, Herbert Fingarette, George Fletcher, Nico Frijda, Craig Haney, Kathleen Higgins, Zoltán Kövecses, Justin Oakley, Keith Oatley, Stephanie Shields, Richard Singer, and Bob Solomon for their works, which we cited frequently, and for their supportive words. We also thank the book series editor, Bruce Sales, and the acquisitions editor at the American Psychological Association, Susan Reynolds, for their encouragement of this project; our development editor, Judy Nemes, for her suggestions and improvements of this work; and the anonymous reviewers for their suggestions. And finally, we both thank Georgetown University for granting us senior faculty fellowship awards, which provided the time and support to complete this work.

I

DEFINING THE GROUND AND PROVIDING A PSYCHOLOGICAL CONTEXT FOR THE EMOTIONS

1

1

WHEN THE LAW'S STORY OF EMOTION AND CULPABILITY IS AT ODDS WITH HUMAN NATURE

Emotions and culpability were linked "in the beginning"—with the first murder (Genesis 4: 1–16)—but not without ambiguity. As Stephen Mitchell translated the story in *Genesis: A New Translation of the Classic Biblical Stories* (1996, p. 9), "Cain was very troubled, and his face fell" when the Lord accepted Abel's offering of "the fattest pieces of the firstlings from his flock" but did not accept Cain's offering of "the first fruits of his harvest." But in *Genesis 1–11: A Commentary*, Claus Westermann (1984) translated the passage as "Cain was very angry and his face fell," (p. 281) and highlighted "burning envy" (p. 297) as the specific emotion in his commentary, though he noted other acceptable translations. And in *The Five Books of Moses: A Translation With Commentary*, Robert Alter's translation was "Cain was very incensed, and his face fell," although Alter noted that these two "locutions for dejection"—which God repeats ("Why are you incensed, and why is your face fallen?")—are "particularly elliptic in the Hebrew, and thus any construction is no more than an educated guess" (Alter, 2004, p. 30).

However, we do not have to guess about what happens next, for the text is quite clear. Cain led his brother into the field, "And when they were

3

in the field, Cain rose against Abel his brother and killed him" (Alter, p. 30). And we know that a culpability judgment of *guilty* followed. For when the Lord puts His query ("Where is your brother Abel?") to Cain and first receives a lie, and then a smart-aleck question back ("I don't know. Am I my brother's keeper?"), His judgment is swift: "What have you done! Listen: your brother's blood is crying out to me from the ground. Now you are cursed . . ." (S. Mitchell, 1996, p. 9).

Yet the biblical and archetypical story of the first murder does not take us as far as we would like into Cain's subjectivity—particularly into his emotions and thoughts, and their interaction—nor do we learn how these elements affected motive and intent, the act that followed, and the culpability judgment rendered. As to his emotions, we have only our inferences from the words *troubled*, *angry*, and *incensed* and from his *fallen face*. Inferences, though, leave us with doubts and questions. For example, (a) what particular emotions did Cain feel, (b) in regard to what, and (c) to whom (or Whom) were they directed? Was the specific emotion envy, jealousy, resentment, anger, or revengefulness—the emotions that fall within the cluster of vindictive passions that Nietzsche called *ressentiment* (Murphy, 2003, p. 14)—or did the emotions fall within the cluster of shame and embarrassment? Was his anger and dejection directed toward God the Father because, in Cain's eyes, He had humiliated Cain by the public slight, or because He seemed to be playing favorites unfairly? Or were his emotions directed toward his brother, the "chosen one," such that he was envious of Abel's superior offering, jealous of God's regard of Abel, and resentful that Abel made him look bad? Or were Cain's emotions directed toward himself, such that he was embarrassed by his public failure, ashamed by his inferiority in the eyes of the Lord, or guilty about having withheld the best of his harvest for himself instead of offering the best to the Lord as his brother had done? Or were his emotions some combination of the above? Unfortunately, the text does not answer our queries.

We certainly sense that Cain's emotions relate to, if not lead to, the killing, but what is meant by *lead to*? Were Cain's emotions the cause, a significant correlate, or merely an incidental concomitant of the act? Did they play their part before the overt act, by driving his motive and distorting his thinking, or did they play their part during the act, by disabling his control? For example, when Cain said to Abel, "Let us go out to the field," what was Cain thinking? Had his emotions already led him to premeditate and deliberate about killing his brother, and was he now performing the first scene of the soon-to-be-executed fatal act? Or had his emotions led only to a "depraved heart," in which state he may have thought about killing, but had not fully deliberated? Or was his invitation to walk to the field more innocent than those possibilities—merely a brother wanting to talk about his feelings? And if the latter, did Abel say or do something in the field that suddenly provoked Cain to a heat-of-passion killing that the Law would consider manslaughter, rather than murder? Once again, the biblical text falls silent about how Cain's emotions affected his subjective intentions (i.e., his thinking and malice) and how these subjective elements led to the overt act of killing.

And what role did Cain's emotions play in the Lord's culpability judgment, His initial sentence of Cain, and His revision of that sentence following Cain's plea? We know the Lord judged him guilty, but to what degree was the judgment based on Cain's emotions, intentions, and act of killing, and to what degree was it based on his lie to the Lord, his failure to own up to what he had done, and his failure to show remorse? We know that the Lord does not kill him, but He offers no explanation for His sentence: "And so, cursed shall you be by the soil that gaped with its mouth to take your brother's blood from your hand. If you till the soil, it will no longer give you its strength. A restless wanderer shall you be on the earth" (Alter, p. 31). And when Cain said to the Lord—"My punishment is too great to bear. Now that You have driven me this day from the soil and I must hide from Your presence, I shall be a restless wanderer on the earth and whoever finds me will kill me" (p. 31)—we are not provided with God's reasons for revising the sentence by putting a mitigating and merciful mark on him instead "so that whoever found him would not slay him" (p. 31). Once again, we get no answers to our questions, this time about how Cain's emotions and intentions affected the culpability and sentencing decisions.

In this book, our focus is not on how and why the Omniscient One makes culpability judgments, but on how and why ordinary human beings do so. By setting our sights earthward and by focusing on the Law and Psychology,[1] we examine where, when, how, and why that most animating psychological concept—emotion—influences culpability. Our primary interest is the emotions of the accused, and our particular focus is on American criminal law and its theories of culpability, which are embedded in statutes, in the reasons and dicta judges give for their decisions, and in the works of legal theorists. We ask why, for example, emotions sometimes aggravate a murder, making it so vile and heinous that it warrants the death penalty, whereas at other times emotions mitigate a murder to manslaughter, or excuse a killing (e.g., insanity) or even justify it (e.g., self-defense). By moving our focus from heaven to earth we do get answers, but not without considerable work, because the Law's earthly theories of emotion and culpability are neither straightforward nor coherent.

INCONSISTENCIES, CONTRADICTIONS, AND INCOHERENCE

We now briefly illustrate some of the inconsistencies, contradictions, and incoherence among modern criminal Law's theories of emotion, as seen

---

[1] When speaking of Law and Psychology as a discipline with a collective consciousness, with aims and intentions to produce, for example, cohesion and coherence among its laws, or achieve valid theories, then we use capital letters. When speaking about particular laws, parts or areas of law, or particular practices or research within psychology, we use the lowercase.

through different crimes, defenses, and doctrines (Dressler, 2001; Fletcher, 1978). Conflicting theories occur within the same crime category (e.g., between premeditated murder and felony murder, within first-degree murder), between abutting crime areas (e.g., first-degree murder and second-degree murder), and among the theories that relate a crime and a defense to one another (e.g., murder and the insanity defense, or murder and self-defense). For an example of conflicting theories within the same crime category, consider murder, beginning with first-degree murder, for herein the law presents the "cold blooded" premeditated murderer who kills without emotion, purposefully and intentionally. But this image conflicts with the facts about many serial killers, the worst of the worst, some of whom receive the death penalty, who at the time of the act often display strong, hot, and unwholesome emotions that oftentimes drive the act, aggravate the offense, and pose grave risks of future violence.

The incoherence grows again when we include the other murder verdicts. When we drop down to second-degree murder, we find the depraved-heart murderer, where emotions clearly come into play; when we drop down yet another notch, there is heat-of-passion manslaughter, where emotions are more significantly involved; and within the insanity defense—whether it be in the 18th- to 19th-century "wild beast" test, or the 19th-to 20th-century "irresistible impulse" tests, emotions are again strongly implicated. What is puzzling is why emotions can (a) aggravate and add to culpability (i.e., enough to warrant a death penalty) for some first-degree murderers; (b) mitigate intent and subtract slightly from culpability, for second-degree murderers; (c) mitigate culpability significantly, as in manslaughter, and negate the possibility of malice; (d) exculpate entirely in insanity, where we hold the actor blameless; or (e) justify the act, as in self-defense.

Such inconsistencies, contradictions, and incoherence strongly suggest that there is no unifying theory beneath these disparate laws, rules, and distinctions. Moreover, when we examine the Law's folk theories of emotion we find many based on outdated notions of psychology and human nature; these findings challenge the validity of the laws that rest on these folk theories. With the validity of many of these legal theories in doubt, and with inconsistencies and contradictions between theories and a general incoherence overall, we are left with disturbing questions about whether such laws will be respected and obeyed. It is time, we believe, to take a different tack, and use some different navigational lights.

SETTING A NEW COURSE

As we have pointed out, the Law has multiple theories about how emotions relate to culpability, and these theories can be found in common law case decisions, treatise writings, appellate decisions, statutes, penal codes, and law review articles and books. It is our contention that the vast majority of these legal theories, when closely analyzed, turn out to be psychological theories—for they advance explanatory claims about the emotional side of our human nature as they relate to culpability. We illustrate our view later in this chapter and in Part II of this volume, in which we focus on specific areas of the criminal law (e.g., murder, manslaughter, insanity, self-defense, mistake), but now, we offer a few words on theory.

As theories go, one theory may cover a narrow topic whereas another may be more comprehensive; one theory may seem to cohere whereas another does not; one may show internal consistency among its parts whereas another may reveal contradictoriness. There is clearly a need to evaluate and compare theories (both within and across areas of the criminal law) in regard to their comprehensiveness, coherence, consistency, and contradictoriness, and this sort of analysis, which we undertake in this volume, takes us inward, into the Law itself.

But as scientists well know, a theory can be comprehensive, coherent, and consistent and still be wrong. This possibility leads us to a different set of questions, and in a different direction. For example, we can ask, on what psychological facts or assumptions does a particular legal theory rest, and are these facts and assumptions valid? Does a theory rest on an antiquated folk-psychology, long ago proven wrong and discarded? Does it rest on a psychology that was fancifully conjured by some judge or treatise writer without any regard for the empirical reality at all? These questions about validity require us to look outward, beyond the Law to the empirical reality. We perform this sort of analysis as well, using two types of sources.

First, we turn to academic psychologists who have accumulated hard facts derived from their empirical investigations of emotion, and who have built their emotion theories from those substantive facts. Second, we turn to the facts and theories ordinary citizens hold about emotions. Although the choice of this second source may seem surprising, we will defend our choice. Citizens have facts—drawn from their own experiences and from what they hear from others, see on television and the movie screen, and read in newspapers, magazines, and books. Although these anecdotal sources, stereotypes, and prototypes are less representative and solid than the scientists' hard facts, nonetheless their folk theories of emotion and *commonsense justice* (CSJ) theories of culpability turn out to be powerfully determinative of how jurors frame a case, understand the legal instructions, and reach their verdict (Finkel, 1995b). These two outside-the-Law perspectives, one from CSJ and the other from academic Psychology, are critical for informing the Law, we submit, but critical in different ways.

Commonsense Justice Informing the Law

When a judge instructs the jury at the end of a trial, the criminal law's theory and the jurors' CSJ theories meet. This meeting may lead to a melding, when these theories accord, but a clash may result if jurors hold to a significantly different theory. If a clash occurs, jurors may nullify the law outright or, more likely, they may reconstrue the instructions to fit their own CSJ theories (Finkel, 1995b; R. M. James, 1959), although the Law wants neither of these outcomes. The Law has a vested interest in seeing that its law is comprehended and followed. However, considerable empirical research shows that jury instructions oftentimes fail to instruct (e.g., Finkel, 2000b; Lieberman & Sales, 1997), whereas other research shows that even when the instructions are comprehended, jurors still may reconstrue or nullify (e.g., Finkel, 1995b).

This fact leads to an empirical point, and then to a theoretical one. If jurors do comprehend the instructions but still reconstrue or nullify, the jurors could be sending the Law a message—one the Law ought to at least fathom, though not necessarily follow. Through empirical work on such cases, researchers can diagnostically determine jurors' reasons for their verdicts (i.e., what constructs, principles, and theories they are invoking), comparing whether CSJ theories make better sense than do the Law's theories. If the jurors' reasons for their decisions do appear to be principled, coherent, and comprehensive, even more so than the Law's, then this situation raises the remedial issue of whether the Law ought to consider a revision of the law along commonsense lines. There are also pragmatic reasons to consider revising the law: if the law departs significantly from community sentiment, then citizens may lose respect for the law and disobey it—outcomes that some legal and social science scholars have predicted (Holmes, 1881/1963; Pound, 1907; Tyler, 1994).

Psychology Informing the Law

The reasons for using academic Psychology to inform the Law are more complex, but we start with the obvious: validity. Psychology's knowledge of emotions derives from systematic studies and controlled experimentation, and this knowledge can inform the Law about the validity of the facts and assumptions that underlie its theories, and about the validity and generalizability of those theories per se. Put simply, solid substance allows the Law to develop sounder theories.

Our second point is not so obvious. From our perspective, the disciplines of Law and Psychology have much in common. It is not surprising that the Law's theories of emotion and culpability turn out to be psychological theories, for the Law is not, nor can it be, an exclusively normative discipline: in significant part, it is a descriptive discipline, dealing with the complexities of human behavior, in both applied and theoretical ways, much as does psychology. Moreover, the Law's analysis of human behavior is neither superficial nor confined to surface acts alone; to the contrary, the Law's analysis plunges into subjectivity, making assumptions and attributions about the mind, malice, emotions, motives, and capacities that underlie and propel acts, much as one would find in psychology.

Although Law and psychology share a sizable common ground, there are notable differences as well. One difference is that those in the Law are generally far more confident about stepping over the *is–ought* divide—into the normative realm—than are those in psychology, who oftentimes embrace the scientist's value-neutral credo. But the Law cannot reside solely on the *ought* side of the line, living high among Platonic ideals, building airy theories divorced from reality—for part of the Law's very purpose is to bridge the gulf between the empirical *is* and the normative *ought*. Thus, for particular laws to be respected and obeyed by its citizens, their normative *ought* story must portray human nature with fidelity, by taking "men as they are," in Rousseau's (1762/1950) words, rather than by propping up metaphorical fictions or outright myths that citizens reject. That the normative must be grounded in fact is a point that philosopher John Rawls (1999) made in *The Law of Peoples*, when he pointed out that what we ought to be depends significantly on what we are.

In light of what we are, psychology has something to offer the Law about emotions, a topic badly muddled within the Law. For example, psychology can provide some guidance as to where, when, how, and why emotions fit within the complexity of human interactions. Our aim, we hasten to add, is not a guise covering hegemonic intentions, for we seek not to replace normative concepts with psychological surrogates. In Professor George Fletcher's words (1988), our aim is "not to defeat the law, but to perfect the law, to realize the law's inherent values" (p. 154).

SOME ISSUES THAT SURROUND AND GROUND THE EMOTIONS

In a traditional legal text on culpability and the law, emotions would not be a headliner; top billing would go to action (the *actus reus*) and intention (the *mens rea*). We reject this traditional casting as narrow and simplistic, for it relegates emotions to background, subtext, or irrelevancy. However, we do not plan simply to elevate emotions from supporting actor to yet another leading actor that joins the established headliners. Rather, in our approach, emotions are integrated within psychological and interpersonal contexts. They are related to motives, cognitions, and control within the psyche, and to actions and relationships in the interpersonal environment. This approach creates a richer fabric for our theory, one that stretches out in space and time and conveys a more complex psychological story. This theoretical approach, we believe, is more consistent with psychological findings, with what the citizenry believe, and with what Lord Coke (who elaborated the murder–manslaughter distinction in the common law) saw at the Globe as he watched those complex Shakespearean dramas of emotion and culpability unfold.

Contradictory Views of Emotions

Emotion is a strange ontological entity, if it is an entity at all. Some conceive its nature to be substantive, others see it as ephemeral; some believe its origins reside in the body, whereas others claim it is the mind, whereas still others believe it transmutes through both. But it has traditionally been cast in the role of disorder and unreason and thus it has never fit comfortably into reason's account of human nature, civic life, or the law. Whether it be within a Freudian psyche, in which the id, ego, and superego manage a precarious balance through uneasy accommodations, or whether it be within the family, in which the savage child is socialized through informal prescriptions, proscriptions, and punishments, or whether it be within "Law's Empire" (Dworkin, 1986), in which formal prescriptions, proscriptions, and punishments promote responsible civic actions—emotion's primordial chaos is traditionally seen as threatening the harmony. On the large or local scale, whether it be terrorists flying planes into the Twin Towers or merely vandals taking the handles, to paraphrase a Bob Dylan lyric, the dominant view has been that savage emotions wear away at civilization and tear down Law's Empire. Put simply, emotions are negative, particularly when they run to the extreme (Shields, 2002).

But this negative picture cannot be the only one. Folk theory also recognizes, for example, that righteous anger, rightly directed, as in the hands of Macduff, can topple the tyrant Macbeth and restore Law's Empire. Moreover, most people acknowledge that our emotions make us feel alive and can make us better souls and citizens, whereas other emotions keep us alive and lead us to defend ourselves and others (Parrott, 2002). Emotions thus have another face, different from disorder and unreason, and the complexity of folk theories must be acknowledged for a more accurate picture to emerge about their function within the psyche and society.

Emotion's Heat, Its Suddenness, and Its Type

To reconcile these contrary folk theories, we summon a venerable legal phrase, *heat of passion*, suggesting that we may see more distinctly when emotions burn hottest. The phrase *heat of passion* takes us into the interior life, connoting a volcanic font, with its molten fluid, on the verge of blowing (e.g., Kövecses, 1995). The phrase's two terms, *heat* and *passion*, both allude to the intensity of emotions, suggesting that the Law's concern kicks in when emotions exceed some intensity threshold. Still, there must be a difference between the two terms, for if not, then the back-end term (*passion*) would be a mere redundancy of the front-end term (*heat*). If our supposition is correct, then what does *passion* convey that *heat* has not already delivered? Does *passion* suggest that only some (unnamed) emotions, lying within passion's orbit, are of concern within the law's culpability analysis? If so, then which emotions are relevant, and why? For example, in subsequent chapters, we show that the Law treats anger and fear quite differently, and thus there must be different implicit theories about how these emotions relate to culpability. Then there is the question of how heat and passion reach a boil. We do not know if the Law's focus is exclusively on "boil and bubble" (e.g., the *of a sudden* phrase that Lord Coke attached to manslaughter), or whether "simmer and stew" will do just as well, as a brooder such as Hamlet may eventually reach the same intensity as that of the hot-flaring Laertes.

Contextualizing Emotions Within Interpersonal and Intrapsychic Processes

In beginning with the dominant view of emotion as the antithesis to reason and in briefly exploring the possible meanings of *heat of passion*, we have greatly simplified our topic by discussing emotions as if they can be isolated from cognitions, motivations, and perceptions. Within the interpersonal and intrapsychic worlds, emotions complexly interact with cognitions, motivations, perceptions, and other emotions, and these interactions play a determinative role in our theory of culpability.

Outer-world actions engage our interest not only as final acts in a drama but also as initiators of the drama. In the Model Penal Code's (American Law Institute, 1962) story of "extreme emotional disturbance," the focus is on the defendant's subjective world, for that is where the disturbance takes place. But in this story the question that naturally arises is, what caused the emotional disturbance in the first place? Two distinct possibilities come to mind. Either these legally troubling emotions arise from some subjective inner process, or they germinate from objective, public circumstances. If the latter is likely, then the heat of passion is an intermediary step in a process involving the defendant construing an external provocation, which then connects and interacts intrapsychically with other variables, which may then lead to a criminal act.

Understanding emotions as a contextualized process leads to a series of specific questions: (a) Which provocations ought to be taken into account in an analysis of legal culpability, if one assumes that some provocations have been normatively or empirically judged by the Law as not warranting either mitigation or exculpation; (b) what are the distinct processes, and their supporting rationales, that lead to exculpation, mitigation, or no remittance of culpability whatsoever; and (c) are these distinctions grounded in supporting science? A comprehensive, coherent, and valid story of emotions ought to provide an account of how those provocative actions, on the front end (i.e., where external stimuli are first perceived and interpreted by the individual), trigger the defendant's intervening emotions. At the intervening stage (i.e., within the individual, before any overt action), it ought to provide an account of how those emotions relate to and affect our thoughts, motives, and propensity to act. And on the back end (i.e., where overt action occurs), it ought to provide a satisfactory account of how those emotions may lead to or trigger criminal actions, and whether reason can insert itself into the process to control those passions and prevent deadly action.

Mechanistic and Evaluative Perspectives

Not only must emotions be considered from both the interpersonal and intrapsychic contexts but their causation can be considered either mechanical or evaluative. Is emotion mechanistically, even unconsciously, set in motion in some hard-wired reflexive fashion, such that, on the front end, certain actions invariably provoke a certain emotion, and, on the back end, emotions turn immediately into action, immune from reason's reach and control? Or, does emotion, by its nature, contain controllable elements, such that an emotion results from a controllable evaluative process, on the front end, and, on the back end, reason can insert itself at the emotion–action nexus to prevent the action from resulting? If we believe in the mechanistic view (as opposed to the evaluative view), very different implications for the law's culpability analysis follow.

The first view is mechanistic, whereas the second is deliberative, rational, or controllable, though Kahan and Nussbaum (1996) called it "evaluative." Both answers start the heat-of-passion process in the objective world, where a provocation occurs, and thus both root the origin of the process in the interpersonal rather than the intrapsychic. But the similarity ends there, for the mechanistic and evaluative theories generate very different psychologies. In a mechanistic account, a provocation arouses the same emotion in different people. In this fungible view, the provocation is all we need to know to predict the aroused emotion and the actions that likely will follow—for the "average person"—although the predictions may not hold for any particular individual. In a mechanistic view, then, the character of the person and the person's evaluations recede into insignificance, leading to an objective account without a subjective assessment.

The evaluative theory, by contrast, leads to a subjective account, which is likely to be highly variable across individuals, because this account will be deeply influenced by the individual's evaluations and character. In the mechanistic–objective account, we can identify the subsequent emotion and action to the provocation nomothetically (i.e., by what the average person comes to feel and do), whereas in the evaluative–subjective account the so-called average person is seen as an oversimplifying fiction that must be set aside, for we can understand the emotion that follows the provocation only by entering the subjectivity of each particular individual, in an idiothetic way.

These surrounding and grounding issues recur throughout the remaining chapters in this volume. Now some illustrations are needed to make some of these issues concrete. Although we can draw examples from case law or academic psychology, we instead reach to the literary, where a master psychologist of emotions, Shakespeare, tells a tale "of one that loved not wisely, but too well." We are about to see whether that depiction is correct.

OTHELLO, AS A "JEALOUS SOUL"?

Let us consider the following two quotations from Othello, The Moor of Venice (Shakespeare, 1938, III, iv, 158–160), beginning with the one from Emilia: "They are not ever jealous for the cause,/But jealous for they're jealous: it is a monster/Begot upon itself, born on itself." The second quotation is from Othello (V, ii, 340–347), who offers his own epitaph before he commits his final act—suicide.

> I pray you, in your letters,
> When you shall these unlucky deeds relate,
> Speak of me as I am; nothing extenuate,
> Nor set down aught in malice: then must you speak
> Of one that loved not wisely, but too well;
> Of one not easily jealous, but, being wrought,
> Perplext in the extreme . . .

There is clearly a tension, if not contradiction, between the outsider and the insider views. Emilia locates the driving jealousy intrapsychically, removed from the world of external causes, "begot upon itself, born on itself." In her view, jealousy comes from the disposition, not from the situation, whereas Othello speaks of being "perplext in the extreme" (i.e., by those external provocations and lies, engineered by Iago and located in the environment), as he claims that his killing of Desdemona was out of his character, for he is a man "not easily jealous."

But does not Shakespeare show that both the external and the internal are necessary? Surely there would be no Othello, no such noble man who smothers his beloved, if not for the external, malevolent manipulations of Iago, whose reverse alchemy draws base emotions from a noble man. But Shakespeare's drama is internal as well, for Othello's nobility may be more the "seeming" sort than that which is deeply rooted in character, despite what he claims. His ego and hauteur were transmuted into real vulnerabilities and deadly violence, as Iago peeled away Othello's husk and found feelings within that Othello did not suspect—feelings that were *in* Othello, despite his being unconscious of them.

As a contrast, let us consider a hypothetical man, also provoked by an Iago-type, but not subject to Othello's inner vulnerabilities. Our hypothetical man may not succumb to murder as his redressing answer to suspicions of betrayal. Perhaps this man questions his Desdemona with a more open mind and questions his own interpretations of the facts more thoroughly and honestly than Othello did his. And perhaps, after his interpersonal and intrapsychic questioning, this man arrives at no judgment of betrayal at all. By contrasting this hypothetical with Othello, we see the role that evaluation and a different subjectivity may play, which reminds us that hoisting the nomothetic average person to explain an idiothetic emotion may be a mistake.

To make other issues concrete, let us consider another variant. Assume that Othello had not taken his own life and had been brought to trial. The prosecution seeks to prove murder, while Othello offers the mitigating defense of manslaughter. Would Othello's claim succeed? By the text, not likely, but let us hold off on judging his Act V, Scene II, smothering of Desdemona to first consider his striking of her, which occurs in Act IV, Scene I.

Through Iago's manipulations and his manufacturing of false evidence, Othello believes that Desdemona has been unfaithful with Cassio. In Act IV, Scene I, with Iago, Lodovico, and Attendants present, Othello misinterprets Desdemona's remark about the "love she bears to Cassio" (IV, i, 229): he becomes enraged and strikes her. Had she fallen, banged her head, and died on the spot, Othello might well offer a manslaughter plea. After all, his act was of a sudden, with heat of passion rising so rapidly that his reason could not check it. It was clearly an out-of-character action, as Lodovico notes, "Is this the noble Moor whom our full senate/Called all-in-all sufficient?—Is this the nature/Whom passion could not shake? whose solid virtue/The shot of accident, nor dart of chance,/Could neither graze nor pierce?" (261–265). Here, in his striking of Desdemona, Othello's manslaughter claim might well be sustained, but not his smothering of Desdemona in Act V, Scene II.

Why not? For one, he has been cautioned on a number of occasions (by Iago, ironically) to use his head and not his passions, and Othello tells Iago that "I will be found most cunning in my patience; But—dost thou hear?—most bloody" (IV, I, 95–96). He kills neither in heat nor in suddenness, but with premeditation and deliberation, and with the reins on his feelings as he and Desdemona "negotiate" the "when" of the killing. At best, for Othello, the killing might amount to second-degree murder, if a jury finds that he did not deliberate sufficiently, but there is no doubt that he premeditated, which nullifies manslaughter's of-a-sudden requirement. Although he does not rein in his emotions at the moment of the slap, he does in the murder scene, where he demonstrates control, rather than the loss of control.

By pointedly questioning Othello's hypothetical manslaughter claim, we make the Law's implicit theories explicit. For example, are mere words, "informational words," in the common-law language of manslaughter, like the love Desdemona "bears to Cassio," the sort of provocation that would satisfy a manslaughter claim, and is the sight of a mere handkerchief (not of an *in flagrante delicto*) the sort of provocation that would satisfy? If yes, why yes, and if not, why not? In light of the fact that only some provocations qualify, what theory does the Law rely on to support these qualifying provocations, and what facts are relied on to support the view that these generate the necessary heat to upend reason and impair control? And in a cross-perspective comparison, do citizens and scientists make the same distinctions and rely on theories similar to those of the Law, or not?

We can also raise within-area questions to get at the Law's theories and distinctions. For example, we can take the Law's notions about emotions cooling following a provocation, and its presumptions about when reason is back in control, and ask, must the act immediately follow the emotion, or can the act come an hour later, a day later, or 2 days later? Can the killing still be manslaughter if it occurs following a rekindling by a minor provocation (which reexcites the old intense heat), even if the minor provocation is not one of the legally sanctioned provocations, and even if it comes weeks (or months) after the major provocation? And finally, can the killing still be manslaughter if the provocation is only imaginary, such that the defendant brooded on slights in his mind? The Law's answers to these questions will reveal its theories, which then can be evaluated for comprehensiveness, coherence, or contradiction.

Still staying within the Law, we can then make a comparison across areas. Imagine that a judge at a bench trial (i.e., where there is no jury) has rejected Othello's manslaughter claim for the killing of Desdemona on the following grounds: (a) that the provocation was neither of the type nor of the intensity to warrant manslaughter to begin with; (b) that too much time had passed following the provocation and before the act, so that reason and control ought to have been reestablished; and (c) that there was no rekindling provocation in the objective reality, for Othello was a brooder who merely imagined slights that did not exist. Now, let us conjure for comparative purposes another Othello who brooded over delusional rejections and persecutory beliefs and who also kills but pleads insanity. Let us further assume that the judge at this second bench trial finds the defendant's insanity claim worthy and renders a verdict of not guilty by reason of insanity (NGRI). We pose the following questions: Is the theory that accepts insanity consistent with the theory that rejects manslaughter; are the two judges relying on different theories of emotion and culpability; and do their theories reflect a mechanistic or evaluative view, an objective or subjective perspective, or a nomothetic or idiothetic analysis?

MURDER AND MADNESS

Manslaughter and its mitigation can be situated on a continuum where, at the end points, sit other legal stories of great interest in the larger story of emotions, culpability, and law. At one endpoint is murder, which remits not a whit from full culpability, yet where emotion is oftentimes present and hot. At the other end point of this continuum is madness, where emotion is nearly always evident and hot, but where a judgment of insanity remits all culpability. Such madness crimes may lead to an NGRI verdict, which is designated as an excusing condition. There is, however, another continuum, running from murder through manslaughter to the end point of self-defense, where emotion is again typically present and hot, and where the verdict is now not guilty by reason of self-defense, which is considered a justifying condition.

Why these great differences and distinctions when emotion is present and hot in all of these cases? Do the distinctions that make a difference have to do with the meaning of emotion, the type of emotion present, or the degree of heat they convey? Then again, are the critical differences not in the emotion's parameters, but in how particular emotions arise in the interpersonal context and interact with those other inner aspects of our psyche?

A "Distempered Cause" Beneath a "Cold-Blooded" Epithet

We pick up the story of emotions, culpability, and law with first-degree murder, the end point of our two continua. Contrary to the prevalent "cold-blooded" epithet, we find some "hot" murderers at this end point. Think of the most heinous murders or serial killers—or think about Macbeth. In *Macbeth* (Shakespeare, 1938), the main character kills and kills, in his blinding ambition to secure and retain the crown. First Macbeth overcomes his hesitancy and his host's obligation to his guest and eliminates King Duncan while the King sleeps in Macbeth's castle. Murder subsequently becomes easier. He eliminates a prophesied rival, Banquo. And then he kills a rival's wife and children, Macduff's "all my pretty ones" (IV, iii, 226). As the body count mounts, he is less and less able to "buckle his distempered cause within the belt of rule" (V, ii, 18–19).

For Macbeth, as with Othello, both external and internal pushes appear to be necessary to produce action. In regard to Macbeth's first kill, there is no question about the external push he gets from Lady Macbeth, who shames him into overcoming his "unmanly" hesitancy. The witches' prophecy can be understood as an external impetus (rather than as an internal hallucination), for Banquo hears and sees the witches as well. From there on, killing gets easier and gorier. By comparison, Othello's deadly deed appears almost genteel and scrupled, in that he would not kill when his victim's spirit was unprepared. Macbeth, to the contrary, cares little about such niceties, nor about any punishments that might be inflicted in the afterlife; rather, his inner savagery grows, as does the audience's sense of horror.

We (as the audience watching this tragedy and as prospective jurors judging it) are likely to be saddened by the Moor's downfall and able to feel some empathy for his mistaken folly, given that Iago's evil principally brings it out. We are not only able to parse our anger but also likely to reserve the greatest portion of it for the one who steals a handkerchief, rather than for the one who smothers his wife, as the subjective *mens rea* becomes the heavier determiner of culpability than the *actus reus*, when weighed on the balance scale of commonsense justice (Finkel, Maloney, Valbuena, & Groscup, 1995). By contrast, we are likely to feel very different emotions for Macbeth. For instance, when Macduff brings out Macbeth's head in the last scene (V, viii) of the drama, the victors' (and the audience's) sense of justice is vindicated. Yet, in terms of the two characters' emotions, why do Macbeth's emotions lead us to ratchet up our desire for a dramatic death penalty? Why not parse our anger once more, reserving a portion for the witches and another for the wife, for both provide contributing pushes?

In this context, the comparison of Othello with Macbeth surely dooms the latter. But let us consider, as contrast, Iago. Might not a clever prosecuting attorney argue that it was not Othello alone, or even principally, who killed Desdemona, but that it was Iago, acting as perpetrator-by-means, who manipulated Othello like a puppet master, pulling the strings so skillfully and malevolently, with deep-seated hatred and malice and with seething emotions of envy and resentment, yet so controlled by reason in the service of his evil motive? Next to Iago-as-murderer, how does the initially hesitant Macbeth look now?

These sorts of questions bring to light a knotty fact: culpability determinations are not simple and easy sums. Jurors (and audiences) do not work from fixed variables, nor do they multiply them with specified weights. It is a complex calculus, without an a priori formula, in which the equation's variables and weights may vary greatly. We strongly suspect that these judgments of culpability involve the defendant's emotions, though the how and the why of it remain unclear. These judgments are likely to involve contextual factors, including other actors who interact with the defendant. And in framing this case, we are likely to situate this defendant alongside others we know, have heard about, or can imagine, as we try to judge culpability.

When Maddening Emotions Dominate, Culpability Takes Its Leave

On the other end of one continuum lies insanity. Insanity defendants share with many murderers the same acts and heated emotions, though not, allegedly, their *mens rea*. Yet many in the press, the populace, and the political sphere note evidence not only of passionate heinous acts but also of planfulness, which seems to indicate that reason was also operative, raising the question of whether jurors or expert witnesses can tell the difference between a madman and a murderer faking madness.

When the jury rendered a verdict of NGRI in the *M'Naghten's Case* (1843), there were harsh questions from the Queen and the populace about the competency of these judgments, and the *Standard* published the following barb reflecting the outrage:

> CONGRATULATIONS ON A LATE ACQUITTAL
> Ye people of England: exult and be glad
> For ye're now at the will of the merciless mad.
> Why say ye that but three authorities reign—
> Crown, Commons, and Lords!—You omit the insane!
> They're a privilg'd class, whom no statute controls,
> And their murderous charter exists in their souls.
> Do they wish to spill blood—they have only to play
> A few pranks—get asylum'd a month and a day—
> Then heigh! to escape from the mad-doctor's keys,
> And to pistol or stab whomsoever they please.
> No the dog has a human-like wit—in creation
> He resembles most nearly our own generation:
> Then if madness for murder escape with impunity,
> Why deny a poor dog the same noble immunity?
> So if dog or man bit you, beware being nettled,
> For crime is no crime—when the mind is unsettled. (Finkel, 1988a, p. x)

Insanity acquittees share the fact that heated emotions were operating not only with certain murderers but also with most manslaughter defendants. So if emotions are present in murder, manslaughter, and insanity, and the degree of heat is similar, then what negates culpability in insanity? The Law's theory, embedded in its test of insanity, ought to provide the answer. In the case of *Rex v. Arnold* (1723), Mr. Justice Tracy revealed the theory embedded in the wild-beast test of insanity:

> It is not every kind of frantic humour, or something unaccountable in a man's actions, that points him out to be much a madman as is to be exempted from punishment: It must be a man that is totally deprived of his understanding and memory, and doth not know what he is doing, no more than an infant, than a brute or a wild beast, such a one is never the object of punishment. . . . (N. Walker, 1968, p. 56)

The key theoretical constructs are some kind of frantic emotions, which remain unidentified, and impairments in understanding and memory that must be total, that liken true cases of insanity to infants, brutes, and wild beasts. This is a tough test to pass.

When we examine some of the symptoms of Mad Ned Arnold, who was known to the townsfolk to be mad, we find that he was hallucinating devils and imps, and he was also delusional, believing that Lord Onslow was directing those devils and imps to torture him out of all peace of mind. In light of his hallucinations and delusion (i.e., the primary symptoms of schizophrenia, and ones that mark someone as psychotic), Arnold seemed to be an excellent candidate to pass the wild-beast test. Yet, in fact, he failed the test, as the prosecution scored big points with the jury by making much of the fact that Arnold bought pistol and shot (ammunition), which indicated that Arnold had a lucid interval wherein planfulness was evident, showing that Arnold was not totally deprived of reason.

But when we turn the clock ahead to *Hadfield's Case* (1800), we find that James Hadfield also bought pistol and shot, and Hadfield further indicated his planfulness by tracking King George III to Drury Lane Theatre, where Hadfield bought an orchestra seat (with an excellent view of the king's box). He stood up from his seat, took aim at the king, and fired, though his aim, like his delusion (which we are about to describe), proved to be untrue. Hadfield was delusional, but in a different way from Arnold: Hadfield believed that Christ's Second Coming was at hand but that Christ would not set foot in England as long as George III was on the throne. From his delusional perspective, the king had to be removed from the throne, and the illegality of killing had to be trumped for the higher, moral good.

In a legal sense, Hadfield knew what he was doing and knew that what he was doing was legally wrong; Mad Ned Arnold, arguably, did not, and on the basis of their symptoms at the time of the act, Hadfield seems less the wild beast and the more planful of the two—yet it is Hadfield, not Arnold, who gets the NGRI verdict. We now briefly take up the question of why Hadfield was found NGRI, along with where and how emotion fits in.

Hadfield's able attorney, Erskine, wove a masterful strategy. Part of that strategy involved attacking the credibility of the wild-beast test. According to N. Walker (1968), Erskine "made great play with Coke's requirement that 'there must be a total deprivation of memory and understanding'" (p. 77). Erskine first argued as follows:

> If a TOTAL *deprivation of memory* was intended by these great lawyers to be taken in the literal sense of the words:—if it was meant, that, to protect a man from punishment, he must be in such a state of prostrated intellect, as not to know his name, nor his condition, nor his relation towards others—that if a husband, he should not know he was married; or, if a father, could not remember that he had children; nor know the road to his house, nor his property in it—then no such madness ever existed in the world. (*Hadfield's Case*, 1800, p. 1312)

According to Erskine, the wild-beast test was a fiction that did not accord with the psychological–empirical reality, for it did not fit with the true nature and essence of insanity.

Erskine's second argument laid out what he believed was the true essence of madness. In madness, he said, "Reason is not driven from her seat, but distraction sits down upon it along with her, holds her, trembling upon it, and frightens her from her propriety" (N. Walker, 1968, p. 77). Embedded within Erskine's words is his theory about strong emotion and its effects—which distracts and frightens reason from her reigning, and, presumably, reining seat. Within these metaphors is a psychological theory of how delusions seduce and take over, and how the madman comes to reason from false premises, "because a delusive image, the unseparable companion of real insanity, is thrust upon the subjugated understanding, incapable of resistance because unconscious of attack" (p. 77).

In his third argument, Erskine offered a mechanistic theory, with highly questionable assertions about how the madman suffers from what Erskine called *motives irresistible*. He tried to fit Hadfield's symptoms into his mechanistic account, augmenting his words with dramatic touches, so much so, perhaps, that his underlying empirical assertions might slide past judge and jury without too much scrutiny. His courtroom strategy began with an established fact, that Hadfield had suffered brain damage. The hole in Hadfield's head from his war wound revealed his brain, which Erskine, in a nice bit of theater, invited the jurors to inspect; during his closing argument to the jury, Erskine rubbed Hadfield's forehead, literally rubbing in the psychological point that Hadfield's capacity had been shot.

But neither Erskine nor the science of the day could bridge the two gaping causal leaps in Erskine's mechanistic argument. First, he made a questionable leap from brain to mind: that the organic brain damage had caused the mental symptoms (e.g., the delusion). The second questionable leap went from mind to the act: that the delusion caused motives irresistible that compelled the act. Erskine portrayed these results as inevitable sequelae, the mechanistic outcomes of the brain injury; this conclusion clearly overlooked the facts that other brain-injured individuals, with similar amounts of damage to the same brain site, did not necessarily develop delusions of Christ's Second Coming, and even though some brain-injured individuals had delusions of grandeur, probably none, save Hadfield, acted on them by attempting to kill the king.

Emotions turn out to be central in Erskine's defense, at the front and back ends. On the front end, emotions subvert and distort rational thinking, turning rational clarity into "thick-coming fancies," (*Macbeth*, V, ii, 37) because reason's threads were severed by a saber cut. Before moving directly to the back end, let us consider the intermediate step: whatever the constituent parts of *motive* turn out to be, they likely involve interacting thoughts and emotions; moreover, having a motive activated, like being aware that one is hungry, increases the action potential, as all motives do, but does not necessarily mean that a person will eat then and there, or steal to eat. Now we move to motives irresistible, and to the back end. Motives irresistible must be a special type of motive, for, once initiated, they cannot be stopped; here, presumably, is where the emotion overrides, overwhelms, or suppresses reason's inhibiting function. When we examine Erskine's defense more deeply, we see a mechanistic view being articulated: emotions arise from a physical cause, unconsciously, without cognitive input; such emotions trigger delusions and motives irresistible, which can block reason's control; and these motives irresistible compel murder or mayhem, because a causative chain has been set in motion.

A LOOK BACKWARD, AND THEN FORWARD . . . TO A NORMATIVE CHALLENGE

In opening this chapter, we began with the question of emotion's place within the Law's culpability story, a story dominated by its conjoined costars, *actus reus* and *mens rea*. Although assigned supporting roles, at best, emotions are scattered throughout the criminal law's script, and they seem relevant to culpability, in some way. In addition, the Law's emotion theories appear to be psychological theories about the emotional nature of our human nature, though whether they are valid theories, or even coherent theories, is open to question.

We then analyzed the emotions, thoughts, and motives that drove the actions of two literary characters, Othello and Macbeth, and two legal actors, Arnold and Hadfield, all men moved by emotion in various ways to attempt or commit murder. Arnold was found guilty, whereas Hadfield, who seemed more "with it," was found NGRI. As for Shakespeare's twosome, if jurors pitied Othello or directed some of their anger to Iago, they might have mitigated culpability with a manslaughter verdict, but had jurors judged Macbeth, a first-degree murder verdict would surely have resulted, with culpability lessened not a whit. All of these men, with strong emotions operating, committed grave criminal acts, yet different culpability assessments result. Thus, we return to our opening question: What theory of emotion and culpability accounts for this?

We hold that the criminal law's theory of emotion and culpability, like the ether alleged to have filled the regions of space, exists nowhere and everywhere. In fact, there is no single theory of emotion and culpability, let alone a grand unified theory. Rather, multiple theories exist, which, problematically, fail to cohere, and oftentimes contradict. This situation raises an obvious question, one that would be of pressing concern in a scientific discipline: What is the cause of this theoretical disorder and chaos?

We find a number of suspects, with the first being the discipline of Law itself. American criminal law, which evolved out of British law, is part normative and part descriptive. These parts developed and changed at different times, in different directions, and through different perspectives, resulting in a mixed bag of legal and folk-psychological theories, "avowed or unconscious" (Holmes, 1881/1963, p. 32). Unlike most scientific theories, these legal theories were often unsupported by empirical facts and were inconsistent when applied to the same crime, to other crimes, or to various defenses and doctrines.

The second suspect we finger is the way the Law has cast the emotions in its culpability drama—emotions that at best have been minor characters, and at worst, cut from the script altogether. In the Law's culpability drama there are two lead actors, *mens rea* and *actus reus*, who conjoin at center stage to enact the tale of how culpability is determined in the moment-of-the-act. The Law's casting and storytelling is actually quite odd, as can be seen by comparing it with the nonlegal theater. For example, Elizabethan theatergoers well understood that it was Macbeth's "distempered cause," which he could not buckle "within the belt of rule" (V, ii, 17–18), that led to murder after murder; that it was Hamlet's distraction within his globe that so delayed his revenge murder; and that it was Othello's jealousy that killed Desdemona. Emotions were center stage in Shakespeare's dramas, bringing characters to life. Moreover, those emotions arose from a complex interpersonal context, which the character construed and interpreted, and the emotions evolved over time and within psychological time, rather than being provoked mechanistically at some snapshot of time. So, too, on the real-world stage, we submit.

A third suspect is the way the modern criminal law focuses the story on the moment-of-the-act and fractionates the story into a small number of elements that must be proved. This framing constrains the drama to Act V, without there being Acts I through IV. This framing and fractionation differ not only from Shakespeare's dramatic storytelling but also from academic psychology's facts and theories of emotion, as well as from how ordinary citizens relate their narratives of crime and blame (Finkel, 1995b).

Therein lies a rub, or two. For example, numerous empirical investigations with divergent methodologies (e.g., archival research, opinion polls and surveys, studies and experiments) have shown that the disjunction between black-letter law and CSJ not only is real but also has serious consequences (e.g., Finkel, 1995b). A particularly dramatic consequence occurs when jurors violate their oath to follow the judge's instructions and nullify the law outright, because black-letter law's theory of emotion and culpability is out of tune with the jurors' sense of people's real emotional nature. Disjuncts between the Law's theories and those held by citizens, psychologists, and dramatists prompt the following question: How and why did the Law create this kind of story?

This question leads to our fourth suspected cause of theoretical disorder in the Law: the Law did not follow one *emotion course*, but many courses, sometimes tacking to port in one criminal law area, contradictorily tacking to starboard in another area, and ambivalently coming about in yet another area, with its forward movement slowed, stalled, or sidetracked into inlets without outlets. This lack of progress results not from lack of rules but from piecemeal changes in the rules—sometimes a modification of the rules, and sometimes the creation of entirely new rules. These rules grew more variant from one another, in part because heated battles were fought between proponents of an objective approach and proponents of a subjective approach; these battles were fought over centuries, crime-by-crime and defense-by-defense, with oftentimes flip-flopping results. The result has been both a lack of theoretical integration and coherence (i.e., no development of a grand unifying theory) and an avoidance of the empirical issues of validity and generalizability.

Finally, there is a fifth suspect—the weaknesses of the Law's core concept, *mens rea*. In determining culpability, the visible criminal act (*actus reus*) is seldom the problem; rather, the problem is usually with the unseen reasons that move the actor. For example, when someone takes a life, is it a tragic accident or a criminal homicide? And if it is a homicide, did it result from malice, mayhem, mistake, or madness? Answers to these questions require an inquiry into certain subjective factors, such as the thoughts, emotions, and motives of the defendant.

Once upon a time, *mens rea* (i.e., literally meaning *evil mind*) was a robust concept, encompassing not only the thoughts in the mind but also the dark motives and roiling emotions that lay beneath. But over time, many learned hands came to view the concept as failing and in need of fixing, although a few diehards held that *mens rea* could carry the freight (Morris, 1982). One significant fix was that malice, which gave *mens rea* its depth, was cut from the concept's core. But because emotions were tied to malice in particular ways, jettisoning the latter weakened the emotions' connection to this new, lightened *mens rea*. Bereft of malice, *mens rea* was reduced to a *general intent*, which made *mens rea* even less emotional. Still later, *general intent* would fractionate and compartmentalize into *specific intents* (*mentes reas*). The net effect of these transformations, in terms of our disjuncture problem, was that the emotions and motives—which so moved the characters of Homer, Aeschylus, Sophocles, and Euripides, the dreamer of Cervantes, and the schemers of Shakespeare—lost their connectedness to *mens rea*, as literary and legal storytelling about culpability parted company more dramatically. And with the advent of the Model Penal Code (American Law Institute, 1962) in the 20th century, *mens rea* splintered into intentions that no longer hung together as a psychic whole. As for the characters' emotions, they would be considered but an emotional disturbance within the code, as cognitive intentionality commandeered center stage.

If legal theories of emotion and culpability are, as we maintain, psychological theories about the emotional nature of human nature, then psychology must be in the legal game, so to speak. Academic psychology can inform the Law about emotion's place within the nature of our human nature, and its findings can address the processing of emotions in this provocative, interpersonal, and intrapsychic context, in which objective and subjective perspectives and emotions, thoughts, and motives all intermix and interact. From its factual findings and theories, psychology can inform the Law about how and why deadly actions may sometimes result, despite one's assumed control, and it can challenge the Law's questionable assumptions and folk theories with hard facts.

We have also noted much common ground between the disciplines of Law and psychology, for both, in their own way, are concerned with the nature of human nature. Still, an *is–ought* divide generally separates psychology and the Law, and on this topic, that divide occurs at *culpability*. Psychologists have traditionally been hesitant to jump into the realm of value judgments, a normative realm in which the Law is at home and quite comfortable. And clearly, *culpable* is a normative judgment about an individual's moral blameworthiness, a judgment that a defendant is legally guilty under the law and is subject to the law's punishment. But it is our position that this culpability judgment is not completely a normative judgment, nor can it be, for its underlying theory of the nature of human nature rests on a psychological theory. Its normative standard, then, about how men ought to be is grounded in part on men as they are. Therefore, the normative *ought* depends, to some degree, on the empirical *is*. Regarding this empirical ground, Psychology and CSJ can inform the Law, for both perspectives offer substantive theories of emotions and culpability that are important for the Law to note.

This opening chapter sets a new course on emotions and culpability. However, we have presented our position without considering an opposing point of view, and there is a strong one. The opposing view sees the Law as essentially a normative, moral, value enterprise, which contrasts with Psychology's position, which is viewed as a scientific enterprise. Law professor Samuel Pillsbury (1998, p. 11) offered these contrasts between the two positions:

> No one claims, at least not explicitly, that the scientific method can provide moral answers. The scientific method seeks to explain human behavior (among other phenomena), while morality critiques that behavior. Science describes while morality prescribes. This means that if we want an objective test for morals, it will not come from science. Science may give us information highly relevant to moral decision making, but never moral answers.

The staunch normative advocate believes that a criminal law can be created that would uphold our cherished values—quite well, thank you—without Psychology's empirical, evolving, and ever-changing contributions regarding emotions. In fact, those empirical facts and theories are quite beside the point: "irrelevant," as opposing counsel would shout, because causes are not reasons, as the philosopher would say. From this normative point of view, Law and Psychology are simply playing two different games, on two different levels, with two different types of analyses—and Psychology's descriptive facts, and its correlations and causal explanations of those facts, are not germane for the normative Law. But the staunch normative goes even further: that Law ought to guard against Psychology making inroads, for the empirical, like an insidious virus that can infect the system, may subvert or pervert the Law from properly carrying out its normative mission.

This argument is devastating, if sustained, for it would be the equivalent of a quick checkmate, sweeping from the board our position that Psychology informs the Law. We obviously have to defend our position, and in chapter 2, we take up this normative challenge.

2

WITHIN A NORMATIVE LAW, CAN PSYCHOLOGY'S PLACE STILL BE DEFENDED?

In this chapter we present our position that Psychology informs the Law, then imagine how it would be critiqued by a normativist. For the normative position, we could have drawn from a number of 19th- or 20th-century judges and scholars who have been critical of, or disappointed by, psychology's offerings to the Law and its courts. For example, we could have picked the Scottish judge of the Victorian era, Mr. Baron Bramwell, who, in R. Smith's (1981) words, "rejected medical views most forcibly . . . because he considered them to be subversive of justice and society" (p. 104). Others argued that medico-psychological expert opinion was usurping the power of the courts and the ultimate decision of the jurors. Even jurists generally open to medico-psychological findings, such as the influential 19-century jurist James Fitzjames Stephen, who hoped that medico-psychological findings could assist his thinking about insanity and responsibility, found that the links "between theory and description were too weak for his purposes" (R. Smith, 1981, p. 58). In the 20th century, we could have picked law professor George Fletcher (1988), who has lamented that "psychology has nearly displaced moral philosophy" as it "fills old moral vessels of guilt and blameworthiness

27

with psychological surrogates" (p. 62). Or we could have even picked Judge Bazelon (1982, 1988), who opened wide the door to psychological input, yet lamented that he often got unsubstantiated conclusions regarding culpability from testifying experts, rather than facts and intermediary conclusions as he had hoped. These criticisms point to either expert psychological testimony impermissibly crossing the *is–ought* divide, or psychological theory not adequately establishing the *is–ought* connection.

But there are problems with all those opinions just cited. Either these judges' and scholars' criticisms were not sufficiently developed and defended, or their criticisms focused on applied testimony rather than theory, or they did not develop their own normative position sufficiently. Fortunately, we found a critic who not only avoids these shortcomings but also, even more to the point, gives emotions a central place within his normative account of culpability. For the opposing view, we highlight law professor Samuel Pillsbury's *Judging Evil: Rethinking the Law of Murder and Manslaughter* (1998), which presents a sophisticated normative theory of deserved punishment, a challenge to "the causal explanations of the human sciences" (p. xi). As we outline Pillsbury's position, comments and questions are interspersed.

After presenting these opening outlines, we set aside the *Law as it is*, for we and Pillsbury (1998) agree that the battleground is the Law *as it ought to be*. On this *ought* ground, the strengths of the normative position are most apparent, as psychology seems relegated to applied areas and sideline issues, at first. But as this normative theory unfolds, questionable concepts begin to emerge, and an analysis of them will reveal the presence of psychology within normative Law's culpability position—there as a fact, and there as a necessity—because there it must be.

PSYCHOLOGY INFORMING THE LAW, BECAUSE THE LAW IS, IN PART, PSYCHOLOGICAL

Our argument makes three points. The first, a preliminary one, is that psychology is already in the Law, and that the Law seems none the worse for it. Our second point is more fundamental and ontological: that psychology is within the Law's culpability schema because psychology is part and parcel of the Law's dual nature. Put another way, the Law has a descriptive (psychological) side as well as a normative side, and these two sides are intrinsically bound in the Law's essence. These sides are essential to one another, such that the empirical side and its connection can be neither ignored nor severed without harm to the normative side.

Our third point focuses on the relationship of the normative and psychological sides, which is more fully appreciated, we argue, once we step outside of a simplistic free will versus determinism debate or a causes versus reasons divide. Once we do, we see that the normative and psychological sides are neither fundamentally, naturally, tautologically, nor irreconcilably at odds over culpability. Rather, they may inform and enhance each other, because, to borrow Kant's famous dictum from *The Critique of Pure Reason* (T. M. Greene, 1957)—"thoughts without content are empty, intuitions without concepts are blind" (p. 57). Psychology's empirical facts can concretely provide objective bolstering (i.e., the content) for the Law's subjective introspections (i.e., the thoughts) about normative values, whereas clear concepts can improve the relevance and validity of psychological intuitions.

Psychology, as we see it, would have little problem applauding and supporting the Law's enduring normative values; nor would it have fundamental problems working within sound normative parameters. For example, psychologists have made contributions to such normative topics as rights and duties (e.g., Finkel & Moghaddam, 2005), justice (e.g., Finkel, 1995b), and fairness (e.g., Finkel, 2001), topics central to "law's empire" (Dworkin, 1986). Still, we recognize that the Law has other options besides listening to, let alone heeding, psychology's informing findings. The Law can, for example, deny psychology's existence or simply choose to ignore psychology's offerings. The problem with the first option is that denying psychology's existence denies part of its own essence. The problem with the second option is that the Law ends up settling for being less than it ought to be, failing not only on empirical grounds but also, ironically, on normative grounds. In the words of law professor George Fletcher (1988), in putting its best input forward, psychology is engaging the Law not "to defeat the law," but rather to improve the law "to realize the law's inherent values" (p. 154).

The Dual Nature of the Law

Our second point concerns the Law's dual nature. The Law's normative side is so luminous, lit as it is by sacred values, that its other, psychological side may be hidden in the penumbra, or glimpsed as something foreign. We shall bring this second side out from the shadow shortly, but first a few words about the first side.

We certainly see the normative side within and about the criminal law. Criminal laws are explicitly proscriptive, for they tell people what they shall not do and what normative judgments will follow if they fail to heed, whereas implicitly they tell people what they ought to do to meet the minimum normative standards for civic, moral, and legal behavior. The Law's normative concerns, if we situate them within a college curriculum, are likely to be found in philosophy, ethics, and theology courses, where values are central.

The Law's normative values are also found within our foundational documents and on the Law's highest building: they are the subjects of the first two paragraphs of Thomas Jefferson's *Declaration of Independence*, whereas the value of "equal justice under law" is etched atop the United States Supreme Court. These values are also represented in iconic form, by the marble statue of justice, by the courthouse itself, and even by the grave markers at Gettysburg, which not only identify those buried beneath but also symbolically point to those lofty principles "for those who here gave their lives that that nation might live." Those normative values, including what it meant to be a "nation," and a "nation, under God," were the subject of that 2-minute address Lincoln gave at Gettysburg, in which Lincoln so wrongly predicted that "the world will little note nor long remember what we say here" (Fletcher, 2001, p. 49). We need not dwell long on the Law's normative side, because its words and images have been ingrained in us.

But the Law, we assert, has a second side, which, unlike the lofty first side, is earthly and human. This second side can be found in the legislators who enact laws and in the jurists who make law through their decisions. Consider that no deity delivers these laws. Plato does not find their forms through introspection, nor does Aquinas find their natural laws through meditation, nor does Kant find their categorical imperatives through pure reason alone. The makers of this law, for the most part, turn out to be elected representatives, who may open their legislative sessions with prayers for divine guidance, but in the compromises they hammer out and the laws they enact leave a pronounced human and pragmatic mark; it was much the same when our Founding Fathers met in Philadelphia to hammer out certain compromises and a constitution, creating new Law. Supreme Court justices also make law through their decisions, but these unelected Platonic Guardians possess no transcendent wisdom either, as their perceptions and judgments remain subject to human error. We all seem stuck in Plato's allegorical cave.

Now we switch from who makes the law to the content of the law they make. If we look at criminal law, this body of law is about human behavior, and the thinking, feeling, and motives that drive that behavior, and about the capacities that ordinarily control (or fail to control) the behavior under certain conditions or situations; these laws are also about human reactions to other humans' actions, and the sorts of provocations, interactions, and situations that bring these actions about.

In yet another aspect of law, when defendants at trial are judged by jurors as to their culpability, social scientists have documented that jury decision making is a psychological process, not one that is logical, syllogistic, additive, or strictly normative (Bennett & Feldman, 1981; Hastie, Penrod, & Pennington, 1983; Kalven & Zeisel, 1971; Pennington & Hastie, 1992; Schklar & Diamond, 1999). And when judges use their legal decision making to decide appellate cases, they are likely using psychological factors, rather than performing a syllogism or a strictly normative analysis (e.g., Dworkin, 1986; Holmes, 1881/1963; Posner, 1990).

Then there is the matter of what factors are given consideration in the creation of new law. When legislators consider a new crime bill, for example, a host of pragmatic and utilitarian factors usually play a part: community sentiment is typically a factor (Finkel, 1995b), but there are economic concerns, deterrent concerns, prison overcrowding concerns, familial–sociological concerns, and more; with regard to these concerns, a phalanx of social scientists, armed with empirical data, are likely to testify before a legislative committee. These empirical facts are likely to affect the bill and how lawmakers will subsequently vote on the bill, as will facts about where community sentiment stands on the proposed law.

In summary, in terms of who makes the law, in negotiating the give and take of constructing law, in the rough-and-tumble politics of enacting law, in the content of law, and in adjudicating a case—we see psychological beings and psychological processes at work, or psychological beings or psychological processes being described and defined. In all of these processes, the second side of Law, the Law's psychological side, is most evident.

Putting This Psychological Side of the Law Into Context

Let us return again to the college curriculum to see where this descriptive Law finds kinship. We have obviously linked the Law to psychology, though Alexander Hamilton, James Madison, and John Jay, the authors of *The Federalist Papers* (1787/1961), might link this descriptive law with the disciplines of government, political science, history, and economics. Less obvious is a link to language, linguistics, and psycholinguistics, in a Wittgensteinian (1958) sense, for Madison (A. Hamilton et al., 1787/1961, p. 37) recognized "a fresh embarrassment," that

> no language is so copious as to supply words and phrases for every complex idea, or so correct as not to include many equivocally denoting different ideas. Hence it must happen that however accurately objects may be discriminated in themselves, and however accurately the discrimination may be considered, the definition of them may be rendered inaccurate by the inaccuracy of the terms in which it is delivered. . . . When the Almighty himself condescends to address mankind in their own language, his meaning, luminous as it must be, is rendered dim and doubtful by the cloudy medium through which it is communicated.

Madison's point is made painfully clear when the Law attempts, through its words, to communicate its theories of culpability to jurors through its *jury instructions* (e.g., English & Sales, 1997; Finkel, 2000b; Horowitz, 1997; Lieberman & Sales, 1997, 2000). Here we confront an empirical question that transmutes into an empirical–normative question: Will the jurors comprehend those words and understand the deeper, underlying theory, as the Law hopes they will, or will the jurors fail to understand (e.g., Elwork, Sales, & Alfini, 1977, 1982), or will jurors understand what the law means, but use the vagueness of language to nullify or reconstrue those instructions because the law does not fit with their values?

A century after the framers fashioned the Constitution, Oliver Wendell Holmes Jr., wrote in *The Common Law* (1881/1963, p. 1) that a judge brings the "felt necessities of the time, the prevalent moral and political theories, intuitions of public policy, avowed or unconscious, even the prejudices which judges share with their fellow-men" to his legal decision making. Law is linked not only to psychology (unconsciously and consciously) but also to sociology. Holmes identified these factors as forces that act on a judge because the judge is part of the community, and through the judge these forces affect the Law. Moreover, the judge can find no island of safety from these forces, because physically he cannot isolate himself and psychologically he cannot compartmentalize; thus, these forces are going to get through and affect the Law.

This point was extended at the beginning of the 20th century by Roscoe Pound (1907), who would be identified with "sociological jurisprudence" and who predicted that in "all cases of divergence between the standard of the common law and the standard of the public, it goes without saying that the latter will prevail in the end" (p. 615). The realist movement of the 1930s (e.g., Frank, 1932; Llewellyn, 1931) pushed the ideas of Holmes and Pound still further, with its call for non-Euclidean legal thinking, meaning, in part, a separating of the *is* and *ought* for purposes of analysis, so that the Law could clearly see and analyze the Law for what it *is*, recognizing that the *ought* of lofty principles and normative ideals could cast a distorted haze over what is.

Almost every law school bulletin today includes courses in *law and economics*, part of a movement that has achieved prominence if not preeminence in the 20th century, supported, now, by a vast literature (e.g., Posner, 1985, 1990). Law has grown close to economics even while economics and psychology have grown closer, as the study of rewards, incentive theories, game theories, market forces, perceptions, and heuristic thinking crosses disciplinary lines (e.g., Kahneman, 1994, 2003; Kahneman & Tversky, 1982). In addition, the Law, particularly international law, has ties to anthropology and to cross-cultural and cultural psychology, with their mutual interests in diverse legal systems and with how others construe rights, duties, justice, and fairness (e.g., Gibson & Caldeira, 1996; V. L. Hamilton & Sanders, 1992; Miller & Bersoff, 1992; Moghaddam, 1998). And if we look at the factual problems that so frequently come before the Law these days, we see the problems of violence, abuse, and neglect, of one sort or another: against children, women, older persons, minorities, people living in poverty, persons with mental illness, the disadvantaged, the disenfranchised (e.g., Levesque, 2001; Perlin, 2000; Stefan, 2001). These are topics studied by those in the social sciences, written about by those in the humanities, and dramatized by those in the arts.

Finally, we note the connection between Law and literature, which takes a number of forms (e.g., Amsterdam & Bruner, 2000; Brooks & Gewirtz, 1996; Posner, 1988; Weisberg, 1984). Of greatest interest to us is not how often writers, such as Shakespeare or Dickens, use legal dramas in their fiction, and not how often lawyers turn to fiction writing and feature lawyers as their protagonists; rather, our primary interest is in how drama and legal cases are emotion stories, containing an implicit theory of culpability, as we illustrated in chapter 1 (this volume).

PILLSBURY'S NORMATIVE THEORY OF DESERVED PUNISHMENT

Having made the opening moves of our position that Psychology informs the Law, we yield to Professor Pillsbury (1998) for the normativist's story, and face a challenge. We are not the only ones challenged, because Pillsbury also challenges the legal view that would tie culpability and punishment to utilitarian considerations, where empirical considerations would gain easy admittance. Addressing this divide, Pillsbury cited Kant's warning approvingly:

> The penal law is a Categorical Imperative; and woe to him who creeps through the serpent-windings of Utilitarianism to discover some advantage that may discharge him from the Justice of punishment, or even from the due measure of it . . . for if Justice and Righteousness perish, human life would no longer have value in the world. (p. 8)

In his own words, Pillsbury (1998) wrote,

> Modern philosophers have used Kant's approach to develop a theory called respect for persons, which holds that the individual's autonomy— his or her ability to make rational choices—must be respected. Under a Kantian approach to punishment, just punishment is what a person deserves according to the individual's choice to disrespect another. Deserved punishment for homicide respects autonomy in two ways: it respects the autonomy of the victim that was wrongly destroyed, and it respects the autonomy of the killer by taking seriously his or her choices to kill. (p. 8)

For Pillsbury (1998), normative values ought to be the basis of the criminal law, and though he would probably grant us most of our *law as it is* facts, he would no doubt find these points beside the point, for two main reasons. First, he might respond that many of the topics we cited in our beginning-to-end survey—adjudication, construction, and passage of new law—are irrelevant for dealing with the content of criminal law and its embedded theories of emotion and culpability. Second, he might remind us that he is dealing with how the Law *ought to be*, whereas our illustrations seem to be about *how the Law is*, which is, again, beside the point.

Comment and Question

The ground Pillsbury (1998) established, the Law *as it ought to be*, poses a tough challenge for psychology, which is why we take it up early in this book. The challenge, from our side, is this: Can we find, within Pillsbury's emerging normative theory, implicit psychological theories of emotion and how they relate to culpability? If we are correct about the dual nature of the Law, and psychology is an inherent part of that nature, then we ought to find the psychological within the normative law, despite Pillsbury's best efforts to eliminate it.

A Question of Values

We have already met Pillsbury's (1998) Kantian positions on autonomy, respect for persons, and the ability to make rational choices, and why, therefore, deserved punishment follows for an individual who has made a rational choice to kill and acted on it—because that individual has disrespected the autonomy of another. With this groundwork, Pillsbury, in his chapter 1, entitled "A Question of Values," continued on to consider the question: "Where do these values come from?" (p. 10). He proceeded to answer this question as if he were being grilled by a utilitarian. He admitted that the answers are not handed down by the Almighty, nor is there a "universal and timeless human consensus" (p. 10). Pillsbury acknowledged that the skeptic is likely to conclude that "value is nothing more than a fancy word for personal preference" (p. 10), but he went on to give it deeper roots. He wrote,

> We find value in our experience of life. From a thoughtful, deeply felt examination of our own lives and those of all around us, we ascertain certain principles that resonate with moral truth. We find value in much the same way we find beauty or ugliness. These are not insights capable of scientific proof or universal affirmation, but this does not render them fictitious. Value is metaphysical; we can usefully discuss its dimensions, but we will find no impersonal, objective methods for proving or disproving its validity. (p. 10)

Pillsbury (1998) described a complex process, involving observations of ourselves and others. These observations have an objective component (e.g., overt behavior and interactions) and a subjective component (e.g., thoughts, feelings, and motives), though most of the process is subjective, involving reflection, contemplation, and introspection. Pillsbury knew that his response

> seems weak because it seems to challenge two of the most powerful sources of authority in contemporary America: science and democracy. . . . If we cannot test an idea by physical measurement or public referendum, we often dismiss it as personal opinion, something that counts for little in resolving questions of public policy. Such skepticism about subjectively derived ideas bodes ill for the value approach to punishment. (p. 10)

Yet this subjective, reflective, introspective approach is the one he set out to defend.

Near the end of the same chapter, in a subsection called "The Importance of Value Talk in Criminal Law," Pillsbury (1998) used the example of changes in Anglo-American rape law to make his point. For centuries, barriers in the law made successful prosecutions for that offense all but impossible. As Pillsbury wrote,

> In order to win a conviction, the state had to prove that the assailant forced the woman to have sexual intercourse, knowing that she did not consent, *and* that the woman resisted "to the utmost." Most jurisdictions required that a rape victim's allegations be corroborated by a second witness. Courts held that the woman's reputation for chastity in the community was relevant to the offense, which meant that defense counsel could freely question her about her previous sexual history. Through these doctrines the law demonstrated not only distrust of women's complaints of rape, but also a judgment that most instances of coerced sex did not involve severe harms to women. After all, the law rendered the majority of sexual assaults virtually unprosecutable. (pp. 15–16)

These laws have changed drastically in the past 30 years, but Pillsbury argued that neither a utilitarian explanation nor one offered by a social historian can give a full accounting for the changes. Such explanations fail, according to Pillsbury (1998), because neither "addresses the value question implicit in rape law. We cannot give a full account of what happened to the law of rape without speaking of how the law *values* women" (p. 16).

Comments and Questions

We, the authors, happen to agree with Pillsbury (1998), and that makes three. But how do we know that the reason for the law's change is that the law changed its values toward women? Did we arrive at this conclusion through introspection, deep reflection, meditation, or some revelation? And is this way of knowing sufficient to convince others?

There is a second question: What is this "Law" that has changed "its" mind and values in the past 30 years? Answer: It turns out to be all those legislators, in all those state legislatures around the country, who introduced these changes in new crime bills regarding rape laws, and voted to enact these bills into law, perhaps in response to the sentiments of their constituents. Question: Do we know if those legislators were voting their conscience, and if so, were their consciences dominated with concerns about value reasons? Or were they voting, with their political futures primarily in mind, in response to the sentiments of their constituents, as they gauged those sentiments from opinion polls? We do not know the answers to these questions, but we know that they are empirical questions, and neither introspection nor meditation on the part of Pillsbury, Finkel, or Parrott is likely to provide us with grounded answers to them.

Our point, here, is that Pillsbury's (1998) value change "conclusion" is but a hypothesis, which is one of the three he mentions (along with the utilitarian's and the social historian's hypothesis). What is most curious, however—from the scientist's methodology—is that Pillsbury ends up self-validating his own hypothesis—which raises our eyebrows. His conclusion surely would have been strengthened had he had some supporting social science empirics to offer, rather than impermissibly declaring his answer valid. Still, the reader might conclude that in regard to the changes in rape law, Pillsbury's conclusion sounds about right.

But we suggest a thought experiment. Had Pillsbury (1998) lived in the 1920s, or the 1820s, and conducted "a thoughtful, deeply felt examination of our lives and those around us" (p. 10) on the topic of Anglo-American rape law, would he come up with the same conclusions he does today about how the law values women? If not, then the value he speaks about is not metaphysical, but changes with changing time and context, advancing as community sentiment is enlightened "by humane justice" (*Weems v. United States*, 1910, p. 350). This is the reason why the Supreme Court, in its Eighth Amendment jurisprudence involving the meaning of *cruel and unusual punishment*, performs its own social science analysis of community sentiment, gauging certain objective indicia, rather than having nine justices closing their eyes to the empirical reality to deeply reflect and meditate.

But now we turn to Pillsbury's (1998) conclusion about the felony-murder rule. On this topic he stated, "Given the obvious and long-recognized problems with the doctrine, why has the felony murder rule proven so popular in this country? Despite judicial and scholarly hostility, it enjoys wide public support" (p. 108). Ah, but does the felony-murder rule enjoy wide public support, and how does Pillsbury know this? In his two sentences, Pillsbury made empirical assertions, not normative ones, but he backed these assertions with only one citation, which turns out to be an outlier study (Crump & Crump, 1985). Had Pillsbury done a more thorough and representative sampling of the opinions of justices, judges, treatise writers, and commentators, he surely would have reached a very different conclusion, for most have been sharply critical of the felony-murder doctrine (see chap. 6, this volume). For example, the 19th-century Victorian judge, Sir James Fitzjames Stephen (1883), called the doctrine "astonishing" (p. 57), "monstrous" (p. 65), with "little or no authority" (p. 75), and with a "credence gained only from repetition" (p. 38); Justice Brennan, in his dissent in *Tison* (*Tison v. Arizona*, 1987), called the doctrine "a living fossil" (p. 159); and Judge Posner (1988) labeled it "a legal fiction that punishes a felon who is not a murderer as if he were one" (p. 81). Legal and psychological commentators have been even more critical (e.g., Dressler, 1979; Finkel, 1990a; Fletcher, 1978; Roth & Sundby, 1985).

Although these citations may be considered weak opinion data, the data get harder and more empirical when we examine the objective indicia that the Supreme Court analyzed—legislative enactments and jury decision data—as proxies for community sentiment in its decisions in *Enmund v. Florida* (1982) and *Tison v. Arizona* (1987). Despite the Court's 5-to-4 splits in these cases, neither the majority's nor the minority's analyses could be read as Pillsbury (1998) does—as indicating "wide public support" for the doctrine (p. 108; Finkel, 1990a).

Finally, using the most controlled methodology, an experiment, which can yield even harder and more discriminating data, Finkel and his associates (Finkel & Duff, 1991; Finkel, Liss, & Moran, 1997; Finkel & Smith, 1993) tested various felony-murder scenarios with college students, adults, and even children, and found widespread lack of support for felony murder in terms of measures of culpability (verdict) and sentencing (punishment), and the participants' reasons for their decisions revealed moral values. In specific terms, the vast majority of these citizens held that deserved punishment ought to be proportional to what each defendant intended and did. The only widespread support for the felony-murder rule comes from prosecutors, who find it ever so easy to gain first-degree murder convictions under this rule, because all they have to prove is intent to commit the underlying felony (e.g., robbery) and that a death occurred in the commission of that offense.

On this topic of felony murder, Pillsbury (1998) has entered the realm of the empirical to support his assertion, but his claim fails because the facts fail to support his contention. But our point should be clear: once the normativist crosses the normative–empirical (*is–ought*) divide into the realm of the empirical *is* to find support for his *ought* notions, psychology's facts would be informing, if not dispositive; on this ground, introspections and deep reflections do not validate.

Moral Choice Versus Moral Capacity

It is time to return to normative ground, to the heart of Pillsbury's (1998) normative culpability theory. This complex theory is hard to explicate, and we will do so in parts, by drawing certain contrasts. We begin with the concept of choice, which has long been mired in a free will versus determinism debate, with various attempts to reconcile that debate. Pillsbury, as a normativist, obviously rejects determinism, which views actions as caused by influences (in the environment or in genetics) that humans have not chosen and do not control; this determinist position would eliminate responsibility and culpability, which is an untenable position for the normativist, who believes humans make choices for which they are responsible.

But Pillsbury (1998) was not going to defend free will by amassing more and better arguments; rather, he adopted the position that both sides have framed the debate to include the assumption of the possibility that free will can be negated—when, in fact, "we cannot live without it" because "our form of conscious, rational life commits us to a belief in responsible choice"

(p. 29). Many determinists are likely to object to this proposition, which they would see as legerdemain—by which Pillsbury's prestidigitation transforms his position into an implicit metaproposition—that allows him to lift it out of the debate and place it into the untouchable category of *a given*. We, however, will grant Pillsbury's assumption, and see where he goes with it.

Where he goes with it is to an illustration, from the 1924 case of Nathan Leopold and Richard Loeb, to make the point that Leopold and Loeb's motives in killing Bobby Franks

> met the basic requirements of deserved punishment because each of them purposefully, without external coercion, and for rational, immoral reasons, participated in the killing of another human being. In so doing, Leopold and Loeb challenged the value of human life that society is formed, in significant measure, to defend. (p. 33)

The two decided to commit the perfect crime, and planned it for months. They had "resolved to kidnap and kill a rich boy and then collect a ransom from his family" (Pillsbury, 1998, p. 32). Pillsbury went on to argue against a view that Leopold and Loeb "lacked the capacity to feel for others, and therefore could not see the wrongness of their conduct" (p. 33). His position shuts the door on any exculpating or mitigating defense for the psychopath. However, Pillsbury wanted to shut the door on capacity defenses generally, for if that door is not closed, then the courtroom would be open to expert testimony about defendants with bona fide mental disorders (American Psychiatric Association, 1994), and about how these disorders impair the defendants' capacities, which would only encourage creative lawyers and imaginative clinicians to come up with new syndromes. Pillsbury did not mention the gatekeeping function of the Supreme Court's *Daubert* decision (*Daubert v. Merrell Dow Pharmaceuticals*, 1993) nor the Court's criteria to aid the judge in discriminating good science from junk science. We presume that Pillsbury would reject that decision and its discriminating criteria as a wrongful decision, or try to cast it as merely the Law *as it is*, although it is hard to see the Court not placing a value on good scientific testimony.

Pillsbury's (1998) primary reason for wanting to shut the door on considerations of capacity in culpability was that such considerations misdirect the law's proper focus from what the defendants did and why they did what they did to considerations of who they are (e.g., they are young) and what they are (e.g., they are sick). However, despite his intentions, Pillsbury could not—and did not—shut the door on capacity considerations completely. He acknowledged that deserved punishment follows because humans (a) are rational moral actors who make moral choices, (b) are members of society with obligations to society, and (c) know the social norms and the laws. To paraphrase Pillsbury, we as humans have experience with choice, with human interaction, and we know enough about how our actions produce reactions: we know that if we inflict harm, someone feels pain. We are moral actors, then, because we understand the moral dimension of our conduct.

Comments and Implications

This is all well and good—for ordinary adults—but we human beings are not born as moral actors, for moral capacity develops. The Supreme Court has recognized and reaffirmed an age line (at age 7), which was fixed in the common law and recognized at the time of the Bill of Rights, in the Court's consideration of the constitutionality of the death penalty for juveniles (e.g., *Thompson v. Oklahoma*, 1988; *Stanford v. Kentucky*, 1989; *Roper v. Simmons*, 2005); this age line serves, however imperfectly, as that moral capacity discrimination line.

Pillsbury (1998), aware of the developmental problem, excused the very young because they have not had the necessary experiences and interactions with life, and have not learned enough of those vital social norms and laws; in short, they have not become full moral choosers. Pillsbury then opened the door to others, implicitly or explicitly, who either have not become full moral choosers or may have been moral choosers at one time but whose moral capacity has now become severely impaired. Although Pillsbury does not specifically mention mentally retarded individuals, presumably some of these persons might fail his requirement test (e.g., *Jackson v. Indiana*, 1972; *Penry v. Johnson*, 1999), because their cognitive and social capacities either have been like the child's since birth or became impaired later as a result of illness or brain insult. Adding to his list of capacity exemptions, he gave examples of "some instances of brainwashing or organic brain damage" (p. 45) that might also fail to meet his requirement. And he mentioned the insane as failing his test as well:

> Even if they are dangerous to others, crazy persons do not engage us in a dialogue about moral meaning. They seem to live in a different reality than ours, making communication by words or actions virtually impossible. In a moral sense, the actions of the crazy seem meaningless. (p. 37)

In regard to the allegedly insane, Pillsbury was more generous than we are (see chaps. 8 and 9, this volume), and, as it turns out, far more overinclusive than the commonsense justice turns out to be.

With grudging recognition and against his professed wish, Pillsbury (1998) recognized that his universal rule must bend to accommodate some obvious exceptions, and even some questionable exceptions (e.g., brainwashing). Thus he ended up opening the door to capacity considerations, and, as a result, many individuals from the groups he listed might fail his test of being a moral chooser, and these individuals may walk out of the courtroom without any culpability judgment rendered for their alleged criminal actions. Each of these groups may be overinclusive, and the number of groups grows beyond Mr. Justice Tracy's "infants, brutes, and wild beasts" (*Rex v. Arnold*, 1723), those who were exempt under the wild-beast test of insanity. Worse yet, for Pillsbury, is who walks into the courtroom to help the Law make this determination, for here is the normativist's worst nightmare: the specter of one psychological expert after another testifying at all those competency hearings about the defendant's capacity and how it relates to culpability—when scientific psychology was supposed to be on the sidelines, out of bounds in this normative Law. Still, this opening of the capacity door, Pillsbury might claim, merely allows psychology to play a role in the applied realm, in *Law as it is*, by assisting in the adjudication process; Psychology, he might claim, is not yet in the content of the normative *Law as it ought to be*, in its theory of emotions and culpability. But in turning to Pillsbury's arguments for "moralizing the passions" (p. 62) and for a "motive analysis" (p. 122), which are the core arguments in his normative theory, we will show that these arguments put psychology into the content of the normative *Law as it ought to be*. In the end, we agree with Pillsbury's normative positioning of emotions and motives in a culpability schema, but we argue that very different implications follow.

Moralizing the Passions, and a Motives Versus *Mens Rea* Analysis

Following his discussion of the Leopold and Loeb case, Pillsbury (1998) gave the reader a foreshadowing of what was to come. He stated that "Punishment is fundamentally a way of making public morality real. It is an argument, backed by force, that autonomy must be valued" (p. 34). This view works, he said, "on an emotional level," for if "our anger is morally based, it provides a legitimate motivation for punishment" (p. 36). Here he began to link emotion and motivation, though in the previous instance, they are jurors' emotions and motives. But at the heart of his culpability theory, he was concerned with the defendant's emotions and motives: emotions that have, at times, moral meanings, and that should not be ignored within a normative Law, and motives that similarly should not be ignored, as they often are ignored under a *mens rea* analysis, for motive goes to the morality of the act and explains why the defendant did what he or she did, and why the culpability judgment and punishment that follow make moral sense.

Regarding moralizing the passions, Pillsbury (1998) was quite aware that he was going against legal tradition, in which the "passions of law" (Bandes, 1999) are generally suppressed, and dicta state that the law ought to act on reason alone, for the passions are typically regarded as primitive, unruly, irrational, bloodthirsty, vengeful, and oftentimes unconscious. In this traditional view, Pillsbury wrote, "Courts generally distrust the influence of emotion because they, like many philosophers, view emotion as the opponent of reason" (p. 65). But in Pillsbury's view, emotions may or may not have moral content, and thus "emotions may assist moral judgment, or hinder it. We need to recognize when emotions have moral content and when they do not" (p. 63). Thus, Pillsbury did not view emotion and reason as "irreconcilable opponents," for he saw them as representing "rival but closely related modes of human understanding, including understanding of morality" (p. 65). In other words, emotions, with their own rationality, should not be ignored in a normative theory of culpability.

Pillsbury (1998), perhaps without acknowledging it, incorporated a view of emotion as old as that of the Stoics, who saw reason and evaluation as central in the formation of emotion. More to the point, he failed to recognize that this evaluative, cognitive view of emotions is quite dominant in modern psychology's view of emotion (see chaps. 3, 4, and 5, this volume). This lack of understanding of the psychology of emotions contributes to straw-man casting of psychology as a mechanistic anathema to making proper moral judgments.

What do emotions, in the positive sense, have to offer the Law? Pillsbury (1998) told us that they "help us make sense of the world"; "connect our inner life to events in the world beyond us"; "ground meaning"; "bring responsibility to life"; and "represent the electric current that connects normative theory—general ideas about right and wrong—to personal experience: how we feel about a particular issue" (p. 66). He then cited the development by philosophers and psychologists of

> cognitive theories of emotion as a way of understanding the particular rationality of emotional reactions . . . [whereby the] emotion depends on a perception of some aspect of the world that can be judged correct or incorrect according to rational principles. Emotion under this view involves a rational assessment of a person or situation, associated with a physical sensation, normally accompanied by a desire to undertake a particular kind of action. (p. 66)

Pillsbury was clearly invoking the deliberative, rational, controllable, and evaluative view of emotions in contrast to the mechanistic view (see chap. 1, this volume).

Understanding emotions is important in two ways, though both pose clear and present dangers. In one way, if we want to understand why a defendant did what he did, emotions serve as useful telltales of motivation, which is what jurors will have to judge in Pillsbury's (1998) theory of culpability. For instance, signs of emotion or lack of emotion would be important in determining whether or not heat of passion or extreme emotional disturbance existed in a manslaughter determination. One danger is that these telltales are not perfectly reliable indicators.

In a second way, it is important to understand one's own emotions, particularly for jurors making culpability judgments on defendants' alleged criminal acts. Such an understanding is important because of the dangers of emotions, and how they may conflict with the law and its requirements: emotions are "personal," "prereflective," and typically involve "simple judgments," whereas the law "consists of universal rules" and "requires deliberate decisions based on articulated reasons," and its "decisions about guilt and innocence are usually complex" (Pillsbury, 1998, p. 67). As Pillsbury noted, the law seeks to guard against "irrational emotions" and "self-deceptive emotions" (p. 68), and through the use of role and rule, the law's best hope is to make the emotive influence self-conscious. Pillsbury made three recommendations to maximize the benefits and minimize the dangers. "In order to moralize the passions of punishment, criminal rules should meet three criteria: (a) they should be clearly stated; (b) they should be morally evocative; and (c) they should be act and not character based" (p. 72).

With the dangers minimized, Pillsbury (1998) made his strong claim for why emotions must have a place within this normative Law. They help make the criminal rules "morally evocative," addressing "the most important moral considerations involved in the wrongdoing" (p. 74). For

> unless the law encompasses our best moral intuitions, it loses its best opportunity for emotive regulation. When the law articulates our otherwise inchoate moral sensibilities, it provides a way of questioning less worthy emotions. It provides a basis for discussion of feelings and the connection between those feelings and proper judgments. (p. 74)

We now turn to the motives versus *mens rea* issue. The problems with *mens rea* are old ones (e.g., in 1477, Chief Justice Brian said, "The thought of man is not triable; the devil alone knoweth the thought of man" [Hart, 1968, p. 188]), and they have been reviewed in detail elsewhere (e.g., Dressler, 2001; Finkel, 1988a; Fletcher, 1978). Pillsbury (1998) objected to *mens rea*, particularly in its analytic style, which seems too dispassionate—for it is denuded of emotions, motives, and morals. Pillsbury contrasted this analytic style with the older allusive style, in which moralistic and emotive terms such as *malicious, depraved, willfull,* or *wanton* were relied on heavily (p. 84). The continuing trend toward the analytic style is exemplified in the Model Penal Code (American Law Institute, 1962), which includes "a hierarchy of four basic forms of culpability: purpose, knowledge, recklessness, and negligence" (Pillsbury, 1998, p. 84).

Pillsbury (1998) went against this trend, favoring a more allusive style, because he wanted the moral meaning of the law to be clear. It is not thoughts or intentions that best make the act's immorality clear, but the motive for the act—why the defendant did what he or she did. As Pillsbury wrote,

> Motive is relevant to culpability in murder because it reveals the depth and nature of the offender's attack on value. The worst motives for killing are those that demonstrate the greatest commitment to individual or community disregard. The worst killings express a philosophy deeply hostile to individual human value and usually to the value of the community. Such a killing expresses the view that human existence has no moral dimension, that life is simply the war of all against all. (p. 112)

Implications

Pillsbury (1998) situated emotions and motives centrally in his theory of culpability for normative reasons, and we have no objection to his placement. But once one commits to a consideration of emotions and motives on moral grounds, one thereby requires these ordinary citizens-turned-jurors to engage in a sophisticated psychological assessment process in which they must make inferences and attributions from overt acts to those inner emotions and motives. Pillsbury acknowledged that

> adding motive to mens rea does make criminal decision making more difficult . . . [as] jurors must not only determine whether a particular motive played a role in the conduct, but also how important a role . . . [and this] does require the decision maker to look further into the background of the defendant's conduct. (p. 122)

Yet he believed that careful definition of motive "will limit the depth of the motive inquiry" (p. 121). But as we see it, Pillsbury's requirements commit the jurors to perform two tasks, in a particular sequence: before they begin their normative inquiry, the jurors' first task must be a psychological inquiry.

Still, our more important point addresses the content of Pillsbury's (1998) theory of culpability, which turns out to be as much a psychological theory as it is a normative theory, for his central concepts of emotion and motive not only are deeply rooted within the scientific discipline of psychology but also function within his theory as psychological constructs. For example, this emotion construct relates to provocations, on the front end; thinking, motives, and bodily states, at the intermediate level; and control, at the back end. A judgment of moral culpability assumes choice, which presumes that the individual made some evaluation of his or her emotions, however fleeting. These emotions could be neither prereflective emotions nor emotions that mechanistically (i.e., reflexively) triggered actions, for the former would fall into that category of "emotions having no moral meaning," whereas the latter would fall into the category of "emotions for which we would find no culpability" (i.e., because they could not be controlled). Thus, what discriminates the moral, culpable emotions from those that have no moral meaning are our psychological judgments. To construct the moral meaning of emotions, we must construct the psychological meaning of emotions from the psychological drama in which they arise.

We shall make our point of disagreement with Pillsbury (1998) more concrete through an example. In the play *Othello*, the characters of Iago, Othello, and Desdemona all have emotions. Yet the key question in Pillsbury's theory is this: Do emotions have moral meanings, in terms of culpability? Does Desdemona, for example, through her emotions, motives, and actions, bear some culpability for what transpired, including her own death? For the readers of the play (i.e., the jurors) to make that judgment, they have to make a psychological assessment, involving inferences from the interpersonal context to the subjective, psychological interior. Only when they construct the character's psychological inner life—of emotions, motives, and thoughts—can they then render the normative judgment. In our analysis of

Pillsbury's schema, psychology has not been eliminated. Far from it. Rather, within Pillsbury's schema, a psychological analysis is both the prerequisite first step and a necessary step to get to the normative.

A BRIEF SUMMARY AND LOOK AHEAD

This psychological aspect within the normative theory was nowhere in sight at the outset of this chapter. However, when the central concepts of emotions and motives were critically examined, the psychological emerged, within the heart of the normativist's theory of culpability. It not only emerged but also provided the underpinning for the normative argument—because determining whether emotions had moral meaning required, as a first step, a psychological assessment of the psychological meaning of the emotions and their psychological interrelations with provocations, thoughts, motives, states, control, and actions.

At the end, we do have some points of agreement with Pillsbury's (1998) normative theory. First, Pillsbury underscored the failure of the analytic approach, which relies on conceptions of *mens rea* and intent that denude culpability of considerations of motive and emotion, an approach that fails to get to the moral meaning of the act. These conceptions are too superficial, reflecting a surface-level approach, when we need to go deeper. Second, his culpability theory is quite psychological, for he brought emotions and motives in as necessary elements for a thorough analysis of culpability, which takes us deeper, to *mens*, at a mid-level. And third, neither Pillsbury nor we are advocating going all the way down to the deepest third level to make a moral judgment on the defendant's deep character, "the most basic evil of character [that] Kant calls 'radical evil'" (Murphy, 2003, p. 11). Though Pillsbury cited Kant approvingly in many places, his position (like ours) turns out to be more Aristotelian, which recognizes that character states "may be basic aspects of character, not because of free choice that one has made but because of the luck of the kind of character education (habituation) experienced by the possessor" (Murphy, 2003, p. 11), and thus our capacity as moral choosers can be limited or diminished. Thus Pillsbury granted certain exclusions.

A major disagreement we have concerns the second, midlevel, where, as we have shown, the psychological assessment is the necessary first step before the moral judgment can be made. The disagreement is over the empirical aspect of the judgment, and then over whether and how the empirical can and should inform the normative. We clearly reject Pillsbury's (1998) assertion, made in a section called "The Psychological Approach," that during

> the second half of the twentieth century a number of Anglo-American jurisdictions were influenced by what may be called the psychological

approach to provocation. Instead of emphasizing the nature of the provoking incident and character of the reasonable man, the psychological approach focused more on the intensity of emotion experienced by the accused and its impact on his choice-making abilities. (p. 131)

Pillsbury's characterization of the psychological approach is far from accurate, for what he claims is not at all the dominant approach of scientific psychology. Pillsbury barely scratched the surface of what cognitive psychologists have contributed to the study of emotions, and he failed to cite any references whatsoever to the enormous literature that social psychology has contributed to the study of emotions. Rather, what his characterization more accurately portrays is the Law's own folk-psychological approach, which is a "psychology" decades or a century out of date, and the Law's folk psychology is the topic of chapter 3 (this volume).

Law professor Samuel Pillsbury's (1998) misunderstanding of academic psychology is not an isolated example. Law professor George Fletcher (1988), whose legal thinking we also respect and whose writings we frequently cite in this work, also miscast psychology as that discipline in this age that has "nearly displaced moral philosophy" (p. 62). Such a review lends support to the subjectivists' false view, says Fletcher, "that guilt and blame must be mirrored in the offender's thoughts" (p. 61), which "consists in a state of mind" (p. 62) rather than "on self-control" and "whether he could and should have acted otherwise under the circumstances" (p. 61). Fletcher claimed that the discipline of psychology (a) does not support self-control, (b) does not see individuals "having the capacity to act other than they have acted," (c) takes the position that if "someone makes a mistake, then the mistake 'must have been in the cards,'" and (d) believes that if "he acts wrongly, then it must have been the case that he would act wrongly" (p. 61). This casting of psychology sees humans as caused, bound, and determined, without evaluative choice to do otherwise, and removed from responsibility for their mistakes and negligence. This casting is also a false caricature of academic psychology.

We have seen that important legal scholars have misunderstood academic psychology's views on emotions and how they both relate to evaluations, cognitions, motives, self-control, and responsibility and exaggerate how psychological surrogates will replace moral concepts and usurp culpability. But the Law oftentimes does not recognize or properly understand the folk-psychological theories it employs, or the folk-psychological theories of emotions that jurors bring with them to the courtroom. This being the case, it is time that we turn our attention directly to the topic of emotions, in some detail. In chapter 3 of this volume, "Emotions in Folk Psychology," we look at the origins of emotion, and of these folk theories, and begin to draw connections to those legal concepts. In chapter 4, "Emotions in Academic Psychology: Implications for Culpability and the Law," we explore different approaches to and aspects of emotions, their effects, and the current contentions within the Law. In chapter 5, "Emotions in Context: Time, Function, and Type," we draw distinctions among emotions that appear relevant for various criminal law issues.

3

EMOTIONS IN FOLK PSYCHOLOGY

The concept of emotion shapes the Law in many ways, but it is not the academic psychologist's concept that has this influence. The Law incorporated ideas about emotion long before academic psychology even existed. Even now, the major source of the Law's ideas about emotion is not academic psychology: it is folk psychology, the ordinary person's understanding of emotion and its effects. Folk psychology can certainly be influenced by academic psychology, but that is just one of folk psychology's many sources. The goal of this chapter is to explore the concept of emotion and its development over history, a goal whose importance can be gleaned by considering some of the ways that the folk concept of emotion influences the Law.

Sometimes the concept of emotion is ingrained in the Law itself. The notion of the *heat of passion* is central to the definition of the crime of manslaughter. The lack of emotional concern for others' well-being constitutes the callous disregard for human life that defines second-degree, *depraved-heart* murder. Beliefs about the nature of strong emotion form the basis of the Law's wild-beast and irresistible-impulse tests of insanity. Even basic legal concepts such as that of the "ordinary, reasonable person" incorporate ideas about when emotion is appropriate and how it should be expressed. Yet, academic psychologists do not speak of depraved hearts, nor measure the heat of passion, nor theorize about the capacity of human nature to be reduced to that of a wild beast. These ideas all derive from folk psychologies that existed during the development of the Law.

In other cases the concept of emotion has led the Law to exclude emotion. The folk category of emotion can appear to threaten the orderly rule of law, for it carries with it the irrationality of primitive impulses and the indeterminacy of subjective states. These perceived threats account for why the Law sometimes omits emotion in favor of more cognitive criteria, for the Law's timid psychologizing with *mens rea*, and for many legal theorists' aversion to academic psychological approaches to emotion (e.g., Fletcher, 1988; Pillsbury, 1998). Yet, as we saw in chapter 2 (this volume), folk understanding of emotions also enters into the thinking of legal scholars. Writers such as Pillsbury and Fletcher drew, knowingly or not, on folk conceptions of emotion even while denying the relevance of academic research on emotion. Legal scholars cannot be expected to be immune from this influence when even the research of academic psychologists and philosophers is influenced by folk conceptions of emotion (Averill, 1974; Parrott & Schulkin, 1993). Before these influences can be understood, then, the everyday concept of emotion must be explicated.

The folk conception of emotion shapes the Law in a third way as well. It seeps into the legal system through the understanding of the people involved in the legal system. Everyday ideas about emotion shape how judges and legislators think about guilt, mitigation, exculpation, and justification. Jurors, untrained in the Law, bring their everyday notions of emotions into the courtroom to make decisions about culpability, even when the Law officially does not. Jurors use folk conceptions of emotion to impose sense on the testimony, to construct an understanding of events and intentions, and to evaluate the culpability of the defendant. To understand these influences, we must turn, first, to folk psychology, and not to academic psychology.

Thus, folk psychology is the primary source of the ideas about emotion that have influenced the Law. Fortunately, folk conceptions of emotion have been the topic of considerable research by academics, not only in psychology but also in other disciplines. Everyday theories of emotion change over time and can differ between cultures, so, before their influence on the American and British legal systems can be understood, it is critical to explore their history, complexity, and cultural variability. Academic psychology has, of course, also researched the nature of actual emotional states, but this research is reserved for subsequent chapters. This chapter sets out to explore how emotion is understood in everyday life, which differs in an important way from how it is understood in psychology. The folk conception of emotion is often not so much about mental states and behavior per se as it is about explaining human behavior. The concern of folk psychology is often more about assigning responsibility than about providing a coherent account of psychological states. Common sense about emotions is one basis of commonsense justice, so we shall explore the former to understand the latter.

THE CONCEPT OF EMOTION: A HISTORY

From the way that some scholars write about the concept of emotion, one would infer that *emotion* refers to a timeless and universal category of human experience. The classic survey of Western theories of emotion is a book by Gardiner, Metcalf, and Beebe-Center (1937) entitled *Feeling and Emotion: A History of Theories*. The book presents dozens of theories, beginning with the ancient Greeks and concluding with the psychologists most prominent in the early 20th century. Their exposition, still valuable today, characterizes the great philosophers' and psychologists' ideas as being about essentially the same category, emotion, in the sense it was understood by the book's English-speaking authors in the mid-1930s.

Is this assumption fair? This book begins with Heraclitus, Empedocles, and Anaxagoras; moves on to consideration of Plutarch and Cicero; and contains detailed treatments of Descartes, Hobbes, Spinoza, Adam Smith, Rousseau, and Kant. Can such a book fairly claim that the philosophers being surveyed were all writing about the same thing that the 1937 book called *emotion*? The authors appeared to think so, although they did not defend their belief. A number of contemporary classicists justify taking a similar approach. For example, Richard Sorabji, writing about the ancient Stoics, asserted that the ancient Greek *pathē* is best translated as the English *emotions* and not *passions* (Sorabji, 2000, pp. 7, 17, 19), and Martha Nussbaum (1994, p. 319, note 4) used the English *emotions* for the Stoics' *pathē*, arguing that there is decently good correspondence between the particular states that are included, such as love, grief, and anger. Thus, some prominent scholars see reasonable grounds for making at least a rough equivalence between *emotion* and terms in other languages from other cultures and historical periods. We would add that, in the case of ancient Greece and Rome, we are considering conceptions that directly influenced those of our own culture, so, with the addition of historical continuity, the notion is not at all farfetched.

Yet, even when there is some rough correspondence between concepts, there can be significant differences in what is included in different categories, and there can be profound differences in the beliefs that are attached to these categories. Consider the following examples, all suggested by Thomas Dixon's (2003) recent study on the origin of the concept of emotion. The ancient Greek text of the Christian New Testament uses not only the word *pathē* but also the word *apithumiai*, yet no major translation of the Bible translates either of these terms as *emotions*; rather, these words are translated variously as *lusts*, *sinful desires*, or *passions*. In another example, Stoic theorists writing in Latin used a variety of terms to refer to *emotion*, including *affectus*, *affectiones*, *passiones*, *motus animae*, and *perturbationes*, and none of these terms really means quite the same thing as *emotion*. For that matter, the modern English word *emotion* usually does not include desires and motives, but the older English word *passions* does.

The point is made even clearer when we consider cultures and languages not directly in the Anglo-American lineage. Recent research by Cristina Casado Lumbreras and José Miguel Fernández Dols (Casado Lumbreras, 2003) has compared the meanings of English, Spanish, Arabic, and Japanese words that have the general meaning of *emotional*. In Spanish, the closest term, *emocionado*, has a more positive connotation and is much less associated with a loss of control than is the English *emotional*; the Arabic *muta'attir* overlaps with some of the connotations of *emotional*, especially its linkage to mixed feelings and a tendency to weep, but it does not include joyful states and a loss of control the way *emotional* does; and the Japanese *kandō shite iru* refers to strong feelings, but only to strongly positive feelings. Linguist Anna Wierzbicka (1999) pointed out that languages such as German and Russian really have no word for *emotion* at all: the German *Gefühl* and the Russian *čuvstvo* both mean *feeling* in a broader sense.

So the equivalence of the category of *emotion* with other categories from different languages, cultures, and epochs, even when they are closely related to contemporary Anglo-American culture, is not at all straightforward. Writers who want to make the wisdom of the ancients accessible to modern readers may need to elide the difficulties of translating from one language and era to another; Gardiner, Nussbaum, and Sorabji certainly had this motive. One should not, however, mistake this motive for an assertion that a universal human nature transcends culture and history but is obscured by folk beliefs and language. That assertion is interesting and debatable, but it does not address the central concern of this chapter. Our concern is with how folk psychology's understanding of emotion influences judges, legislators, and jurors, and for our purposes, what matters are the beliefs existing in particular cultural and historical contexts—not the underlying psychology, which may or may not vary by culture.

The error we want to avoid is what Kurt Danziger (1997) called *ahistoricism*—an orientation that encourages psychologists to view mental phenomena "as historically invariant phenomena of nature, not as historically determined social phenomena" (p. 9). We therefore wish to avoid mistakenly projecting contemporary English concepts for mental phenomena onto other times and cultures, as if they refer to timeless categories of human psychology. Our aim is the contrary: to highlight the ways *emotion* is commonly understood to see how it is used in legal discourse, the assessment of culpability, and the judgments that follow. Let us then examine the cultural and historical variability of the concept of emotion in closer detail.

Passions and Emotions

The word *emotion* is a rather recent addition to the English language. It was imported in the mid-16th century from the French *émotion* and derived from Latin *e-* (out) + *movere* (to move). The earliest usages concern physical movement. Among the examples cited by the *Oxford English Dictionary* (*OED*; 2002) is a 1603 reference to "the divers emotions" of the Turks, meaning migration. But the earliest usage cited by the *OED*, from 1579, refers to a public commotion: "There were . . . great stirres and emocions in Lombardye." This first usage associates the word with disturbance or agitation, even if not a mental disturbance or agitation.

Much older than the English word *emotion* is the word *passion*, which entered into Middle English from Old French. According to the *OED* (2002), the earliest uses of *passion* in Middle English (as well as in French) pertained to Christian theology, specifically to the suffering of Christ. The original Latin word *passionem* meant "suffering," and Middle English usage included that meaning as well. Other meanings of the Latin word *passionem* that developed referred to feelings and desires, such as lust and rage, that powerfully affect the mind. These were given Christian interpretations by philosopher–theologians such as Augustine and Aquinas and these meanings were transferred from Latin to Old French and Middle English. Examples of all of these meanings of *passion* can be found in the writings of Chaucer in the mid-14th century.

Thus, the original function of *passions* in both English and French was to capture whatever meaning the Latin word *passionem* had in the Christian theology of Augustine and Aquinas. *Passionem* was used by those theologians to express ideas they derived from their readings of Plato, Aristotle, the Stoics, and the Bible. The passions were contrasted with the intellect in a variety of ways, but generally the passions were linked to a "lower," more animalistic and sensory part of the soul, whereas the intellect was linked to a "higher," more uniquely human part of the soul that, in the Christian scheme, was closer to God. Passions were based on sensation, whereas the intellect was based on reason. The passions were involuntary—truly passive as their name would imply—whereas the intellect was governed by the will. The passions were of the realm of animals and the body; the intellect was of the realm of angels and the soul.

It was this set of Christian connotations that carried over to the English word *passion*. With respect to the relation between emotion and culpability, it is most interesting to note that the concept of the passions was inherently evaluative: by definition, passions were based on morally tainted impulses, and thus to categorize a state as a passion was to cast theological judgment on it.

So what has happened to that now-archaic sounding term *passion*, and where did our word *emotion* come from? The first writer to use *emotion* extensively was David Hume (2000) in his *Treatise of Human Nature*. It is interesting that this usage occurs in a large section of the book entitled "Of the Passions." Quite likely, Hume borrowed the term from Descartes' *émotions*, who also used the term *passions*. Exactly what Hume (and Descartes) meant by these terms is the topic of a large exegetic literature, but he seems to have used *emotion* to stress the noncognitive, sensory qualities—feelings or agitations (Neu, 1977). In fact, the concept of passion was on its way to being replaced by being split into parts: emotion and motivation (Danziger, 1997). But in Hume, as in Descartes, the new term *emotion* did not replace the term *passion*, which still figured in his theory and still retained its Christian connotations of being based in the less noble aspects of the body.

The real inventor of the modern concept of emotion, according to Dixon (2003), is Thomas Brown, a physician and professor of moral philosophy at the University of Edinburgh. Brown's *Lectures*, published shortly after his death in 1820, was the first philosophical work to abandon the passions altogether. Dismissing the traditional account of mental powers or faculties of the soul, Brown divided the mind into sensations of the outside world, intellectual states of mind, and emotions. Emotions (basically, feelings) were passive and nonintellectual, whereas intellectual states were active and cognitive. The choice of the word *emotion* rather than *passion* by such early 19th-century writers as Thomas Brown and Alexander Bain was initially motivated by hostility to traditional religious beliefs (Dixon, 2001). *Emotion* gradually became the standard word in psychology and *passion* faded from use because the new term was free of the religious connotations of the old term.

It is interesting to note that *passion* still appears in contemporary legal usage, as the term *crimes of passion* is still retained (partly because the phrase predates the coinage of *emotion*), though the debate over whether *passion* ought to have a sanctioned place with the Law continues (e.g., Abramson, 2004). For example, in the appeal of the death sentence of sniper John Allen Muhammad, his attorney argued that the presentation of victim-impact testimony was an unfair effort "to excite the passions of the jury regardless of the lack of facts" (Jackman, 2004, p. B5). The attorney's argument echoed both the Supreme Court's majority in *Booth v. Maryland* (1987), which held victim-impact testimony in death penalty cases to be impermissible, and the Supreme Court's dissent in *Payne v. Tennessee* (1991; note that the High Court reversed its position 4 years later). The choice of terminology is as significant in legal parlance as it is in philosophical and psychological parlance. To condemn someone as acting under the influence of passions implicitly brings to bear a network of religious ideas about sinfulness, whereas to describe someone as acting under the influence of strong emotions, although not entirely free of the older moralistic notions, does more readily access newer notions of science, psychology, evolution, and biology.

In fact, the modern concept of *emotion* turns out to be very broad. It obliterates some distinctions made by ancient and medieval philosophers (Dixon, 2003) and mixes connotations of the old moralistic and the new scientific perspectives. The way to avoid confusion is to identify the different worldviews and metaphors that attach to this concept.

Higher and Lower, Smarter and Stupider

Aspects of the concept of passion have been transferred to our modern concept of emotion to produce one of the major strains of our modern folk theory: the tendency to think of emotion as being opposed to (and inferior to) reason. The history and pervasiveness of this idea have been well documented in an essay by James Averill (1974). Averill argued that emotions (and their conceptual predecessors such as *passions*, *passionem*, and *pathē*) have been closely linked to the body as opposed to the mind, and that current psychological theories of emotion continue to be colored by this association. He found this idea in the earliest Greek philosophers, and meticulously traced it through 2,500 years of Western thought about first passion and then emotion. The basic link between emotion and physiological processes expresses itself in a number of contrasts between emotion and the intellect. Emotions are thought to be irrational, involuntary, and animal-like, whereas the intellect is rational, voluntary, and distinctly human. From Plato we get the idea that emotions are mortal, located in the heart, and concerned with hunger and lust, whereas reason is immortal, located in the head, and concerned with truth (Averill, 1974; Parrott & Schulkin, 1993).

Yet, it would be a profound mistake to believe that the passions and emotions were consistently conceived as being inferior to rationality or as lacking in cognitive content. First, let us consider their inferiority. Even as emotions are considered primitive and animal-like, they are also considered to be sources of wisdom and intuition. People trust their emotions as a way of learning their true opinions and desires and of freeing themselves of self-deceptive rationalization. The Romantic movement broke from the Enlightenment by celebrating the authenticity of emotion over detached reason. Thus, the modern folk theory of emotion is not consistent in depicting emotion as inferior to reason.

Nor is folk theory consistent in depicting emotion as devoid of cognition. Parallel to the tradition of opposing emotion and reason is another, equally important tradition depicting passions as involving beliefs and perceptions. Aristotle, especially in his *Rhetoric* and *Nicomachean Ethics*, depicted passions as involving cognition as an intrinsic aspect of their nature (Fortenbaugh, 1975). Emotional states do not generally arise willy-nilly; rather, they arise from a certain interpretation of events. For example, anger results from the judgment that one has been deliberately transgressed by someone; fear results from the perception of an impending destructive or painful thing; we feel pity when we believe that another person faces a destructive or painful circumstance and does not deserve to have it happen. Thus, passions were depicted by Aristotle as being aroused by certain beliefs and as dissipating when those beliefs cease to be held. In his *Rhetoric*, Aristotle applied his theory to achieve practical effects, instructing orators how to arouse the passions of their audiences by manipulating their beliefs. In a court of law, for example, an orator can prevent jurors from feeling pity for the defendant by arousing incompatible passions: fear can be induced by emphasizing the suffering of the victim and the similarities of the victim to the jurors, and envy can be induced by depicting the defendant as receiving undeserved fortune that is desirable to the jurors (Nussbaum, 1994; Sorabji, 2000).

The cognitivism of Aristotle was greatly elaborated by the Stoics. Chrysippus made the bold claim that passions actually were a type of judgment. In particular, the Stoics claimed that two value judgments were inherent in emotional states such as fear or distress. The first was a judgment that benefit or harm is present (at least as a possibility), and second was a judgment that it was appropriate to react to the first judgment. Later Stoics, such as Cicero and Seneca, provided elaborate analyses of passions that emphasized the central role of evaluative judgments, and these cognitive aspects were central to the Stoic belief that passions were generally based on mistaken judgments. A wise person, therefore, would be free of most passions (Sorabji, 2000).

The co-occurrence of these two approaches to the passions in ancient thought—one disapprovingly noncognitive and the other more integrated with cognition and character—is well illustrated in discourse on the *heat of passion*. One interpretation would construe passion and reason as distinct processes. By this account, passion would overwhelm reason when it is hot, but would allow reason to operate once it has cooled. Such an interpretation was offered by the ancient Greek philosopher Posidonius, who revived Plato's metaphor of reason as a charioteer who must control the two horses of irrational anger and appetite (Galen, 1984).

Yet, quite another interpretation is also possible. Alternatives to Posidonius' interpretation existed in the ancient world. Chrysippus argued that judgments change over time and therefore emotions change with them (Sorabji, 2000). Rather than splitting the soul into two distinctly different opposing forces, reason and passion, Chrysippus spoke of a unified soul oscillating between different interpretations. As he put it in one of the few known fragments of his writing, the soul is "not the conflict and civil war of two parts, but the turning of a single reason in two different directions, which escapes our notice on account of the sharpness and swiftness of the change" (Nussbaum, 1994, pp. 383–384). By this account the person in the heat of passion is not at all devoid of cognition but rather is consumed with a particular way of understanding the situation. Passion is understood as involving cognition, as entailing a focus on certain aspects of the situation and involving certain beliefs about what happened and what the key actors intended. The person's mind is fixed on one interpretation of events, but can typically remain so fixed only for some limited period; gradually, then, as the blood cools, the perspective broadens, alternative interpretations are considered, and judgments of importance diminish.

This more cognitive view of passions can also be detected in the writings of the Christian theologians whose conception of passion passed into Middle English. Augustine provided an account of recovery from grief that more resembles Chrysippus than Posidonius, pointing out that over time new experiences displace a person's attention and alter his or her expectations so that a person is changed cognitively as well as emotionally (Sorabji, 2000). In more fundamental terms, the distinction between intellect and passion made by Augustine and Aquinas was not a distinction between intellect and what we now call emotion. The theologians maintained that the higher region of the soul had emotion-like desires of its own (e.g., love of knowledge, of virtue, of truth, and of God), distinguished from the lower soul's more animal-like passions by being called affections (*affectiones* or *affectus*). Thus, not the presence or absence of cognitive content but, rather, the source of the appetite distinguished affections from passions. Affections were based on the higher, intellectual appetite of the upper, rational soul, whereas the passions were based on the lower, sensory appetite of the lower, animalistic soul (Dixon, 2003). This difference seems more evaluative than qualitative.

The Psychologist of Avon

We find these themes continuing into the Renaissance. Shakespeare also portrayed passion as overwhelming the intellect. Elizabethan folk theories of emotion inherited the ancient and medieval ideas, and good illustrations can be found in Shakespeare's plays (Anderson, 1927/1966). In *King John* (Shakespeare, 1938), the title character claims that his angry aggression was instigated by the sight of a weapon:

> Witness against us to damnation!
> How oft the sight of means to do ill deeds
> Make deeds ill done! Haddst not thou been by,
> A fellow by the hand of nature marked,
> Quoted, and signed to do a deed of shame,
> This murder had not come into my mind. (IV, iii, 220–224)

In *The Merchant of Venice* (Shakespeare, 1938), a song sung while Bassanio contemplates the caskets demonstrates the Elizabethan folk belief that infatuation (*fancy*) enters a person through the senses, by way of the eyes, and not through the action of the intellect:

> Tell me where is fancy bred,
> Or in the heart, or in the head?
> How begot, how nourishèd?
>
> . . . .
>
> It is engendered in the eyes,
> With gazing fed; and Fancy dies,
> In the cradle where it lies. (III, ii, 63–65)

And in *Macbeth* (Shakespeare, 1938), Macbeth's fear of Banquo's ghost disappears when the ghost is gone:

> Approach thou like the ruggèd Russian bear,
> The armed rhinoceros, or th'Hyrcan tiger;
> Take any shape but that, and my firm nerves
> Shall never tremble. . . .
> Hence, horrible shadow,
> Unreal mock'ry, hence! [*Exit Ghost*]
> Why so, being gone,
> I am a man again. (III, iv, 99–102, 105–107)

Ancient Greece, ancient Rome, medieval Christianity, and Renaissance England all left their mark on contemporary Anglo-American conceptions of emotion. Yet, folk conceptions have continued to evolve, and contemporary notions are not identical to those of the cultures that have influenced them (Parrott, 2000). For example, consider some Elizabethan ideas about the physiological aspects of passions. In Elizabethan folk psychology, the liver, spleen, and gall were all believed to have functions in the passions. The liver, when supplied with blood, was believed to cause love and courage. Activity of the gall produced anger and bitterness. The spleen's action produced laughter and could dispel melancholy. These beliefs may be found in Shakespearean plays, too, but rather than seeming apt for modern readers, they require footnotes to understand. Consider Grey's remark to the king in *Henry V* (Shakespeare, 1938; II, ii, 29–31): "Those that were your father's enemies/ Have steeped their galls in honey, and do serve you/With hearts created of duty and of zeal." The meaning of this remark was transparent to theatergoers in the 17th century, but enemies with galls steeped in honey no longer suggest abandoned anger or bitterness. Or, from *Measure for Measure* (Shakespeare, 1938; II, ii, 123–126), consider Isabella's description of man: "His glassy essence, like an angry ape/Plays such fantastic tricks before high heaven/As makes the angels weep, who, with our spleens,/Would all themselves laugh mortal." The spleen was considered the seat of mirth, so, if angels had spleens they would laugh at human follies. Our present folk psychology of emotions no longer has a place for spleens or galls. In the next section, where we examine our contemporary notions about emotion, we shall see many themes familiar from older conceptions of passion, but some new ones, too.

CONTEMPORARY FOLK PSYCHOLOGY OF EMOTION:
METAPHORS AND CONTRASTS

"The meaning of a word is its use in the language," according to the famous dictum of Wittgenstein (1958, p. 20), and if we look at how the word *emotion* has been used during the few centuries of its existence, we can learn much about its meaning. Here we highlight examples in everyday speech, in the media, and in literature.

Metaphor

Folk conceptual systems have been found to be fundamentally metaphorical in nature (Lakoff & Johnson, 1980). One useful way of investigating concepts of emotion is therefore to examine the metaphors that are used in our everyday linguistic expressions. Zoltán Kövecses (2000) has conducted an extensive analysis of contemporary metaphorical expressions about emotion and concluded that most of them can be understood as expressing an underlying "master metaphor" of emotion, namely, that emotion is a sort of force. Kövecses' analysis suggests that two aspects of emotions draw on this master metaphor. The first is the cause of emotions. Events and situations are often construed as forces that initiate emotional responses. A speech might *stir up* our feelings; unexpected bad news might *hit us hard*; we can be *attracted to* or *repelled by* people or ideas. These examples depict the cause of emotions as physical agitation, as a physical impact, or as a magnetic force.

The second aspect of emotion to draw on the force metaphor is the emotional response itself. Once an emotion is initiated, it has a force of its own. This force might be physical, as when we are *swept off our feet* with infatuation. Or it might be described as heat or fire: once our emotions have been *kindled*, we can be *hot* with passion, *burning* or *on fire* with emotion, *smoldering* with resentment, or *boiling* with anger. Emotion can be depicted as internal pressure within a container. We are *filled* with emotion, and can *overflow* or *explode* with emotion if the internal pressure is sufficient. The force of emotion can be construed not only inanimately but also animately: as a wild animal (we feel emotion's *tug*) or as an opponent (emotion can *grip* us) or as a social force (emotions can *govern* or *rule* us). Emotions can also trick us, as when we are *fooled*, *misled*, or *deceived* by our emotions. The force can be sufficient to produce mental incapacitation, as when we become *crazy* or *mad* with emotion (Kövecses, 2000).

Implicit in these metaphors are important components of our everyday understanding. Some emotions are clearly desirable whereas others are undesirable. Good emotions elicit metaphors of upwardness, light, warmth, and high value, whereas bad emotions elicit metaphors of downwardness, darkness, cold, and low value. Variations in intensity are clearly allowed by the metaphors of containers, heat or fire, physical force, and social force (Kövecses, 2000).

The metaphor of emotion as a force got a considerable boost from Sigmund Freud. Freud, along with Josef Breuer, developed a 19th-century metaphor that likened emotions and other human motivations to hydraulic forces (Breuer & Freud, 1893/1982). In their famous account, the symptoms of hysteria were understood as expressions of repressed emotional memories. The energy of these blocked emotions could not simply dissipate; rather, their pressure continued to build and build until they escaped through an alternative route, which produced the symptoms of hysteria. This hydraulic model of hysteria draws on many of the metaphors delineated by Kövecses (2000). The treatment for hysteria developed by Breuer and Freud was also consistent with these metaphors: using techniques such as hypnosis and free association, Breuer and Freud helped their patients bring repressed emotional memories to consciousness, which resulted in an outpouring of pent-up emotion that they termed *catharsis*. Once released in catharsis, the emotion was discharged (like a contained pressurized gas or fluid) and the neurotic symptoms disappeared. The Freudian notions of repression and catharsis have influenced the contemporary folk psychology of emotion, and there is reason to believe that some of the metaphors documented by Kövecses owe their prevalence, if not their existence, to the writings of Freud (Averill, 1990; Tavris, 1989). For example, a current folk belief holds that it is unhealthy to hold in one's emotions, and that one ought to express an emotion if one feels it.

The metaphors analyzed by Kövecses (2000) depict the emotional person as being passive (i.e., being overcome by emotions), on the one hand, yet at the same time characterize emotions as something that people have some ability to control. For example, emotion may be an internal pressure, but we often try to *keep the lid on it* and *hold it in*. Emotions, like wild animals, can be *reined in*. Emotions, as social forces, can be *rejected*; as emotional opponents, they can be *grappled* or *wrestled* with. Yet, these efforts at control are not always successful, and the wild animal *carries us away*, the natural force *overwhelms us*, the container *boils over*, and our opponents *get the better of us*.

What is striking about these ways of talking is that emotion is depicted as something that is different from and often opposed to oneself (i.e., we may try to keep the lid on it, but this *it* is something apart from *us*). It would seem that the concept of emotion can be used as a way of expressing mixed feelings about emotion and control, though not all metaphors have this implication. Before we leave this subtopic, it is worth considering another study undertaken by James Averill (1990).

Like Kövecses (2000), Averill (1990, p. 113) found several metaphors that depict emotion as primitive or irrational. For example, Averill referred to emotion(s) as a "driving force or vital energy," as "diseases of the mind," as "physiological responses," and as "the animal in human nature." Thus, fear *drives* people (like a force), *paralyzes* them (like a disease), gives them *cold feet* (like a physiological response), and must be *subdued* (like an animal). Yet, Averill pointed out that these metaphors neglect important qualities of emotion. First of all, emotions are not entirely private, inner experiences; they are public, occur in social situations, and are subject to social rules. Second, people are not completely passive when it comes to experiencing emotion; they cultivate their emotions and call them up when appropriate or necessary. So Averill suggested another metaphor—emotions as social roles.

In everyday life, people play different roles depending on how they are interacting with others; these roles express a person's identity and moral values. The metaphors of social roles draw on the language of the theater: people *act* hurt or angry; they *put on* a cheerful face; they *play up* their anxieties; they *work themselves* into a fury. People *put on* their demeanor as if it were clothing, as if they were dressing themselves appropriately for an occasion or to make a certain impression. These metaphors bring out aspects of emotion not captured by the metaphors analyzed by Kövecses (2000), aspects that are strategic and at least partly under a person's control.

The aspects of emotion that are captured by Averill's role metaphor may be less noticeable in everyday life because people's acting, when convincingly done, is not noticeable even to themselves. To be convincing to others, they may try to forget that they were acting in the first place. Yet, people tend to acknowledge the volition and control they exert over emotions when asked whether they have ever tried to fall in love or to slow the speed at which they fall in love. People will acknowledge working themselves into feeling scared, putting themselves into the mood to go to a party, or adopting the proper demeanor for attending a solemn ceremony. The metaphor of emotion as social role aptly captures these aspects of emotion, which are quite distinct from those of force or animality emphasized by Kövecses (2000). Indeed, we would propose yet another metaphor of emotion that was neglected by Kövecses: emotions are self-initiated. We humans *work ourselves into* a rage, *get ourselves into* a mood (or *the* mood), *wallow* in self-pity, are *in love with the idea of being in love, cling* to hope, *cultivate* a grudge, *nurse* a resentment, *work up* our courage, and *puff up* our pride.

Thus, metaphors for emotion depict them both as different from ourselves and definitional of ourselves, both as opposed to ourselves and as constitutive of ourselves, both as primitive and base and as direct and unclouded, both as irrational and as rich in interpretation, both as overpowering and as self-initiated. This impression may be pursued further by moving from the study of metaphors of emotion to consideration of some other aspects of emotion talk, particularly contrasts between emotion and nonemotion.

Contrasts

We have already seen how in medieval times *passion* was contrasted both with *intellect* and with *affection*. The contrast with *intellect* has carried over to the modern term *emotion*, although the distinction between emotion and affection has been lost (Dixon, 2003). We also sometimes speak of the *heart* and the *head* as if they are two mental faculties, one associated with feeling something and the other associated with knowing something. When the head–heart distinction is applied in this way, feelings are sometimes depicted as being at variance with one's knowledge or reason.

The following three examples help illustrate this contrast. The first is a statement by T. S. Eliot (1932, p. 118) on the function of poetry: "Poetry is not a substitute for philosophy or theology or religion . . . ; it has its own function. But as this function is not intellectual but emotional, it cannot be defined adequately in intellectual terms." The second example is a statement from Michael Stutz, a psychologist who specializes in treating athletes, speaking about race car drivers: "On an intellectual level, they know there's a risk. On an emotional level they just don't feel it. . . . There is a significant amount of denial. . . . It's a way of self-protection" (MacPherson, 1994, p. 12, ellipses in original). A final example comes from an episode of the television program *Civil Wars* (brought to our attention by a former student, Jennifer Groscup). In an episode that aired in 1992, a judge refused to grant a divorce to the plaintiff (the wife) who in the past had been raped while the husband was held at gunpoint. Under cross-examination she seemed to reveal that she blamed her husband for not being willing to die for her. The judge stated, "I do not believe Mrs. Reardon blames her husband intellectually, but I do believe she blames her husband viscerally."

In these quotations, the intellect or the head is contrasted with the emotions or the gut or viscera as two different ways of knowing that can conflict with each other. T. S. Eliot seemed to think that the intellect and the emotions are different ways of knowing, different routes to truth. The judge on *Civil Wars* seemed to think that the plaintiff felt blame but disavowed there being any basis for it—a genuinely irrational emotion. The example of race car drivers supplies an interesting twist: the athlete's intellect knows about the danger, but his or her "emotional level" fails to feel the corresponding emotion; in this example, the absence of emotion is contrasted with an intellect that seems to have all the information necessary to justify strong fear. Folk wisdom does not consistently depict one of these modes of understanding as being superior to the other. On some occasions the head is considered superior to the heart, which can be irrational, yet on other occasions the heart is preferred, as when someone is urged to follow his heart, or when philosopher David Hume (2000) stated in his *Treatise of Human Nature* that "reason is, and ought only to be, the slave of the passions" (II, iii, 3, p. 266). In these cases the distinction between the head and the heart seems to refer to two ways of knowing, one perhaps more analytical, the other more intuitive.

Not all contrasts between the head and the heart fit this pattern, however. Consider the following statement made by a patient telling his therapist about his jealousy: "Of course, in my head I want her to be free. I believe in freedom. I hate smothering relationships. But in my gut I can't let her have an inch of freedom" (T. Moore, 1992, p. 103). Like the previous examples, this one presents a contrast between the head, which "wants her to be free," and the "gut," which does not. But notice that this head does not "think" or "believe" she should be free—it "wants" her to be free. The jealous man assigns his possessiveness to his gut, but is that because his possessiveness involves emotions and his belief in freedom does not? Actually, he sounds rather passionate about the general importance of freedom, though unable to muster very much of this passion when it comes to his girlfriend. The gut clearly has the stronger feelings, but in this case the head seems to have feelings, too—it *wants* her freedom, it *hates* smothering relationships. Thus, this example introduces other elements, which lead us to believe that the head–heart distinction can involve something more subtle than simply a distinction between intellectual knowing and emotional feeling.

Let us examine two other cases in which head–heart contrast involves pitting two emotions or feelings against each other. Consider a statement found in Herman Melville's short novel *Billy Budd, Sailor* (Melville, 1924/1986), spoken by the character Captain Vere:

> But let not warm hearts betray heads that should be cool. Ashore in a criminal case, will an upright judge allow himself off the bench to be waylaid by some tender kinswoman of the accused seeking to touch him with her tearful plea? Well, the heart here, sometimes the feminine in man, is as that piteous woman, and hard though it be, she must here be ruled out. (p. 362)

This quotation begins with the head–heart distinction and then adds a second simile, that of a tearful woman trying (through "victim impact"!) to persuade a disciplined male judge. Captain Vere is arguing for strict adherence to the role of judge: "Our vowed responsibility is in this: That however pitilessly that law may operate in any instances, we nevertheless adhere to it and administer it" (p. 362). Yet the entire speech is quite emotional! Captain Vere passionately insists that certain passions should not be allowed to influence him in his role as judge. The "feminine" emotion of pity is contrasted not with an unemotional masculine judge but with other, more appropriate emotions, such as dutifulness, pride in doing one's proper job, and fear of the chaos that would come from subordinates questioning the orders of superordinates at sea.

As a final example, let us consider the case of a student in the nursing school at Georgetown University who was working with premature infants in the nursery. One day she had to care for an infant who had been coded as DNR (*do not resuscitate*, meaning that no extraordinary measures would be taken to prevent a natural death from occurring). The nursing student cared for the infant for several weeks, and during this time became very attached to the infant. When anticipating the possibility that the infant would start to die and she would not be able to intervene, the student felt strong conflict. She stated, "On the one hand, I am a nurse and must respect the parent's wishes. Also this infant is hooked up to so many machines that there is very little hope that the infant could survive on her own. On the other hand, I feel a bond to her and cannot imagine just sitting there and watching her die." She described the situation as one in which her heart pulled her in one direction (saving the infant) and her head pulled her in another (allowing her to die). It would not be accurate to say that cold reason dictated allowing the infant to die whereas emotions urged the student to try to save the infant's life. Surely there are emotions favoring the DNR code, about being a good nurse, about respecting parents' wishes, and about not prolonging a life that involved much suffering. Yet the assignment of head and heart to the two sides of the conflict does not seem random.

Even though there appear to be thoughts and emotions on both sides, it sounds wrong to reverse the head and heart in either example. It does not sound quite right to say, "Although her head said she should do anything to try to save the infant's life, in her heart she knew she should let the baby die." Nor does it sound right to say, "Although the judge's head told him that he should not let the murderers go free, his heart told him that due process required that rules be followed exactly."

In these cases, the head properly corresponds to whichever inclination is consistent with the societal role the actor is supposed to be playing, that of nurse or captain, whereas the inclination properly called the heart is the one that is at variance with the sanctioned societal role. The distinction between the head and the heart, in these cases at least, is not so much between intellect and feelings as it is between socially sanctioned and unsanctioned courses of action, both of which entail a rich mixture of beliefs and motivations. We talk about heads and hearts in this sense when we are ambivalent. We assign the label *head* to what we are supposed to do, to actions that are often motivated primarily by emotions such as fear of the consequences of not following the socially sanctioned role and doing one's duty. We assign the label *heart* to what we want to do instead, to actions that typically are motivated by emotions corresponding to one's wishes and desires (Parrott, 1995).

Evaluative Aspects of the Category of "Emotion": Emotionality and Gender

As the preceding discussion indicated, the *heart* sometimes refers to emotions as a category separate from nonemotion, and other times refers only to emotions that are socially unsanctioned. The word *emotional* also has this dual potential in everyday language. The connotations of describing oneself as *emotional* were investigated in a study by Parrott (1995), in which 70 students completed a questionnaire asking them to describe a time when they considered themselves to have been emotional. They were then asked to specify why they considered their state to be emotional, and how their feelings, thoughts, and actions would have differed if they had not been emotional. Analysis of their answers provided a picture of the meanings of *being emotional* in everyday American English. This concept was found to subsume a number of connotations, which often occurred in combination.

The most common theme was of irrationality, which was found in nearly half of the questionnaires. Episodes of emotionality typically featured an inability to think clearly or to cope effectively, and the students tended to blame themselves for their irrationality, whether it consisted of reacting to improbable possibilities, exaggerating the importance of an event or comment, or failing to take into account another's point of view. Another common theme, mentioned in more than one third of the episodes, was of being out-of-control, with mental distraction, rash or impulsive actions, and feelings arising quickly and spontaneously being examples of out-of-control reactions. Other themes cited as characterizing emotionality were high intensity, a confusing mixture of emotions, and the occurrence of weeping.

Psychologist Stephanie Shields (2002) has pointed out that the same expressions and behaviors that get labeled *emotional* in one context may not receive this label in a different context. The label *emotional* tends to be used when the expressions are inappropriate or uncontrolled, but what counts as appropriate or controlled can change depending on the context. For example, a display of anger may be described as emotional when displayed by a woman but not when displayed by a man. Such labeling differences demonstrate how the concept of *emotional* can be evaluative, and not merely descriptive.

The previous example suggests another way in which emotionality can be evaluative: cultural norms of emotion are an important part of cultural norms of gender. Notions of gender are as culturally and historically variable as are those of emotion, but the two are usually intertwined. Shields (2002) surveyed a range of attitudes, from those of Aristotle to those of the Victorians, and showed how these notions continued to evolve up to the late 20th century. Recent research by psychologists, anthropologists, and sociologists has shown that women are expected to experience most emotions more intensely than are men and generally to be the "emotional sex." There are exceptions, however: anger and hate are considered more appropriate for men. Men's emotions are interpreted differently than are women's—they are considered to be more important, and to originate more from the situation (whereas women's emotions tend to be interpreted as part of their nature). Women's emotionality is more associated with physiological attributes (such as hormones), with excessive or hysterical intensity, and with immaturity (Hochschild, 1983; Lutz, 1988; Shields, 2002; Tavris, 1989). In short, in many respects the contrast between *male* and *female* entails many of the same characteristics of the contrast between *rationality* and *emotion*, that were seen earlier in the quote from Melville (1924/1986, p. 362): "The heart here, sometimes the feminine in man, is as that piteous woman, and hard though it be, she must here be ruled out."

But just as the rationality–emotion contrast does not entirely favor rationality, the male–female contrast does not entirely favor males. Although female emotionality has negative connotations of irrationality, weakness, and immaturity, it also has positive connotations for interpersonal interconnectedness, engagement in relationships, and nurturing. Furthermore, it is seen as the source of deep spirituality, energy, and toughness.

Research on folk conceptions of female emotionality thus reveals an ambivalence about gender and emotion. The topics surveyed throughout this chapter reveal an equivalent ambivalence about emotion more generally, because emotion, whether female or male, is conceived as part of two distinct dichotomies: one is that emotion is opposed to reason; the other is that emotion is the essence of being alive. These conceptions would not seem contradictory except that they imply opposite evaluations: reason is good, so emotion's being opposed to reason makes it bad; yet, life is good, so emotion's being aligned with vitality and opposed to death is good. Thus, in the contemporary folk theory, emotion is both bad and good.

This contradiction has been carefully analyzed by anthropologist Catherine Lutz (1988), who summarized the paradox succinctly:

> To say that someone is 'unemotional' is either to praise that person as calm, rational, and deliberate or to accuse them of being withdrawn or uninvolved, alienated, or even catatonic. . . . These two views represent both a cultural contradiction and a necessary feature of any dualism whose simplicities cannot hold in the face of the demands social processes will put on it. (p. 56)

One of the demands that social processes put on the folk conception of emotion is in helping to determine culpability. The problem, for the Law's theory of emotion and culpability, is in wisely navigating these cultural contradictions.

LOOKING BACK, LOOKING FORWARD

When jurors, judges, and lawmakers include emotions in their culpability decisions and in the criminal code, it is the everyday conception of emotion, not a scientific one, that guides their actions. This chapter has explored the everyday concept of emotion, drawing on an abundance of research by psychologists as well as by historians, philosophers, linguists, and anthropologists.

We have seen that the term *emotion* is actually of quite recent origin, and that this concept is culturally malleable. The general superordinate category for emotions has changed in significant ways throughout history, and reviewing this history reveals the sources of today's multifaceted concept. The modern concept encompasses a number of senses, each of which consists of a rich mix of disparate (and sometimes discrepant) connotations. Emotion can be contrasted with reason, and within this contrast it can be evaluated as either bad or good; as bad, it is linked with physiological processes and infrahuman animals and understood as irrational and primitive; as good, it is linked with natural vitality and understood as authenticity and power. Emotion can alternatively be understood as being melded with thought, in which case it may be linked with point of view, intuition, understanding, judgment, and character. In this more cognitive sense, the folk evaluation can also be either good or bad: sometimes the emotional way of knowing is superior (direct from the heart, intuitive, free of the intellectual fog of alienated rationalization) and sometimes it is inferior (impulsive, sloppy, short-sighted, stimulus-bound, or motivated by fearful denial, prideful self-protection, or anxious self-deception). In either understanding, emotion can be understood as being under one's control or as overwhelming one's control.

Emotion is typically understood as something experienced passively, that is, as something that happens to oneself. Yet, there are important senses in which emotion is understood as being active, that is, as something that one brings about intentionally. In this active sense, people speak of using their emotions to accomplish their goals, to motivate thought and action, to influence other people. Emotions are put on for certain social occasions, and are part of professional behavior and gender roles. One of the most important social functions of the category of emotion is to excuse, justify, or mitigate behavior that normally is not allowed. When a person's behavior is attributed to emotion, a person is allowed to apologize and remain in good standing because the behavior is construed as not characteristic of the person's real self.

All of these senses share the idea that emotion is a distinctive psychological state, be it cognitive or not, controllable or uncontrollable, passive or active. This chapter, however, has uncovered other usages that do not imply any contrast between the state of emotion and other types of psychological state. In these usages, the term *emotional* is applied to a feeling, urge, or course of action that is believed to be unreasonable or socially inappropriate. This emotional inclination is often contrasted with another that is judged more reasonable or appropriate, but both inclinations may involve states of mind that could be termed *emotions* in one of the previous senses. Perhaps because of this evaluative meaning, in everyday language the term *emotional* tends to be associated more with unpleasant feelings and with undesirable characteristics, such as irrationality, uncontrollability, and inappropriateness.

Although our exploration of the concept of emotion has developed the material richly enough to permit us to evaluate in the next chapter how emotion is used by the Law, the present chapter's content is incomplete in two important ways, both having to do with the abstractness of its topic. First, the concept of emotion is a superordinate category that includes all of the particular types of emotion (e.g., anger, fear, jealousy, shame, and so on). We are saving the specific types of emotions for chapter 5 (this volume), but at this stage we must point out that much of our knowledge about emotions is found not at the global level of emotion in general but at the more specific level of particular types of emotion. Second, the concept of emotion is abstract in a second sense as well, in that it tends to isolate a state of mind from the context in which it occurs; as we have indicated, it is important to reintegrate emotion with its context.

In exploring definitions, folk theories, metaphors, and contrasts, we focused on what linguists would call the *semantics* of the word *emotion*. We have presented a detailed analysis of what is meant by *emotion* and *being emotional*. But we have also seen that some of the uses of *emotion* do not so much refer to a type of mental state as judge the appropriateness of mental activity. Such uses do involve semantics, but much of their import entails what linguists would call the *pragmatics* of the word *emotion* (White, 2000). In everyday discourse, the concept of emotion plays a part in evaluating a person's actions. Emotion is part of a story in which a character's thoughts and actions are judged, or in which a character negotiates with others to gain acceptance of boasts, excuses, apologies, and other accounts of his or her behavior and character (Parrott, 2003). As shall be seen in chapter 5 (this volume), the specific emotion words can also play these roles, and researchers have found it necessary to represent their meaning as scripts or stories to capture how they are processes that unfold. That emotion words play a role in accounts of behavior and character suggests that they also can play an important role in judgments of responsibility and culpability. To that we turn in the next chapter.

4

EMOTIONS IN ACADEMIC PSYCHOLOGY: IMPLICATIONS FOR CULPABILITY AND THE LAW

In the preceding chapter, we used the methods of academic psychology, philosophy, and social sciences to explore the folk theories of emotion that underlie legal conceptions of culpability. In the present chapter, in which we discuss the nature of emotion itself, we turn to academic research and ask whether the facts about emotion support legal traditions about how an actor's emotions influence his or her culpability.

At this early point, an objection might be lodged asserting that culpability is a legal, not a scientific, concept and that therefore science has nothing to add. We have already met a version of this "Stop! Do not enter, for your facts are irrelevant to the legal judgment of culpability!" in Pillsbury's (1998) normative theory (see chap. 2, this volume), although, in our critique, we demonstrated how Pillsbury nonetheless drew on the psychology of emotion. Now, we examine this objection more broadly. First, this objection is correct in a sense. A judgment about culpability is arrived at by understanding a culture's values and standards for legal responsibility and applying them to a specific situation. Scientific research on emotion indeed cannot establish how culpability *ought* to be conceived, and independent of normative values, no objective test can measure how much culpability a person should receive. But neither of these empirical failings is the sense in which we are proposing to apply scientific findings about emotions. Science has important roles in the study of emotions, culpability, and the Law that do not deny or usurp the normative nor attempt to make the normative disappear by folding it into the scientific.

What Psychology can do is examine the assumptions about emotions that lead the Law to include emotions in determinations of culpability. Psychology can help us understand how people make judgments of responsibility and culpability. It can be used in an examination of folk assumptions about the nature of emotion and help us decide in what ways those assumptions are supported by fact. In short, the cultural, moral, and legal traditions that have shaped notions of culpability make assumptions about the nature of emotion, and these assumptions can be examined objectively and empirically. None of this presupposes that science can tell us what responsibility or culpability is, only that it can tell us how better to apply the notions of responsibility and culpability that we already have. In this chapter we survey the scientific study of emotions and explore the ways this study can inform the Law.

THE PSYCHOLOGY OF EMOTIONS: BIOLOGICAL, COGNITIVE, AND SOCIAL APPROACHES

The roots of scientific research on emotions are to be found in the same historical movements that led to the abandonment of the term *passions* and the adoption of the word *emotions*. The 19th-century shift from a religious to a secular psychology was marked by an interest in adopting the ontology and methods of the physical sciences and applying them to the biological aspects of emotions. The important emotion theorists of the 1850s to 1880s (e.g., Herbert Spencer, Alexander Bain, and Charles Darwin) focused on the role of the nerves and the brain; they emphasized the muscles, glands, and viscera; they discussed biological evolution and the commonalities between humans and animals; and they paid particular attention to the emotions displayed by the uncivilized humanity represented by infants, "savages," and those judged insane (Dixon, 2003). Darwin's (1872) interest in emotions was limited primarily to arguing against theories of divine creation; he therefore focused on evidence that emotions were inherited and not terribly useful (Fridlund & Duchaine, 1996). William James's (1884) theory posited that emotional feelings arose from sensing bodily activities, such as trembling, clenching, visceral stirrings, dilation of the blood vessels, and raising of gooseflesh. According to W. James, emotional feelings were nothing other than the perception of such bodily changes.

Although these emphases were helpful in divorcing the scientific study of emotion from earlier ethical and theological traditions, it was immediately recognized that emotion consisted of more than physiology alone. W. James's famous article appeared in the April 1884 issue of the new psychology journal *Mind*. In the very next issue of this quarterly journal in July 1884, James's friend Edmund Gurney pointed out a problem in James's theory by questioning how the body could know which response to produce in any given circumstance. In James's account, the body simply reacts to a situation by instinct, and the perception of the bodily change produces the emotional state. Gurney questioned the immediacy of the bodily response by raising the example of emotional responses to music. If a person feels an emotional chill when listening to Beethoven but not when listening to Clementi, the music must have been judged or evaluated first. For Gurney, there seemed a logical necessity that some cognitive process occur between the musical stimulus and the bodily response. The theory of William James entirely neglected the crucial role of cognition. As Gurney put it in July 1884, "Why should my brain-centres know better than I, and send down a summons to my body to reverberate when Beethoven is 'right,' and not when Clementi is 'right'?" (Gurney, 1884, p. 426).

As the psychology of emotion developed over the next 120 years, psychologists worked out a consensus that emotions must be considered and analyzed at multiple levels. Emotions can be studied as biological phenomena, as cognitive phenomena, and as sociocultural phenomena. In this respect, emotions are no different from perception, memory, or any other topic in psychology. Each level of analysis yields insights, but no one level is fundamental, and none yields a complete account of the phenomenon in question. The different levels of analysis complement each other and together lead to a more complete understanding. So too do different levels of analysis of psychological research about emotions: discoveries about brain structures that regulate emotional reactions do not diminish the relevance of observations about the cognitive aspects or social functions of these very same emotional reactions.

In the next section we embark on a brief survey of psychological approaches to the emotions. Our goal is to illustrate some of what psychological science has learned about emotions. We do not attempt to produce a comprehensive summary of theories and knowledge, for that is not the purpose of this book, and such a comprehensive summary would be impossible to do in just a few chapters. (Consider that the two most recent scholarly summaries of current emotion research—Davidson, Scherer, & Goldsmith, 2003, and M. Lewis & Haviland-Jones, 2000—had an average length of 900 pages and of 50 chapters!) Instead, we illustrate the major psychological approaches to the emotions by applying them to the emotions of a well-known murderer we met in a previous chapter: Macbeth.

In the second scene of Shakespeare's (1938) *The Tragedy of Macbeth*, King Duncan, delighted at the news of Macbeth's victory against the King of Norway and the traitor Macdonald, decides to bestow on Macbeth the title

Thane of Cawdor. Macbeth appears on stage in the next scene, when he and Banquo come upon the three witches, who greet him not only with his current title of Thane of Glamis but also as Thane of Cawdor and as "Macbeth, that shalt be king hereafter!" (I, iii, 46–48). The witches tell Banquo that his children shall be kings, and then disappear. Afterward, two noblemen, Ross and Angus, arrive to inform Macbeth that the King has awarded him the title of Thane of Cawdor. The remainder of this scene allows Macbeth a number of asides to display a sequence of emotional reactions that define his character and start him down the path that leads to murder and ruin.

The first emotion is a brief flash of incredulity, shared by Banquo, that the witches could have foreseen this award: "The Thane of Cawdor lives. Why do you dress me/In borrowed robes?" (I, iii, 106–107). Macbeth's incredulity quickly yields to belief in the witches' prophecy, however, and he betrays a new emotion, a joyful hopefulness, by projecting it onto the still skeptical Banquo.

> MACBETH [Aside]:
> Glamis, and Thane of Cawdor.
> The greatest is behind. [To Ross and Angus] Thanks for your pains.
> [To Banquo] Do you not hope your children shall be kings
> When those that gave the thane of Cawdor to me
> Promised no less to them?
> BANQUO:
> That, trusted home,
> Might yet enkindle you unto the crown,
> Besides the thane of Cawdor. But 'tis strange,
> And oftentimes to win us to our harm
> The instruments of darkness tell us truths,
> Win us with honest trifles to betray's
> In deepest consequence. (I, iii, 114–124)

Macbeth, however, does not heed Banquo's warning that believing the prophecy could "enkindle" his desire to be king. Instead, Macbeth gives in to this wish, feeling the emotion of joyful anticipation that the third prophecy, that he will become king, will come true: "Two truths are told/As happy prologues to the swelling act/Of the imperial theme" (126–128).

But Macbeth gives in to more than happy anticipation; he no sooner considers the "swelling act of the imperial theme" than he imagines killing the king to bring the imperial theme to hellish actuality. The thought of murdering King Duncan triggers a completely different emotion—that of moral revulsion—for Macbeth is fully aware of how wrong this killing would be. His immediate reaction shows how natural to him is this decent response.

> MACBETH [Aside]:
> This supernatural soliciting
> Cannot be ill, cannot be good. . . .

If good, why do I yield to that suggestion
Whose horrid image doth unfix my hair,
And make my seated heart knock at my ribs,
Against the use of nature? Present fears
Are less than horrible imaginings:
My thought, whose murder yet is but fantastical,
Shakes so my single state of man that function
Is smothered in surmise; and nothing is
But what is not.
BANQUO [*To Ross and Angus*]:
Look, how our partner's rapt.
MACBETH [*Aside*]:
If chance will have me king, why, chance may
crown me,
Without my stir. (I, iii, 129–130, 133–143)

For Macbeth, his fantasy of murdering the king yields a "horrid image" that so frightens him that it makes his hair stand on end and his heart pound. Although the murder is only imagined, his thought of it scares him more than something present and real, and his fantasy so absorbs him that he is oblivious to those around him. At the end of his aside, he appears to reject the thought of murder, and speculates that he may become king without his having to kill Duncan.

Shakespeare's language touches on all three levels of analysis in describing Macbeth's emotions. The physiological level is used to characterize the strength of Macbeth's horror at the thought of committing murder—the pounding heart and the piloerection. The effects of emotion are also apparent on the cognitive level: Macbeth's fear involved not only his pounding heart but also his mental distraction, his attention directed at his fantasy and away from the social setting. The cognitive level is also the source of his emotions, which arise from Macbeth's assessment of events and possibilities. In psychology, the word *appraisal* is used to designate interpretations of the significance of events that lead to emotions (Roseman & Smith, 2001). His happy anticipation is brought about by his new belief that the witches were indeed telling the truth and that he therefore can realistically expect that in the future he will become king. His horror is brought about by his reaction to the thought of murdering Duncan, which, we can infer, he interpreted as ghastly and immoral. These thoughts point to the social and cultural level of analysis, because Macbeth's evaluations draw on his social connection to King Duncan—they are cousins—and on the values he has learned from his culture, such as that murder is wrong.

As Act I continues, Macbeth's aversion to murder is soon weakened. First, he is angered when King Duncan announces that the heir to his throne will be his son Malcolm, which reignites Macbeth's "black and deep desires" (I, iv, 51) to gain the crown by violent means. Second, when the angry Macbeth rushes back to his castle to prepare for a royal visit, he receives the encouragement and assistance of his charismatic wife. Lady Macbeth has no aversion to murder, but she does doubt that Macbeth is sufficiently evil to fulfill his ambitions by murder. Because she believes him to be "too full o'th' milk of human kindness" (I, v, 15), she will "pour my spirits in thine ear" (I, v, 24) to bolster his will. In this sequence all three levels of analysis continue to be illustrated. The social level is necessary to understand the perceived slight from King Duncan and the goading from Lady Macbeth. We see the physiological level in the increased energy and purposefulness that result from the exertion of Macbeth's hurried ride. Psychologist Dolf Zillmann (1979) has shown how bodily arousal can be transferred to increase the intensity of hostility and aggression. We see the cognitive level in Macbeth's response to the information of Malcolm's becoming heir and to his inference of its import for his goal of becoming king. Psychologist Keith Oatley (1992) has shown how emotions tend to arise when there is a significant change in one's assessment of the outcome of a goal or plan.

During King Duncan's visit, while the banquet is in progress, Macbeth begins to have reservations about going through with the murder, which he expresses in a long soliloquy. Some of his reservations are pragmatic: he doubts that the murder would lack repercussions. He is willing to accept repercussions in the afterlife, but even in the present life the assassination of Duncan would set an example for others who would likely assassinate him later. Other reservations concern the morality of the murder. Macbeth considers the reasons why it would be wrong to kill Duncan. First, Duncan is his own kin. Second, Macbeth is Duncan's subject. Third, Macbeth is Duncan's host, "who should against his murderer shut the door,/Not bear the knife myself" (I, vii, 15–16). Fourth, Duncan has been blameless as king, so his murder would only give rise to great pity and grief in others, not to any sense of justice. So when Lady Macbeth enters, Macbeth announces to her, "We will proceed no further in this business" (I, vii, 31). But this blunt announcement proves no deterrent for Lady Macbeth, who berates Macbeth with contemptuous taunts about his being unreliable, cowardly, and unmanly. She then proposes a plan to frame the King's chamberlains so they will appear guilty of the murder, and Macbeth goes along with it.

These scenes vividly illustrate the social aspects of emotion. In Scene V, when Lady Macbeth calls on spirits to "unsex me here,/And fill me from the crown to the toe top-full/Of direst cruelty" (I, v, 39–41), her murderous determination and ruthlessness seem contagious, just as social psychologists have found emotions to be in social settings (Hatfield, Cacioppo, & Rapson, 1994). In Scene VII, Macbeth's conviction that he should not proceed with the murder is completely undone by the taunts of his lady. She rebuts his rationale, construing his motives not as those of prudence and honor but rather as those of fear and cowardice.

Macbeth's objections crumble before this onslaught. His pragmatic objections are assuaged by the apparent likelihood that Lady Macbeth's plan to frame the chamberlains will succeed. His moral objections are overwhelmed by Lady Macbeth's skill at equating moral qualms with vacillation, hesitation with cowardice, and murder with manliness. Lady Macbeth's forceful presentation of these equations is social, face-to-face, and puts Macbeth to shame. His moral objections seem not to be strong enough. His reservations seem too much based on pragmatic fear of failure. His idea of manliness is too dependent on the views of his wife. His brief defense of his manliness in lines 46 and 47 ("I dare do all that may become a man;/Who dares do more is none") soon dissolves into the belief that his wife personifies manliness better than he does. His capitulation begins with lines 72 to 74: "Bring forth men-children only,/For thy undaunted mettle should compose/Nothing but males." It is the nature of social interaction that definitions—definitions that are often expressed in emotions such as contempt, anger, and shame—are negotiated (Parrott, 2003). This scene concludes Act I, and, by its end, Macbeth's qualms are "settled."

The psychology of emotion tells us much about Macbeth's emotions and about Shakespeare's depiction of them, but what does it tell us about Macbeth's culpability? To answer that question, we must consider the psychology of emotion in light of our folk and legal conception of culpability. Five central aspects of the folk conception of emotion have been particularly important in shaping legal notions of culpability. The Law's treatment of emotions has been shaped by assumptions about whether (a) people can be considered responsible for their emotions, (b) emotions can be controlled, (c) there is a distinction between single emotions and long-term emotions, (d) emotions involve thought, and (e) emotions are objective or subjective. We will consider each of these issues, in each case drawing on the academic study of emotions.

RESPONSIBILITY AND EMOTIONS

The scholars and judges who would keep Psychology out of the Law seem to fear that Psychology's entrance will precipitate culpability's exit. From their standpoint, psychologists seem to be excuse-providers for criminals (D. O. Lewis, 1998), for psychological understandings that depict behavior as being caused seem incompatible with explanations that allow for choice and free will, which are necessary for responsibility and culpability. Consider the following examples. Psychologists and psychiatrists have claimed that serial murderers often have a history of being severely abused as children, and that the pattern of their abuse in childhood often resembles their characteristic method of killing as adults (e.g., Pincus, 2001). Genetic abnormalities, such as the XYY chromosome configuration, were once widely (but incorrectly) believed to be associated with criminal behavior (D. O. Lewis, 1998). The viral encephalitis that causes rabies leads to uncontrolled attacks of rage, as can temporal lobe epilepsy and tumors located in the part of the brain known as the limbic system (Mark & Ervin, 1970). Neurologists have proposed a dyscontrol syndrome, in which disorders of the limbic brain (MacLean, 1949; Papez, 1937) lead to uncontrollable violence, associated with repeated traffic violations and accidents, impulsive sexual behavior, and domestic violence (Mark & Ervin, 1970).

Some who learn of such research and theory have concluded that criminal behavior can be directly linked to structural or functional abnormalities in regions of the brain that are linked to emotion. Some have even proposed that the outcome of a simple test of brain function, the electroencephalogram, be considered sufficient grounds for incarceration in the absence of criminal action (Wexler, 1972).

There are good reasons to resist the conclusion that such claims diminish responsibility and culpability, however. First and foremost, the association between brain abnormalities is only a hypothesis: the XYY hypothesis is now discredited, and the association between electroencephalogram abnormalities and violent tendencies is nowhere near perfect (Mark & Ervin, 1970). Even if the association between brain abnormalities and violence is real, the association would be only a correlation that need not imply causation; indeed, the original formulators of the dyscontrol syndrome cautioned that the head injuries could have been the result of violence rather than the cause, for the majority of the violent criminals sampled sustained multiple head injuries from their fighting (Mark & Ervin, 1970). And even if the dyscontrol-syndrome hypothesis, the child molestation hypothesis, and others of that ilk were correct, they would apply to only a fraction of people who do criminal violence; furthermore, not all of these people who have the alleged syndromes necessarily do criminal violence.

For the more general case of a person with normal brain functioning, we must recognize that explanations from the biological or social sciences are compatible with responsibility and free choice. Consider a voluntary movement, such as pointing a finger at this line of the book. It is not surprising that a reader's decision to point or not point can, without contradiction, be understood as a decision involving responsibility, as the result of brain processes, and as the outcome of prior life experiences. Yet the decision seems no less free for being so. So biological and developmental explanations do not necessarily eliminate responsibility. We must consider what else about emotions might incline people to say that people are or are not responsible for them. There are two issues worth considering: the first is whether people in everyday life hold others responsible for their emotions; the second is whether people *ought* to hold others responsible.

The first of these questions has been addressed by psychological research. The general finding is that people do in fact hold people responsible for their emotions—under certain conditions. Attributions of responsibility for emotions was the topic of two of Matthew Spackman's (1998) studies. Respondents were asked to rate an emotion that had recently occurred, with half of the respondents recalling and rating an emotion that they themselves had experienced and the other half rating an emotion experienced by someone else. In one study, the respondents in this latter condition described and rated an emotion that they had actually observed someone else having, whereas in the other the respondents rated an emotion that had been reported by the person who experienced it. The results revealed that respondents had no difficulty in rating the extent to which a person was responsible for his or her own emotion.

By analyzing the ratings, Spackman (1998) determined what factors best predicted whether a person was held responsible for his or her emotion. These factors—essentially a folk theory of responsibility for emotions— included the degree to which a person could control his or her emotion and the degree to which a person intended the actions he or she performed while having the emotion. It is interesting to note that the criteria that predicted the degree of responsibility were somewhat different when others' emotions were rated as compared with when one's own emotions were rated. When respondents rated their own emotions, the best predictor of their rating of personal responsibility included information that is not readily available to observers, such as their subjective experience (i.e., the degree to which their thoughts at the time were intentional, or the extent to which outside forces caused their emotion). When respondents rated others' emotions, responsibility was determined more on the basis of observable cues than on subjective experience. Others were deemed more responsible for their emotions when their emotions were inappropriate or low in intensity. In a related study, Spackman and Parrott (2001) examined descriptions of emotions they had extracted from classic American novels. These accounts, although fictional, could be understood as expressing everyday conceptions of emotion. Ratings of the texts revealed that responsibility was again related to the appropriateness and intensity of the emotions, with responsibility being highest for the least appropriate and least intense emotions.

Regardless of whose emotions were being rated, respondents consistently tended to allocate responsibility for emotions as if there were a finite amount of overall responsibility for an emotion; if one person is judged to have much responsibility, other people are judged to have less, and vice versa. This pattern of dividing a fixed portion of responsibility between actors has been observed by other researchers as well (Finkel & Groscup, 1997b; V. L. Hamilton & Hagiwara, 1992).

Thus, research suggests that people will hold others responsible for their emotions, at least under circumstances when the emotion could reasonably have been avoided. In this respect, then, the folk attribution of responsibility for emotion is remarkably similar to the general approach to responsibility that enjoys wide acceptance in the fields of philosophy and law (Hart, 1968; Oakley, 1992). It is also similar to psychological research on the attribution of blame (K. G. Shaver, 1985). In each of these fields, the notion of controllability is important to responsibility, so we now turn to the question of whether emotions are controllable.

EMOTION AND CONTROL

Most psychological research on the controllability of emotions centers on the ability to control emotional expressivity. For example, Gross and Levenson (1993) showed undergraduate students brief films that depicted medical procedures; one showed the treatment of burn victims, the other the amputation of an arm, and both elicited strong disgust. The students all watched the burn film without special instructions, but for the amputation film half were instructed to try their best not to let their feelings show. The students were videotaped as they watched the films, and their behavior was carefully analyzed. The analysis revealed that students were remarkably successful in suppressing their expressions of disgust.

Yet, when asked how disgusted they felt, students who tried to conceal their feelings reported just as much disgust as did students who did not try to conceal their feelings. However, the act of suppressing emotional behavior increased sympathetic nervous system activation. Gross and Levenson (1993) found that the students, while controlling outward expressions of their emotion, had greater increases in their skin conductance (often associated with inhibition of behavior), greater quickening of their pulse transmission speed (indicative of increased arterial blood pressure), and greater decreases in the amplitude of their pulse—all of which are signs of greater arousal of the sympathetic nervous system.

The facial and bodily responses studied by Gross and Levenson (1993) are not exhaustive of emotional reactions, however. When one is first exposed to an emotion-eliciting situation, one's initial appraisal of its significance can be quite spontaneous. People evaluate stimuli without intending to do so, without knowing that they do it, and sometimes without even being aware of the stimulus that they are evaluating; their attention can be grabbed by the arrival of an object that is spontaneously evaluated as desirable or as threatening. These evaluations can be so quick and automatic that they interfere with the task that a person is trying to accomplish (Pratto, 1994).

In addition to these evaluative and attentional reactions, a variety of bodily reactions can proceed so quickly and automatically that they can be difficult to control. Threatening stimuli can elicit startle and freezing responses that are the result of evolution. Joseph LeDoux (1994) has proposed that two categories of emotional behaviors can be distinguished. Type I responses are immediate, evolved, quite similar between different individuals of the same species, and largely involuntary. In the case of fear, the neural circuitry controlling Type I responses is in a part of the limbic system called the amygdala. Type II responses reflect an individual's past experiences, can occur alone or following Type I responses, and are under volitional control. In the case of fear, Type II responses also involve the amygdala, but in connection with other brain areas.

LeDoux's (1994) proposal is intriguingly similar to one made 2,000 years earlier by the Stoic philosophers, who distinguished emotions from what they termed *first movements*. First movements are involuntary reactions, which are brought about by an initial appearance and which cannot be controlled by reason. They are described as *shocks, jolts,* or *bites*. They can be either mental (such as the perception of injustice) or physical (such as blushing). But the Stoics did not consider first movements to be emotions. Emotion, they argued, requires the additional step of approving the appearance. Because this approval could be controlled by reason if suitable habits of thought were cultivated, the Stoics maintained that emotion per se could be controlled (Sorabji, 2000).

LeDoux (1994) defined emotion differently than did the Stoics, proposing that "the emotional reaction may have both voluntary and involuntary components" (p. 272). Nevertheless, LeDoux would agree with the Stoics that the involuntary aspects of emotion tend to occur quickly and that the more controllable aspects tend to occur later on in the sequence. It is worth noting that the time scale is quite short. LeDoux's most famous discovery shows that two neural pathways lead from sensory organs to the amygdala (where many fear responses are controlled). One goes directly to the amygdala from incoming sensory pathways without benefit of much interpretation. The other goes from incoming sensory pathways to the sensory cortex, where it receives significant amounts of analysis before proceeding to the amygdala. These pathways have been termed the *low road* and the *high road* by LeDoux (1996, p. 164). The low road, which is about twice as fast as the high road, permits only crude analysis of sounds and sights before determining whether fear should be elicited, whereas the high road, which lags by about one tenth of a second, is capable of much finer discriminations. The low road might seem to be maladaptive because it yields fear responses that are frequently pointless—such as freezing at the sight of a leaf blowing in the wind and jumping at the sound of a stick snapping—but LeDoux argued that this cost is outweighed by the benefits of speed, because occasionally those reactions will be correct, and there is a large benefit to reacting quickly to a real threat.

The findings of ancient Stoics such as Seneca and of contemporary neuroscientists such as LeDoux seem to imply that some emotional impulses initially are impossible to control but after a fairly brief interval are controllable to some degree. However, it is interesting to consider that Gross and Levenson (1993) actually found that some signs of emotional control can appear *before* the emotion begins. In their experiment, some of the physiological signs of emotional suppression tended to start before the film of the amputation even began; merely anticipating the onset of an event that one wished not to react to initiated some of the mechanisms of self-control. Thus, under some circumstances probably no aspect of emotion is completely uncontrolled.

For this reason, emotion theorists often describe emotions as being a process in flux, not a state that is constant (e.g., Lazarus, 1991). The environment is constantly being appraised, as is one's ability to cope with what the environment holds. Emotion theorists consider self-control to be present throughout the emotion process. One particularly influential theorist put it thus:

> There is regulation of confrontation with events: Emotional events are sought and avoided. There is appraisal regulation: Appraisals can be modified within a considerable range by selective attention and self-serving cognitive activities. There is impulse control: Emotional urges can be suppressed so as to disappear from consciousness as well as from behavior, and they can be amplified. Overt response can be checked, or attenuated, shaped, or replaced by some other response. (Frijda, 1986, p. 401)

Some emotion theorists tend to equate uncontrollable responses with innateness and controllable responses with experience, but this equation is false. It is clearly possible for a learned response to become habitual, automated, and thus difficult to control. Cognitive psychology demonstrates that complex, learned mental processes such as reading, once practiced, can become so automated that they will occur without conscious attention. These facts about controlling emotions have implications for culpability that we shall return to later in this chapter. The nearly continuous possibility of control, and the possibility that choices of thought and self-regulation can form habits that shape emotional responses, are topics that we shall return to after we have considered some other issues concerning emotions and culpability, such as the cognitive nature of emotions and the objectivity of emotions.

THE COGNITIVE NATURE OF EMOTIONS
(OR, ZAJONC VS. LAZARUS)

Are emotions evaluative or are they mechanistic? Put another way, are they cognitive or not? The language of the Law often seems split between these two incompatible views of emotion (Kahan & Nussbaum, 1996). It is interesting to note that Psychology is also split, as shown by a famous debate in the 1980s. The debate was launched by Robert Zajonc (1980) in a feisty anticognitive article, "Feeling and Thinking: Preferences Need No Inferences," published in the journal *American Psychologist*. Zajonc proposed that cognition and emotion should be conceived as two independent systems, often working together, but capable of being completely at odds. Two years later, Richard Lazarus (1982) published a rebuttal in the same journal. Lazarus defended the idea that the beginning of an emotion requires an evaluative perception of the nature of the situation, known as an appraisal. An emotional appraisal evaluates events or objects as significantly affecting a person's concerns, goals, or values in a positive or negative way. The debate continued for several rounds, with Zajonc (e.g., 1984) critiquing Lazarus's position and Lazarus (e.g., 1984) rebutting Zajonc's.

Although the debate has never fully been resolved, considerable progress has been made in understanding the underlying issues. It is generally agreed that one source of disagreement involved incompatible definitions of the two key terms in the debate. *Emotion* was used somewhat narrowly by Lazarus (1982, 1984), to refer to prototypical emotions such as anger or jealousy, whereas Zajonc (1980, 1984) used it much more broadly, to include a range of affective phenomena such as preferences for consumer products and free-floating moods. Also critical was the difference in the debaters' use of the term *cognition*. Zajonc meant it in the extremely narrow sense of deliberate, verbal, controllable cogitation, whereas Lazarus used it in the quite broad sense of *information processing* such as is generally used in modern cognitive psychology (Parrott & Sabini, 1989). Any statement about the cognitive nature of emotions, then, requires a careful discussion of just what is meant by *cognitive*.

The thinking that leads to emotion is usually called an *appraisal*. Appraisals are characterized by an assessment of the current situation and the implications it has for the well-being of oneself and of the things that one cares about. The classic experiments demonstrating the importance of appraisals in emotions were performed by Richard Lazarus (1966), who asked people to watch movies showing extremely unpleasant scenes of people being mutilated in primitive rites or in woodworking accidents. Before viewing the films, some of the people were encouraged to interpret the filmed events as harmful and painful, whereas others were encouraged to deny the extent of the harm and interpret them as benign, and still others were encouraged to distance themselves mentally from the victims and to view the scenes in a more detached, intellectual manner. All of the people then viewed the same films, yet the first group experienced more stress and more intense, negative emotions than did the other two groups. After the film Lazarus asked the viewers to describe how they were feeling, and he also measured certain physiological symptoms of autonomic nervous system activity; the groups differed on both the self-report and the physiological measures. These experiments demonstrated how changes in cognitive appraisal could produce differences in the intensity of emotions that occur (Lazarus, 1966).

There is controversy, however, over the type of judgments that should be included in the concept of appraisal. Some appraisals are quite careful and deliberate, as when a person thinks through a remark and only gradually realizes that it was inconsiderate (and then becomes angry), whereas other appraisals are very quick, outside conscious awareness, and independent of one's rational faculties. The latter situation spurred Zajonc to propose that emotion results from a system independent from the cognitive system, and it has been claimed that the "low road" and "high road" proposed by LeDoux (1996) correspond to the emotional and cognitive systems originally postulated by Zajonc (see Zajonc, 2000). However, LeDoux does not agree. LeDoux used the term *emotion* in a manner much more like Lazarus did than like Zajonc did by maintaining cognition is involved in both low and high roads; the difference between the two is not that only one is cognitive, but that for one road the cognition is cursory and poorly elaborated whereas for the other road the cognition is more elaborated. If this is the case, then the low road and high road are capable of reaching different conclusions about the emotional significance of a stimulus, and, because the low road is faster, it can initiate its emotional reaction before the high road registers its disagreement.

Zajonc's (1980) proposal, however, generally fails to explain a number of ways in which cognition and emotion are intertwined (Parrott & Sabini, 1989). For example, although certain emotions are often called—and believed to be—irrational, this would not make sense if emotions did not intrinsically entail beliefs. Also, emotional development seems to require cognitive development (e.g., children don't get embarrassed until they know about social roles and appearances), and such cognitive dependencies are not consistent with Zajonc's independent systems. As numerous philosophers and psychologists have pointed out, most emotions are *about* something, such as *being insulted* or *being threatened with a knife*, but it seems necessary for something to be cognitive if it is to be about something. In short, there is a host of problems with proposing a separation between emotion and cognition (Lazarus, 1982; Solomon, 1976). The most important problem is that the way in which a person thinks about a situation obviously affects how he or she feels.

The cognitive alternative to Zajonc's (1980) dual-system solution is suggested by theorists such as Lazarus (1982), who views emotion as intrinsically linked to cognition. The key to such a solution is to be clear that *cognition* is a broad term that includes a variety of information processing, not all of which is conscious, deliberate, or verbal (Parrott & Sabini, 1989). Such cognition can be difficult to control, and therefore can explain why emotion and reason can be in conflict; this view nevertheless conceives of emotion as involving cognition.

As we have described, the concepts of passion and emotion have long histories of being understood both as bodily and as cognitive. When the Law draws on folk conceptions of emotion, it often gives the appearance of drawing more heavily from the body-based tradition than from the cognitive tradition. When the Law distinguishes murder from voluntary manslaughter on the basis of whether the accused was acting in the *heat of passion* or whether enough time had passed for the accused's *blood to cool*, the Law is clearly drawing on everyday metaphors of emotion as a type of force. When the Model Penal Code (American Law Institute, 1962) allows murder to be downgraded to manslaughter when the accused was subject to extreme emotional disturbance, it also seems to emphasize the primitive aspects of emotion, depicting emotions as a "disturbance" akin to temporary insanity.

In the case of the common law terms *heat of passion* and *cooling time*, it seems possible that these heat metaphors are not intended literally. Anger may take time to dissipate just as a heated skillet takes time to cool, but that fact need not imply that anyone actually believes that anger is caused by elevated blood temperature, or that thermal insulation, say, provided by a heavy winter coat, may prolong anger. Perhaps these phrases merely express in compact form a more complex phenomenon whose nature may involve thinking and attention but is not specified or fully understood by the speaker.

In an important law review article, Kahan and Nussbaum (1996) argued that these metaphors can be deceiving. Even though the Law's language may suggest a view of emotion that is distinctly primitive, bodily, and mechanical, they argued that the Law's logic suggests an evaluative understanding of emotions. Kahan and Nussbaum claimed that the presence of emotions such as rage can be mitigating not because of a mechanical loss of control but because the rage expresses values that are proper in the situation, even if they do not justify killing. In folk theories of emotion, anger is the result of being transgressed. Anger can be mitigating because an angry reaction to certain transgressions (e.g., insulting one's honor or attacking one's loved ones) seems appropriate, thus making the killing a result of a mixture of appropriate and inappropriate values. By Kahan and Nussbaum's account, it is conceivable that the Law expresses understanding of emotion's cognitive aspects even as it draws on noncognitive metaphors to describe it. The way that jurors arrive at decisions about murder and manslaughter suggests that they understand the defendant's emotions as expressing judgments about interpersonal, psychological situations, which requires those emotions to be understood as involving cognition of some type. The cognitive approach to emotion advocated by theorists such as Lazarus provides a scientific basis for such an approach.

The cognitive approach to emotion also supplies a way in which people can be held responsible for their emotions. If emotions are based on appraisals of circumstances, and if appraisals can be influenced by the information sought, then people are responsible for their emotions in the sense that they are responsible for the influences they choose to expose themselves to, as well as for what they choose to selectively ignore (Solomon, 1980).

Thus, the cognitive nature of emotion can supply a way to link emotion to responsibility. But the link relies on these appraisals, interpretations, and judgments being refutable, and this can be so only if they are objective. Yet, emotions are often thought of as being subjective, not objective, and subjective feelings are not refutable. Thus, we must examine the objectivity and the subjectivity of emotion.

OBJECTIVITY AND SUBJECTIVITY

Throughout Shakespeare's plays, a recurrent theme is that passion can cloud reason. In *Troilus and Cressida* (Shakespeare, 1938), Troilus is questioned by his brother Hector about his passion for keeping Helen: "Is your blood/So madly hot that no discourse of reason,/Nor fear of bad success in a bad cause,/Can qualify the same?" (II, ii, 115–118).

The folk belief that judgment can be clouded by emotion encompasses more than powerful emotional states; it also includes long-term desires and self-centered points of view. Judgment is believed to be biased not only by states such as anger but also by the wish to maintain high self-esteem and the normal human tendency to pay greater attention to one's own efforts and problems than to other people's. Thus, this folk belief is related to one of the meanings of the head–heart dichotomy that we described in chapter 3 (this volume): it has to do with a contrast between what a disinterested person would believe and what one's personal cares and concerns incline one to believe—which is essentially the contrast between objectivity and subjectivity (Sabini & Silver, 1982).

A classic account of how passions promote a bias away from an objective viewpoint was given by James Madison in *The Federalist Papers* (A. Hamilton, Madison, & Jay, 1787/1961, Madison, No. 10, p. 79, italics in original):

> No man is allowed to be a judge in his own cause, because his interest would certainly bias his judgment, and, not improbably, corrupt his integrity. With equal, nay with greater reason, a body of men are unfit to be both judges and parties at the same time; yet what are many of the most important acts of legislation, but so many judicial determinations, not indeed concerning the rights of single persons, but concerning the rights of large bodies of citizens? . . . The inference to which we are brought is, that the *causes* of faction cannot be removed, and that relief is only to be sought in the means of controlling its *effects*.

The remedy for the excesses of subjectivity is greater objectivity, and Madison argued that a republican government would protect from passions more so than would a pure democracy. This preference for objectivity in legal settings extends even to behavior in the courtroom. Sally Engle Merry's (1990) research on the legal perceptions of working class Americans provides interesting examples of how everyday emotional discourse is screened out of the courtroom:

To the people who work in the lower courts—the judges, prosecutors, and clerks—interpersonal cases are unwelcome. . . . These problems are . . . difficult because they are so emotional. The people themselves are likely to get out of control, to violate the rules of appropriate behavior in court. The telltale sign is an angry victim who brings up other issues. A prosecutor who regularly handled interpersonal cases said it can be very embarrassing to bring cases like this to trial, and she tries to avoid it, for if people start shouting at each other in the courtroom, the judge will say to her: "Why did you bring this crap in here?" . . . Prosecutors and clerks prefer to send cases such as these to mediation rather than to bring them to trial. Nor do judges like getting involved with them. . . . In contrast, a clean case, such as a breaking-and-entering case or an unprovoked assault and battery in which the incident occurs between strangers, does not raise these hazards. Everyone but the parties seems anxious to keep emotional cases out of the courtroom. (pp. 14–15)

The history of Anglo-American law reveals a strong preference for objective rules, and the need for objectivity presses for the Law to exclude emotions. But exclusion is obviously not possible for many alleged crimes and defenses, so containment has been the typical stratagem, with emotions being included only in the most rigid, rule-like manner possible. That general reluctance to deal with emotion, we suggest, along with the desire to avoid the appearance of subjectivity as much as possible, has inclined the law toward the more mechanical, physical, bodily aspects of everyday emotion language.

Yet, it does not have to be this way. Everyday notions of justice involve appraising the motives of the defendant; they involve understanding a moral story that allows the defendant's culpability to be appraised (Finkel, 1995b). Jurors' application of mechanical-sounding expressions such as *cooling time* is best understood as assessing the appropriateness of the defendant's emotions within the context of a nuanced matrix of social norms (Kahan & Nussbaum, 1996). Elements of folk theories of emotion make emotions suitable for this subtle task.

The more cognitive aspects of emotions are crucial, obviously, and these we have already discussed. In the present context it is important to add that everyday emotion concepts can be understood as having objective meaning as well as involving subjective points of view. The concept of anger, for example, can be used in both subjective and objective senses. In the subjective sense, if someone says he or she feels angry, then that is how he or she feels, regardless of the reasonableness of the emotional appraisal or the morality of the action tendencies that are part of his or her anger. But everyday emotion talk can take on an objective dimension, too. Someone who reports feeling anger (in the subjective sense) can be told that he or she has no right to feel angry, that it is not reasonable to feel angry, or that he or she is being oversensitive or arbitrary in his or her expectations. These replies are expressions of objective rules concerning the conditions under which one is entitled to be angry. In this objective sense, anger is not a feeling but rather a social role that one is entitled to play under specific circumstances.

James Averill, who proposed the metaphor of emotion as a social role (described in chap. 3, this volume), has analyzed hundreds of reports of everyday anger. On the basis of this research, he generated a complex list of rules and norms governing anger (Averill, 1982, chap. 14). For example, people are entitled to become angry at intentional wrongdoing, as well as at unintentional misdeeds if due to negligence; they are not entitled to be angry at events beyond a person's influence or at events that can be remedied in conventional ways. Anger should be used to restore equity or to prevent reoccurrences, but not to achieve selfish ends or to inflict suffering. The list of rules, which goes on for two pages, specifies standards for angry behavior (e.g., it must be proportional to the instigation). It is interesting that anger must be enacted so as to be spontaneous and heated—anger that is deliberate and cool is not allowed, because the point of this social role is to entitle the angry person to special rights on the grounds that the person is in a special emotional state and his or her behavior is to be interpreted as passion, not as action, for which he or she therefore is not held fully responsible. This state cannot last more than a few hours or days at most, and it must cease when "the target apologizes, offers restitution, or gives assurance that the instigation will not be repeated" (Averill, 1982, p. 325).

These standards are subtle and complex, but they are objective. By Averill's (1982) account, people who display anger without following the rules will not be entitled to the special privileges accorded to angry persons—they will not have a right to be angry, so their claim of feeling angry would not be validated socially; it would merely be a report of subjective anger and would not count as objectively justified anger.

The existence of such objective standards for emotions means that emotions need not threaten the impartiality and reliability of court decisions. Jurors can judge emotions such as anger by the standards of everyday society, subtle and complex though they be. Emotions that meet the standards may mitigate or incriminate, whereas those that do not can be disallowed or discredited. The "ordinary, reasonable person" need not be an unemotional person, just a person whose emotions meet the objective standards for their elicitation and enactment.

BRIEF EMOTIONS, LONG-LASTING EMOTIONS, AND THE FORMATION OF CHARACTER

As we have seen, the controllability of emotions is most limited in the short term. One reason for this is the element of surprise: an emotion brought on by unexpected circumstances is one that people would not be prepared to restrain. Another reason is that people can be mistaken about circumstances and that it can take them time to ascertain that they were in error.

When emotions are long-lasting, however, there is opportunity to recover from surprise, rectify errors of judgment, restore perspective about the relative importance of competing values, and engage in methods of self-control. A long-lasting emotion can therefore appear to be a choice, the result of self-control designed to nurture the emotion, not to dispel it. The contrast to Othello's flash of jealousy is Iago's long-standing resentment and hatred. When such long-lasting emotion contributes to a criminal act, it can make a person seem more culpable, not less.

Emotions can reveal a person's character in three ways. A person's emotions can reveal something about that person's true values because appraisal reveals a person's habitual cares and goals. Keith Oatley (2000) puts this insight into the language of the cognitive approach to emotion: "People's actions and thoughts flow from interpersonal goals that are habitual, and hence somewhat predictable by self and others. We define character, and its effects, in terms of such habitual goals" (p. 4). Second, when an emotion continues under circumstances that permit regulation, suppression, or moderation, then the emotion begins to involve an element of choice. In choosing not to engage in self-regulation, a person reveals a commitment to the view implicit in the emotion. Such a choice therefore communicates a person's values (Planalp, 1999). Finally, because self-regulation of emotions can involve efforts to match one's appraisals with one's rational assessment of the truth of events and of their importance, the speed and direction of one's struggles with emotion can further reveal one's values.

According to Kahan and Nussbaum (1996), the aim of jurors' assessments of emotions is to judge the values of the defendant:

> A good person not only values the right things but values them in the right amount in relation to other goods. We might expect a person who is snubbed by a colleague in a professional setting to be angry; anger reveals that she properly values her honor and dignity. At the same time, if this person became *more* angry at this slight than at, say the wrongful infliction of an injury upon her child, we would say that her relative valuations are skewed; the intensity of her anger would then reveal that her love of honor is excessive in relation to her love of her child. The "heat of passion" requirement accommodates assessments of an offender's relative valuations. The existence of passion demonstrates that the offender values the good . . . sufficiently in relation to other goods. If a man dispassionately killed his wife's paramour—much as he might dispassionately kill an annoying mosquito—we would suspect that his beliefs about what is important are skewed: the absence of anger would show us that he invests too little value in fidelity; his act of killing without anger would show us that he invests too little value in others' lives. (pp. 315–316)

By this account, emotions express values because they are based on cognitive appraisals of how situations impact the people and goals that one cares about. Emotions that are displayed in inappropriate circumstances or to an inappropriate degree are judged as showing inappropriate values and thus count against a defendant. Thus, in appraising the emotions of another, what comes to light is the other's psychology, through which the person's thoughts, judgments, intentions, motives, and morals are seen, so to speak, and only thereafter is a normative judgment made. This psychological evaluation *first*, followed by the normative evaluation *second*, was what Pillsbury (1998) was not acknowledging in his normative view. The legal phrase *heat of passion*, by this analysis, displays a cognitive and moral subtlety that belies its primitive, mechanical imagery.

The legal phrase *cooling time* can be similarly analyzed:

> When an offense is fresh, we tolerate—indeed, expect—strong anger; it is precisely because a person *ought* to value fidelity intensely that the law is prepared to mitigate the punishment of the cuckold if he kills shortly after learning of the adultery. But if the cuckold continues to be obsessively angry for days, weeks, months, or even years, then we will regard his view of what's important in life as skewed. Unshakable rage reveals that he values something—honor, control—too much. It also reveals that he values other things that matter—like the life of the victim and the lawful resolution of disputes—too little. If a person has good character, he won't stop valuing fidelity as time passes, but he will take the steps necessary—perhaps divorcing his wife, or possibly notifying authorities of the transgression of the offending man—to restore "tranquility of . . . judgment" in a way that reflects an appropriate valuation of all the goods and interests at stake. (Kahan & Nussbaum, 1996, pp. 317–318)

Thus, it is not the subjective existence of anger per se that matters in determining culpability. It is the objective adherence to the rules of anger and the moral implications of that adherence (or lack thereof) that influences judgments of culpability in commonsense justice. Put another way, what is evaluated in judging culpability is the degree of integration of thinking, feeling, motives, and values, and not just the emotions as a separate entity or element.

People can reveal their values in their initial emotional reactions, as well as in their longer term struggles with their emotions. But there is still another way in which people take responsibility for their emotions. Aristotle (1984) argued that it is possible for a person to train his or her emotions. By immersing oneself in situations likely to induce certain appraisals (say, developing sympathy for others) and by practicing emotions that we approve and discouraging those that we disapprove, we can gradually train our emotional natures and shape our moral character so that we become better people (Oakley, 1992). Parents, of course, attempt to educate their children's emotions by instructing them about the appropriate way to interpret events (Sherman, 1989). People continue this process throughout life, developing insight into their emotional reactions and developing new habits of thought (Peters, 1970). In short, despite limited means of directly controlling one's emotions, there are an abundance of ways in which to influence them indirectly.

Because this potential for regulating emotion exists, because people always face choices about what reactions to allow themselves to have, it is crucial to realize that emotions and the law are not fully separate entities. One factor that potentially can influence people's choices about emotional reactions is the Law itself, which sends important signals that can shape the emotions of the citizenry. People have some choice in forcing themselves to consider another person's point of view or in directing their attention to other issues. Whether the Law states that killing shortly after finding one's spouse *in flagrante delicto* will be treated lightly or whether the Law states that such killing will be treated harshly potentially matters a great deal. However, we do not claim that a threat of punishment will always deter crime; our claim is only that the Law delivers a message about what is acceptable, understandable, forgivable, or not. The Law is part of the system of cultural norms that influences choices about how to behave, and therefore it is, in principle, impossible to consider the effects of emotion on behavior as if they were independent of the Law.

It should be noted that our claim is different from the standard one, in which punishments influence crime rates by imposing a "cost" on crime, but that potential criminals either discount the probability of getting convicted (the cost) or overweight the benefits of committing the crime. Kahan (1997) persuasively contrasted this type of "economic" conception of deterrence with what social psychologists call *social influence* and *social meaning* and how these factors influence individuals' decisions to commit crimes. Social influence refers to ways that people's choices are affected by what they see other people do; social meaning refers to how the Law affects the significance of compliance and criminality. Kahan argued that variables that have little effect on the cost of committing a crime nevertheless have significant impact on individuals' decisions about whether to engage in criminal behavior. Social influence works by setting public examples that establish social norms. Public policies, such as preventing visible disorder (e.g., graffiti), have no effect on the cost of committing a crime but can nevertheless lower crime rates by creating the impression that most people do not engage in criminal activities. Likewise, the Law imparts meaning on actions by conveying what a community values and condemns, what it deems moral and immoral. These meanings can influence crime rates, such as when laws against possessing a gun reduce the public display of guns which thereby reduces guns' value for conferring status, but they may not necessarily reduce crime rates (Kahan, 1997).

Our proposal is that the effect of laws that address emotions is not merely to accommodate human frailties and punish human vices, but to influence behavior through social influence and social meaning. This view of emotions and the Law is most consistent with the psychological theory of social constructionism, which holds that social practices influence human psychology (Harré, 1986). In the case of emotions and the law, the constructionist thesis is that the effects of emotions, such as the degree to which people find that their emotions overwhelm their ability to obey the law, will to some extent be determined by the laws themselves. For this reason there exists a motive for the Law to be somewhat conservative in allowing mitigation or exculpation based on the presence of an emotional state. Human nature is not an invariant that the Law must accommodate; rather, the Law's accommodations can actually shape human nature and thereby facilitate the very crimes that the Law mitigates or excuses.

One might ask, then, why the Law permits any mitigation of emotions whatsoever. If human nature is actually malleable, why not use the Law to improve human nature by just abolishing the category of voluntary manslaughter altogether? One answer is that community sentiment would not favor making all the changes that such a strict standard would require. As Kahan and Nussbaum (1996) argued in the passages quoted previously, people's sympathy toward crimes of passion is aroused not by the uncontrollability per se of the emotion, but by the values that give rise to the emotion. Society and the Law want people to value human life, but also to value marital fidelity, personal honor, and so on, and these additional values require accommodation. From this perspective, the reason why the Law allows the mitigation or excusing of crimes of passion is that the community has sympathy for the person who is torn between two important values that are both endorsed by the community.

The emotion theorist Averill (1982) advanced a similar argument when, speaking of anger in particular, he observed that people face conflicting sets of norms. On the one hand, deliberate acts of violence are condemned, but, on the other hand, retribution against perceived wrongs is proscribed:

> By attributing his response to anger (or temporary insanity), an accused killer is in effect asking the jury to judge him not by the standards that prohibit the deliberate taking of life, but by the standards (sometimes called the "unwritten law") that encourage protection of home and honor. There is a problem, however. The proscription against homicide does not allow many exceptions. The killing itself must therefore be redefined: No longer is it the act of a normal human being; rather, it is the result of an irrational, animal-like impulse (anger) or the symptom of a disease (temporary insanity). (p. 124)

The role of emotion, Averill suggested, is to allow violence to be treated as a passion rather than as an action if it conforms to the rules of anger. The demand for retribution is thereby fulfilled without violating the proscription against deliberate acts of violence. If the rules are not met, however, the defendant's claim of passion can be disallowed. The violence is then treated as an action for which the person can be held culpable under the law.

CONCLUSION:
MACBETH AND THE PSYCHOLOGY OF EMOTIONS

When Macbeth commits regicide in Act II, he has experienced a series of emotions that inform the audience about his motives and character. Do these emotions mitigate the blameworthiness of what he has done? Should a jury modify its verdict if Macbeth were to plead that he had been provoked by Duncan and the three witches, shamed by Lady Macbeth, or at least shown to be less than evil by his reluctant ambivalence? The intuition of the person watching the play is not to find any mitigation in Macbeth's emotions, and the psychology of emotion we have reviewed provides a number of justifications for this intuition. Far from mitigating his crime, Macbeth's emotions help establish his culpability. His anger at Duncan will not mitigate his crime because the action that offended him did not objectively justify anger, as Averill's (1982) analysis shows. There is no objective obligation to choose Macbeth as heir to the throne, and, objectively, Macbeth's reaction cannot be justified anger; it was merely frustration at being blocked from his personal goal of becoming king. As for the witches' prophecy of his becoming king, Macbeth could simply have waited, as Banquo was content to do. Furthermore, Macbeth had ample opportunity to engage in self-control, which he demonstrated by successfully deciding to "proceed no further in this business" (I, vii, 31). Macbeth demonstrated he had knowledge of what is right, but he also demonstrated that he did not value it enough (as Kahan & Nussbaum, 1996, would put it). His reasons were partly principled, partly pragmatic. His desire to be king was at least as strong as his desire to value being a subject, kinsman, and host, and it took only Lady Macbeth to push him away from what is good toward murder in the name of becoming king. Rather than use his powers of self-determination to choose the right path and better himself, he actually chose to make himself evil by nurturing habits of thought and action that made it easier and easier to seek power ruthlessly.

On this final point, Shakespeare's psychology surpasses that of modern academic psychology (Parrott, 2000). Critics such as Harold Bloom (2003) have pointed out that Shakespeare's characters develop over the course of a play. Shakespeare's Macbeth began the play a brave and loyal supporter of the king. He brought himself, with much effort and horror, to kill the king. Throughout the rest of the play, he practiced ruthlessness, using the techniques for building character to become increasingly evil. He was responsible for one more death, that of Banquo, and then for even more, including Lady MacDuff and her children. By the end, he no longer feels horror or remorse; killing has become easy for him. He retrained his emotions to become a character different from the one he once was.

5

EMOTIONS IN CONTEXT:
TIME, FUNCTION, AND TYPE

In the previous two chapters we discussed emotion in general: as a concept in folk psychology, and as a topic studied in academic psychology. This approach, however, was doubly abstract. The first source of abstraction derives from the way the broad category of "emotion" overarches a myriad of particular emotions. Most psychological research tends to be about particular emotions (with an emphasis on the plural). Yet before we discuss what contemporary research says about emotion, we need to discuss the differences between emotions.

The previous two chapters were abstract in a second way, too. Discussion of the nature of emotion can make it seem to be a static state of mind whereas, in fact, emotions develop over time. People are continually reappraising their circumstances and regulating their emotional state, and, as a result, their emotions are continuously in flux. Furthermore, new emotions arise as circumstances change, and people also have new emotions in response to their previous emotions. These sequences of emotions become a narrative of developing evaluations, concerns, and motivations, and this temporal sequence often characterizes a person's motives and character in ways relevant to culpability. So in this chapter we continue to explore the psychology of emotions, but with two new elements that will bring us closer to understanding the role emotions can play in legal culpability.

EMOTIONS IN THE PLURAL: ANOTHER LOOK AT FOLK AND ACADEMIC PSYCHOLOGY

It is difficult for most people to answer the question, what is emotion?, but it is easy to answer the question, could you name some examples of emotions? No problem there: love, anger, hate, depression, fear, jealousy, happiness, passion, affection, sadness, grief, rage, aggravation, ecstasy, sorrow, joy—this is just to name the first 16 from a list of 213 that were rated in a now-classic study by P. Shaver, Schwartz, Kirson, and O'Connor (1987). These researchers culled their list of English emotion words from several published sources, and then asked college students to rate how confidently they could rate each one as being (or as not being) an emotion. Emotion is the superordinate category; the 213 nouns in this study were all subordinate to varying degrees, and the students' ratings showed these words to vary widely in how clearly they belonged to the superordinate category. The 16 words previously listed were the ones with the highest ratings, which were among the words that, according to the raters, *definitely* would be called an emotion. Examples of words with more moderate ratings are *glumness, irritation, contempt,* and *astonishment*. At the bottom of the rankings were words regarded, at best, as poor examples of emotion: *alertness, carefulness, deliberateness,* and, at the bottom, *intelligence*.

P. Shaver et al. (1987) then selected the top 135 words and asked college students to sort them into groups of similar emotions. The frequency with which any pair of words ended up in the same group was used as a measure of the words' similarity, and this measure was used to construct a hierarchy of emotion words with the statistical technique of cluster analysis. The output of this procedure is a large, branching tree structure that depicts the way that the domain of emotions can be divided into subgroupings at various levels of detail. At the bottom of the tree structure are all 135 emotions. Above that are small clusters that combine the most similar words (e.g., *apprehension* and *worry, grouchiness* and *grumpiness*). Above that are a smaller number of larger clusters, still quite homogeneous (e.g., *rage, wrath, hate, spite, vengefulness, dislike, resentment*), that combine the most similar of the smaller clusters. As this tree diagram nears the top, at a certain point only five large clusters contain virtually all the emotions: these clusters—termed *affection, happiness, anger, sadness,* and *fear*—are what the researchers judged to be the basic level of categorization.

These distinctions were made by college students, not by psychologists or emotion experts, so the findings demonstrate that the contemporary American folk psychology of emotion recognizes the different categories of emotion as having important standing in their own right. People naturally use basic-level emotion words in their everyday conversation. Young children learn basic-level emotion words (*happy, sad, mad*) before they learn the superordinate (*emotion*) or subordinates (P. Shaver et al., 1987).

In academic psychology, early theorists, such as W. James (1884), Papez (1937), and MacLean (1949), tended to treat emotion as a general phenomenon and a unitary category. Contemporary researchers continue to talk about the general category, but their research much more carefully addresses the differences between different emotions. There are two primary reasons for this shift in emphasis. The first is that the category of emotion actually is quite heterogeneous, at all levels of analysis. There turns out to be no single *emotion center* in the brain, but rather an assortment of brain regions governing a variety of components of different emotional reactions (Panksepp, 1998). The cognitive effects of emotions are different for different emotions, as we shall see later in this chapter. The social effects of anger are not the same as those of embarrassment or guilt (Parkinson, Fischer, & Manstead, 2005). So this heterogeneity across all levels of analysis has led researchers to distinguish specific types of emotion in their research.

The other reason for the increasing emphasis on basic and subordinate levels of analysis has been the emergence of an important new theme in emotion research: functionalism. Emotions are generally understood not to consist merely of feelings but to have physiological, cognitive, and social effects. Many aspects of emotion can be understood physiologically as changes in "action readiness" (Frijda, 1986). For example, changes in muscle tension and blood flow facilitate quicker and more energetic responses. In a cognitive manner, emotions may influence people's expectations and what they pay attention to. Memory can be biased, judgment altered, and even one's style of thinking affected by the emotional state one is in (Forgas, 1995). Each of these could impair or facilitate perception, decision making, and action under certain circumstances. In the social arena, emotions can help harmonize and coordinate social interactions by nonverbally communicating a person's desires and intentions. Emotional expressions often induce similar or complementary emotions in others, and thus serve as powerful means of interpersonal influence. Behavioral changes can lead to approach or avoidance, dominating or submitting, caution or self-protection, nurture or censure (Keltner & Haidt, 1999; Tiedens & Leach, 2004).

To a reader accustomed to the everyday associations of the term *emotional*, it may seem odd that academics have come to think of emotions as playing useful functions, but the academic conception of emotion has grown apart from the everyday folk definition. Functionalism applies to both positive and negative emotions, and functionality lies not in the pleasantness of the feeling but in the usefulness of the emotion's effects (Parrott, 1993a). Positive emotions, such as exuberance, happiness, and contentment, are functional not because they feel good but because they can have effects such as increasing exploration and creativity, promoting sociability, and recovering from the effects of stress (Jamison, 2004; Tugade & Fredrickson, 2002). Negative emotions, such as anger, fear, or shame, are obviously not pleasant, though they can be functional: negative emotions signal the existence of a problem and can function to rectify that problem. Many negative emotions prepare for withdrawal or escape, although some, such as anger and contempt, prepare for confrontation. The action readiness of negative emotions is often evident in a lowered threshold for initiating that action: the angry person is irritable; the fearful person is skittish; the sad person is withdrawn and difficult to energize (Parrott, 2002).

Functionalists assume that emotions' consequences must on balance be helpful, or at least that they used to be helpful at the time in evolutionary or cultural history when they came into being. This assumption is held by researchers across the range of approaches to emotion. Those who emphasize the biological and genetic basis see emotions as the product of biological evolution, whereas those who emphasize the learned and cultural basis see emotions as playing a role within a cultural system. Emotions seem too elaborate to exist by accident (although Darwin, 1872, famously maintained that some did).

Nevertheless, the functionality of emotions exists as a potential, not as a certainty. In reality, emotions can be either helpful or harmful. The functions that emotions can serve provide the best explanation of why they exist, but that does not mean that emotions are always useful (Parrott, 2001). In some cases, responses that once were usually functional now are usually not. An example would be some reactions to stress, such as increased heart rate and cortisol levels, which were much more useful for fleeing from predators than they now are in coping with busy schedules. And even responses that are still quite useful, such as focusing attention on threats, will not necessarily be useful every time (for example, when one does not notice solutions in the periphery). For many reasons emotions that have a function can nevertheless sometimes cause more harm than benefit. First, there is an element of probability to functional responses. Just as it is usually functional for moths to fly toward light because it increases their chance of reproductive success, it may, at other times, lead moths to flames. This is also true for emotions, which may frequently be useful but occasionally are not. Consider the effects of adrenaline release triggered by fear, which can be helpful for gross motor actions such as fleeing from attack or rescuing a wandering child but only make matters worse when what one fears is an indelicate performance of Beethoven on one's violin. Emotions can also be dysfunctional when they are mismanaged (Parrott, 2002). Emotions can be expressed in a variety of ways, and habits and choices about how to express them can make a big difference. Anger at one's boss can motivate career-saving professional assertiveness or a career-destroying wisecrack: both are expressions of anger, but only one would yield more benefits than costs.

There are still other reasons why emotions can go astray (Parrott, 2001). One involves the accuracy of the appraisal. Emotions' functions fit the circumstances that normally elicit the emotions: anger from transgression, fear from threat, sadness from loss, and so forth. Yet, if the appraisal of the situation is incorrect, the emotion will occur in a context for which it is not at all suited and thus is unlikely to be useful. Another problem can involve situations with multiple, simultaneous concerns. An emotion that is perfectly appropriate for one situation in one's life can nevertheless cause problems in other aspects of one's life, as when distraction resulting from marital problems causes poor performance at one's workplace. Functionality also depends on how one copes with one's emotions. Anxiety about a major project at work could be functional if one copes with anxiety by focusing greater attention and energy on the problem, but it could be dysfunctional if one copes by getting drunk.

The basic point, for our purposes, is that the functions of emotion are not constant across the superordinate category because different emotions have different effects, which serve different functions. Most of what one can say about how emotions function must be said at the basic level or lower. To discuss specific functions, one must address specific emotions. Later in this chapter, we consider a number of specific emotions that are particularly relevant to the Law, but before we begin our survey, we must introduce a second element of this chapter's less abstract approach to emotion.

EMOTIONS IN TIME: PERSPECTIVES FROM FOLK AND ACADEMIC PSYCHOLOGIES

Just as we have moved from the superordinate, *emotion*, to the basic level of particular emotions, so too must we move from considering emotions as static states to considering how they change over time. Such an approach is found in folk psychology as well as in academic psychology. The evidence about folk psychology can once again be found in the seminal paper by P. Shaver et al. (1987), who, in a second study, asked their students to report five incidents of emotion in great detail. Each student provided a description of fear, sadness, anger, joy, and love. Some students were asked to remember an actual incident from their own lives, whereas others were asked to describe a typical episode of one of these emotions. In all cases, students were prompted to report what caused the emotion; what their thoughts, feelings, actions, and utterances were; and how the emotion was resolved. They wrote narratives about an event that causes each of the particular emotions they were asked about. P. Shaver et al. analyzed the stories and generated a list of features often present and organized them into a temporal structure.

The outcome of this analysis was a prototype for each of the five emotions, a representation of what people consider typical about each of five basic-level emotions. The prototype was something like a script or schema for a story (e.g., Schank & Abelson, 1977). It had a narrative structure (with a beginning, middle, and end), and took place across a period of time. The beginning part of the prototypical emotion episode consisted of what might be called *antecedents*, or the typical causes of the emotion. Let's use fear as an example: the antecedents included the possibility of social rejection, failure, loss of control, and threat of harm, as well as being alone, in the dark, or in an unfamiliar situation—the typical causes of fear. The middle part of the episode consisted of the emotional reaction itself, which typically included behaviors, physiological reactions, verbal and nonverbal expressions, and cognitive symptoms. For prototypical fear, these reactions included trembling, looking around, and feeling jittery; screaming or having a shaky voice; hurrying, fleeing, or hiding; and imagining a bad outcome and losing focus. The final part of the episode consisted of self-regulation of the emotion. For prototypical fear, this part included trying to calm oneself and hiding one's fear from others.

Thus, in contemporary folk psychology, emotions appear to be conceived as having a narrative structure and evolving over time. Converging evidence has come from several researchers who have noted that people use narrative structures to describe their own emotions. When studying first-person accounts of jealousy and envy, Parrott (1991) observed that a person's description of his or her own experience of jealousy followed the structure of a narrative. There was a description of the situation that existed before the emotion began, the events that led to the emotion, a chain of emotional responses that included others' reactions, reactions to their reactions, emotions about emotions, and attempts to cope with emotions. There were subsequent events, and eventually some sort of resolution. The term *emotional episode* was coined to capture the complex, narrative structure that appeared to be the natural unit in such accounts (Parrott, 1991).

Quite independently, a team of Dutch researchers asked people to report on a recent emotional experience, and they were struck by the duration of the emotions and the complexity of the reports they received (Frijda, Mesquita, Sonnemans, & Van Goozen, 1991). Durations ranged from under a minute to more than a week. Complexity was evident in their finding that many of the reports mentioned more than one emotion; for example, an anger report might also mention feeling fear of retaliation, satisfaction at harming the opponent, hurt feelings, and hopelessness. Some of the emotions reported were reactions to events, but others were long-standing emotional tendencies, such as losing trust in another person or being afraid of spiders. It is interesting to note that these researchers also used the phrase *emotional episode* to capture the heterogeneous, story-like structure of these reports.

We would conclude that the everyday folk theory does not distinguish focused emotional reactions from the extended narrative in which they take place. In the example of anger cited previously, the anger, fear of retaliation, satisfaction, hurt, and hopelessness are all wrapped up together in an episode of being angry at someone. What holds these disparate reactions together is the narrative structure: "It all started when. . . ." It makes sense for ordinary people to structure emotions in this manner, because people care about the problems and triumphs of their lives, not about identifying the units of their reactions that can be precisely defined and examined in a replicable manner.

Academic psychologists do have these cares, but in pursuing them, they, too, have found that emotions are processes that develop over time. Psychologists have learned that, even when emotions are identified with a single appraisal of events, emotions are processes, not a unitary psychological response. When events are examined in a fine-grained manner, as if in slow motion, there does not seem to be a single moment when an emotion begins, but instead there seems to be a process of developing emotionality (Ellsworth & Scherer, 2003). At the beginning of an emotion, there is a moment when it is first noticed that something is happening, though all one may realize, at first, is that there is novelty. At this moment a person could not properly be said to be angry or afraid or overjoyed, but the person is nevertheless different from before. Once the person is alerted to something unexpected, attention shifts, ongoing activity is interrupted, information is sought. Is this good or bad? How certain can one be about what is happening? Does this event affect things the person cares about? Is it caused by another person, and does this person intend what he or she is doing? The answers to these questions are all components of emotional appraisal, but these questions do not get answered all at once. As a result, emotionality is fluid. When all the components for an emotion are present, the resulting emotion corresponds to a prototypical emotional state, but it is necessary to recognize that anger, fear, joy, and the rest come in a variety of shades and degrees that are in flux.

A potential conflict between folk and academic conceptions, on the one hand, and the Law's views, on the other, can already be foreseen. The Law, with its typically narrow focus on the moment of the act, tends to see emotions statically and as simplistic stories, rather than as complex narrative episodes in which appraisals develop and change across time, situations, and circumstances, and in which the very emotion may transform into another emotion. This conflict is addressed in chapters 11 and 12 (this volume).

FOUR EMOTIONS

Having described the reasons for examining specific types of emotion, and having portrayed emotions as changing over time, we now consider four types of emotion. These four are especially relevant to legal culpability: anger, envy, jealousy, and fear.

Anger

When people think about emotions that are associated with criminality, anger usually comes first to mind. In both everyday and academic thought, anger is closely associated with physical aggression and violence. In reality, however, human anger is compatible with a wide range of responses, and physical aggression is relatively rare. In a survey of experiences of anger, Averill (1982) found that physical aggression or punishment was characteristic of only 10% of incidents, although people reported aggressive impulses 40% of the time. It clearly is not uncommon for anger to produce an urge for physical aggression, but such urges are usually not expressed. Social norms dictate the ways in which anger can be expressed, and physical aggression is rarely condoned. American social norms became less tolerant of violence during the 18th century and those norms have remained fairly consistently strict for the past 200 years (C. Z. Stearns & Stearns, 1986).

Nonphysical forms of aggression are more permissible, and Averill's (1982) survey reveals that they are by far more prevalent, both as felt urges and as behavior. Verbal aggression occurred in half of all cases, and impulses toward verbal aggression were reported by a whopping 82%. Other more indirect forms of aggression, such as removing a benefit, were frequently reported (40%). The most frequently reported actions, however, were talking about the incident with a third party without intent to harm the offender, and engaging in activities intended to calm oneself down—both occurred in about 60% of cases. In 40% of cases the angry person discussed the incident with the offender without exhibiting hostility. Anger was overwhelmingly directed at people or human institutions, and although anger may commonly be thought of as involving hatred, in fact most anger is directed at acquaintances, friends, and loved ones (79%).

Perhaps the most striking finding from Averill's survey was that 75% of respondents rated the overall effect of their episode of anger as adaptive. Lest this result be construed as self-serving, Averill (1982) conducted a parallel survey concerning incidents in which the respondent had been the target of someone else's anger, and about the same proportion evaluated the episode as being beneficial overall. Anger was described as having a range of benefits: the target of anger often changed his or her attitudes and behavior, came to realize his or her faults, gained respect for the angry person, and did something good for the angry person, and mutual understanding between the parties increased. Thus the angry episode strengthened the relationship 75% of the time, whereas 25% of the time it was harmful to the relationship: the target lost respect for the angry person, and the relationship cooled. Overall, the evidence suggests that some form of aggressive impulse usually occurs during anger, but physical aggression is usually inhibited and usually takes socially approved forms.

Because animals and infants display reactions that seem anger-like, this emotion is sometimes considered to lack a moral dimension (e.g., Berkowitz,

1993). However, studies of human anger show that it is strongly cognitive and moral (Haidt, 2001; Parrott, 1993b). The prototypical anger narrative begins with a judgment that a situation is illegitimate, unfair, or wrong, and that someone is blameworthy, or that one has lost status or been insulted (Averill, 1982; P. Shaver et al., 1987). This judgment can be facilitated by pain, frustration, failure, stress, or fatigue, but the effect of these factors appears to be mediated by the cognitive and moral judgments of unfairness and blame. In a social setting, anger communicates perceived injustice and motivates people to try to correct it (Planalp, 1999). The prototypical anger response may involve physical attack, but, as mentioned, this stereotype may be more the ideal than the reality because the impulse is not always physical, and when present it is usually inhibited, fantasized, or displaced. Expressions of anger include threatening gestures, nonverbal expressions such as slamming doors, and verbal attacks accompanied by obscenities, yelling, and complaining; they may also involve weeping, social withdrawal, or preoccupation with the situation.

In humans, the link between anger and violence has strong cultural influences. In cultures that place a high value on personal reputation and integrity, it is frequently considered proper to resort to violence as a way of defending one's honor against insult. Cohen and Nisbett (1994) have proposed that societies without effective law enforcement tend to develop an emphasis on honor and a social norm of responding to insults and threats with retaliation. They posit that the southeastern United States was settled by immigrants from such cultures, and demonstrate that the modern population of this region has attitudes toward violence different from those of the rest of the United States. When personal honor or defense of family and property is at stake, violence is considered more legitimate in the southeast than elsewhere.

In American culture, anger is considered more typical of men than of women. Research shows, however, that this norm is also more of an ideal than a reality (Shields, 2002). When people report emotions shortly after experiencing them, there appears to be no difference between the frequency or intensity of men's and women's anger. When people are questioned after considerable delay, or when asked how much they typically or generally experience anger, the expected difference between men and women becomes evident, probably because respondents draw on the stereotype rather than actual experience to answer the question.

Envy

Envy can refer to a variety of specific emotions, but in the context of criminal law it generally refers to a malicious resentment of a person who is perceived as having status, ability, possession, or other advantage that the envious person desires but lacks. *Jealousy* is often used as a synonym for envy, but we avoid using it in this context because it can also refer to other emotions that we discuss later. Envy involves a comparison between two people, the envious and the envied, but not all social comparisons result in envy. The envious must perceive that the envied enjoys some superiority, but other factors must be present as well. The superiority of the envied must be in some domain that the envious person cares about, and it must have the potential to make a person feel inferior. If a person simply feels inferior, there is no malicious envy—a person may be sad, depressed, hopeless, dejected, and worthless, perhaps, but not malicious. The hallmark of malicious envy is that the envious person finds a path from inferiority to hostility (Parrott, 1991). This path is not always taken, but, when it is, it often seems plausible that there is a motive for doing so. Feeling inferior and deprived is unpleasant enough, but feelings that one's inferiority and deprivation are one's own fault are more painful still, and a motive for malicious envy might be to construe circumstances so that they are the fault of the envied, not the envier. If the superior person is held to be undeserving of his or her advantage, one's deprivation becomes the result of unfairness, not inferiority, and that may in some way feel better (R. H. Smith, 2004). Once the situation is so construed, malicious envy is the result. The accomplishment of the superior person is disparaged, depressed inferiority is replaced by angry resentment, and the very thought of the superior person elicits hatred. It is for this reason that the emotion *schadenfreude*, joy at another person's misfortune, is often associated with envy.

Shakespeare (1938) paints a compelling portrait of envy in the character Cassius from *Julius Caesar*, a portrait that exemplifies the various facets of malicious envy, according to Richard Smith (2004). In the second act of the play, Cassius' envy unfolds from inferiority to resentment to hostility. As the scene opens, Caesar enters in a victory parade, with his conquests, popularity, good fortune, power, and honor all on full display. Cassius fumes about the contrast between their lots: "Why, man, he doth bestride the narrow world/Like a Colossus, and we petty men/Walk under his huge legs, and peep about/To find ourselves dishonourable graves" (I, ii, 136–139).

But Cassius does not simply feel inferior because of the difference between their lives—he feels that the difference is unfair. As evidence of the unfairness of his present superiority, Cassius recounts how he once saved Caesar from drowning and how he once observed Caesar weakened by a fever: "And this man/Is now become a god, and Cassius is/A wretched creature, and must bend his body/If Caesar carelessly but nod on him. . . ./Ye gods, it doth amaze me/A man of such a feeble temper should/So get the start of the majestic world,/And bear the palm alone!" (I, ii, 117–120, 130–133). In the final lines of the scene, it is clear that the resentment that has been eating at him has resulted in malicious hostility: "And after this, let Caesar seat him sure,/For we will shake him, or worse days endure" (315–316).

The clearest link between envy and the Law comes from what sociologist Helmut Schoeck (1966/1969) called *crimes of envy*, instances of which he has carefully documented and cataloged. Among murders of envy, Schoeck documented a series of fires at Cornell University targeting dormitories of students in a special program for gifted students, as a result of which eight students and one professor were killed; the murder of a high school student just elected class president; and even the envy of the living by those committing suicide whose second-to-last act is to ensure that others cannot live, either. Then there is vandalism brought about by envy: slashed tires on luxury cars by those who cannot afford them and broken windows in buildings that are nicer than the ones the vandals live in. The goal of envious crime, believes Schoeck, is not to benefit personally but to prevent others from enjoying what one cannot.

Cultural norms strongly influence the acceptability of expressing envy, and Schoeck (1966/1969) believed that a society's economic growth and development requires that envy be inhibited. In societies where envy is considered inevitable and can be freely expressed, the most talented and successful members of the society must constantly fear the envy of their neighbors, so they inhibit their talents and hide their successes. In societies where envy is considered illegitimate, taboo, or unseemly, the most talented members of the society are less inhibited and can pursue achievements that likely will benefit society and themselves.

Envy provides a particularly good example of the ways in which emotions can be understood both as subjective states and as objective social categories. One can speak of envy as a subjective state, in the sense that a person can report feeling envious regardless of whether he or she has an appropriate cause for envy. But envy is primarily understood in an objective sense, as an explanation for a person's hostility (Parrott, 1991). In this sense, envy refers to hostility that is not justified by the rules of anger but is plausibly understood as a defensive reaction to comparing poorly to another person in a self-relevant domain. The objective category of envy is thus pejorative: "Don't take her insults personally," people reassure the target of the envious remark. "She's just envious." The irony of objective envy is that in many situations the envy is clear to all parties except for the envious person, who will adamantly deny the envy and insist that he or she is justly resentful. In such a case one could say that the envious person was objectively envious but subjectively righteously angry.

Jealousy

Jealousy, as we use the word here, can be contrasted with envy in several ways. Jealousy arises in social situations in which there are three people: the jealous person, the partner with whom the jealous person is, was, or hopes to be in a social relationship, and a rival who threatens to take the jealous person's place in the relationship with the partner. Thus, jealousy involves a triangle of three people whereas envy involves only two, and jealousy typically involves the fear of losing a relationship, whereas envy concerns an object or quality that one lacks (Parrott, 1991). Despite these differences, these two emotions are commonly confused. The ambiguity of the English word *jealous* is partly to blame, because it can refer to either emotion. Another source of confusion is the fact that situations that produce jealousy also often elicit envy. The very triangle that can lead to jealousy about the possibility of losing an important relationship also offers the jealous person the opportunity to feel inferior to and hostile toward the rival, who, after all, is in the enviable position of attracting the attention and possibly the affection of the partner. Research on actual experiences of jealousy reported the co-occurrence of envy in 59% of the cases (Parrott & Smith, 1993).

Jealousy can be represented as a prototypical emotional episode much as P. Shaver et al. (1987) did for other emotions (Sharpsteen, 1991). The emotion typically begins with the appraisal that there is a rival for one's partner. The experience of jealousy depends somewhat on whether that threat is only suspected, say on the basis of flirtatious giggles, or whether it is unambiguously real, say on the basis of their moving in together; the former is termed *suspicious* jealousy, and the latter is called *fait accompli* jealousy (Parrott, 1991). In either case the prototypical relationship is romantic, though it is worth pointing out that any type of relationship (e.g., child–parent, friend–friend, student–teacher) can give rise to jealousy when one is threatened by a rival.

There is some controversy as to whether jealousy is a unique emotion or whether it is a composite of other emotions, but both may be true (Parrott, 1991). The feeling of anxious insecurity that comes from the shake-up of the sense of self that comes from the transfer of a partner's attention and devotion to another person may be a unique emotion, encountered in no other context. At the same time, plenty of other emotions typically arise during episodes of jealousy. Appraisals of betrayal yield anger; appraisals of loss elicit sadness; appraisals of uncertainty and change elicit anxiety (Sharpsteen, 1991). The episode can involve stages of reactions, much like grief, that can continue for weeks or months. The initial shock and numbness on discovering the betrayal is followed by recriminations and feelings of hurt, anger, and sadness, along with anguished preoccupation, before a search begins for meaning, adjustment, and, eventually, recovery (Hupka, 1991).

Jealousy arises in the context of the Law as a motive for violent assault and murder. For example, some husbands and boyfriends threaten and use violence to achieve sexual exclusivity or, failing that, to punish or retaliate against their wives, girlfriends, and rivals. Evolutionary psychologists argue for a genetic basis for this violence in light of the evolutionary pressure on males to be vigilant about sexual infidelity because of uncertainty of paternity (e.g., Daly, Wilson, & Weghorst, 1982). Other psychologists argue against evolutionary explanations, pointing out that cultural variables better account for patterns of jealous violence. It can be argued that differences in economic, political, and legal power, customs concerning monogamy and divorce, and rules about gender roles and honor all are related to the practice of violence when jealous (Hupka, 1991).

Within Anglo-American culture, norms for jealousy have shifted over time. In the early 19th century it was increasingly acceptable to display jealousy, but after the American Civil War norms prevented such free expression (P. N. Stearns, 1989). Until the 1890s courts tended to excuse the slaying of one's wife's lover (but not of one's husband's lover). English and American common law traditionally recognized four provocations for crimes of passion, known as the *19th-century four*, which led to exoneration, and one's wife's adultery shared this appellation with being violently assaulted, engaging in an unplanned mutual quarrel, and being subjected to unlawful arrest (Averill, 1982). Beginning in the 1890s, courts began to reject this defense, and some states replaced the husband with the state by enacting laws against adultery. Jealous murder of one's wife's lover was no longer exonerated, but it was eligible for mitigation to voluntary manslaughter. The justification for these rules tended to be stated in terms of uncontrollable passion, but clearly conceptions of honor played a role. Most laws allowing men to kill in response to marital infidelity were repealed by the 1970s, reflecting continued changes in attitudes toward expression of jealousy, but also societal attitude changes toward women, the death penalty, divorce, and sexual behavior (P. N. Stearns, 1989).

Fear

Fear occurs following an appraisal of threat or danger. The prototypical episode of fear, described earlier in this chapter, involves antecedents that involve threat of harm, plus conditions that heighten vulnerability, such as being alone or in the dark. The symptoms of fear are often divided into somatic and cognitive groups. Somatic symptoms include sweating, shallow breathing, and heart palpitations. Cognitive symptoms include worrying, rumination, and intrusive thoughts (Öhman, 2000). Fear and anxiety have been found to affect the way that people pay attention to their environments by making them especially attentive to threatening stimuli. People notice threats more readily, and find it difficult not to pay attention to them (Mogg & Bradley, 1999). When they are anxious, people's attention is riveted by threatening words, facial expressions, or pictorial scenes. There is evidence that this anxious vigilance occurs automatically, quickly, and, in the early stages at least, without people's awareness, making it extremely difficult to control. It can also be fairly specific, so people with social worries will selectively attend to words suggesting social threats (e.g., incompetent) more than to words suggesting physical attack (Mogg & Bradley, 1999). Once a threat is detected, attention can zero in on that stimulus so much that peripheral features of the environment are not noticed.

Fear is generally understood to function adaptively to help people es-cape from danger. The somatic symptoms prepare the body for energetic flight or attack. The cognitive symptoms prepare the perceptual systems for the earliest possible detection of threat (Öhman, 2000). Extreme danger can elicit a powerful emotion, including panic, and can produce long-lasting con-sequences, such as posttraumatic stress disorder. Nevertheless, cognitions play an important role in eliciting and controlling even strong panic. For ex-ample, a belief that one can control one's situation, even if false, is highly protective against panic attacks (Öhman, 2000).

Fear has significance for the Law in that the occurrence of this emotion can be seen as mitigating or excusing homicide. A plea of self-defense may be more persuasive if the defendant was afraid, which would reinforce the claim that the defendant genuinely appraised the situation as threatening. A plea of extreme emotional disturbance (EED) may rest on any emotion at all, but Finkel (1995a) had data suggesting that mock jurors impose lighter sentences on defendants who kill when afraid than on those who kill when angry. In Kirschner, Litwack, and Galperin's (2004) review of EED cases in New York County, they found that cases in which the defendant was afraid were more likely to receive a verdict of not guilty by reason of EED than were cases in which the defendant was angry.

For a variety of reasons, a fearful person might elicit more sympathy than, say, an angry person would. Being afraid is perceived as involving a very low level of power and little control over one's environment, whereas being angry is perceived as involving high levels of both control and power (Ellsworth & Scherer, 2003). People tend to extend sympathy to a person who has suffered and to nurture those who are powerless (Planalp, 1999), and a fearful person is both suffering and powerless. Sympathetic reactions to fear may help explain why the emotion of fear is more successful than other emotions in EED defenses.

TOWARD CRIMES AND DEFENSES: EMOTIONS, CONTEXT, AND CULPABILITY

Particular emotions, such as the ones we have described, play a role in determinations of legal culpability, but the role is neither fixed nor straight-forward. The isolated fact that a defendant felt angry or humiliated does not by itself mitigate, aggravate, exculpate, or justify the act. Instead, the reason-ableness of the emotion and its fit within the larger context determine the emotion's effect on culpability. In this final section of this chapter we con-sider the manner in which an emotion's context may be taken into account, as well as the reasons why context matters in determinations of culpability.

Previously in this chapter we described how emotional episodes can be represented by a narrative structure. Narratives capture not only how emotions develop over time but also how emotions are related to a broader context. We find a suggestive parallel in the psychology of juror decision making: it has been shown that jurors impose a narrative organization on information presented during a trial (Pennington & Hastie, 1986). By asking mock jurors to think aloud while reaching a decision about a verdict, Pennington and Hastie found that jurors tried to make sense of complex evidence by imposing a narrative structure on it. For example, a mock juror for a murder trial might decide that the defendant had been frightened during an altercation with the decedent and fled home to get away. While home, the frightened defendant picked up a knife, just in case, and later used it to defend himself when again threatened by the decedent, killing the decedent incidentally. But another mock juror, hearing the same evidence, might impose a different narrative structure: in this story, the mock juror might decide that the defendant became angry during the initial altercation, formed a plan to injure the decedent, went home to get the knife, then searched for the decedent and used the knife to kill him. These two stories yield two different verdicts: first-degree murder in the second story, but manslaughter or not guilty by reason of self-defense in the first. It is interesting to note that most mock jurors were not aware that another narrative existed that would fit the available evidence. They proceeded to try to match the story they constructed with the available decision alternatives presented in the judge's instructions.

Narratives exert a strong influence over the perception of responsibility and culpability. For example, there is evidence that the order in which evidence and witnesses are presented influences how juries structure the information. Experiments in which the order of presentation are systematically varied suggest that whichever side—the prosecution or the defense—presents its case in narrative order will prevail when the other side does not use narrative order (see Pennington & Hastie, 1990). Other research on narratives confirms the power of storytelling. When McGregor and Holmes (1999) asked college students to write a biased or an unbiased account of an actual incident involving a friend that made them angry, upset, or hurt, the story they told affected how upset they felt 8 weeks later; those who told a story biased toward their own point of view reported being more angry and hurt than did those who told an unbiased story.

Emotions appear to have a central role in organizing stories. In Pennington and Hastie's (1986) research, the first-degree-murder story was also an anger story, whereas the not-guilty-by-reason-of-self-defense story was also a fear story. In McGregor and Holmes' (1999) research, the biased story was often one of righteous anger at a fully blameworthy person by a completely innocent party, whereas the unbiased story was often one of frustration and irritation in which blame was shared.

Thus, there is a parallel between research on emotions and research on jury decision making regarding the use of narratives in understanding responsibility and culpability. It is interesting that the differences between ordinary people and experts in each field are also roughly analogous. Emotion researchers conceive of emotions as reactions to focal aspects of events, agents, and objects (Ortony, Clore, & Collins, 1988). Ordinary people, in contrast, think of emotions as narrative episodes (P. Shaver et al., 1987). Legal experts conceive of jury decisions as a concatenation of judgments about the identity, intention, and provocation of the defendant (e.g., Pennington & Hastie, 1986). Ordinary people, in contrast, assess the actions of the defendant by assimilating the facts into a narrative. It is significant that there seems to be overlap between emotion narratives and culpability narratives, because culpability narratives often incorporate emotion narratives into their structure. In both domains, the narrative structures chosen by laypersons are used for different purposes than are the more analytical schemes of the experts: whereas the experts seek to abstract from particulars, the laypersons set out to place the incident into its context.

This contrast between abstraction and contextualization has been the topic of considerable attention. Psychologist Jerome Bruner (1986) has argued that there are two modes of thinking, each of which provides a distinctive way of representing reality. One, called the paradigmatic mode, seeks truth through categorization and formal and empirical proof, its ideal being the transcendence of the particular into the universal. The other, called the narrative mode, seeks a believable account by placing human intentions and actions into a specific time and place, its ideal being to locate the universal in particular events, actions, and states of consciousness.

A similar dichotomy has been noted in the realm of ethics and the Law. Philosopher Stephen Toulmin (1990) has documented how events of the 17th century led to the celebration of abstraction and rationality and to the derogation of the less abstract Renaissance humanists. Yet, Toulmin argued that prior to the 17th century scholars were as concerned with the concrete circumstances of human actions as they were with abstract theory. Medieval scholars were strongly influenced by Aristotle's (1984) concern with "the 'circumstantial' character of practical issues, as they figure in problems of medical diagnosis, legal liability, or moral responsibility" (p. 26). The rhetorical analysis of persuasive speeches was held to be as important as the validity of their logic; case ethics and casuistry had reputations equal to that of formal ethics.

> The Renaissance humanists . . . declared that . . . "Nothing human is foreign", and they set out to do this in rich detail, which was new at the time, and has rarely been equaled: the political analyses of Niccolò Machiavelli and the dramas of William Shakespeare are among our permanent inheritances as a result. In the 14th century, the accepted ways of thinking had still constrained new ideas of human character and motives: in the last decades of the 16th century, they no longer placed limits on the creator of Othello and Hamlet, Shylock and Portia, Juliet and Lady Macbeth. (Toulmin, 1990, pp. 27–28)

What narrative episodes accomplish that analysis cannot is to provide a rich context in which to evaluate the human significance of events. Episodic structures provide a framework in which actions can be understood (Harré, 1972). Such context is essential for assessing the moral significance of emotions. Philosopher Justin Oakley (1992) argued that the moral significance of emotions requires knowing more than merely which emotion a person experienced, and he distinguished two levels of moral significance. *First-level moral significance* refers to an emotion's potential to figure importantly in human virtues and vices. Some emotions—such as envy, compassion, resentment, sympathy, fear, and self-pity—frequently play a role in human relationships and influence human flourishing, but other emotions do not have much moral potential; these, according to Oakley, would include embarrassment, awe, nostalgia, and intrigue. But first-level moral significance will not determine whether an emotion is right or wrong on a given occasion. The rightness or wrongness of an emotion will depend on the object toward which it is directed and the circumstances in which it is elicited. To evaluate the rightness or wrongness of the object and circumstances, Oakley appeals to Aristotle's concept of *phronesis*, or *practical wisdom*, which is "the capacity to deliberate well such that one realises virtuous ends in one's responses to particular situations" (Oakley, 1992, p. 81).

Thus, in moral philosophy as in folk psychology, the moral significance of emotions is bound up in the particularities of their context. In everyday life, people think of emotions in narrative episodes because they are concerned with what emotions say about events, responsibility, and character, and when ordinary people enter the courtrooms as jurors, they frame evidence in narrative episodes (often in emotional episodes) because they are concerned with assessing culpability in the context of the "story" in which it occurs.

In the chapters that follow in Part II, we explore how emotions influence the Law's culpability theories and the culpability judgments that follow, focusing on a number of crimes and pleas within the criminal law: murder, manslaughter, insanity, self-defense, and mistaken self-defense. We draw on the research and theories of emotion that we presented thus far, along with additional research on citizen–jurors' theories of emotion and culpability. We compare these emotion and culpability theories—from Law, Psychology, and commonsense justice—and look for coherence, consistency, and validity, but where we find contradiction between the Law's views and those of Psychology and commonsense justice, we "inform the Law" to improve the Law.

II

ANALYSES AND COMPARISONS OF THE LAW'S EMOTION AND CULPABILITY THEORIES

6

ANOMALIES IN MURDER: CONFLICTING VIEWS OF MALICE, EMOTIONS, AND MOTIVE

We speak of a lost language in the Law, muted for almost a millennium now, though once upon a time in Anglo-Saxon England, words such as *bot*, *wer*, *wite*, and *wergeld* were used and understood (Finkel, 1988a; Hermann, 1983). Today, these words stir neither meanings nor emotions in ordinary citizens, nor in most lawyers, likely, though some legal historians will feel a resonance, from "a time out of mind." In that time before the Norman Conquest, when there was no common law in England (Pollock & Maitland, 1968), there was a world in which "crimes" were seen as personal feuds (e.g., *wergeld*), and the operative Saxon system was summed up in the phrase "buy off the spear or bear it" (N. Walker, 1968, p. 15).

WILD JUSTICE, WHERE VICTIMS GET THEIR DAY IN COURT, AND DUE PROCESS

Why open with a lost language from an uncivilized world where "wild justice" reigned (Jacoby, 1983), a world long since civilized by the rule of

Law? Because we believe that some germinal notions were bred out of this "dead land" (Eliot, 1934)—notions that were expressed in those words now weeded from modern criminal law's language. These notions took root in folk theories and in citizens' commonsense justice (CSJ) notions, and shoots from those notions have now reached into modern criminal law and have begun to infect it.

Today's highly elaborated criminal law began to evolve a millennium ago, and it is our contention that to see the Law *as it is* and *as it ought to be*, we must begin where it began—at its roots. Understanding the historical context helps us recognize when *time past* becomes *time present*, and we believe this is so, *now*, as the criminal law wrestles with a problem that has come back to haunt: What to do for victims and victims' families?

A Civil Answer Is Trumped, a Victim Is Finessed, and Modern Criminal Law Pays for the Trick

In recent times, victims, and the family members of victims, have felt left out of the criminal law, a situation they see as neither right nor fair (Finkel, 2000a, 2001). Of late, they have taken their grievances to legislatures and courts seeking redress, and both branches of government have responded. For example, state legislatures have passed *victim impact statement* statutes, whereby victims (or their family members) can speak at sentencing hearings. In addition, the Senate Judiciary Committee responded by holding a hearing on a constitutional amendment to ensure that victims of violent crimes have rights in criminal proceedings; as a *Washington Post* editorial commented: "This is a bad idea whose time, unfortunately, may have come" ("Rights and wrongs," 2003). These responses and symptoms have been discernible in the Supreme Court, in biting opinions and dissents in highly contentious victim-impact statement cases (*Booth v. Maryland*, 1987; *Payne v. Tennessee*, 1991; *South Carolina v. Gathers*, 1989). If these responses are diagnostic that *time past* has broken into *time present*, as we claim, then we suggest that a connection between the old forgotten answer and the modern problem may be found by going back to a wergeld, a blood feud, and following it.

In Anglo-Saxon time, if I (or my family members, or my property) were harmed by another, I had the right to pick up my spear and seek redress or revenge, for surely I saw myself as the aggrieved party, the victim, and my passions not only mattered but also needed assuaging and satisfaction. But what about the perpetrator (the alleged defendant, to use the modern criminal law language)? His guiding maxim was "buy off the spear or bear it," which offers a choice between negotiating or fighting: if he chose the former, he could offer me some satisfactory payment to end the feud (e.g., a *wer* was an assessment for a killing, and a *bot* was a compensation for injury to the victim or the property); in a similar way, the word *murdrum* referred to the payment, "a fine imposed for an unexplained homicide" (Green, 1985, p. 51). This evolving "law," then, turns out to be civil rather than criminal, as it offers a compensating answer to the victim, rather than a culpability determination for the defendant. Local customs grew as to what the usual and customary bot and wer fees were for various offenses, and we may assume that these compensations were enough for many a victim to sate his loss and blood lust, thereby ending the feud and bringing peace to the local community.

Beyond the bot and wer outcomes, the value of the process must be considered. In this system, the victim gets to confront the wrongdoer, so he gets his say and his passions have their day. Translated into modern legalese, he gets his day in court and his due process, as he can put forth his case directly, deliver his victim impact statement, and vent his spleen.

But this private feud (i.e., a wergeld) was intruded on by a third party, which leads us to the *wite*, a term critical for understanding how and why criminal law emerges out of this civil law: the wite was a payment the "king or public guardian could obtain . . . for the breach of the King's Peace" (Hermann, 1983, p. 61). The harm became more than some private tort matter between two citizens, because the harm was also to the king, the state, the general peace. In a relatively short time, historically, the king's (or state's) claim would come to trump the victim's claim.

Now we jump ahead centuries, to a modern criminal law trial involving the same harm, to see how, once the State has played its wite trump card, the victim gets finessed. At this modern criminal trial, the victim's voice has been silenced and his compensation has vanished: whereas once upon a time he was the major player bringing his claim with spear at the ready, now he is repositioned in the gallery, as a mere spectator. Today, the focus of a criminal trial is on the defendant, who is the major player. The defendant enters the courtroom armed with a host of "rights," about to do battle. But against whom? The case headlines as *People* (or *State, Commonwealth,* or the *United States*) v. *Defendant*; the very title tells the story, by omission, of the victim's displacement. Many victims are angry about this, claiming that the state's interests do not represent their interests, and they have been particularly critical about plea bargains between the state and the defendant. Although victims may object to such arrangements, their objections can be brushed aside as irrelevant, for they are no longer a party to the case.

The victims' rights movement of the late 20th century reflects, in part, victims' discontent with their loss of voice, impact, effect, and due process. This harkens back, we believe, to that Anglo-Saxon civil law process that gave victims voice and validation, as well as some compensating satisfaction. But perhaps this is as it should be. Empirical research (e.g., Orth, 2003) shows that victims' goals do not reflect "community sentiment," for they do not align with those of third-party observers. Victims are often motivated by revenge, and their emotions of anger, fear, and guilt are not felt to the same degree by nonvictimized citizens. Moreover, victims' moral goals tend to accent retaliation and recognition of their victim status more, whereas their instrumental goals favor the protection of victims' security more and rehabilitation of defendants less, when compared with nonvictims.

But empirical findings do not solely answer here, for the question involves normative values. In philosopher Jeffrie Murphy's (2003) book, *Getting Even: Forgiveness and Its Limits*, he offers reasons why the vindictive passions have value, when they are not motivated by hate or evil passion, while recognizing that "the temptations of self-deception here are enormous" (p. 104). Murphy cited the values of self-respect, self-defense, and respect for the moral order, and made these arguments for them.

> A person who never resented any injuries done to him might be a saint. It is equally likely, however, that his lack of resentment reveals a servile personality—a personality lacking in respect for himself and respect for his rights and status as a free and equal moral being. (This is the point behind the S. J. Perelman quip . . . "To err is human; to forgive, supine.") Just as indignation or guilt over mistreatment of others stands as emotional testimony that we care about them and their rights, so does resentment stand as emotional testimony that we care about ourselves and our rights.
>
> This is a very important point to emphasize: moral commitment is not merely a matter of intellectual allegiance; it requires emotional allegiance as well, for a moral person is not simply a person who holds the abstract belief that certain things are wrong. The moral person is also *motivated* to do something about the wrong—and the source of our motivation lies primarily in our passions or emotions. (p. 19)

Whether the Law ought to base its procedures and punishment goals on victims' sentiments remains an open question. But Murphy's concluding thoughts provide a partial defense, within limits, for the victim's place and passions. He wrote,

> I think that the main message of this book has been this: Even as we rightly preach the virtues of forgiveness, we should recognize that victims deserve to have their vindictive passions respected and to some degree validated. Even if these passions should not be the last word, they have a legitimate claim to be the first word. Even when they should not control, they should be listened to with respect instead of met with pious sermons and sentimental, dismissive clichés. (p. 117)

This issue, although unsettled today, foreshadows what is to come in this chapter: for when the Law forgets, finesses, or otherwise fails to deal adequately with matters relevant to its culpability theory, those matters do seem to come back and demand some due.

Anglo-Saxon law provided some relief and release for the victim, which got lost in the evolutionary advance of the criminal law. When this relief and release is lost, citizens come to feel shut out of the law, and their CSJ notions are likely to grow estranged from the law's perspective. Citizens may come to lose respect for the law, and if so, they may disobey the law. The effects, however, may be felt "inside" the law as well, for citizens—in that sanctioned role of jurors—may be more apt to reconstrue the law to fit with their commonsense notions rather than follow the law as the judge instructs them to do, or, at the extreme, they may nullify the law outright. As we said in our opening chapter, it is not just the Law's theories we consider in this work, but CSJ's theories, for when they are at odds with the Law's theories, they may demand some due.

Problems Without Compensations, and Problems Without Answers

Whatever successes Anglo-Saxon law may have achieved, its many failures greatly outweighed its answers. For example, there were problems (e.g., *botless* crimes) that could not be solved with compensation, and problems, such as culpability, that it did not even address, but needed to. A criminal law addressing culpability was an inevitability, and an infant criminal law eventually crawled out of this uncivil civil womb. The patchwork of courts and jurisdictions and divisions of authority of king, church, feudal lords, and ancient communities would come to coalesce under a strong monarch. The advent of jury trials (Green, 1985) came around 1200. Within a few centuries, distinctions would be made among crimes, among homicides, and, in a few more centuries, a separation of manslaughter from murder would result.

One of the bigger problems with the old Anglo-Saxon law, which relates to why we put the word *crime* in quotation marks in the first paragraph, is that these feuds (*wergelds*) were often initiated over actions that caused harms, but were not necessarily crimes as modern law defines them. For example, harms could result from accidents in which no one is at fault, and harms could result from honest mistakes to which we may attribute no fault. Two related points underscore this distinction between *harms* and *crimes*. First, this early law focused on the overt, be it the harm or act, rather than considering those subjective inner facts in its culpability equation. And second, at the nexus of act and harm, the liability was *strict*, such that if the harm followed from the act, there was culpability, regardless of concurring circumstances or intervening intentions. Even though a few *strict liability* offenses are still on the modern books (e.g., Dressler, 2001), as the philosopher H. L. A. Hart (1968) noted, strict liability offenses are "generally viewed with great odium" (p. 20).

Opposing the objective liability view was one that held that culpability ought to be grounded on the moral blameworthiness of the act, and in this view, culpability must be sought and found on inner subjective ground. This moral view, of course, did not arise with the demise of Anglo-Saxon law, but was rooted "in the beginning," in those culpability stories of Genesis, like the story of the first murder, of brother slaying brother and being marked for it, with which we started. And it was this moral view of culpability that would push its way back into the evolving criminal law.

MURDER EMERGES FROM BREACHES OF THE KING'S PEACE

In this black-and-white wite world of good and evil, we need make only one distinction: Did the man breach the king's peace or not? If he did, then he was culpable and punishable, and if not, then he was innocent and not punishable at all. From our modern perspective, in which we are accustomed to shades of gray and degrees of culpability, we might ordinally arrange breaches of the king's peace on a culpability continuum, from low-end to mid-range to high-end breaches, with treason being the highest breach, for it directly threatened the king. But that early law made no culpability distinctions among types of crimes, as culpability was either total or none, and the punishment was uniform and draconian: the one committing treason, along with the murderer, pickpocket, and forger, all breached the king's peace, and all were subject to a death sentence.

If the law of that time made no second-order distinctions regarding culpability, then third-order distinctions, such as differentiating one type of treason case from another, were even further away. But let us consider a Shakespearean audience at the beginning of the 17th century watching *King Richard The Third* one evening, only to return to The Globe the next month to see *Macbeth*, two plays both dealing with treason (Shakespeare, 1938). In Richard's opening soliloquy, this deformed man, angered at his lot, announces that "I am determined to prove a villain" (I, i, 32) and that "I am subtle, false, and treacherous" (I, i, 39); thus, this son of York will bring upon King and State no King's Peace, but a "winter of discontent" (I, i, 1).

With seething emotions and expressed malice revealed at the outset, Richard has no second thoughts about the evil he is hatching. By contrast, Macbeth, as we have noted, has second thoughts about killing King Duncan, and when Lady Macbeth enters, Macbeth declares that he has had a change of heart: "We will proceed no further in this business . . ." (I, i, 30). It is Lady Macbeth who then shames and humiliates him, and urges him to "screw your courage to the sticking-place, and we'll not fail" (I, i, 66). Surely, this 17th-century audience, having seen the two plays, recognized the culpability distinction between Richard's and Macbeth's degree of malice.

From an Evil World . . . to a World of Intentions

This early criminal law world was morally inchoate, as major and minor crimes were treated indiscriminately. Discriminations would come, as they would have to come, to bring order to this chaos. That order would be founded upon a moral blameworthiness view, in which culpability would be hinged not just to the overt act, and not just to the intent to do the act, but to an evil mind. As law professor Richard Singer (1986) put it in the opening sentence to his article titled "The Resurgence of Mens Rea,"

> Prior to the nineteenth century, the criminal law of England and this country took seriously the requirement that a defendant could not be found guilty of an offense unless he had truly acted in a malicious and malevolent way—that he had not only "the" mental state for the crime, but that, more generally, he manifested a full-blown mens rea: an "evil mind." (p. 243)

This was the robust concept of *mens rea* (see chap. 1, this volume).

We are about to introduce the common law's definition of murder, and its key construct, *malice aforethought*. But to first provide context and contrast, it is instructive to jump to the present day and open a modern text, such as Dressler's (2001) *Understanding Criminal Law* (3rd ed.), for herein we find a disconnect between the modern Model Penal Code's (American Law Institute, 1962) terms relating to criminal homicide and murder and those of the old common law. In the Code, the issue in murder is whether that person kills another "(1) purposely or knowingly; or (2) recklessly, under circumstances manifesting extreme indifference to the value of human life" (Dressler, 2001, p. 540). Under this definition, the common law's malice aforethought vanishes from the Code's definition (Dressler, 2001, p. 540), and depraved-heart murder, typically considered second-degree murder under the common law, also disappears. The Code's defining terms have been "denuded" of the older, moral meanings, the "allusive style" (Pillsbury, 1998, p. 84) that features motive and emotion, and what is left, in psychological terms, is the cognitive—what the actor thought, and how far and deeply the actor thought (or did not think).

When malice (the evil) vanishes from the core construct, a host of emotions vanish as well. Furthermore, when malice is denuded, the evil that motivates the action is also lost, and *mens rea* loses that which makes the criminal act a moral crime, leaving only the cognitive element of intent. And when emotions are removed, what is left is the cold-blooded killer prototype (e.g., Finkel & Groscup, 1997a; V. L. Smith, 1991, 1993; V. L. Smith & Studebaker, 1996; Stalans, 1993), which does not fit many of the worst killers, whose killings are hot and heinous.

This new cognitive, intentional act becomes an ill-fitting caricature for many in the "murder group," who are more hot, heinous, and variable. This new picture reflects discredited folk theories that contrast thinking with emotion, see emotion as devoid of cognition, or hold that when there is strong emotion there cannot be deliberation and premeditation (see chap. 3, this volume). These discredited psychological folk theories are embedded in other legal doctrines, such as provocation in the common law and extreme emotional disturbance (EED) in the Model Penal Code (American Law Institute, 1962): if the defendant shows strong emotion, and one can link that emotion to a provocation at the time of the act, then, under the common law, the defendant is likely to be facing the mitigated murder charge of manslaughter rather than murder charges; and if strong emotion arises within the defendant at the time of the act, even without a linkage to a provocation under the Code's EED, he or she is likely to be facing manslaughter rather than murder charges; so under either the common law or the Code, emotion seems to negate the crime of first-degree murder, leaving first-degree murder a *cold*, pristine *thought* crime.

If we were to accept the Model Penal Code's (American Law Institute, 1962) definition of murder, then this volume would have little to say about this thoughtful, intentional, purposeful murder—for emotion (along with malice) has been made immaterial. We cannot, and do not, accept this. Rather, following Pillsbury's (1998) recommendation, but with our own methods of discovery and analysis, we are going to dig for the *malice*, which was once the core construct of murder, for in finding malice and the meanings it carried we also find the conveyed emotions.

Finding Malice, and the Emotions

Dressler (2001) stated that "the common law definition of 'murder' is 'the killing of a human being by another human being with malice aforethought,'" and then he stated that "manslaughter is 'an unlawful killing . . . *without* malice aforethought'" (p. 503). Regarding *aforethought*, Dressler stated that "In very early English history, the word 'aforethought' probably required that a person think about, or premeditate, the homicide long before the time of the killing. It gradually lost this meaning, so . . . 'aforethought' is now superfluous" (p. 503). As for *malice*, Dressler stated that

> "Malice" is a legal term of art with little connection to its non-legal meaning. As the term developed, a person who kills another acts with the requisite "malice" if she possesses any one of four states of mind: (1) the intention to kill a human being; (2) the intention to inflict grievous bodily injury to another; (3) an extremely reckless disregard for the value of human life; or (4) the intention to commit a felony during the commission or attempted commission of which a death results. . . . [E]ach mental state involves an extreme indifference to the value of human life. (p. 503)

To find the nonlegal meaning of *malice*, we start with the dictionary (*Merriam-Webster's New Collegiate Dictionary*, 1966), roughly concurrent with the Model Penal Code (American Law Institute, 1962):

> ILL WILL; *specif*: intent to commit an unlawful act or cause harm without legal justification or excuse; **syn** MALEVOLENCE, ILL WILL, SPITE, MALIGNITY, SPLEEN, GRUDGE: MALICE may imply a deep-seated

and often unreasonable dislike and a desire to see one suffer or it may suggest a causeless passing mischievous impulse; MALEVOLENCE implies a deep and lasting hatred; ILL WILL may suggest a briefer feeling of antipathy and resentment often with cause; SPITE implies active malevolence together with envy or meanness of spirit; MALIGNITY stresses the intensity and driving force of malevolence; SPLEEN implies ill will together with hot temper; GRUDGE implies a cherished feeling of resentment or ill will that seeks satisfaction.

Here we find the evil, ill will, and desire to see another suffer. Here we also find an array of emotions, from deep-seated and cherished ones, to impulsive and passing ones, which include anger, envy, resentment, and hate, along with grudges, dislikes, and antipathies. This is the stuff of Shakespearean dramas (and chap. 5, this volume), and not the cold-blooded prototype of murder the modernist Code story leaves us with.

But we do even better with the *Oxford English Dictionary* (2002), wherein older meanings of *malice*, dating from the 12th and 13th centuries, are found. In its noun form, we again find the "malicious intent," "the intention or desire to do evil or cause injury to another person; active ill will or hatred. In later use also in weakened sense: mischievous intent, the desire to discomfort." Illustrating the stronger sense is this 1393 quote from Gower's *Confessio Amantis* (Fairf.) I. 605: "He that was a Lomb beforn Is thanne a Wolf, and thus malice Under the colour of justice Is hid." And as this *malice* related to Law, especially in *malice aforethought* or, formerly, *malice prepense*, it meant a "wrongful intention generally," or "the state of mind required for a person to be found guilty of certain criminal offences (esp. of murder)." But the term also related to "malicious character, power, or action" and to "malicious conduct; a malicious act," and *poison* is given as an example of the latter. And more generally, the definitions come back to "badness (chiefly in moral sense) wickedness" with phrases such as *to bear malice*. As an adjective, it means "poisonous," or "full of wrath or ill will," and when used as a verb, "to speak maliciously of, to malign," or "to regard with malice, to bear malice towards; to seek or desire to injure."

These definitions do not paint simply a picture of someone who, purposefully or knowingly, intends to kill. In this picture we find that a wolf may be beneath the lamb, where beneath the thoughts are poison, bile, ill will, malevolence, anger, envy, resentment, badness, and more, all roiling about and suffusing this person's spleen, heart, soul, and moral fiber. This is the portrait Richard III paints of himself in his soliloquy that opens that play. It is also the portraiture of Iago, who holds malevolent emotions deep within, a wolfish ill that will move between the lion (Othello) and his beloved lamb (Desdemona), bringing both down (Shakespeare, 1938). This malice, and the emotions that come with it, which the Model Penal Code (American Law Institute, 1962) has denuded, must surely be affecting if not driving the cognitive thoughts. Yet the Code has chosen exclusively to highlight thoughts and intentions closest to the surface, while ignoring the wolf's motives and emotions beneath.

DISTINCTIONS AMONG MURDERS

We move the story to 1794, when the Pennsylvania legislature passed a statute dividing murder into two degrees. Today, some states, including Pennsylvania, divide murder into three degrees, though other states (Dressler, 2001) follow the Model Penal Code's (American Law Institute, 1962) path "which rejects the degrees-of-murder approach [and] divides criminal homicide into three crime categories (murder, manslaughter, and negligent homicide)" (p. 505). We will follow the degrees-of-murder approach, for this path pursues malice openly, and makes a noteworthy distinction.

Under Pennsylvania's model, the worst types of first-degree murder were committed by means of poison or by lying in wait. The second type of first-degree murder, which involves slightly less culpability than the first type, involved a "wilful, deliberate, and premeditated" killing. And the third type of first-degree murder was felony murder; according to the statute, a homicide "that occurs during the perpetration or attempted perpetration of a statutorily enumerated felony (in the original version: arson, rape, robbery, and burglary) is murder in the first degree" (Dressler, 2001, p. 506).

There was some debate, as Dressler noted, about whether the second type subsumed the first type, for killers who lie in wait or use poison must surely premeditate and deliberate, yet the statute separated the first from the second type. A reasonable inference is that there is a particularly loathsome evil in the psyche of this stealthy wolf—in the depth or degree of the emotions, motives, and moral depravity that drive this sort of murder, which merits the most severe penalty—more so than in the second type, in which the requisite volitional and cognitive elements are met but this "value-added malice" of the first type is lacking. We find this value-added malice in Shakespeare's *Hamlet* (1938), in the character of Claudius, Hamlet's uncle, who was a stealthy wolf, three times over: he was lying in wait for King Hamlet; he used poison on the king; and he did this while the king slept. In committing treason and murder, Claudius took the king's life and crown, and took the king's wife *en passant*. That 17th-century audience watching the drama would have understood the malice, in its depth and nuances.

Suppressing the Emotions and the Malice

Dressler acknowledged that states that grade murder by degrees differ on how to interpret the phrase *wilful, deliberate, premeditated*—whether to treat it as a whole, and what the whole means, or whether to treat it as three separate terms, and what each term means. As Dressler (2001) noted,

> Most jurisdictions understand "wilful, deliberate, premeditated" to mean more than intention to kill . . . [and] that the division of murder into degrees is meant to separate the most heinous forms of murder, which deserve the most severe penalties, from those which, although "intentional" in some sense, lack the gravity associated with the first degree murders. (p. 508)

Although the distinction remains conceptually meaningful, Dressler noted that the distinction "loses practical significance" (p. 508), because all intentional killings are first-degree murder, and these crimes end up being treated the same.

With malice and emotions moot, courts turned to the cognitive elements of deliberation and premeditation, and made psychological distinctions between them. *Deliberation* would come to be associated with the quality of thinking, a depth of thinking, a "cool purpose," as one court put it (Dressler, 2001, p. 509), whereas *premeditation* came to be associated with the quantity of time needed in which a person thought about the murder beforehand, but the minimal time was indefinable. Though the meanings of the two terms are distinct, they are obviously related, for to think deeply (i.e., to deliberate) one needs a certain amount of premeditation time, although one could premeditate without deep deliberation. Yet, if jurors were to infer malice, it would likely be through deliberation. Still, to infer the quality of the defendant's deliberation, the jurors would have to enter the defendant's subjectivity deeply.

In the evolution of first-degree murder from the 18th-century common law to the Model Penal Code (American Law Institute, 1962), the law's language is denuded of such potent and evocative terms as *malice*, *emotions*, and *motive*. As a result, the *mens rea* concept not only constricts dramatically but becomes more cognitive, and the Law is left with fewer determinative factors in its culpability consideration. In terms of the criminal law's new implicit psychological theory, the law no longer considers the whole of the psyche, but only a part of it, restricting its focus to intentions residing within the head.

Implicit Theories and Internal Contradictions

This implicit theory extends as well to second-degree murder, known as "depraved heart" murder in the older language, and Dressler offered a number of citations illustrating what the old language conveyed:

> As one court put it, "more visceral[ly] than intellectual[ly]"—as conduct demonstrating "an abandoned heart," "an abandoned and malignant heart," a "depraved heart," or (to change bodily organs) "a depravity of mind." Some courts have characterized this form of malice in terms of both the heart and the mind: "wickedness of disposition, hardness of

heart, cruelty, recklessness of consequences and a mind regardless of social duty." (p. 512)

This older language, unlike the new denuded language, reveals the visceral, the emotional, and the evil. It reveals a person who neither feels for other individuals nor genuinely cares about the sanctity of another life, for the heart of this killer is so abandoned, malignant, and depraved that it has room for none but the self. Notions of a civic duty would not penetrate this heart, for malice, depravity, and a selfishness fill the key organs.

But this language reveals even more: we find depraved emotions positively correlating with a depravity of mind, whereas in the theory of the cold-blooded first-degree murderer, they negatively correlate. The assumption of a negative correlation seems a general rule within the law. For example, as the emotions get hotter in heat-of-passion cases, the crime is more likely to fall from the murder category into manslaughter. In a similar manner, if strong emotions interfere with thinking or volitional control, *diminished responsibility* (in England) or *diminished capacity* defenses (Fletcher, 1978) may be raised, which also bring the crime down to manslaughter. And if the emotions more seriously interfere with thinking and control to the point of exculpation, then the insanity defense comes into play (Finkel, 1988a). This sampler of the negative correlation reflects an old folk theory that has been discredited by academic Psychology (see chap. 4, this volume).

The implicit theory in depraved-heart murder offers a different theory of emotions and intentions, for here strong emotions and the intention are positively correlated, interrelating within the psyche. This theory contradicts the mutually exclusive theory offered—in which the presence of strong, hot emotions eliminates the possibility of the cool, deliberate intentions needed for first-degree murder. Yet, if we can have the combination of malice, strong emotions, and depraved thinking at second-degree murder, why not at first-degree murder? And why maintain a fiction at the culpability phase—that strong emotions were not (or could not be) present and operating for first-degree murder to result—only to turn around and introduce the hot emotions in the capital sentencing phase, to show that the act was particularly heinous?

WITHOUT THE INTENT: THE ANOMALY OF FELONY MURDER AND ACCESSORY FELONY MURDER

Finally, under first-degree murder types, we turn to an anomaly under either the common law or the Model Penal Code (American Law Institute, 1962): under the common law, felony murder appears to be a murder without the required malice, whereas under the Code, it appears to be a murder without the required intent. This type of murder was defined under that 1794 Pennsylvania statute as a homicide that occurs during the perpetration or attempted perpetration of one of the statutorily enumerated felonies. We have met this controversial topic before (albeit briefly, in chap. 2, this volume), when we summarized the sentiments of justices, judges, treatise writers, and commentators who had written on the felony-murder doctrine and also briefly summarized the results from controlled experiments assessing the sentiments of ordinary citizens. That sentiment was quite negative, as felony murder was judged to be distinctly different from the previous types of first-degree murder. One California court (*People v. Washington*, 1965) identified a distinguishing feature, noting that the felony-murder rule "erodes the relation between criminal liability and moral culpability" (p. 446). This is where we pick up the story.

Consider a hypothetical case of a man with a plan, whom we will call the triggerman (D). He intends to rob a store at gunpoint, and he enlists three associates to join him: a sidekick (C), who will accompany him into the store; a lookout (B), who will stand guard outside the store; and a getaway driver (A), who will be in a car across the street. As the robbery begins, the storekeeper, at the sight of D's gun, falls to the floor and dies of a heart attack. In legal terms, a death (a homicide) occurs during the perpetration of an enumerated felony, and D is charged with felony murder. In addition, through the doctrine of *accessorial liability* or *conspiratorial liability* (Fletcher, 1978), A, B, and C are also charged with felony murder (accessory felony murder), as they conspired with D to commit the underlying felony (the robbery), and they, according to the theory, bear equal culpability for the death that resulted.

It apparently does not matter, pragmatically, that the defendants did not purposefully or knowingly intend to kill, did not express the malice required for first-degree murder, and had only the lesser malice and motive to commit a robbery. But theoretically, how does this robbery escalate and become murder, and first-degree murder at that? Moreover, if one is judging the actions and intentions of the accessories, it would be hard to infer the malice for *extremely reckless* homicide or *depraved-heart* murder, which is second-degree murder; on its face, it would seem that the accessories committed a less serious crime than second-degree murder. So again, how is this crime first-degree murder?

This was one of the questions that appellants Stamp and Koory raised before a California Court of Appeals (*People v. Stamp*, 1969) when they appealed their felony-murder convictions. The facts were as follows: the defendants, while robbing the General Amusement Company with a gun and blackjack, ordered the employees and the store owner, Carl Honeyman, to lie on the floor while they took the money, which took some 10 to 15 minutes. Stamp and Koory then told the victims to remain on the floor for 5 more minutes so that no one would get hurt. After the robbers had left, Honeyman, a 60-year-old obese man with a history of heart disease, who was under a great deal of pressure from the competitive nature of his business, had trouble getting up off the floor and steadying himself. As the court noted, "He was short of breath, sucking air, and pounding and rubbing his chest," and "he said he was having trouble 'keeping the pounding down inside'" (p. 601). When the police arrived, he told them he was not feeling well and that he had a pain in his chest, which was about 15 to 20 minutes after the robbery had occurred; 2 minutes later, he collapsed and was pronounced dead at the hospital; the coroner listed the cause of death as heart attack.

The appellants contended that the evidence was insufficient to prove that the robbery was the factual cause of the death, but three doctors testified that an immediate upset to his system must have precipitated the attack, and the court held that the appellants' claim regarding the factual cause of the death lacked merit. But our main point in citing this case involves the court's reason for rejecting the appellants' contention that the felony-murder rule was inapplicable to the facts of their case. The court rejected their claim as being without merit, noting that

> The [felony-murder] doctrine is not limited to those deaths which are foreseeable. . . . Rather a felon is held strictly liable for *all* killings committed by him or his accomplices in the course of the felony. . . . In this respect, the robber takes his victim as he finds him. (p. 603)

This court advanced a *strict liability* justification for the crime of felony murder, which, as noted earlier, are crimes "generally viewed with great odium" (Hart, 1968, p. 20). Strict liability crimes are throwbacks to Anglo-Saxon time, for they make intent and malice irrelevant. Rather, the premise and conclusion are as follows: if the defendants attempted the underlying felony (which they surely did), and if a death resulted (as the court ruled), then, QED, the defendants are guilty of felony murder.

Other courts and treatise writers, however, have rejected strict liability as a justification for felony murder, and have tried, instead, to use either *transferred intent* or *constructive malice* to provide theoretical support to the felony-murder doctrine (e.g., Roth & Sundby, 1985). In transferred intent, the mental state required for the underlying felony (e.g., robbery, burglary, arson) is transferred for the mental state required for the homicide. But this transfer is highly suspect, for the state of mind that prompted the underlying felony (e.g., robbery) does not constitute the particular *mens rea* required for first-degree murder, and Perkins and Boyce (1982) claimed that it has "no proper place in criminal law" (p. 921). Constructive malice, as a theoretical justification, does not work much better, for in this view, one presumes the malice for the homicide from the mental state required for the commission of the underlying felony. But as with transferred intent, the malice implied in committing the underlying felony, say robbery, may be quite removed from the malice involved in committing murder. In the constructive malice account, "'malice' is stretched from the improbable to the implausible" (Finkel, 1990a, p. 820). In sum, neither strict liability, transferred intent, nor constructive malice can do the theoretical work, and thus felony murder remains a doctrine without a supporting rationale.

WITHIN-LAW COMPARISONS, AND SOME PSYCHOLOGY VERSUS LAW COMPARISONS

In the criminal law of the 18th century, though the Anglo-Saxon civil law focus on the interpersonal process and a compensatory outcome was gone, its theory of culpability had a decided inwardness. Within this law, we must plunge deeply into a subjective, psychological, and moral inner world, captured by the robust concept of *mens rea*. To do this culpability analysis, we must consider whether harms were meant, whether there were malice, ill will, and emotion beneath them, and whether forethought and deliberation were behind them. In psychological terms, the law's "nature" of human nature, and its implicit psychological theory, had become far more complex and Shakespearean, if you like.

The leading literary lights of the time, as well as the Law's leading lights, recognized that humans are morally, emotionally, and psychologically complicated beings, whose thoughts, feelings, motives, and actions interact in exceedingly complex ways. Some people could act evilly and murderously because certain emotions and malice so dominated their nature that they could plan, carefully manipulate others, lie in wait, and use poison, as Iago, Richard III, and Claudius seem to demonstrate. Yet for others who could kill with malice, malice can wrestle with conflicting second thoughts and different emotions in a seemingly divided psyche, but, in the end, temptations, burning ambitions, and an external goad are enough, as Macbeth seems to demonstrate. Still others could murder with lesser malice, because certain provocations brought certain repressed or compartmentalized feelings out of that nature, as Othello illustrates. And others could be duty-bound to revenge a killing, even if such an action went against the inner nature, as Hamlet illustrates. The Bard showed that we human beings are complex and variable, and those ordinary human beings watching these dramas were no doubt discriminating among these various murderers in terms of their degrees of malice, their motives and emotions, the quality of their deliberateness, and the degree of distraction or madness that reigned within their globes. So, too, did the legislators in Pennsylvania, who wrote their statute distinguishing types of first-degree murders: the worst of the worst killed by lying in wait or by using poison, which had an added malice beyond those who killed in a wilful, deliberate, and premeditated way.

In comparison, the Model Penal Code (American Law Institute, 1962) offers a far more circumscribed and segmented theory of the psyche when it comes to murder, for the Code elevates the cognitive to a position of hegemony, while it denudes the psyche of malice, emotions, and motive. Under the Code's psychological theory, murder becomes even more cool and cold-blooded, a purposeful and knowing killing, a crime from *the neck up*. But without looking into the heart, so to speak, murder becomes divorced from its moral evil, its deep-seated emotions, and its core motive.

A COMMONSENSE JUSTICE COMPARISON

Felony murder and accessory felony murder are first-degree murders in most states. Furthermore, a conviction on this charge may lead to the death penalty in a number of those states, under certain circumstances (e.g., *Tison v. Arizona*, 1987). But as noted earlier, there are theoretical problems with the underlying assumptions that support this "murder." Now we switch to an empirical analysis, as we examine four of these underlying legal assumptions from the perspective of ordinary citizens, who may sit on juries and decide such cases, and who bring their CSJ with them to the jury box.

The first assumption the criminal law makes is that it equates the culpability of the felony-murder triggerman with that of the first-degree (pre-meditated and deliberate) triggerman, as both get first-degree murder convictions. Second, the law assumes an equalist position regarding the accessories and the triggerman, for all are judged equally culpable under the theory of accessorial liability. And third, the law treats these defendants as a conspiratorial whole, as if they were fungible, rather than judging them individually, for which culpability would be based on each defendant's actions and intentions; in an individualized assessment, culpability would be graded proportionately, according to each defendant's moral blameworthiness. The fourth assumption is that jurors will follow the *conclusive presumption* of the law, as it is given by the judge: in this case, if the jurors find the defendants guilty of the underlying felony (attempted robbery), and if they find that a death occurred in the commission of the felony (which clearly happened), then, according to the presumption, the jurors should find all these defendants guilty of felony murder. The question is whether CSJ will accept or reject the law's assumptions and premises.

In an empirical test of these assumptions, Finkel and Duff (1991) had *death-qualified* participants (college students and adults) serving as mock jurors; they read one of four randomly assigned cases; made verdict decisions for the triggerman (D), sidekick (C), lookout (B), and getaway driver (A) for the crimes of robbery (the underlying felony) and felony murder; and then made sentencing decisions for these defendants. The four cases varied *how* the victim dies. In the first case, called *heart*, the elderly storekeeper, at the sight of the gun, dies of a heart attack. In the second case, called *accident*, the elderly storekeeper grabs at the gun, and as D tries to pull the gun back from the clerk's grasp, the gun discharges, and the bullet hits the clerk, who subsequently dies from the wound. The third case, *heinous*, begins like the second case with the clerk grabbing the gun, but after they briefly wrestle for the gun, D pulls it away; however, a stock boy testifies at trial that "D went wild, smashing the gun again and again into the face of the elderly clerk," even when the clerk has fallen to the floor with blood covering his face, and then D fires all six shots, in rapid succession, into the clerk as he lies on the floor. The fourth case, *premed* (premeditation), was a baseline control condition for the triggerman: in this case, the clerk hands over the money, and C says to D, "let's go," but D says "no, I've been waiting to nail this old guy for 2 years, and I'm not leaving any witness around"; with that, D opens fire on the clerk, as C stands by, and the clerk is hit with six bullets and subsequently dies. In *premed*, D is charged with first-degree murder, for deliberating and premeditating the crime unbeknownst to his accessories, whereas C, B, and A are charged with felony murder.

The felony-murder verdict was one of the key dependent measures, and mock jurors had the option of finding a defendant not guilty, guilty of felony murder, guilty of second-degree murder, guilty of voluntary manslaughter, or guilty of involuntary manslaughter (the last three guilty verdicts were collapsed into a lesser offense category). Given that mock jurors overwhelmingly found all of the defendants guilty of the underlying felony, given the uncontroverted fact that a death occurred during the commission of the felony, and given that they received the conclusive presumption in the judge's instructions, the mock jurors should deliver a guilty verdict on the felony-murder charge. Thus, Finkel and Duff (1991) considered a significant percentage of not guilty and lesser offense verdicts to be an indication that mock jurors were nullifying or partially nullifying the conclusive presumption of the felony-murder rule.

The not guilty verdict percentages across the four cases for the four defendants were 89% (A), 40% (B), 15% (C), and 2% (D), whereas the felony-murder guilty percentages were 2% (A), 15% (B), 48% (C), and 77% (D), whereas the conviction rate for the premeditated D was 92%. Finkel and Duff (1991) interpreted these results as revealing four things: first, that mock jurors were rejecting the felony-murder rule, for there were significant not guilty verdicts, indicating outright nullifications, and a significant number of partial nullifications (i.e., lesser-offense verdicts), particularly for B and C, but even for D; second, mock jurors were clearly rejecting the equalist justice notion embedded in accessorial liability, for they distinguished the accessories from the triggerman; third, mock jurors were making individualized culpability judgments, grading culpability proportionate to each defendant's blameworthiness; and fourth, they were making a clear discrimination between the felony-murder triggerman and the premeditated triggerman.

The sentencing results, particularly the death sentences given, were another key dependent measure. The death sentence percentages for the four defendants across the cases were significantly different: 0% (A), 1.9% (B),

5.6% (C), and 16.5% (D). But there was a significant difference by case: the majority of death sentences were given in the *heinous* case. And there was another significant difference between types of triggermen: the death sentence percentage for the premeditated triggerman (64.3%) turned out to be four times greater than that for the felony-murder triggerman (16.5%).

Finkel and Duff (1991), thinking that perhaps their task favored nullifications, tried to stack the deck the other way by asking some participants to play the part of mock justices; participants got one of the four cases but under very different conditions: they were told that all of the defendants had been convicted on the felony-murder charge and had been given the death sentence, and now all of the defendants were appealing their death sentence. In this "ninth justice paradigm," they were told that their Supreme Court was split 4 to 4, and they, as the "ninth justice," had the deciding vote, and the question was whether they would "let stand" the death sentence, or "reverse and remand." In addition, participants were given a list of reasons for letting stand or reversing and remanding, reportedly from the other justices, though these reasons were drawn from the arguments Supreme Court Justices raised in *Enmund v. Florida* (1982) and *Tison v. Arizona* (1987). The participants not only had to make a decision for each defendant but also had to write their reasons for their decision.

Across cases and defendants, 77% voted to "reverse and remand," and the percentages for each defendant were 97% (A), 83% (B), 69% (C), and 53% (D); only in the *heinous* case, for D, was "let stand" (68%) the majority decision. A cluster analysis of their reasons for "reversing and remanding" revealed three factors: that felony murder was disproportionate for minor accessories; that the death penalty was disproportionate for felony murder; and the death penalty is unjust when a defendant lacks the intent to kill.

In a second experiment, in which Finkel and Duff (1991) attempted to increase felony-murder convictions and death sentences, they had the sidekick carrying and firing a gun, such that he appears to act with "reckless indifference to human life," and in several of their new vignettes, a police officer, who arrives on the scene, dies in a gunfight. Although felony-murder convictions increased slightly, nullifications and partial nullifications still persisted at significant levels, whereas the death sentence and "reverse and remand" percentages were almost unchanged.

Finally, Finkel and Smith (1993) empirically tested the Supreme Court's empirical assertions about where community sentiment stood on the death penalty for felony-murder accessories (Finkel, 1990a) in its 5 to 4 decision in *Tison v. Arizona* (1987), using a mock juror paradigm with multiple variations of the Tison case in two experiments. Finkel and Smith found that by "a wide majority, community sentiment rejects the death penalty for such an accessory [i.e., one who shows reckless indifference to human life] and rejects equal treatment of principal and accessory" (p. 129).

A LOOK BACK, AND A LOOK FORWARD

Although first-degree murder would anchor the high end of a culpability scale, neither the common law nor the Model Penal Code (American Law Institute, 1962) can theoretically account for the anomaly that is felony murder. It does not fit among the worst of the worst. But even when we ignore this anomaly, we still have problems. The first-degree murderer is most often portrayed as the prototypical cold-blooded killer, who kills without emotion or feeling for another, a portrayal that finds support in the Code's definition, denuded of emotion and malice, in which the killer's actions are cognitively driven, "purposely" and "knowingly," as cognitions become the determinative element under this constricted *mens rea*. If strong and hot emotions were present, they would seem to negate a purposeful homicide, knocking the crime down into a lesser category—into the next chapter on manslaughter.

But that narrow view of *mens rea* has not always held sway, for once upon a time malice (and the emotions that accompany it) was the central construct of murder. In the era of common law, *mens rea* had a deeper meaning, in which much more of the psyche was considered and finer distinctions among types of first-degree murderers were made. The common law's implicit psychological theory of murder, with its consideration of malice, emotions, and motive, and how these interact with intentions, is at odds with the implicit theory embedded in the Code.

Outside the Law in the 17th century, this broader theory of human nature was played out on the stage in Shakespearean dramas, as citizens watched and understood. This commonsense perspective comes into play within the Law, through the jurors. Citizens bring to that role a subtext— their commonsense notions of justice and fairness (e.g., Finkel, 1995b, 2001)— and these notions may, at times, be at odds with the law's notions. This subtext, we believe, was clearly evident in the empirical research presented on felony murder and accessory felony murder, in which citizens overwhelmingly disregarded many of the law's assumptions.

In the next chapter we move to *manslaughter*, to that area of the Law in which *heat of passion* is legally at home, in which there can be no pretense that emotions are not present, or if present, they are there only within "reckless indifference to human life." If emotions are to be given a more central position in a culpability scheme, then what are the Law's theories? And are they internally coherent, and are they consonant with the theories that Psychology and CSJ hold? This is our next topic.

7

MANSLAUGHTER'S FAILING THEORIES OF MITIGATION: EMOTIONS BOUND BY OBJECTIVE RULES, OR AN UNRESTRAINED SUBJECTIVITY?

In going from murder to manslaughter, our story ought to get psychologically richer and subjectively more interesting, for the emotions that had been relegated to subtext in modern murder now take center stage. However, in moving into manslaughter, things get "curiouser and curiouser," as Lewis Carroll (1978) put it, for we enter a looking-glass world, where perspectives reverse, factual questions transform into legal ones, and a psychological flux becomes frozen.

In the previous chapter, we saw that the common law's theory of murder took malice, emotions, and motives seriously, which required a deep subjective analysis of *mens rea*. However, the common law's theory of manslaughter was a contradictory flip-flop, for it was dominated by objective rules about *provocations* and *time* that would make a subjective analysis of emotions, control, motives, malice, and *mens rea* moot, leaving the rich psychological inner life simplistically and mechanistically fixed. But things only get curiouser and curiouser.

In the Model Penal Code's (American Law Institute, 1962) definitions of murder, we found that the common law's elements of malice, depraved heart, and the emotions were jettisoned, as the Code's subjective *mens rea* analysis narrowed to specific intentions. Yet, in the Code's treatment of manslaughter, we get another flip-flop and contradiction, this time in the subjective direction. Emotions, according to the Code's definition of extreme emotional disturbance (EED) arise *ex nihilo* and become reified and personified as entities—unconnected from objective provocations in the outer world, and disconnected from thoughts, motives, and control in the inner world. Alone, within the psyche, they brood, seethe, and then suddenly explode—as if they have minds of their own.

Our story of the story of manslaughter law begins with the common law, as a theoretical study of emotions cast in the objective extreme. Then our story switches to the Model Penal Code (American Law Institute, 1962), as a theoretical study of emotions cast in the subjective extreme. As the objective common law story progresses, it becomes a story of how case decisions and commonsense justice (CSJ) begin to create exceptions to those rigid objective rules, increasingly adding more subjectivity and psychology to the picture. At the other end, as the EED standard's subjective story progresses, it becomes a story of how jurors injected their own commonsense rules and objectivity into this unrestrained subjectivity, inserting a "sense" to this story when there was none. In the end, with more balance, context, and psychology added to the CSJ story, a more complex culpability theory emerges about why people mitigate in manslaughter—a theory the Law has yet to fully grasp.

THE COMMON LAW'S OBJECTIVE RULES

At its earliest beginnings, when the common law was first differentiating manslaughter from murder, Lord Coke (1628/1979) held that manslaughter differs from murder in both the objective act and the subjective intent, for the act occurs "of a sudden" (p. 55), from chance medley situations, in which the actor's intent, unlike the murderer's, does not involve malice aforethought. By Coke's definition, the nature of the act necessarily constrains the intent, because there was "no time for the defendant to establish hatred or ill will toward the deceased"; thus "a killing done upon chance medley is *by definition* not done with malice" (R. Singer, 1986, pp. 251–252, emphasis added). This definition features a certain type of provocation (e.g., chance medley) and a limited time frame (which we shall designate as $\Delta t1$) between the provocation and the killing act.

We shall add two related variables to complete this model. The first, *heat of passion*, was added early in manslaughter's development by a number

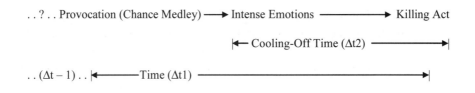

Figure 7.1. The common law model of manslaughter.

of treatise writers (R. Singer, 1986), as this variable, which features intense emotions, intervenes between the objective provocation and the killing. Through this variable one can enter the defendant's subjective, psychological, inner world, where emotions arise quickly and hotly from a provocation, which may override reason's controls and prompt the killing. But this emotional variable leads to another variable, for heated emotions eventually cool, and, at some point during the cooling process, reason and control reestablish; this new variable was called the *cooling-off time* (which we will designate as $\Delta t2$), for the Law would consider, to paraphrase Coke's words, whether the blood had time to cool, for if it did, then that would make the killing murder. We put these variables into a model (see Figure 7.1), and examined its components.

Provocations

The treatise writers drew an objective line as to which provocations would qualify for manslaughter's mitigation and which would not. "Sticks and stones" (e.g., assaults and batteries) that produced physical harm were on the qualifying side, and "names" that did not harm (e.g., mere words, wry faces, and gestures) were on the nonqualifying side. Under this objective theory, only certain physical provocations were viewed as legally sufficient to ignite the intense heat needed to override reason's control, produce deadly action, and warrant mitigation.

Yet we know, from empirical facts, that when it comes to deadly violence, there is great variability among individuals. For example, names, words, wry faces, or gestures—whether they be aurally or visually delivered on a playground, in prison, during a road rage incident, or in a family violence episode—can produce intense emotions in some individuals that lead to a sudden killing. We also know that individuals differ in their character and temperament, with some being quick to ignite. In the *Iliad*, Homer provides such an example: Achilles, with his wrath on the rise, was about to draw his sword and slay Agamemnon on the spot, when Athena swooped down and grasped him by the hair to check his fury (Homer, 1950, p. 38).

But what provocation was Achilles reacting to? King Agamemnon had come to Achilles's tent to claim Achilles's spoil of war (his concubine

Briseis)—which was Agamemnon's prerogative to do, as king. The provocation, then, involved only words, and therefore would have been illegitimate under the common law's rule. Common law judges and treatise writers were undoubtedly aware of between-subject variability and that there were hot responders, like Achilles, but they were unwilling to take manslaughter down that individualized, subjective road for fear that such a path would lead to no objective rule at all.

Yet empirical considerations of variability do enter the common law's considerations, for most people do not kill when subject to physical provocations. In fact, those who kill probably make up a small but significant subset of cases. We surmise that had these killings been even rarer, the Law might have set the mitigating bar higher and lessened the amount of mitigation; however, had these cases been more frequent, representing what the "average person" did, the Law might have increased the amount of mitigation and perhaps moved manslaughter closer to insanity's exculpation.

But variability entered the common law's rules most significantly and problematically through exceptions to the rules, and the adultery exception was there from the beginning: a man (and only a man) who caught his wife "in bed with a lover, and killed one or both of them, was entitled to a reduction to manslaughter" (R. Singer, 1986, p. 256). Though this provocation was likely to produce sudden and intense emotions in the cuckolded spouse, the provocation was only visual. If this provocation (which led to mitigation) was interpreted as a physical assault on the husband's property (rather than on his person), then the rule was bending; if it was interpreted as psychological provocation (i.e., the sight being an emotional betrayal triggering rage), then the rule was broken, because the Law is crossing the physical–psychological distinction it has created, which it now obliterates. This instance of rule-bending foreshadows what is yet to come.

Intense Emotions

One might think that intense emotions would be the place within the process where the traditional subjective inquiry into *mens rea* would begin. But the Law's objective, mechanistic, and nomothetic positions on provocations make a traditional subjective analysis into emotions moot. Once the Law knows that an objective provocation is legally adequate, then, by its mechanistic theory, the Law also knows that this provocation is sufficient to trigger intense emotions, and by its nomothetic position, the Law knows that these intense emotions will occur in "the average individual." In light of this theory, the Law saw no need to put what is a psychological, fact question (i.e., Did sufficiently strong emotions arise in this defendant to override his reason and his controls?) before the jury; instead, the treatise writers substituted their psychological judgments (based on their naive folk-psychology theories), thereby turning a fact question into a matter of law. This pattern would repeat for the objective rules about time and cooling-off time, as empirical, psychological, and subjective fact questions about whether the defendant had malice or could control his emotions and actions would again be settled as matters of law. Under this scheme, the Law ends up assessing a prototype rather than a particular individual, and a subjective analysis of *mens rea* is bypassed entirely. Had the fact question been put to the jury, and had a subjective analysis been required, one jury might have found that Achilles's wrath was hot enough, whereas another jury might have found, for another defendant hearing similar words, that his emotion was not hot enough.

The Time ($\Delta t1$) Between the Provocation and the Killing

This was Lord Coke's "upon a sudden time," which was critical in his analysis, for it seemingly closed the door to malice's entrance, precluding a murder verdict. But we must take a closer look at chance medley, and this $\Delta t1$, for there are unexamined assumptions here. The chance medley pattern begins, according to R. Singer (1986), "with a verbal argument between A and B, which escalates into use of non-deadly force, and then deadly force" (p. 251). But looking at this pattern as one that unfolds and develops over time, we ask, How long did this verbal argument go before it escalated to nondeadly force? And how long, following that, did the nondeadly battle last, before it escalated to deadly force?

When we ask these questions, we realize that the killing might not have been all that sudden. For example, what if, contrary to the assertions of Coke and Singer, this chance medley did not begin with a verbal argument? What if it had a history, in which a prior provocation occurred in $\Delta t - 1$? Under this possibility, the current provocation not only becomes a last-straw incident but also reignites the bad blood and malice prepense already there between the two actors. But under the objective rule about time, only $\Delta t1$? (i.e., the time between the current provocation and the killing) is considered, and this time must be of a sudden; under this theory, prior provocations were irrelevant, for they occurred objectively too long ago to affect the killing.

Yet there was a prior provocation in Achilles's case: Agamemnon was forced by his fellow Greeks to give up his concubine to appease the god Apollo, and Achilles led that effort. With ill will already between them, when Agamemnon subsequently demands Achilles's concubine, Achilles likely hears this, from a subjective perspective, as tit-for-tat payback. Once we extend time into the past $\Delta t - 1$, the of-a-sudden time dilates, and an interpersonal history previous to the chance medley reframes the story differently. However, the of-a-sudden $\Delta t1$ is critical under Coke's objective theory, for it allows the Law to automatically rule out malice (i.e., there was not enough time for it to form) and to automatically conclude that control and reason did not reassert themselves, because the time is too short and the emotional intensity too great. But even in a very short time reason and control can be present. Consider Achilles once more. As Homer (1950) wrote, "and the anger arose in Peleus' son. His heart within his shaggy breast pondered two courses—whether, drawing his sharp sword from his thigh, he should disperse the others and slay the son of Atreus, or should quell his wrath and curb his spirit" (p. 8). But in pondering his two courses, Achilles demonstrates control over his wrath: he can quell it, or give in to it. In reflecting on his options, some reason is demonstrated, but more, Achilles reveals himself as a chooser in this short time, even with his wrath. Homer's portrayal is contrary to Coke's view, for in the latter's portrayal there is no chooser, no control, and no malice whatsoever (Finkel, 1995a, 1996).

Malice may also have been present in manslaughter, although to a lesser extent than in murder. But how much less would not be factually assessed, for again such a subjective analysis was foreclosed, with malice deemed non-existent by definition and dicta. Furthermore, there is an apparent contradiction between the common law's theories of murder and manslaughter: it seems contradictory to hold, for murder, that, as a matter of law, a minimum time necessary for premeditation cannot be fixed, yet hold, in Coke's manslaughter formulation, that this $\Delta t1$ is too short for malice to form, as a matter of law.

The Cooling-Off Time ($\Delta t2$)

If ever there was an empirical and idiothetic question, it is the one concerning the cooling-off time ($\Delta t2$), the time it takes for provoked individuals to be back under control (i.e., to be reasonable once again). Individuals are certainly variable here. Yet the legal rule about cooling-off time treats people as fungible, as if there is no variability among them. Again, the Law takes a fact question that ought to be decided by the jury and turns it into a question of law, which is then decided by a general rule applied to all defendants with the same provocation.

But what if, as a matter of fact, some people do not cool off? For example, what if, during the nondeadly part of a chance medley fight, a man named Stagger Lee breaks off the fight with Billie, goes home and gets his .44, and returns to the bar 15 minutes later, still as hot or hotter than when he left—and shoots Billie to death? In this scenario, both $\Delta t1$ and $\Delta t2$ have stretched a bit, which raises specific factual questions about whether malice and control inserted themselves in that interval. But a stretched-out scenario raises broad, deep, and critical questions about whether an objective, nomothetic theory—which ignores the subjectivity of Stagger Lee and ignores the interpersonal context to this story—can properly evaluate Stagger Lee's culpability. We do not believe it can, because this objective, mechanistic, and nomothetic theory (a) limits the context and foreshortens the act in psychological spacetime, (b) constricts the number of determinative elements needed to make a sound culpability judgment, and (c) by not including the subjective perspective in its analysis, eliminates the story of the story.

A Short Summary

Manslaughter is a compromise verdict. The Law mitigates culpability, but it does not exculpate. The Law acknowledges our human frailty and lessens culpability, recognizing that we are not at our psychological and legal best when our passions get the best of our thinking and control. However, the Law does not go all the way to exculpation, and by not doing so, the Law is claiming that our passions have not overturned our reason and control to the point of insanity and blamelessness. But on what factual basis does that claim rest? Put another way, do the theoretical grounds for granting mitigation (but no more) rest on something substantive? That question, we submit, has not been answered satisfactorily through the common law's rules.

Looked at from the other end, this compromise verdict of manslaughter remains a guilty verdict. As such, the Law is saying to such a defendant— psychologically and normatively—"you could have, and should have, done better." Somewhere, then, in the Law's folk-psychology theory as well as in its normative expectations, there is the belief that control over one's emotions is psychologically possible and normatively expected: the Law believes, then, that these defendants could have (and should have) followed a law-abiding course, even when hit by physical provocations that arouse intense emotions. If this is so, then why remit anything from culpability? Either way we pose the question, we are still in search of a satisfactory theory of the emotions and their interplay with provocations, thinking, control, and motives.

The early common law theorists avoided a subjective, evaluative, and idiothetic approach, fearing, perhaps, that a law so grounded might end up having to grant mitigation to the weakest, vilest, or least controlled of its citizens, just the types the Law most wants to restrain "within the belt of rule." In going in the extreme objective direction, the common law's theory selected and defined variables in such a way that subjectivity and psychology were squeezed out of the picture, but the Law's resultant picture became a still-life snapshot rather than a moving flesh-and-blood story, for context and time were limited to an of-a-sudden act that occurs at a moment in time. This creates a false and simplistic framing of the problem. In effect, there was no story to this story. In this legally foreshortened picture it was as if Agamemnon suddenly appeared at Achilles's tent out of the blue, without history and prologue, and as if Hamlet (Shakespeare, 1938) stabs the king with his poisoned sword in Act V acontextually—as if Acts I through IV had no effect on what happened.

Achilles and Hamlet, both brooders, were also *rekindlers*, for new provocations, ones that the common law would deem legally inadequate, reignited older provocations that still roiled within. Yet the common law closed the legal door to consideration of these older provocations, once those earlier emotions had cooled, for its theory of time stopped the chronological clock and made those events irrelevant, moot, and dead. Some provocations, though, do not die easily; rather, they may come back from the dead when reignited by a small spark.

But change was coming within the Law. Common law cases were forcing the Law to elasticize to accommodate exceptions, and the rules were bending and amending. The Law's prototypical caricature began to crumble, along with the objective theories supporting it, as the Law began a slow slide toward subjectivity.

SUBJECTIVE BREACHES IN THE OBJECTIVE RULES

John Royley (*Royley's Case*, 1666) was not battered himself, and he did not witness the beating that the boy John Derman administered to his son William, such that William's "nose bled." In Richard Singer's (1986) summary and analysis of the case, what Royley heard were William's words, "telling and complaining to him of that battery" (p. 254).

The Subjectivizing of Provocations: Informational Words

John Royley (*Royley's Case*, 1666), with those *informational words* in mind and with heated passions propelling him, "goes a mile to find [the young John Derman], and there, in revenge of his son's quarrel, strikes the boy with a little cudgel" (R. Singer, 1986, p. 254), killing Derman. The court ruled "it was but manslaughter," as the killing was "upon that sudden occasion" (p. 255).

Although mere words had been excluded as an adequate provocation, this court drew a new distinction, and held that informational words, when aurally delivered about a battery, were an adequate provocation. But in moving from a physical and visual provocation to an aural one, Royley ran with an imaginative picture, a subjectively conjured provocation, and the beating he imagined in his mind was no doubt far worse than what the Derman boy actually delivered to Royley's son.

But by finding that this was manslaughter—because the killing occurred "upon that sudden occasion"—this court ends up stretching out $\Delta t1$, for it is a fair assumption that it took this father some 10 to 15 minutes or so to travel the mile to get to young Derman. This decision also stretches out the cooling-off time, $\Delta t2$, for Royley has both the time and opportunity, during the run, to reflect and realize that this was merely a quarrel between two boys, amounting to no more than a bloody nose, and that a father intervening to revenge this boys-will-be-boys quarrel was an inappropriate escalation. Had

Royley had any of those thoughts, his reason and control might have stopped him in his tracks. Moreover, there is no indication that the court, given the factual $\Delta t1$ and $\Delta t2$ in the case, asked the normative question: Should Royley have asked himself whether his avenging run was appropriate?

But when Royley gets there and is standing over the young John Derman, with the disproportionate size difference evident, and with a disproportionate cudgel in his hand, about to have his nonchance medley with Derman—what is he thinking, and what should he be thinking? We know from the court record that Derman does not physically attack John Royley, so there was no objective physical provocation, save for what was subjectively still in Royley's mind, which was not freshly of a sudden anymore. For this verdict to make any sense (and we believe it was faulty on many counts), the jurors must have heavily weighted Royley's subjectivity—subjectivity rooted in the images and emotions those informational words stirred in his mind and in a mind that could conjure, inflame, and keep the fire burning over a run of time, in spite of a face-to-face encounter with a much smaller adversary that should have given him reason to pause—or at least reason to put down the cudgel.

This informational-words exception began to appear more frequently in case decisions until it became the rule, though a contradictory exception remained for adultery cases. In the North Carolina case of *State v. John* (1848), the defendant tried to introduce evidence that witnesses had aurally told him that his wife was having an adulterous affair, but the court excluded the evidence, claiming that the affair had to be visually witnessed. Although aural information about a battery (e.g., *Royley's Case*, 1666) and a sodomy (e.g., *Regina v. Fisher*, 1837) was judged reliable, aural information about an adultery was not deemed reliable in *State v. John*. But this adultery exception was soon to crumble.

In *Regina v. Smith* (1866), William Smith killed his wife after she "violently abused him, taunting him with her preference for Langley" (p. 910), a man with whom she had lived in adultery, but who was now dead. Beyond taunting and using foul language, she may have "spat in her husband's face," although in the next sentence the case record indicates that whether she "actually spat on, or only at him, did not appear" (p. 910). The ruling in *Regina v. Smith* was manslaughter, as the court suggested that words spoken could aggravate the provocation, as could the spitting, whether the spittle lands or not. This court seemed to be either expanding what could be an adequate provocation or suggesting that a current but inadequate provocation may serve to subjectively trigger an old provocation from the past.

The Subjectivizing of Time

In *Regina v. Fisher* (1837), Fisher hears from his 15-year-old son that he was sodomized by a man named Randall, and, like Royley, Fisher takes off to avenge what happened; however, unlike Royley, Fisher takes off the next day, not immediately. When he meets up with Randall, he first beats him with a short stick, and then stabs him to death with a table knife. Justice Park ruled that this was murder, and he cited the cooling factor, for whether "the blood had time to cool or not, is rather a question of law" (p. 454), and the Justice ruled that the blood had cooled by the time Fisher confronted Randall. Fisher's run was apparently a day late, according to the Law's theory.

In a Texas case, *Pauline v. State* (1886), Pauline gets a letter on January 5 informing him that his wife is having an adulterous relationship with the victim, whom he kills on February 7. The court held that too much time had passed between the provocation and the murder, as a matter of law, with the blood having plenty of time to cool. But on rehearing the case, the *Pauline* court learns that the letter had actually been dated February 5, not January 5, and this corrected fact changed the verdict to manslaughter, for it "establishes the killing on the first meeting after the appellant had been informed of the adultery of the appellant's wife and the deceased" (p. 464).

We are now going to examine these common law cases relating to time. The *Royley* court found 10 to 15 minutes to be sufficient for manslaughter's mitigation, whereas the *Fisher* court found 1 day to be too late. However, the *Pauline* court found 2 days to be within manslaughter's mitigating range, which contradicts the *Fisher* holding. But the *Pauline* case is not just contradictory, it is revolutionary, for it actually obliterates objective time entirely: it says, in effect, the clock does not begin to run until the defendant first sees the victim. But this first meeting could come 2 days later, as it did in the actual case, or it could come 5 days, 50 days, or 5 years later, raising the question, does objective time really not matter at all? If not, then the underlying theory behind this ruling is not that the defendant's emotions stayed hot for all that time without any cooling (a rather absurd proposition), but rather that *Pauline* is in actuality a rekindler case, for the first sight of the victim reignites Pauline's dormant (but not dead) emotions, linked with the old adulterous provocation, and this becomes legally sufficient for manslaughter. Put another way, the defendant subjectively connects new and old provocations in psychological time, for only in the psyche can one turn "time past" into "time present"—in an instant—as the poet T. S. Eliot (1934) well understood.

IS THE LAW'S SUBJECTIVITY
LAGGING BEHIND THE JURORS' SUBJECTIVITY?

In a seminal case in Michigan, *Maher v. People* (1863), the defendant was charged with "an assault with intent to kill and murder one Patrick Hunt" (p. 215). Maher acted under the belief, arrived at through visual and informational evidence, that Hunt was having a relationship with Maher's wife: "first, on the morning of the assault, he saw his wife and Hunt going into the woods together and coming out an hour later, just before he followed Hunt into a saloon and fired; second, before entering the saloon, a friend informed Maher that his wife had had sexual intercourse with Hunt the day before in the woods" (Finkel, 1995b, p. 757). From the objective perspective, however, both pieces of evidence were problematic: though Maher had visual evidence suggesting that something provocative may have been happening, Maher did not see the act, and though someone else did witness the sexual intercourse, Maher had only an informational report of it. According to the adultery rule, mere information or inference does not add up to witnessing the *flagrante*.

What makes this a seminal case in the Law's turn toward subjectivity was Judge Christiancy's speculations about how the jurors likely heard Maher's two pieces of evidence. Judge Christiancy believed that they would have used the subjective vantage point and put the two pieces of evidence together to find "sufficient evidence of provocation" (p. 225), indicating that the Law's formal rules were out of tune with what "men of fair average mind and disposition" (p. 220) would construe.

Judge Christiancy went to the subjective nature of provocations when he noted that they "must depend upon the nature of man and the laws of the human mind" (p. 222). If each man construes a provocation uniquely, idiothetically, depending on his nature, history, and disposition, then only a subjective, psychological *mens rea* inquiry can unearth how that particular provocation is construed and evaluated, what degree of emotion is engendered in this person's mind, and how quickly or slowly emotion cools for that individual. If this be so, then an objective, ordinal scale of provocations— with physical assaults at the top, adulterous relationships in the middle, and mere words at the bottom, and with provocations producing set amounts of emotion and set rates of cooling—was nonsense. As Christiancy wrote,

> The passion excited by a blow received in a sudden quarrel, though perhaps equally violent for the moment, would be likely much sooner to subside than if aroused by a rape committed upon a sister or a daughter, or the discovery of an adulterous intercourse with wife; and no two cases of the latter kind would be likely to be identical in all their circumstances of provocation. (p. 222)

But Judge Christiancy's subjective perspective was at odds with the objective perspective that a Washington court held in *State v. Gounagias* (1915):

> This theory of the cumulative effect of reminders of former wrongs . . . is contrary to the idea of sudden anger as understood in the doctrine of mitigation. In the nature of the thing, *sudden* anger cannot be cumulative. A provocation which does not cause instant resentment, but which is only resented after being thought upon and brooded over, is not a provocation sufficient in law to reduce intentional killing from murder to manslaughter. (p. 9)

This clash of perspectives is best illustrated through the facts in *Gounagias* and how they were interpreted.

Gounagias, a Greek immigrant and a small man, worked in a restaurant where he was sodomized by a coworker, a much larger man. Adding insult to injury, the attacker told the defendant's friends of the sodomy and taunted Gounagias for 3 weeks. When Gounagias returned to the restaurant to pick up his pay and saw his attacker, he stabbed and killed him. Gounagias attempted to introduce evidence at trial that he had been sodomized by the deceased and taunted for 3 weeks, but the evidence was excluded, and the Washington Supreme Court held that this evidence had been properly excluded because though the defendant might in fact have killed in passion, it was not of a sudden. But as Finkel (1995b) stated,

> The *Gounagias* court, beneath its legalities, announces a psychological theory that dooms the brooder and the rekindler . . . [for] strong provocations like sodomy, if not acted upon immediately, fade into history and irrelevancy, such that only the current context matters. In such an analysis, a new and weak provocation, like a taunt, cannot produce the sudden, red-hot passion for mitigation. As for the nexus between present and past anger, the court severs it: the old anger fades and cools, so there is no cumulative storehouse waiting for a last taunt to ignite. (p. 760)

The *Gounagias* decision reverts to the objective rules about provocations, cooling time, and the moment of the act as the context. This decision stands in contrast to the decision in *Pauline* and the commentary of Judge Christiancy in *Maher*, which, by making subjective, psychological connections between new and old provocations, expanded the context: the *Pauline* court, by contrast, understood the importance of psychological time rather than chronological time, and Judge Christiancy understood that provocations were construed subjectively, based on an individual's history. From the subjectivist's vantage point, a fundamental question remains in doubt: Did the jurors truly pass judgment on Gounagias if they never heard about the sodomy and the 3 weeks of taunts?

In this growing clash within the Law between objective and subjective perspectives, we take up a final case, a British case, *Director of Public Prosecutions v. Bedder* (1954), in which the 17-year-old Bedder, who was told by doctors that he was impotent, hired a prostitute in the hope of being able to perform; when he was unable to perform and the prostitute ridiculed him, he "slew her in what was undeniably true rage" (p. 1119). At trial, the judge held that Bedder's impotence was irrelevant, and the jury was instructed not to consider or weigh that fact. On appeal, Bedder claimed that his impotence produced his sensitivity, and that when the prostitute taunted and hit him "in a fracas about his inability to perform the negotiated sexual act" (Fletcher, 1978, p. 248), he reacted to the provocation not as an ordinary man might, but as a highly sensitive man would, and lost control. The House of Lords, however, rejected Bedder's claim and affirmed the trial court's ruling. As Law Professor George Fletcher (1978) wrote, "One can hardly say that the jury passed judgment on Mr. Bedder if they did not even consider the most significant facts that influenced his loss of control" (p. 248), which is the same point we made about the jury judging Mr. Gounagias.

WHEN COMMONSENSE JUSTICE DOES GET TO PASS JUDGMENT

A case oftentimes raises intriguing psychological and legal questions— hypotheses, in scientific language—which, unfortunately, cannot be tested scientifically and systematically in that case, for case facts are fixed, and key variables cannot be experimentally manipulated in that setting. What we need are multiple variations of that case to make an adequate test.

Finkel (1995a) tested a number of hypotheses about the *Bedder* and *Gounagias* cases in an experimental design with mock jurors, in which he systematically manipulated variations so he could see their specific effects. To test Bedder's contention that jurors would have reached a more lenient verdict had they heard and weighed the contextual information about his impotency, Finkel manipulated the variable *context*, so that mock jurors got either a vignette stating the facts of his impotency or one in which the impotency information was left out (an impotency vs. no-impotency context comparison). Bedder's "sensitivity" argument—that his impotency sensitized him to the provocation—was also tested as an interaction effect with the second variable, *provocation*: mock jurors heard that he was laughed at by the prostitute (called "taunt"), in one condition, or laughed at and slapped by the prostitute (called "slap"), in a second condition. This second variable tested the taunt versus slap provocation. As for the interaction effect, a physical provocation (slap) should have a greater mitigating effect than the taunt condition, but if information about his impotency (impotency condition) sensitizes the jurors sympathetically, then the taunt–impotency condition might be as equally mitigating as the slap–impotence condition, more so than in the taunt–no impotence condition. Finally, Finkel tested his own hypothesis regarding the type of emotion Bedder experienced by having mock jurors read that he was either enraged following the taunt or slap, or frightened, such that an "anger" or "fear" condition was manipulated. In this $2 \times 2 \times 2$ factorial design, Context × Provocation × Type of Emotion was manipulated, and mock jurors made verdict and sentencing decisions as culpability measures and gave their reasons for their decisions.

Overall, 68% of the verdicts were second-degree murder, and 32% were manslaughter. There were no significant verdict differences for any of the variables, and there was no support for either of Bedder's hypotheses. However, when we examined the finer measure of sentencing, we found significant differences for provocation and type of emotion as well as a significant

Provocation × Type of Emotion interaction effect: sentences were higher for taunt (195 months) when compared with the slap (140 months) condition, and higher for feelings of anger (223 months) than for fear (113 months). For the interaction effect, fear reduces the sentence to the lowest point when paired with either laugh (113 months) or slap (112 months), but anger paired with slap reduces the sentence only to 167 months, whereas anger paired with taunt leaves the sentence at its highest, at 278 months; thus the emotion of fear, rather than the physical provocation of slap, produces the greatest mitigating effect. Finally, though the effect did not reach significance, the sentence was higher (184 months) in the impotence condition, interestingly, than in the nonimpotence (151 months) condition.

Analyses of the mock jurors' reasons for their decisions were revealing. First, they tell us that jurors do consider his impotence, do sympathize with the young man, and do agree with Bedder's argument that he was sensitive, but nonetheless hold him culpable in a way that the Law does not consider in manslaughter. In their analysis of the story, they first widened the traditional moment of the act and considered his culpability before the act for bringing about the act: what these jurors were focusing on was his negligence or recklessness for putting himself in a situation that he should have known was a high risk for danger, given his sensitivity.

Second, these results support the common law's objective position regarding provocation, because the physical slap was judged worse and more mitigating than a mere taunt. But subjectivity mattered as well, for what was more surprising, and even more potent, was the type of emotion felt (see chap. 5, this volume): mock jurors showed a mitigating sympathy for fear and an antipathy for anger, with the subjective fear mitigating more than did the objective slap. Thus, in the mock jurors' subjective analysis, it was not merely a question of emotion's intensity, but its type.

Turning to the *Gounagias* case, Finkel (1995a) tested eight variations of the case, and the results can be summarized this way. Overall, the majority of the verdicts were manslaughter, and the results reveal that mock jurors clearly rejected the suppositions of the *Gounagias* court. When a nonsodomy and taunt condition (which is how the court said we should see this case) was compared with a sodomy and taunt condition or with a sodomy and frequent taunt condition (the actual case, which involved frequent rekindling), there were significant differences between the former and the latter two; in fact, the rekindling conditions showed almost as much mitigating effect as an immediate heat-of-passion killing.

It is clear that mock jurors connect the recent taunt with the distant (3-week-old) sodomy provocation (that occurred in $\Delta t1$), as they see a powerful unbroken nexus between the two that explains the killing. Unlike the court's moment-of-the-act view, jurors widen their perspective, take in relevant context, and create a meaningful story, which is a psychological story. They affirm that subjective psychological time is what matters, rejecting the

Gounagias court's objective claim that the cooling time clock had expired, such that the sodomy was history and did not matter. In fact, when Finkel extended the rekindling time to 6 months following the sodomy, the mock jurors still connected the recent taunt with the distant (6-month-old) provocation, as the nexus remained and the mitigating effect still held.

Where the mitigation effect did not hold, however, was for the brooder conditions; when there was no objective taunt, but only something imagined in the defendant's mind, the mitigating reduction was much less than for the rekindler versions, which indicates that objectivity does matter in regard to the new provocation, and that subjectivity has its limits. Said another way, the jurors want to "see" some provoking event in the real world to validate the psychological nexus. And finally, in two conditions where the historical context was opened wider and further into the past, where information was provided that Gounagias had suffered abuse as a child, this information added nothing to mitigation. These results indicate that jurors circumscribed the context to those elements that they judged to be psychologically relevant to the killing, and ancient history was deemed too far removed for relevancy.

In the experimental work of Spackman, Belcher, Calapp, and Taylor (2002), the researchers gave one of three cases to mock jurors, who rendered either a murder or manslaughter verdict. These mock jurors received either an objective or subjective jury instruction. The verdict results did not significantly differ by jury instruction, as mock jurors construed the instructions to fit with their commonsense notions of murder and manslaughter. But the findings on the three cases were different, and surprising. When the defendant "intended to kill," jurors, as expected, tilted toward the murder verdict, but two other factors had even greater effect: whether there was a history of violence between the defendant and the victim and, the most powerful variable, whether the defendant dwelt on his or her emotions—two factors not ordinarily considered within the common law's objective factors.

These results support the findings of Finkel (1995b) and add complexity to CSJ's culpability story. Again, context matters, for the interpersonal history between defendant and victim matters because it extends the story back in time and space and raises questions about the defendant's and victim's earlier culpability for what ultimately happened. And when the defendant dwells and broods over past incidents, this makes matters worse—setting himself up to emotionally ignite in response to a provocation that should not have triggered a lethal outcome. Spackman et al.'s (2002) mock jurors, like Finkel's mock jurors and like Elizabethan theatergoers, were widening the Law's culpability considerations by weighing a greater number of determinative elements, having a psychological spacetime that expands the Law's moment-of-the-act focus, and having a subjective perspective—all of which create a wider, longer, deeper, and richer story.

This culpability analysis that mock jurors are doing is complex. And though the story they fashion is decidedly psychological and steeped in subjectivity, they do not get lost in a subjective Wonderland (Carroll, 1978); rather, they anchor their story to objective reality at a number of points. We see that they circumscribe their story to relevant grounds, rather than falling through a hole into distant past. We also see that the brooder loses where the rekindler wins, for the latter reacts to an objective taunt whereas the former reacts only to his subjective imaginings. In a similar manner, mock jurors see the one who dwells on his emotions as one who is more likely to be aware of his emotions and who should be able to control them. In a similar vein, they did not yield to their sympathies for the teenage Bedder's impotency and sensitivity, for once Bedder knows about his problem and sensitivity, he then has a duty to consider others and the risks he takes.

These mock jurors' *mens rea* stories clearly have a subjective coloring, but with some balancing objectivity to it. Yet their picture is noticeably wider and more modernist, for both context and time open beyond the moment of the act, as significant connections between past and present events are drawn in the mind, as types of emotion, not just their heat, are discriminated, and as different types of culpability are considered, more so than we find in the Law's culpability analysis. It is the story of a unique person with emotions, whose psychology is connected to objective interpersonal events, past and present, subjectively construed and connected in the mind to thoughts, feelings, and motives. It is a story wherein an ending action has a beginning psychological prologue, which may be a history of violence between the defendant and victim. This story has more breadth, depth, and nuance than what the Law puts forth, or seemingly allows. Yet, by bending and breaking objective rules, the courts in *Smith*, *Pauline*, and *Maher* seemed to be moving slowly toward that subjectivity and psychology, that wider view that connected new aggravations and old provocations—in mind.

EXTREME EMOTIONAL DISTURBANCE: SUBJECTIVITY ADRIFT

The Model Penal Code's (American Law Institute, 1962) definition of manslaughter is as follows:

> a homicide which would otherwise be murder [is manslaughter when it] is committed under the influence of extreme mental or emotional disturbance for which there is reasonable explanation or excuse. The reasonableness of such explanation or excuse shall be determined from the viewpoint of a person in the actor's situation under the circumstances as he believes them to be. (§ 210.3(1)(b))

This definition clearly tilts toward subjectivity in its language and the viewpoint, for even though it mentions the objective-sounding "reasonable explanation," the next sentence subjectivizes the matter, for we must view the actor's explanation from his subjective vantage point, as "he believes [the circumstances] to be." So much for objective reasonableness.

The Model Penal Code's (American Law Institute, 1962) subjectivizing direction was also evident in its abandonment of the common law's objective approach of limiting adequate provocations and its abandonment of cooling-off time as a matter of law; instead, such questions were submitted to the jury (R. Singer, 1986, p. 292). But what guidance did the jury have under this new EED standard? Consider the guidance provided by two Connecticut cases—*State v. Zdanis* (1980) and *State v. Elliot* (1979)—for both dealt with brooders who killed victims without a provocative act by the victim. As R. Singer (1986) related the facts of the *Zdanis* case and the appellate decision,

> The defendant had learned that his eight-year-old niece, to whom he apparently was deeply attached, was dying of cancer. After some days "brooding" about the news, the defendant entered his own house, threatened to kill his wife and killed his step-daughter. There was no provocative act by the victim. Indeed, there appeared to be no explicable reason for the killing. Although the murder conviction was upheld by the appellate court, the court strongly suggested that if the fact-finder had found the defendant guilty only of EED manslaughter, that verdict also would have been upheld. (pp. 294–295)

The appellate court in *Zdanis* made it clear the jury was free to consider any reaction to any stimulus in an EED jurisdiction, yet this jury, like the mock jurors in Finkel's (1995b) experiment in the brooder conditions, found no objective provocation and brought in a murder conviction, despite instructions that seemed to free them from such a need.

The appellate court in *Elliot* (1979) went even further:

> The defense [of EED] does not require a provoking or triggering event; or that the homicidal act occur immediately after the cause or causes of the defendant's extreme emotional disturbance. . . . A homicide influenced by an extreme emotional disturbance is not one which is necessarily committed in the "hot blood" stage, but rather one that was brought about by a significant mental trauma that caused the defendant to brood for a long period of time and then react violently, seemingly without provocation. (p. 8)

The appellate court's dicta is great news for the brooder, though whether jurors will be willing to go this far is an open question. Both the *Zdanis* jury and the mock juror research suggest that jurors may still be looking for some objective provocation, even if it be but a taunt that connects the EED on the front end with the killing on the back end.

If we look for the EED standard's underlying psychological theory, we find none, for it fails to offer an explanation for problems on the front end, the back end, and in the middle (the interior). Under the EED standard (that the Model Penal Code [American Law Institute, 1962] gives us and the *Elliot* court embellishes), emotion becomes a psychological entity within the mind, disconnected from any interpersonal context or objective provocation in the external reality, having a nexus with nothing; yet, this disembodied interior entity can rear up, at any time, for any or no reason, and can reach out into the external world and produce mayhem, murder, or manslaughter.

There is nothing, theoretically, to explain how such a disembodied and disconnected entity has come into being or comes to affect other human beings. Neither folk nor academic theories of emotion treat emotions in such a subjective manner, as we saw in chapter 4 (this volume). Nor is there any theory to explain where and how this free-floating entity is situated within the intrapsychic nexus of cognitions, motives, malice, judgment, and control; rather, it seems that this entity is isolated from the rest of the psyche, with a will and mind of its own. This is not the sort of dynamic and discursive "mind" academic psychologists (e.g., Harré & Gillett, 1994) research and write about, a mind that is "embedded in historical, political, cultural, social, and interpersonal contexts" (p. 25). This is not even bad "pop psychology," which at least puts on a pretext of theory. No, in evoking this EED entity, the Law dives into pure subjectivity without a bungee cord and without a theory, with a concept out of a sci-fi movie. As detached and frightening as the *Elliot* court's EED standard is, the question naturally arises: Why is this not an insanity defense? Without a theory indicating where and how some partial control exists over the emotions and actions, this sort of brooder takes on the look, from society's vantage point, of a wild beast within its midst.

HOW JURORS USE THE
EXTREME EMOTIONAL DISTURBANCE STANDARD

We assert that the EED standard is really no standard at all. By throwing off all of the objective rules, and by throwing the key decisions to the jurors to decide from the defendant's vantage point, the Law is, in effect, asking jurors to perform a task in which they are to leave their own reality behind, like Alice (Carroll, 1978), and enter the Wonderland world of the defendant's EED, to see and feel as the defendant did, and then to judge whether the defendant's excuse was reasonable. This task calls on jurors to be more than exquisite psychotherapists, for it asks them to set aside not only their own judgments at the outset but also their own personalities to adopt that of another. This is an impossible task for ordinary citizens, and for Alice, because we carry our self into Wonderland and cannot magically dissociate to the abracadabra of the judge's instruction. The Law's psychological expectation goes beyond curiouser and curiouser; it is unrealistic.

We now present some findings from an empirical study done by Kirschner, Litwack, and Galperin (2004), who did a qualitative analysis of all cases in New York County during a 10-year period in which defendants pled the partial defense of EED to charges of intentional murder or attempted intentional murder. Their analyses attempted to distinguish those factors that discriminated "successful" cases (i.e., those ending in manslaughter or attempted manslaughter) from "unsuccessful" cases (i.e., ending in murder or attempted murder). During this period, there were 24 cases: 9 successful (S) and 15 unsuccessful (U). It is interesting to note that there were no significant differences between the S and U cases in terms of the defendant's psychiatric diagnosis. In the U cases, 10 of 15 victims were wives, girlfriends, or fiancés, whereas for the S cases, only 1 of 9 were. Pursuing this difference, the researchers found a deeper type of emotion difference that separated the U and S cases: in the U cases, the dominant emotions of the defendants fell in the anger, jealousy, and revenge category, whereas for the S cases, the defendants were motivated more by fear. This finding was quite consistent with what Finkel (1995a) found in his experimental work with mock jurors and consistent with what academic Psychology finds (see chap. 5, this volume): there is a sympathy toward fear and an antipathy toward anger.

These researchers also concluded that jurors did not accept the EED claim of mitigation based simply on strong, intense emotions; rather, they evaluated the reasonableness of the emotions under the circumstances, and did so not just from the defendant's point of view, as the EED standard requires, but from the community's point of view and from their own commonsense point of view. In other words, they did not leave their own self or the objective world behind. Rather, the jurors considered and weighed the objective reasonableness of the emotions in the given situation, along with the subjective construal and reaction, as they created some degree of subjective–objective balance in their analysis despite the legal instruction that clearly tilted toward the subjective. Thus, in the absence of legal guidance, jurors created their own guidelines, insisting that a manslaughter story be reasonable and plausible, in which the defendant's emotional reactions, thoughts, motives, and actions had to be connected in some reasonable way to the interpersonal events, however tenuously construed. Furthermore, in their own story construction model for manslaughter, angry and vengeful reactions were not judged as an acceptable or justifiable reaction to the events that transpired.

Finally, these findings are supported by a laboratory study by Spackman, Belcher, and Hanson (2002), in which mock jury deliberations under either objective or EED instructions were tape recorded and qualitatively analyzed. Though there were no significant verdict differences by instructions, both types of jurors were reconstruing the instructions a third way: not objectively (by using the "ordinary, reasonable person" standard), and not subjectively (from the vantage point of the defendant), but by adopting a third perspective—wherein they ask themselves and one another whether they would have killed in the situation.

A LOOK BACK, AND A LOOK FORWARD

Some 400 years ago the Law began to create its theory of manslaughter, and after all this time, and after flip-flopping betwixt the extremes of objectivity and subjectivity, the Law has made little headway in offering a coherent, psychologically grounded account. Without such an account, it is not clear why it makes good theoretical sense to mitigate (but not exculpate) culpability in these situations. R. Singer (1986) stated that common sense seems to understand "that persons in extreme situations normally do not 'intend' very much of anything; they merely wish to end the stressful situation" (p. 310). Perhaps that was the commonsense intuition that guided treatise writers such as Coke at the beginning of manslaughter's evolution. But theoretically explaining this intuition became the rub, and what the Law would offer, under either the common law or the Model Penal Code (American Law Institute, 1962), rubbed the wrong way.

It is ironic that these crimes would be called "crimes of passion," because the common law's objective rules never allowed for an individualized examination of these intervening passions. Its theories never accounted for how defendants subjectively interpreted those interpersonal provocations; nor did these theories deal with which emotions arose, nor how those emotions linked with the defendant's thoughts, intentions, motives, and malice; and as these emotions and motives pushed toward killing acts, these theories did not explain how and why reason did not, would not, or could not insert control and quell the emotional heat short of homicide. With an objective rule that established those legally adequate provocations, and with a mechanistic theory that fixed their provoking emotional intensity above the threshold sufficient to weaken both reason and control in the nomothethically average individual, the Law knew all it needed to know about the passions' intensity and their of-a-sudden rising. When coupled with its objective rule of cooling-off time, the Law knew all it needed to know about whether malice had time to form. As it turned out, then, subjective *mens rea* was never analyzed for the particular defendant, for it was already known from the objective givens. This theory rests, then, on the Law's nomothethic, folk-psychology assumptions.

Yet, to its credit, this common law theory was an attempt to develop a theory, though the treatise writers' "psychology" was not good psychology. This naive psychology was turned into a matter of law, which put the actual defendant on the sidelines of his own trial; the defendant had good company on the sidelines, for the jury was there as well, as what should have been factual matters at trial were transmuted into legal matters as the Law applied its rules to a fungible caricature. As it turned out, these objective rules ran afoul of case facts and exceptions arose, as rules were bent and interpreted in more subjective ways by some courts, such that psychological interpretations of provocations, the connections between provocations, and a psychological view of time and context began to move this objective law in the subjective direction. As a result, an actual defendant, and the jury, were creeping back into the picture.

The Model Penal Code's (American Law Institute, 1962) EED answer to the problem of manslaughter turns out to be the opposite extreme—a subjectivity unrestrained—with not even the pretext of a supportive psychological theory to back it up. The Code would throw the decision, with little guidance, to the jurors who would be given the near-impossible task of having to enter the defendant's EED to see and judge the reasonableness of his or her explanation or excuse from the defendant's vantage point and situation, as the defendant believes them to be. As it turns out, from some limited empirical work, jurors seem to be doing a decent job in their qualitative analyses of these difficult cases, though they do not follow this subjective guideline entirely; rather, they bring their own commonsense demands for objective reasonableness into this story. This finding—that jurors do a credible job—redounds positively to the jurors, we submit, and not to the EED standard.

Right from the beginning, the Law drew the wrong picture. First, Lord Coke drew the upon-a-sudden context to manslaughter, a narrow picture that leaves out the nexus between new and old provocations and falsely distills a psychological interpersonal situation down to objective provocations and a moment-of-the-act event. Manslaughter law has yet to recover from this limitation. Second, in its 400 years of manslaughter jurisprudence, even as the Law swung from the extreme of objectivity to subjectivity, the Law has failed to realize that manslaughter is not just a crime of passion, as it has been advertised, for it involves a partial failure of reason (Finkel, 1995a). We have seen, from the mock jurors' analysis of the *Bedder* case, that reason may falter before the action even begins, when the defendant makes a bad choice and puts others at risk because of his greater sensitivity. Reason may also falter in the way provocations are interpreted, and the illustrating example of this is what Royley had in mind (or should have had in mind) while running to revenge his son's bloody nose. And reason may falter further along in the process, when Royley confronts and towers over the boy with a cudgel in his hands, when his reason fails to assess and control his disproportionate anger and action.

Neither the old common law nor the new EED standard has a psychological theory that goes to the heart of this reason–emotion interplay, and how this interplay affects control. The EED standard offers no theory, and the *Elliot* court's account of the EED standard makes manslaughter law indistinguishable from insanity's irresistible impulse, raising the question, why not exculpate?

To reject exculpation, the Law needs a theory showing that reason and control, at least to some degree, were partially operable. The old common law's objective rules do not do much better, for if sufficient heat of passion has been triggered but the cooled-off setting has not been reached, then why is this not an irresistible impulse? To counter, one would have to argue and theorize either that reason and control were not totally impaired by the intensity of the heat to begin with, or that the blood had cooled sufficiently for some modicum of reason and control to be operable, more so than would be present in insanity cases.

Insanity, our next stop, is the end point on this culpability continuum, and at this extreme we face a profound question about personhood: Is there even an agent, a self, a legal actor—acting—one who is still morally culpable and blameworthy? If we believe the actor is not blameworthy, then what psychological, commonsense, legal theory supports exculpation, and how does this theory explain the interplay of emotions, reason, and lack of control? Whereas we are concerned with successful insanity cases, we are also interested in the unsuccessful cases, those that have fallen short of exculpation, for here we may yet find answers to the still-open questions that we leave behind—as we exit manslaughter and enter madness.

8

INSANITY I:
THE PROTOTYPIC, YET PROBLEMATIC,
EXCUSING CONDITION

The 2003 trial of sniper Lee Boyd Malvo (*Commonwealth of Virginia v. Lee Boyd Malvo*, 2003) dominated the headlines in the National Capital Area, as did his actions of the prior year, when a reign of terror fell on citizens of Maryland, the District of Columbia, and Virginia. On the eve of his trial, many who had experienced fear were puzzled by a report in *The Washington Post* (Oldenburg, 2003) that the defense was going to argue that the 17-year-old Malvo was insane during that time, and therefore was not culpable with regard to the charges of capital murder and violating Virginia's antiterrorism law for 13 random shootings, involving 14 victims and 10 deaths. Meanwhile, in another Virginia county, Malvo's alleged father-figure and mastermind accomplice, John Allen Muhammad (who did not invoke the insanity defense), had already been convicted on the same charges, and that jury would return two death sentences for him within days. But it is Malvo's case that particularly interests us in this chapter on insanity, for Malvo not only claimed insanity but also asserted an extreme form of that extreme defense: he claimed that he was brainwashed by Muhammad.

INSANITY *IN EXTREMIS*: EXTERNAL CONTROL (BRAINWASHING) NEGATING CULPABILITY?

Controversies have attached to brainwashing ever since newspaper journalist Edward Hunter (1951) used that metaphorical and misleading term in his book's title, *Brain-Washing in Red China*, to describe "a system of befogging the brain so a person can be seduced into acceptance of what otherwise would be abhorrent to him" (Oldenburg, 2003, p. C2). In the 1950s, there was also the account of Cardinal Mindszenty, head of the Roman Catholic Church in Hungary, who had been "so manipulated and processed by his Russian captors that he . . . falsely confessed and falsely accused his colleagues" (M. T. Singer & Lalich, 1995, p. 55). As the scientific community began to study this phenomenon, the terms *thought reform* (Lifton, 1963) and *coercive persuasion* (Schein, Schneier, & Barker, 1961) began to supplant (though never entirely erased) *brainwashing*. Investigations spread to cults (M. T. Singer & Lalich, 1995) and the processes of control, though camps remained divided as to whether this was science or junk science.

It was a 1962 movie, *The Manchurian Candidate*, that dramatized for the viewing public the idea of an externally controlled assassin conditioned and triggered to act. Once he saw the conditioned stimulus cue (the queen of diamonds), which was followed by a command, he then performed the commanded act. Internally, following the conditioned stimulus cue, the movie character entered a dissociative state, devoid of all emotion, and in that state he single-mindedly carried out his mission, albeit unconsciously. This chilling fictional portrayal transmogrified into hot and horrific fact in 1969, when Charles Manson "manipulated a band of middle-class youths" into committing "multiple vicious murders" (M. T. Singer & Lalich, 1995, pp. 55–56). Life had gone beyond art, putting the Law on alert that a brainwashing defense would eventually come to the courtroom. And it did, when

> the Symbionese Liberation Army (SLA), a ragtag revolutionary group, kidnapped newspaper heiress Patricia Hearst and abused her psychologically and otherwise. The SLA used mind manipulations as well as gun-at-the-head methods to coerce Patty into compliance. They manipulated and controlled her behavior to the extent that she appeared with them in a bank robbery and feared returning to society, having been convinced by the SLA that the police and the FBI would shoot her. (M. T. Singer & Lalich, 1995, p. 56)

But clinical psychologist Margaret Thaler Singer, called as a court-appointed examiner of Patricia Hearst, never got her testimony before the jury, and the jury rejected that diminished capacity defense, based on brainwashing, put forth by Hearst's attorney, F. Lee Bailey. The court, and these jurors, apparently remained skeptical that capacity and culpability could be diminished or undermined to the point of blamelessness.

Decades have passed since the Hearst case, and times have changed. More to the point, receptivity to the brainwashing insanity defense may have changed as well, for certain phenomena, and a prototype that could accommodate them, may have been embedded in the public's consciousness. For example, "aerial photos of 912 brightly clad followers of Jim Jones, dead by cyanide-laced drinks and gunshots in a steamy Guyanese jungle, were shown in magazines and on television, reappearing with each subsequent anniversary of the end of Jonestown" (M. T. Singer & Lalich, 1995, p. 3). In addition, there have been news accounts of, and research on, coerced-compliant and coerced-internalized false confessions (e.g., Kassin, Goldstein, & Savitsky, 2003; Kassin & Kiechel, 1996; Wrightsman & Kassin, 1993), in which those who did not do the crimes nonetheless confessed under certain interrogation procedures.

Such phenomena raise broad questions: Are these individuals truly themselves? Are their minds, emotions, and motives their own? Are their actions of their own volition and free will? The specific question we track is, did Muhammad turn Malvo into today's Manchurian Candidate, and would a jury in 2003 be receptive to his brainwashing defense?

WRESTLING THE PROTEUS, GRASPING ITS PARAMETERS, AND TRYING TO PIN DOWN ITS ESSENCE

Insanity anchors the extreme of one of our legal continua, for a successful insanity defense excuses the defendant as not blameworthy for the act. Insanity also represents the extreme on a psychological dimension, for any attempt at its explication requires that we plunge deeper into subjectivity than we have plumbed before: we must go beyond symptoms, and beyond those segmented parts of thoughts, emotions, and motives, to the very core and meaning of the self. Insanity, though, is a legal, not a psychological, concept, and although the insanity test has changed many times across some 280 years of Anglo-American insanity jurisprudence, these tests must rest on psychological facts and folk theories. The problem has been that many medicopsychological experts maintain that the Law's theories have not been grounded in the nature of human nature.

Insanity's essence has been difficult to pin down, for insanity manifests in so many forms that it has been likened to the shape-shifting Proteus (Sass, 1992), with many seeming to see only its mythical faces (Perlin, 1989–1990, 1990, 1994). Some adventuresome wrestler-types who have entered the ring to pin the Proteus have found themselves in a labyrinth, facing a beast with no way out; others have found themselves in Plato's cave, seeing only shadows; but most have ended up back at the surface, holding onto skin symptoms that the Proteus elusively shed like a snake, that were codified into law—until the Law revised or discarded those tests.

Our analysis and explication of insanity extends over two chapters, for the issues and perspectives that entwine—legal, psychological, philosophical, and commonsense justice (CSJ)—are complex, confusing, and confounding. In this chapter, we must do a considerable amount of ground-clearing to remove what obscures, to expose what is central. By chapter's end, we will arrive at *delusion*—not as a symptom, but as a more fundamental splitting of the self—for this is the psychological place, we believe, wherein the essence of insanity lies. But pinning the essence of this Proteus will come in the next chapter, where we will draw on the insights from psychology, philosophy, and CSJ regarding self-deception, disconnection, and the nature of the self.

We begin our analysis with two cases separated by 200 years, for which the background facts, the alleged crimes and mental disorders, and the proffered claims appear to be eons apart. If the insanity defense is situated at the extreme of culpability's continuum, then our first case, Malvo's case, sits at the extreme of this extreme, for this seldom raised and controversial brainwashing defense rests on the precarious claim that an agent external to the psyche—through psychological indoctrination and control—seduced, dissociated, and transformed the defendant's self to kill, while the defendant remains blameless. In modern light, by contrast, our second case, *Hadfield's Case* (1800; which we sketched in chap. 1, this volume, along with Erskine's three empirical arguments), appears to be a typical insanity case, for here we have a defendant who suffers from a delusion, and the seduction and transformation come from within the psyche. Moreover, whereas delusional defendants such as Mad Ned Arnold and Hadfield may have a variety of emotions (e.g., fear, anger, rage, excitement, ecstasy) depending on the nature of the delusion (e.g., a delusion of persecution vs. a delusion of grandeur), in Malvo's case it would be argued that the brainwashing and dissociation left him devoid of emotion, a mere automaton.

But modern light can create revisionist history, and we must understand the symptoms and story of James Hadfield as the Law and jurors did in 1800—through the context of the existing law and prevailing prototypes of insanity of that time. In light of the depth and variety of psychological theories that Erskine proffered then, and the likely reasons why the jury rendered a not guilty by reason of insanity (NGRI) verdict, this case was extreme in its time. In effect, both cases pushed against the prevailing law, and pushed past the dominant prototype of insanity in citizens' minds, to find a more accommodating prototype.

We shall organize our analysis around starter questions, for they bring the immediate issues, empirical and normative, quickly to the surface. In pursuing these questions, our ground-clearing goals are to expose and analyze those long-standing, problematic, and contentious issues that have surrounded and confounded this most maddening matter of madness, issues that continue to haunt the Law's insanity jurisprudence and confuse the Law's culpability theory. The starter question—Is the defendant's disorder produced from without (Malvo) or within (Hadfield)?—deals with a cluster of issues relating to the origin, source, cause, nature, reality, and legitimacy of this mental disorder, which arose at both trials. There are also contentions regarding insanity's breadth (Is insanity a total or partial condition?), the prototypes of insanity in citizens' minds, and the opinions in the experts' minds about mental disorders and in the Law's mind about the experts' opinion testimony. Then there is a contention and confound about whether there is a second type of culpability—for bringing about one's disability of mind (DOM)—that would widen the time frame and context and add a new layer to culpability. There is a contention about fakery, and whether this can be detected. And when we add the issues of mitigation and disposition to the mix, we begin to understand why pinning the Proteus will not be easy.

QUESTIONS THAT CHALLENGE THE LAW'S TEST AND THE JURORS' PROTOTYPES OF INSANITY

We begin with two compound questions: the first part of each reflects the question in the citizens' minds, and the second part reflects our question about the prototypes in jurors' minds. Could Muhammad, this external agent, really produce a dissociative state in Malvo that completely obliterated his moral sense and agency, leaving him blameless for the alleged criminal acts that resulted, and in the psychological world of the jurors, could such a possibility be accommodated within their existing prototypes? And second, could there be any validity to Hadfield's claim of partial insanity, which contradicted the existing law and prevailing prototype of the wild-beast test that demanded total insanity for exculpation, and did not Hadfield's lucid moments, when his planfulness was so evident, prove his claim false?

What Prototypes Are, What They May Do, and Their Root Sources

At the CSJ level, modern research has shown that citizens have prototypes (i.e., images and notions of crimes and criminals) in mind when they enter the courtroom, and these prototypes may powerfully affect their construal of the case and their verdicts (e.g., V. L. Smith, 1991; Stalans, 1993; Stalans & Diamond, 1990). Moreover, these researchers and others (e.g., Finkel & Groscup, 1997a; J. V. Roberts & Doob, 1990; Skeem & Golding, 2001; Tversky & Kahneman, 1974) have found that citizens' prototypes are often extreme, extraordinary, and saturated by available heuristics, be they from recent high-profile cases that appear in the media (e.g., Hans, 1990), or from Hollywood movies and popular fiction. As a result, prototypes are often off-base from the law's definitions of the crime. And in research most pertinent to this chapter, Finkel and Groscup (1997a) have shown that these extreme, extraordinary, saturated, and off-base findings are common for prototypes of insanity.

Media, movies, and pulp fiction are not the only root sources of proto-types. The Law is a source as well. When Erskine and his client Hadfield confronted the Law and the jurors in 1800, they were facing the wild-beast prototype, which had long ago entered the Law and the public's conscious-ness. Mr. Justice Tracy's articulation (see chap. 1, this volume) of this *total insanity* standard (*Rex v. Arnold*, 1723) was merely a recapitulation of Lord Coke's notion of more than a century previous that there must be a total deprivation of memory and understanding, and Coke's notion recapitulated *furiousus* (e.g., raging, frantic, full of fury), a notion dating back to the an-cient Greeks. The challenge, for Erskine, was to get the jurors to accept *par-tial insanity* as a legitimate instantiation of insanity, whereas Malvo's attor-neys had a more uphill climb, needing to convince the jurors that an external agent could cause insanity.

Still other sources of prototypes are myths and archetypes, which may devolve into law, and the following example might have provided assistance to both Hadfield and Malvo. In *The Iliad*, Homer (1950) portrayed a world where the gods frequently intervene. In *Wild Beasts & Idle Humours: The Insanity Defense From Antiquity to the Present*, D. N. Robinson (1996) picked up the Achilles versus Agamemnon conflict in Book XIX, in which the two antagonists seek to reconcile; however, though Achilles owns his anger, Agamemnon disowns his actions and offers "one of the earliest recorded in-sanity defenses":

> It was not I that did it: Zeus and Fate, and Erinys that walks in darkness struck me mad when we were assembled on the day that I took from Achilles the prize that had been awarded to him. What could I do? All things are in the hand of heaven, and Folly, eldest of Zeus' daughters, shuts men's eyes to their destruction. She walks delicately, not on the solid earth, but over the heads of men to hurt them or to ensnare them. (D. N. Robinson, 1996, p. 8)

Here is a world where everyone, from the weakest to the mightiest, is subject to external control by the whims of the gods, who are powerful, un-predictable, and sometimes crazy. In this world, maybe we humans are as the gods are: If they can be wild beasts for a short time—totally mad and out of control in a moment, a saturnalian night, or even a fortnight—then why not we? A jury of Homeric Greeks might accept Agamemnon's insanity claim and let him off the hook. But what sort of claim is Agamemnon making? In descriptive terms, he is making a partial-insanity claim—that he was totally mad for a brief time. If a 19th-century jury had that prototype in mind, then Erskine's argument for the legitimacy of Hadfield's partial insanity might have fallen on receptive ears. But Agamemnon's claim is also a causal one, involving an external agent: he was not to blame because the gods were, and thus resistance was futile. If external gods can cause insanity, why not a pow-erful father figure indoctrinating a susceptible teenager starved for a father's love? With this prototype in mind, then 21st-century citizens may be receptive to Malvo's claim.

But let us not forget Achilles, for he made several transformations in consciousness in *The Iliad*. As discussed in our previous chapter on manslaughter, Achilles's earlier claim that he was uncontrollably provoked to wrath by Agamemnon turns out to be false, for his own reflections on his choices reveal otherwise (e.g., Finkel, 1995a). But he goes further in his transformation, for he now avows this other side of his self which once he disavowed, as he owns his anger. Here a more complex self emerges from this man-of-action with quick-rising wrath, a man who was not prone to self-reflection or "overhearing" himself, as Hamlet was (Bloom, 2002; Shakespeare, 1938), yet who finally recognizes his self-deceiving delusion. Thus, when it comes to the handling of emotions, there is variability even among Homeric men, as there is among the gods.

Prototypes: What Initially Comes to Our Mind, About Their Minds

Finkel and Groscup's (1997a) findings reveal that citizens have a variety of prototypes for insanity cases, and three of note were (a) the wild beast (i.e., the image of the insane person as totally out of it), (b) delusions (i.e., a partial on-again, off-again insanity), and (c) uncontrollable emotions/motives producing violent acts. These prototypes fit nicely with Erskine's arguments. We know that the wild-beast prototype, still prevalent in the minds of 21st-century jurors (Skeem & Golding, 2001), was in the minds of the 19th-century *Hadfield* jurors, but we believe that the second prototype of "delusions" was present as well. And we know that Erskine ridiculed the first prototype (see chap. 1, this volume) as a fiction that fit no one in the real world, for no one is totally deprived of memory and understanding.

Hyperbole aside, if totally-out-of-it people—who couldn't tell a gun from a guava melon—existed, they were few, and likely to be rocking in their own private worlds. But if, by some chance, one of these totally insane individuals did make contact with this world, this individual was not likely to have the psychological wherewithal to track the king to Drury Lane Theatre and buy an orchestra ticket with clear sight of the king's box as Hadfield did; rather, such a "wild beast" would more likely eat the ticket, or eat the gun. No, if this murderer were insane, he had to be capable of enough planfulness to execute his delusion. Partially insane individuals did exist, and the medical men of 1800 certainly knew of them. Most citizens probably knew of them as well, with King George III a prime example. If partial insanity was a fact of science, and a fact within the common experience, then the Law's prototype was out of touch with reality.

Finally, another prototype that emerged from Finkel and Groscup's findings bears mention. The researchers asked groups of participants to write their narratives under different conditions: some were told to write cases that ended successfully (an NGRI verdict) or unsuccessfully (a guilty verdict) for the defendant. Most of the scenarios that ended successfully did so because participants constructed these as "true cases" of insanity, which the juries saw that way. But some participants wrote successful cases that were not true cases, in which the experts and juries were fooled because defendants were faking insanity, and thus wrongful NGRI verdicts resulted; here, the prototype of the "faker" emerges: a criminal and an imposter, who puts on an antic disposition to escape culpability entirely. We merely note this prototype now to foreshadow an issue yet to come.

Jurors, and Their Prototypes and Commonsense Justice, on Trial

From the usual vantage point, "the story" of an insanity trial typically focuses on a defendant and the Law. However, if we view an insanity trial from the perspective of the jurors who ultimately decide the culpability of the defendant, then an insanity trial is also a trial for—and of—the jurors. Most jurors come to trial without extensive knowledge of people with severe mental disorders, and so, at the outset, they sit in the jury box with little more than their prototypes to help them make sense of the unfolding story. Their prototypes are likely to be battered about by the bizarre facts of the case, the bewildering expert testimony, the competing stories of the prosecution and defense, and the judge's instructions as to the legal test of insanity. For example, after the testimony and the closing arguments by counsels, the judge will ask jurors to set aside their prototypical notions of insanity for the legal one. For another example, during the trial, psychological experts from both sides may throw multiple diagnostic labels at, and over, the jurors' heads, offering penultimate conclusions that amount to the ultimate conclusion about this defendant's culpability (e.g., Fulero & Finkel, 1991). And for still another example, the opposing attorneys, through their opening and closing arguments, will ask the jurors to see the defendant's acts and his unseeable *mens rea* in contradictory ways. In spite of these pressures on the jurors' prototypes and "personal conceptions of insanity" (Skeem & Golding, 2001, p. 561), will jurors do as the judge directs, or will they yield their ultimate decision to the experts, or will they swallow one or the other counsel's story, or will they use their CSJ to fashion a verdict that best fits their own culpability analysis of the case? The answer to this question may be *the story* of the story of insanity.

COMMONSENSE JUSTICE'S OPENING OF THE CONTEXT VERSUS BLACK-LETTER LAW'S NARROWING ON "THE MOMENT OF THE ACT"

In both *Hadfield* and *Malvo*, a considerable amount of testimony concerned the past history and prior actions of these defendants, particularly as they related to the origins (etiology and development) of their alleged mental disorders. For instance, an officer from Hadfield's former regiment testified that Hadfield had been an excellent soldier before he was wounded, but afterward he had been incoherent, with "manifest symptoms of derangement," and the regimental surgeon recalled "how he had been compelled to have Hadfield tied to a bed for a fortnight" (N. Walker, 1968, p. 76). In the Malvo case, there was much more of this sort of testimony regarding Malvo's past. But why all this testimony focused on origins, when the Law focuses on the defendant's *actus reus* and *mens rea* at the moment of the act?

The Illusion of the Legal Burden Versus the Reality of de Facto Law, as Two Stories Compete

Until recently, the prosecution has had the burden of proving that the defendant committed the *actus reus* and had the requisite *mens rea* at the moment of the act (Finkel, 1989). The prosecution's story, then, could ignore the past because the origin issue was moot in light of what it had to prove. The answer to the "why" of this testimony begins to emerge in the following quote (N. Walker, 1968) regarding a defense expert witness in *Hadfield*:

> Erskine then called Dr. Creighton from Bethlem to the stand who testified that in his medical opinion Hadfield's madness was probably the result of his wounds, and although in law it did not matter what the cause was . . . we can guess that this must have made a favourable impression on a war-time jury. (p. 76)

Though it did not matter under *de jure* law, the fact that the defense introduces origin testimony suggests that under *de facto* law (e.g., Finkel, 1990b) it may be necessary for jurors to hear about a disorder's origins. But again, why?

Our answer, from either a commonsense or dramatic perspective, is that to know only that an individual is troubled or "distempered" is not ultimately satisfying. It does not satisfy Macbeth (Shakespeare, 1938), so he sends the Doctor to find out why Lady Macbeth is troubled, and from the Doctor he learns that she is troubled from "thick-coming fancies that keep her from her rest" (V, iii, 37). It doesn't satisfy King Claudius either, who sends Rosencrantz to ask Hamlet, "What is your cause of distemper?" (III, ii, 354), though Hamlet will not give up his mystery. People want to know the reasons why—the story behind the disorder.

We believe that the legal issue—of which side (prosecution or defense), according to *de jure* law, bears the burden of proof in an insanity case—is a fictive one, particularly from the jurors' *de facto* law vantage point. When we consider what jurors are likely to need and want to make the insanity versus sanity determination, we see both sides have a burden—albeit a different one—because both are trying to convince the jurors of two different stories.

From the jurors' vantage point, the defense's burden has always been considerable, because most citizens presume defendants to be sane and responsible actors, hence culpable for their criminal actions, and thus jurors need clear and convincing evidence that this person is not a legal actor, but one who warrants excusing. It is the defense, then, that typically widens the context to bring in the origins story, not for legal reasons, but to make its claim most effectively with the jurors.

The defense, of course, needs to counter the prosecution's story by showing (a) that this defendant did indeed have a serious mental disorder operating at the moment of the act and (b) that this disorder negated either *actus reus* or *mens rea* at that moment. But we argue that the defense must also show (c) that the defendant did indeed have a legitimate mental disorder; this additional requisite, borne by the defense, makes for a different story than the prosecution's, for it leads into time past, where the origins and development of the disorder are to be found. If this additional requisite, c, was unnecessary, then Dr. Creighton's expert medical opinion that Hadfield's act, at the moment of the act, was a result of a delusion that negated *mens rea* should have sufficed. In a similar manner, the Malvo defense experts' testimony that Malvo had a dissociative disorder that negated *mens rea* at the time of the act should have sufficed as well. Yet most of the Malvo experts' testimony, much like Dr. Creighton's, focused on the past, when Malvo's indoctrination began and developed. What this origin evidence conveys to the jurors is illustrated in the next example.

The Legitimacy of the Disorder, Within a Context That Plausibly Explains Its Origins

If the first author, a clinical psychologist, had been summoned through a time machine by Erskine and sent back in time to the battlefield in France to perform a mental status examination on Hadfield soon after he came out of restraints (in 1794), and then went a little forward in time to testify at his trial (in 1800) about the disorder, what would that testimony be like? It might go like this:

> On the basis of my battlefield examination, even without detailed knowledge of the specific site, amount, and effects of the damage to Hadfield's brain, put in terms of the modern *Diagnostic and Statistical Manual of Mental Disorders* (DSM; 4th ed.; American Psychiatric Association, 1994), Hadfield was psychotic and suffered from delirium, caused by a general medical condition. The language of the older DSM (3rd ed., rev.; American Psychiatric Association, 1987) would have called this an "organic brain disorder," and no doubt there were organic brain syndrome impairments (e.g., affect, judgment, memory, intellectual functioning, and orientation) that cut across a broad spectrum of mental functioning, which were etiologically linked to the organic brain damage. Furthermore, the

acute effects of delirium and psychosis had obviously abated enough after 2 weeks that it was judged safe to take him out of restraints and prepare him to be sent back to England. Yet permanent brain damage, and
a chronic brain syndrome, would, in all likelihood, leave residual psychological impairments well beyond the acute stage. But which impairments would manifest 6 years later, and whether the impairments would
be mild, moderate, or severe, would be impossible to predict with any
degree of medical certainty. That would have to be assessed at that later
time.

So, what are the prime functions of this sort of testimony? Surely to
relay not specific etiological details to the jurors, but what such details
signify—that Hadfield had a legitimate mental disorder, rooted in an organic
brain disorder. Though Dr. Creighton's imprimatur and rooting connection
may not have been that crucial for the *Hadfield* jurors—because they could
see Hadfield's damaged brain for themselves—this imprimatur and connection would likely be critical in Malvo's case, in which there was great suspicion as to the legitimacy of his disorder, and whether it could in fact trigger
criminal acts.

This type of testimony also serves a second function critical for the
jurors: it puts the mental disorder into a storied context while providing a
plausible explanation for its being. For the *Hadfield* jurors, this type of testimony grounds the delusion in the physical brain, rather than leaving the
lingering suspicion that the "delusion" is one that Erskine is conjuring whole
cloth. In Malvo's case, by contrast, the defense experts root the dissociative
disorder not in the physical brain but in a psychological indoctrination: this
story leaves an insubstantial explanation and a wide opening for the prosecution to claim that this disorder was faked and that the defense's origin story
was pure fantasy.

ERSKINE'S THEORIES, CONTENTIOUS ISSUES BENEATH, AND
WHAT COMES BACK TO HAUNT

Establishing the legitimacy of Hadfield's chronic organic brain disorder
was not the problem; rather, establishing that this disorder was operating 6
years later at the moment-of-the-act was problematic, given the on-again–
off-again feature of Hadfield's partial insanity. Erskine tried, through testimony, to connect Hadfield's alleged criminal act to intervening delusional
acts as well as to the original delusional acts following the head wound, thereby
establishing a pattern and proclivity. Then, through his psychological argument, he defined *delusion* as the essence of insanity, and through his mechanistic–causal argument, he claimed that this delusion produced motives irresistible that caused the criminal act.

Some Conflicting Stories of Hadfield's Story

But no one knows precisely what happened to Hadfield during those intervening 6 years. We do not know what symptoms he manifested, or their severity, or whether they waxed, waned, or went on-again–off-again. There are contradictory accounts as to whether his delusional thoughts formed early or late, with what degree of specificity, and what role an external agent played in their development. In the accounts that follow, most pick up Hadfield's story within days of the shooting, and though similar in certain respects, they also have key differences.

In *Witnessing Insanity: Madness and Mad-Doctors in the English Court*, Eigen (1995) stated that Hadfield's delusion stemmed from millenarian beliefs that his death (at the hands of the state) was required to effect the Second Coming. He had apparently come under the sway of another True Believer, Bannister Truelock, who told him that he was a true descendant of God and that Hadfield "might be a very great man . . . by becoming [His] son" (p. 50). In *Psychology & Law: Can Justice Survive the Social Sciences?*, D. N. Robinson (1980) claimed that Hadfield was a "nondescript fellow of labile temperament and active imagination" who met Truelock in a field days before the crime, and that Truelock convinced Hadfield that the Savior's coming was but a "short time away," though Jesus not only would be outraged by the state to which the faithful had fallen but also would find England's sovereign to be an especially repugnant symbol of all that had gone wrong in the world (p. 41). Thus it was any good Christian's duty to rid the world of said monarch so that the Redeemer might find a more wholesome civilization upon his return. On the strength of this revelation, Hadfield headed off to Drury Lane where he fired on but failed to harm the king.

Although these two accounts differ about the specificity of the delusion, both point to the strong influence of Bannister Truelock, this external agent influencing, inculcating, or instilling a delusion into Hadfield's mind, which bears some similarity to the Malvo situation. But Eigen (1995) reported that Erskine called battlefield witnesses who testified that "immediately following" his head injury, which occurred 6 years prior to firing his pistol at King George III, "Hadfield had 'constant intercourse' with the Almighty, who told him that the world would end soon unless, like Christ, he would sacrifice his life for others" (p. 50). This evidence documents that the delusion was forming long before Truelock entered the picture, although the focus on King George III is not yet incorporated. However, consider N. Walker's (1968) report on the trial testimony of Hadfield's brother and sisters-in-law, "who described his periodic fits of terrifying madness, in one of which he had threatened to kill his own child because God had told him to" (p. 77). From these witness accounts, Hadfield looks little like the "nondescript" fellow that D. N. Robinson (1980) portrays, and N. Walker concluded that Erskine "had little difficulty in establishing his client's insanity" (1968,

p. 77). It may be that the external agent Truelock only nudged Hadfield in a direction that the inner delusion was already taking him.

This evidence of an intermittent pattern of delusion-inspired behaviors, particularly the testimony from close relatives, probably persuaded the jurors that the act resulted from the delusion. This is an inference, though, from past to present, and not a logical proof, and for Malvo, the inference is more tenuous. Still, for jurors to render an insanity judgment, they must come to understand the power of a delusion over the mind—when two minds (e.g., distraction and reason) occupy one and the same space—which is not an easy concept to grasp. Erskine had to help them grasp it.

Erskine's Psychological Argument for Delusion

Erskine explained a delusion for a jury in this way (N. Walker, 1968):

> Reason is not driven from her seat, but distraction sits down upon it along with her, holds her, trembling upon it, and frightens her from her propriety. 'The madman is deluded, he reasons from false premises,' because a delusive image, the unseparable companion of real insanity, is thrust upon the subjugated understanding, incapable of resistance because of unconscious attack. (p. 77)

The imagery is of a seduction: the siren not only calls from within but also distracts with powerful emotions and false premises, coming at her from below the belt by stealthy unconscious attack; this delusional complex embraces, envelops, and finally topples reason and her virtuous volitions.

Erskine's deep insight shows delusion not as a symptom but as a fundamental rent within the self. Standing alone, this argument is purely psychological, which we can see if we strip Erskine of two of his best assets, sequentially: first, let us close the hole in Hadfield's head, so Erskine has nothing to show the jury and nothing to rub in his closing argument, and second, let us remove the brain syndrome entirely, leaving only a psychological delusion. Now, can Erskine win his case with only his stand-alone psychological argument? We believe he can, but it is no sure bet, because the jurors will have to enter Hadfield's subjectivity and make the correct inferences.

Erskine's Mechanistic Argument for Motives Irresistible

Erskine was not willing to bet it all on just his psychological theory, so he went back to the physiological level where he etiologically grounded Hadfield's criminal actions on the organic brain damage and, in a causal sequelae, a theory intended to produce an irresistible QED: the organic brain damage caused the mental defect of reason (the delusion), the delusion caused motives irresistible, and the motives irresistible caused the criminal act (which could not be controlled). However, for his brain $\rightarrow$ mind $\rightarrow$ motive $\rightarrow$ behavior causal chain and conclusion to hold, the if–then linkages had to be steely. The problem was that the gaps were gaping. If that modern psychologist were summoned back through time to testify, this time by the prosecution, here is how he would attack the linkage assertions:

Regarding Erskine's first alleged connection, between brain and mind, we could no doubt find many soldiers on the battlefield with brain damage similar to Hadfield's—with damage to roughly the same site of the brain and with roughly the same amount of damage—yet most of these soldiers would not develop delusions, and of those that do, probably none, save Hadfield, develops the delusion of Christ's Second Coming. In regard to the second alleged connection, even if we found one or two with Hadfield's specific delusion, I doubt that we would find motives irresistible to kill the King to pave the way for Christ—save for Hadfield. There is great variability between brain damage and the mental symptoms and motives that may manifest, rather than direct one-to-one, cause-and-effect relationships. Regarding Erskine's third connection to the behavior, one can go into any psychiatric hospital with a sizable population of schizophrenia patients and find those with grandiose delusions, yet very few of them kill (or do harm). Thus, with the correlations between delusions and compulsion to kill and delusions and attempts to kill falling far short of 1.00, there is no credible scientific proof for delusions causing motives irresistible, which in turn necessarily cause criminal acts to follow.

INSANITY'S CULPABILITY CONFOUNDS

An insanity case—as it plays out in the courtroom, in jury deliberations, in media headlines, and in public opinion—is seldom just about the defendant's culpability at the moment of the act. Frequently coming into play are other issues that may confound a culpability judgment; these extra-legal issues, as they are called, are not the sanctioned ones that the judge instructs jurors to consider, though there is evidence that jurors sometimes give these factors weight (e.g., Finkel, 1988a, 1995b). As a theoretical and normative matter, there is the question of whether some of these potentially confounding factors ought to come into play. The issues that we examine next concern matters that arise after, before, or during the trial, but whatever the preposition, all may affect and confound the culpability determination.

How the "After Issue" of Disposition Becomes a Culpability Confound

The jury found Hadfield NGRI, but the prospect of Hadfield walking the streets was totally unsatisfactory, as Judge Kenyon feared for the safety of "every man of every station, from the king upon the throne to the beggar at the gate" (N. Walker, 1968, p. 78). This unsettled "dispositional issue" was addressed quickly, as

> Parliament hastily drafted the *Insane Offenders Bill* (1800) to take into strict custody those who were acquitted 'on grounds of insanity,' until 'His Majesty's pleasure to be known'; retrospective phrasing in the Bill's language made it applicable to Hadfield, who was eventually committed to Bethlem. (Finkel, 1988a, p. 16)

This was how the Law settled the issue.

But how does CSJ settle this forward-looking dispositional issue? Under black-letter law (BLL), this issue is not something jurors should consider in their backward-looking considerations of the defendant's blameworthiness at the time of the act. However, there is some evidence they do. The testimony of the *Hinckley* (*United States v. Hinckley*, 1981) foreperson before the Senate Subcommittee on Criminal Law of the Committee of the Judiciary (1983) provides a vivid example of where the disposition issue not only entered the jurors' culpability determination but also confounded it. As Ms. Copelin explained, "We knew that the gentleman was guilty of his act, but we also knew that there was a mental problem. But we could not do any better than what we did on account of your [verdict] forms." What she was referring to was the fact that the jury had only two options, guilty and NGRI; to the jurors, guilty meant prison and no treatment, but NGRI meant incarceration in a psychiatric hospital (where the community would be protected) but where Hinckley would get the needed treatment. So only the NGRI option satisfied both the jurors' treatment and incapacitation concerns, which confounds with culpability.

Confoundings Occurring During the Trial: Seeing Degrees and Types of Culpability

Before Malvo's trial began, skeptics had strong reservations about an external agent controlling another to the point of murder when that brainwasher did not have total physical control of the subject's environment—particularly when the two were physically separate, when the control could only have been psychological because the subject could walk away. Other skeptics realized that the alleged indoctrination had to take time to develop, because it wasn't some instantaneous spell that was cast—which meant that the subject had the time to make moral judgments and reject the indoctrination, and walk away.

However, perhaps some would be more receptive if the indoctrination claim was proffered for young children, whom we regard as particularly vulnerable and susceptible. If some potential jurors saw the 17-year-old Malvo fitting into this "vulnerable and susceptible" class, given his history and background, they might want to register a mitigating culpability judgment between the extremes of "fully culpable" and "completely blameless." This miti-gating betwixt-and-between judgment presents a dilemma because insanity is—and, for almost the entirety of its Anglo-American history, has been—a categorical yes or no decision, with no mitigating middle ground. These ju-rors have a problem, then, for neither of the two extreme choices adequately reflects their graded culpability judgment. If we imagine that these jurors pick NGRI as the best of two, armchair jurors watching court TV may con-clude that this verdict is wrongful, whereas we argue it is confounded.

A Second Type of Culpability

But let us consider other jurors who reach the opposite judgment re-garding so-called susceptible individuals—seeing them as culpable for bring-ing about "their disability of mind," as Fingarette and Hasse (1979) called it, which may not excuse them entirely. This type of culpability is different than the traditional moment-of-the-act culpability, and to tease the two types apart and understand clearly what this DOM is, let us focus on that time interval when Malvo's alleged indoctrination process begins yet before the reign of terror starts.

During this indoctrination time, Malvo told the expert witnesses for the defense that Muhammad's plan was to create a utopia in Canada and recruit child soldiers to kill, as a way of improving the lives of Black people, and to eventually demand $10 million in exchange for an end to the shootings. But Malvo admitted to these experts that he had doubts about the sniper plan, that he believed that killing was wrong, and that he "tried to shoot himself" (Jackman, 2003a). In preparing for this mission, Muhammad had Malvo perform a "test killing" of 21-year-old Keenya Cook in Tacoma, Wash-ington, on February 16, 2002, and Malvo reportedly was in conflict about this beforehand, and "was a mess afterward," one expert testified (Jackman, 2003c). These facts, from Malvo's lips to the experts' ears, contradict the automatism portrayal and contradict a fully indoctrinated portrayal, for they show Malvo with conflicted emotions, including guilt, from which we can infer he had some sense of right and wrong when he was making fateful deci-sions at that earlier time.

Now if this DOM issue had been legally connected to the insanity and culpability determination, then the prosecution would have widened the context to bring in this evidence, claiming that (a) the defendant's sense of right and wrong was not impaired, (b) that his mind and moral sense were not washed away, and (c) that his emotions and volitions were still very much under his own control. The prosecution would then have argued that Malvo made conscious choices and fateful decisions to join with Muhammad, despite what those choices may have been doing to him mentally and emo-tionally. In other words, he chose, negligently or recklessly, to disregard the deterioration of his own mental health (i.e., his DOM) and the harmful effects this might have on others; thus he bears culpability for what follows. This situation is similar to that of individuals who, when functioning well, make fateful decisions to stop their psychotherapy or stop taking their medications, which lead to their deterioration (DOM) and then to criminal acts, or, to paraphrase the words of law professor Paul Robinson (1985, p. 1), cause the conditions of one's own defense. But under historic and existing insanity law, jurors are not asked to make this type of culpability judgment, yet empirical evidence shows that they do make this CSJ judgment (e.g., Finkel, 1988a, 1991; Finkel & Handel, 1989; Finkel & Slobogin, 1995). Now we reach the dilemma (and confound) for jurors who have no separate place to register their assessment of this second type of culpability independent of the first (and only) type of culpability judgment, as the verdict form asks for only one culpability judgment.

A Confound Before the Trial Begins: The "Faking" Overlay

Sometimes, even before an insanity trial begins, looming large is an overlying question about whether the defendant is faking, simulating insanity to escape conviction and punishment. Here, the prototype of the faker emerges. As context for this discussion, we first need to recognize that faking occurs in many situations, most having nothing to do with insanity, for very few people fake that they are mad. Moreover, except in unexpected circumstances (e.g., Rosenhan, 1973), most who attempt to fake madness generally overdo it or just do it badly, typically mixing symptoms from different disorders not usually seen together; even when more knowledgeable fakers stay with just schizophrenic symptoms, they typically manifest the dramatic positive symptoms (i.e., Type I schizophrenia, which includes delusions, hallucinations, and prominent thought disorder) and ignore the negative symptoms (i.e., Type II schizophrenia, which includes impoverishment of everyday functions, flat affect, minimal speech, loss of volition). With this picture of most fake attempts, diagnosticians can usually (but not always) discriminate the true patient from the actor delivering an over-the-top or poorly researched performance.

In a criminal law scenario not involving insanity, when a guilty person tries to fake being an innocent person, we have two prototypes in question. In chapter 1 (this volume), we drew an example of this from Shakespeare's *Othello* (1938), in which Iago simulates so well, hiding his evil beneath the appearance of "innocent person," that no one within the play suspects that he is the guilty perpetrator-by-means, until the tragedies befall. And if there were a truly gifted psychological assessor, who, by seer, sign, or lie detection device, could perfectly detect the criminal faker, well, there would be no need for the jury to pass judgment on that poseur, for the assessor would have not only exposed the fraud but also answered, in effect, the ultimate question of his guilt: the assessment of faking would amount to a judgment of guilt.

But when insanity enters the picture, the assessment task is not identical with the culpability task. Moreover, when a defendant manifests a partial insanity such as delusion, and the defendant comes to believe that what he or she says is the truth (though it be false), we find that there is a realm between telling the truth and lying, which adds a significant complication. And further, when a delusional defendant manifests both bizarreness and planfulness, the latter may be mistakenly taken as indicative of fakery, an erroneous assessment that can undercut a legitimate insanity claim. As both a consequential and an assessment matter, the faking problem is important, for a wrongful verdict will result if the verdict tracks either of the two possible false assessments: a false negative (i.e., predicting that the defendant is not a guilty criminal when, in truth, the defendant is) or a false positive (i.e., predicting the defendant is a guilty criminal, when in truth the defendant is not). Psychological experts have been trying for almost a century to come up with lie detection measures to differentiate the real from the fake, and the trail has followed the emotions.

The "Holy Grail" quest is to find a way to accurately discriminate the true emotions that lie beneath the surface from those emotions within the lie. The early history of polygraphs started with a physiological measure as a proxy for emotion, as William Moulton Marston noted that systolic blood pressure increased when subjects told untruths. However, knowing that subjects were telling untruths was just what the assessor was trying to find out (e.g., Wrightsman, Greene, Nietzel, & Fortune, 2002). Pulse rate, respiratory changes, and galvanic skin responses were added on the assumption that these measures were good proxies for emotions, and that those emotions and lying were very highly correlated. Empirically, however, those correlations turned out to be considerably less than perfect, and those emotions could result from innocent reasons (Saxe, 1991). More problematic was the fact that the best review of the scientific validity of 250 empirical studies of polygraph testing found only 10 studies that met adequate scientific standards (Saxe, Dougherty, & Cross, 1985), which is one of the main reasons why courts (with but the rarest exceptions) have not accepted this evidence.

Other lie detection assessors have tried to use the subject's voice as a telltale, and the psychological stress evaluator (PSE) claims to measure variations in emotional stress that come through in words and phrases when a person is lying (Lykken, 1985), though validity for the PSE has been lacking. When voice and physiological telltales fail, others have tried to read body language, nonverbal cues, facial signs, the eyes, and the gaze (Ekman, 1985; Ekman & O'Sullivan, 1991), but here, too, the search for a "lie response," conceived of as some clear manifestation of various negative emotions, has been unsuccessful, as well as conceptually and psychologically muddled: the emotions of fear, guilt, and anger, for example, may appear to an observer as similar, though they may feel quite different and convey different psychological meanings to those experiencing them, and the presence of any of them may not indicate lying.

Something Between a Lie and the Truth—A False-Belief–Delusion

Within this black-and-white world of truth and lie is an in-between realm, which adds graying complications and confounding possibilities to insanity. First, let us look at this phenomenon for which insanity is not in question. In the courtroom, and in laboratory and field studies, some children will recount memories of an event that contain falsehoods, yet they firmly believe they are telling the truth; this situation involves more than merely making mistakes.

Ceci and Bruck (1995) investigated how this phenomenon might come about through a number of clever experiments with younger and older preschool children, in which all the children saw the same man ("Sam Stone") during a 2-minute visit to their nursery school classroom, and nothing unusual happened. Then all of the children were interviewed multiple times over the next 2 months about that visit: some children were in the "free recall" group, others were exposed to an initial stereotype about Sam suggesting that he was clumsy, but were interviewed in the free-recall manner; others were not exposed to the stereotype, but were interviewed in a highly suggestive manner; and the last group got the stereotype and the highly suggestive interviewing. During the final interview for all the groups, the researchers asked the children if Sam Stone had ripped a book, and if he spilled anything on a teddy bear. The results for the last group were the most dramatic. At first, 72% of the younger children believed Sam did things to the book and teddy bear, though when asked if they saw Sam do these things, only 44% answered in the affirmative; finally, "after being challenged, 20% of the younger preschoolers and 11% of the older ones maintained that they actually saw Sam do these things" (Ceci, 2003, p. 861).

But the relevant point for us is in regard to the assessors' abilities to discriminate the "true" from the "not true but believed to be true" is made by Ceci:

> To assess whether the children's claims were convincing to experts, we showed videotapes of children's final interviews to over 2,200 researchers, judges, law enforcement officers, psychiatrists, and psychologists and asked them to judge which of the events actually transpired and to rate each child's credibility. Most of the professionals were inaccurate. Despite their confidence in their judgments, experts could not reliably determine the accuracy of a child's testimony. This shows how difficult it is to separate fact from fiction, even for trained professionals, when the children have been repeatedly interviewed in a suggestive manner, especially when these interviews were accompanied by congruent stereotypes. (p. 861)

With these findings in the background, consider the back-and-forth-and-back-again arguments of the prosecution and defense in the Malvo case over the issue of faking. The prosecution claimed that beneath the defense's story of a 17-year-old who was indoctrinated and brainwashed into a dissociative disorder lay a criminal mind who fashioned this lie, who knew right from wrong all along, and who chose to kill. The defense, however, pointed to a still deeper self beneath the surface, a self flawed in a different and more profound way, by being psychologically fragmented and disconnected, and thus not legally to blame. To the defense, the prosecution's casting of this as merely a criminal mind faking insanity was superficial, for it missed the disconnected selves that lie deeper beneath. But the prosecution countered with letters Malvo wrote to a fellow inmate about attempting to manipulate the system, in which he stated (Jackman, 2003b): "I play the stupid fool" and "Look at how I act and speak, everybody underestimates me. . . . It gives me the edge I need to study, conquer and overcome." Malvo's writings and advice to an inmate were "almost like a course in dissociation," said one prosecution expert witness, who saw Malvo as a rational criminal who knew right from wrong (pp. B1, B4).

The verdict came as no surprise to most who followed this case closely, those who knew the success rate for the insanity defense in general or for brainwashing in particular, or those who knew the facts about Virginia juries and how their verdicts generally tended to go. And when the verdict came in, the community's response accorded and applauded, by press accounts. But the verdict does not close our story entirely, for on December 23, just before Christmas, the jury returned a surprising verdict in the death penalty decision, sparing Malvo from death, a decision that, from initial press reports, seemed quite at odds with community sentiment as the press reported it. This death penalty decision was shocking, given that Virginia juries were not terribly squeamish about delivering death sentences in the past, even for 17-year-olds, and most Virginians, according to polling reports, thought that if ever there was a "death-worthy" 17-year-old, it was Malvo.

A DISSOCIATIVE DISORDER?

We must examine one more issue: Malvo's diagnosed dissociative disorder, which all the defense experts were in agreement about. We argue that the proffered diagnosis was in error, for when we compare Malvo's symptoms with typical dissociative disorders, Malvo does not fit. If he was not a fake but did have a legitimate mental disorder, we argue that the best-fit category lands Malvo in "delusions," which moves this brainwashing extreme case closer to the Hadfield case, and to what Erskine had to say about delusions.

Malvo's actions (and mind) look nothing like that portrayed in *The Manchurian Candidate*. In one scene from that film, when this conditioned, programmed assassin is playing solitaire and turns over the queen of diamonds (the cue), he happens to hear in the background a bartender telling a customer a story in which the bartender says, "Go jump in the lake in Central Park," which was taken as a command, whereupon the titled character suddenly (unconsciously, somnambulistically, as if sleepwalking) leaves the bar and travels (in this fugue state) to the lake and jumps in. He is, however, amnesiac during the entire episode, his consciousness returning only when he is wet in the water, but he has no memory of how or why he got there. Though this scene is from a Hollywood film, it captures the amnesia, fugue, somnambulism, and automatism that have been characteristic and diagnostic of dissociative disorders historically. Malvo, by contrast, neither shows nor claims these characteristics—nor could he—for his actions (e.g., shooting, spotting, or planning, executing, and eluding police roadblocks) require so much awareness, vigilance, and conscious contact with reality that to claim that he was unconscious seems farfetched.

Moreover, Malvo's actions were nothing like the dissociative act of Esther Griggs, the defendant in an automatism case that went before a British grand jury in 1859 (N. Walker, 1968, p. 168), which found no "true bill against her," holding her not responsible. Esther Griggs threw her baby through a pane glass window to the street, and the baby died—but she did this while in a sleeping state, in a dream about the house being on fire, with the need to save the child. Apart from not having the requisite *mens rea*, Griggs's behaviors did not amount to an act in the legal sense (Austin, 1885), so she failed to meet the *actus reus* requisite, which is something Malvo's defense never claimed regarding his acts, nor could it be claimed, from the facts.

Nor does Malvo's condition look like the multiple personality disorder variety of dissociative disorder (e.g., *State v. Bianci*, 1979), for Malvo's experts were not claiming that another "personality" did it, only that Malvo's sense of right and wrong had been completely replaced by Muhammad's vision of right and wrong. So what does his condition look most like? With his lack of amnesia and his vigilance heightened at the time of the acts, it appears as if he had come to believe and embrace those new world order beliefs of Muhammad's as his own: that by random acts of killing, terrorizing, and extorting fantastic sums of money, they could bring this new world into being. Malvo, we submit, bought into the delusion.

A LOOK BACK, TO A SELF DISCONNECTING, AND A LOOK FORWARD, BEYOND PARTS

This chapter began with seemingly disparate defendants and claims: Malvo's, at insanity's extreme, and Hadfield's, at insanity's center. The former claimed that his culpability was negated by an external agent who brainwashed the moral agency right out of him, whereas the latter claimed that a partial insanity generated from within negated his culpability. Yet in pursuing the Proteus, these two cases converged, in the end, on "delusions."

In looking at these cases and defendants from the jurors' perspective, through their prototypes, story construction, and need for more context and explanation regarding the origin of the disorder, we saw that they wanted a wider story than the Law's moment-of-the-act tale. Yet, beyond their desire for greater breadth and depth, those who made the culpability decision held to a *de facto* law different from *de jure* law, for they had differing expectations about insanity's presumptions, burdens, requisites, focus, and origins, and they applied their complex views (CSJ) in ways that significantly departed from BLL at times (Finkel, 2000b). For example, jurors considered two types of culpability, the mitigating possibility, and the dispositional question within their complex culpability analysis (Finkel, 1988a).

With the two defendants' disorders converging on "delusion," wherein emotions may swing to extremes, our thoughts return to the psychological theory Erskine metaphorically sketched for the *Hadfield* jury. If the Proteus is to be found anywhere, it is likely within delusion's lair, according to Erskine. Had the Law grasped Erskine's insight about the disconnect within the self, rather than latching onto surface symptoms and segmented parts of the psyche, subsequent legal tests of insanity might have been grounded on a sounder theory of the self, and the law might have aligned with the findings of Psychology and CSJ.

Still, neither of Erskine's two theories of insanity was complete, for both theories lacked detailed explication and supporting empirical facts. For example, when Erskine rubbed Hadfield's exposed brain, implying that Hadfield's "capacity" had been shot, a key question remained unanswered: What is the nature of that incapacity that disconnects Hadfield's delusional nucleus from what the community endorses, from what the law enforces, and from what parents inculcate in their young children as they develop into moral agents and responsible citizens? In the next chapter, we explore that incapacity and how the disconnect comes to be, and that inquiry begins with a question that has long puzzled psychologists and philosophers: How is it that we can seduce and deceive ourselves?

9

INSANITY II: ITS DISCONNECT, "DEFECT OF REASON," AND INCAPACITY

At the end of chapter 8 (this volume), we claimed that Erskine's (*Hadfield's Case*, 1800) argument for delusions pointed to where the Proteus was likely to be found. In his formulation, one inhabitant of the psyche, an entity called *distraction*, uses false premises, frightening images, and an unconscious process to seduce and topple the other psychic inhabitant, *reason*. Through this process, a disconnect within the psyche results, and with the psyche now controlled by delusions, the person begins to disconnect from reality and the "shared background nexus" (which includes knowing the accepted law and morals regarding right and wrong). The latter disconnect (i.e., from legality, morality, and reality) is the essence of insanity, whereas the disconnect between distraction and reason is the cause and process of insanity.

But at the end of chapter 8 (this volume), we held that Erskine's theory was less than satisfactory, for it leaves us with two entangled problems—ones that Sigmund Freud later wrestled with unsuccessfully, and philosophers still wrestle with today: the problem of two selves inhabiting one and the same person, and the problem of self-deception. To make these problems clearer, we start with an unanswered question within the story that Erskine spun, which begins with two selves already existing within the psyche. Erskine offered no origins or process account of how this "distraction self" got there, only that it is there, as another self, with thoughts, passions, and motives in opposition to reason. In relation to reason, distraction turns out to be a seducer and cad: it deviously frightens reason, yet it appears instantly as her comforter, sitting down beside the now trembling reason as she shakes with fright; then, while she is in this vulnerable state, this siren sings its soft song, one that mixes gossamer images and false premises, as it subjugates her through its unconscious attack. We could well understand such villainy and treachery if it was perpetrated by an outside other, such as Iago or Richard III. But what is harder to understand is a deception that is a self-deception (i.e., between two parts of one psyche). Erskine failed to offer an explanation of why this deception works.

We now turn our attention to reason, that other psychic self within his theory. In Erskine's drama, reason is portrayed not as the wise Athena—but as a 13-year-old ingenue, slow on the uptake, with emotions that overwhelm. This easily frightened maiden remains oblivious to distraction's ploys, unconscious to its thinking, and blind to its scheming aimed at her upending. But how can this be, if she shares the same psychic space with this distraction character? More broadly, as reason, how can she be unaware that this other reasoning is going on? This is the problem of self-deception, which, like the problem of how and why the split that produced distraction occurred in the first place, remains unsolved.

WHY ERSKINE'S THEORY FAILS, YET SELF-DECEPTION STUBBORNLY STANDS

The philosopher Herbert Fingarette (1974) started his article, "Self-Deception and the Splitting of the Ego," with these two questions: "Who can doubt that we do deceive ourselves? Yet who can explain coherently and explicitly how we do so?" (p. 80). The problem with Erskine's account—like Freud's account of the ego repressing an id impulse while we remain unconscious of it—is that it is a process of self-deception that shouldn't deceive at all. In "Mauvaise Foi [bad faith] and the Unconscious," Sartre (1974) criticized Freud's account that cuts the psychic whole into two—"I *am* the ego but I *am not* the id," as Sartre put it, which created the possibility "of a lie without a liar" (p. 75). This possibility should not work, according to Sartre, because "I must know in my capacity as deceiver the truth which is hidden from me in my capacity as the one deceived . . . [and thus] the lie falls back and collapses beneath my look . . ." (pp. 72–73). These two philosophers would argue that Erskine's "distraction self" has to know the truth to fashion the delusional lie it tries to foist upon reason. If one self knows, then a claim that *mens rea* was negated is false, for the lie is ruined by the self that knows the truth.

But what should not stand, according to Sartre (1974), does stand, and the philosopher Fingarette recognized the conundrum when he asked, "Who can doubt that we do deceive ourselves?" We do not doubt it because we know that the phenomenon is real: we recognize it when we see it in others (e.g., our children, spouses, students, colleagues), though we may be slow to recognize it in ourselves, because the process of acknowledging it may involve embarrassment, pain, and shame. Moreover, therapists know that self-deceptions and delusions are stubborn, for they do not collapse easily, contrary to what Sartre predicts. For example, it certainly took Achilles quite some time to own his anger and to see his sulking for what it was, whereas Agamemnon never owned to his self-deception, claiming to the very end that the gods had brainwashed him.

Modern therapists would no doubt regard Agamemnon as a poor candidate for therapy, one who was not committed to integrating the self. If we are going to unravel self-deception, we would do better by starting with a young man who is a good candidate for psychotherapy—one who is deeply committed to integrating the self and does not allow himself the luxury of self-deception. Yet this young man has a weighty problem: he has received a "command hallucination" to kill.

The young man grieves over the recent loss of his father, sees himself as homeless and the world as pointless, thinks of suicide, and acts bizarrely. Our young man "will talk to everyone but listens to no one, except perhaps the Ghost" (Bloom, 2002, p. 27), and when there is no one to talk to, he talks to himself, which he doesn't mind, because he finds himself the most interesting subject anyway. In the present, he is focused on listening to his self, though he (and we) are not always sure which self he is hearing. Being a reflective type is an asset, given his aim, but it can also be a liability, for this sort of person could easily slip anchor from the external world and slide into the deepest waters of his subjective world, from which he might be shipped out to a psychiatric world with a diagnosis of schizophrenia—because he already manifests the symptoms of overinclusive thinking, hyper-reflexivity, alienation, solipsism, detachment, irony, self-referentiality, derealization, impersonal subjectivism, self-estrangement, fragmentation, and unreality (Sass, 1992).

However, two factors anchor him to the external reality and save him from falling into Bedlam's netherworld. First, his consuming desire to piece together his differing selves requires that he check his interpretations for consistency with his actions in this world. And second, the command hallucination to avenge his father's murder will force him to make contact with the external reality somewhere in the future. Unfortunately, these same factors (e.g., Bowers, 1940; Hallett & Hallett, 1980) may push him deeper into madness.

HAMLET'S CASE: SELVES UNDER "SORE DISTRACTIONS," WITHIN "A DISTRACTED GLOBE"

This Hamlet (Shakespeare, 1938) truly is a piece of work, and we have many reasons for bringing him into our work. Our reasons relate to problems in Erskine's argument about the powers and limitations of distraction and reason, reason not knowing, and this self-deception process. Our reasons also relate to Malvo (*Commonwealth of Virginia v. Lee Boyd Malvo*, 2003) and his alleged faking, for Hamlet feigns madness while having an underlying type of madness known as distraction. Our reasons also relate to the fact that this is a play in which all the major characters try to unlock the mysteries in Hamlet's mind, which raises the question of how far any person can see into another person's mind, which is a central question at an insanity trial, and which has led some legal thinkers (e.g., Gerber, 1984; Morris, 1982; Wootton, 1959) to propose abolishing the insanity defense precisely because people cannot know another's thoughts. And, finally, they relate to Shakespeare's "method" of "overhearing," by which Hamlet keeps discovering selves every time he speaks.

In Harold Bloom's *Genius: A Mosaic of One Hundred Exemplary Creative Minds*, Bloom (2002) gave "the first position" to Shakespeare, in part because he has given us one of the greatest of all literary characters, for

> Hamlet's study of himself is an absolute, and diminishes what is outside the self as a sea of troubles. Incessantly pondering his own words, as if they were and were not his own, Hamlet becomes the theologian of his own consciousness, which is so wide that its circumference never can be discovered. (p. 29)

In this process of discovering these emerging selves, Hamlet "notoriously changes every time he hears himself speak" (p. 28), but this process involves more than hearing—for "self-over-hearing, in Shakespeare, is the royal road to change" (p. 27). Bloom distinguished *hearing* from *overhearing* this way:

> Dictionaries define "overhear" as hearing a speech or speaker without the speaker's awareness or intention. To overhear oneself is to be initially unaware that one is the speaker. That unawareness is so brief that self-overhearing seems more metaphoric than not, yet the moment of literal nonrecognition is authentic. (p. 28)

Shakespeare illustrated a modern psychotherapeutic method 300 years before Freud and almost 400 years before modern psychotherapists had "chairs of eminence and couches of opulence in the finest universities and neighborhoods in the Western World" (London, 1964, p. v); his psychological theory of selves that change with different positions, situations, and circumstances is quite modern as well (Harré, 1998; Harré & Gillett, 1994; Harré & van Langenhove, 1999; Sabat, 2001). We focus now on his theory, for our purpose is to contrast Shakespeare's account of distraction, the psyche, and self-deception in *Hamlet* with Erskine's account in Hadfield's case.

To make this comparison, first we must understand *distraction* in the context of what those knowledgeable Elizabethan theatergoers knew as they sat in the audience watching *Hamlet*, seeing and hearing far more than any jury would. That audience certainly knew the law of 1600 (when *Hamlet* was staged), which made a revenge killing a crime (murder), and they knew Christian teaching, which made revenge killing morally wrong, an act that theologians and poets claimed led the revenger to the deepest part of hell. But this audience also knew the older civil law code of blood feuds (see chap. 6, this volume) wherein revenging the killing of a kin was once justified, and therefore they would have understood that under that older code Hamlet had a legitimate claim to "pick up the spear." The legal realists in the audience might have realized that even under the new criminal law, Hamlet has no Law to appeal to (i.e., because Claudius did the killing and now wears the crown), and they would recognize that Hamlet, the Prince of Denmark, is the rightful (if not lawful) one to revenge the death and purge the corrupted state and Law. And yet, the most sophisticated of all might recognize that Shakespeare has set up, for Hamlet, a conflict between Law and morality.

There is still more context to consider. Frequent theatergoers would recognize that Shakespeare's *Hamlet* was following the patterns and motifs of traditional Elizabethan revenge tragedy (Bowers, 1940), with the ghost, a command, the delay, the play-within-a-play, and the death of the killer and the revenger. The particular motif we highlight is the revenger's madness (Hallett & Hallett, 1980, pp. 9–10), because one form of this madness is distraction:

> The revenge tragedy can be understood in terms of the revenger's efforts to free himself from the restraints that forbid the act of vengeance, a process that involves moving from sanity to madness. . . . The change must be gradual. And it must include a radical shift in the way the psyche views the world. . . . Since the objective world resists the changes the revenger would impose upon it, the world he alters is unfortunately the subjective world. The delay might be defined as the pause necessitated by the revenger's need to construct this world-within-a-world, that private, self-justifying world which will foster the act the external world would never sanction.

Thus theatergoers knew that revenge leads to madness, though its form could vary. The revenger's insanity may descend into barbaric cruelty, which happens to Hieronimo in Thomas Kyd's *The Spanish Tragedy* (1592/1966), whereas in Cyril Tourneur's *The Revenger's Tragedy* (1607/1966), the revenger loses his humanity and focus as the killings spread and he becomes vengeance itself, as indicated by his name, Vindice. But revenge could also lead to a form known as *distraction*—the very term Erskine used 2 centuries later in his argument—and the term Shakespeare used again and again to describe Hamlet (e.g., he is infected "with sore distraction"

[V, ii, 229], "in this distracted globe" [I, v, 97]). According to Hallett and Hallett (1980), what sets Hamlet apart from other revenge protagonists, however, is that he does not descend into total madness or legal insanity because he does not allow himself "the luxury of self-deception" (pp. 122–123). But in stark contrast with Shakespeare's story, in Erskine's metaphorical story and in his real-life client, there is no evidence that Hadfield used his reason to question his delusion.

Hamlet (IV, iv) confronts himself with questions that were no doubt in the audience's mind: What, within him, dulls his revenge? Have all the different selves, with their different voices and conflicting positions, come round to confuse him? This cannot be simply a case of an intellectual type intellectualizing himself into a temporary paralysis, for an individual with Hamlet's keen mind should have been able to resolve this sort of conflict; thus, he may be deceiving himself despite his efforts to know.

Is he maddened, then, by revenge's excessive passions, that have infected him with "sore distraction," which distorts his vision? We find evidence for this distortion when we examine all the collateral damage Hamlet inflicts. For instance, when he is summoned by his mother to her chamber because of the affront his play-within-a-play caused, he is not contrite or subdued; rather, his emotions are wild: he accuses her and orders her to sit down, while she voices fear that he will murder her. When next he hears a noise, Hamlet stabs through a curtain and kills Polonius, mistakenly, but it was an act of recklessness nonetheless, pushed by his unchecked emotions. When Hamlet sees Polonius's dead body, he dismisses Polonius (and his own act) with the words, "Thou wretched, rash, intruding fool" (III, iv, 36)—words that might describe Hamlet at this moment.

And earlier, does his "sore distraction" not lead him (in the nunnery scene) to overgeneralize from his mother to all women, and to see evil in Ophelia, where there is none? His madness and self-deception are compounded by the antic disposition he puts on, for when his underlying feelings erupt, the distinction between role and reality blurs, as he desperately grasps "at the role to disguise emotions that are about to overwhelm him" (Hallett & Hallett, 1980, p. 192). He then suddenly turns from hot to cold and callously pushes Ophelia away, which is the push that sends her into madness, and then into suicide. Still, Hallett and Hallett (1980) claimed that Hamlet, unlike other revenge protagonists, never descends into legal insanity because he continually brings his madness under control "through the scrutiny of his reason" (p. 199). This claim may be accurate, over time, yet we would argue that "scrutiny by his reason" is clearly belated, for when he turns on Ophelia he has deceived himself, as his later remorse at her graveyard scene attests.

Finally, Hamlet deceives himself in distracted self-righteousness when he relays to Horatio his hand in the deaths of Rosencrantz and Guildenstern. He tells Horatio that he deliberately and knowingly created the Bellerophontic letter (i.e., a letter that says, "kill the bearer of this letter") that sends

Rosencrantz and Guildenstern to their deaths, yet he now asks Horatio to approve of his act as justified. Horatio does not give him the approving answer, but rather answers (and judges) Hamlet by changing the topic.

As Bloom (2002) stated, "Hamlet becomes the theologian of his own consciousness," but that subject matter is so vast it "never can be discovered" (p. 29). Hamlet may want to see his self clearly, but a maddening distraction results from having to execute a duty he can neither avow nor disavow, which may split the ego in the process of defense and create the possibility of self-deception despite his professed intentions.

AN EGO NUCLEAR COMPLEX, SPLIT OFF BY THE EGO IN THE PROCESS OF DEFENSE

Fingarette (1974) took the position that the self (i.e., the personal identity one claims) is "a synthesis, an achievement by the individual" (p. 83). But the self-deceiver refuses to avow certain engagements as his, and thus these actions are not synthesized into the personal identity he claims. "Having disavowed the engagement, the self-deceiver is then forced into protective, defensive tactics to account for the inconsistencies in his engagement in the world as acknowledged by him" (p. 81). If one continues to disavow certain engagements as part of the self, then "a nuclear, dynamic complex" is likely to be "split off from the more rational system (i.e., the system which is defended)," said Fingarette, with this nuclear entity being "a complex of motive, purpose, feeling, perception, and drive towards action" (p. 93). Regarding the split within the psyche, Fingarette thus gave an answer to the *how* question, but what remains is the question of *why* this happens.

In regard to the *why* question, Fingarette stated,

> It is because the incompatibility between the ego-nucleus and the current Ego are so great, relative to the integrative capacities of that Ego, that the latter gives up any attempt to integrate the ego-nucleus itself. The Ego . . . says, This is *not me*. The Ego treats this unassimilable but still ego-like system as "outside" rather than "inside." (p. 93)

If Fingarette is right about how and why the "counter-ego-nucleus" comes into being, then his account reverses Erskine's story, for it is the Ego (reason) that creates the counter-ego-nucleus (distraction) by giving up on any attempt to integrate it into the self. In other words, reason gives distraction its life, so to speak, by turning its back on it, disavowing it, and making it not-me. By isolating this counter-ego-nucleus "from the civilizing influence of the Ego," wrote Fingarette, this nucleus is less concerned with "strict logical, causal, temporal, and other rational relationships," and this isolation from the Ego makes this nucleus "much cruder," more "primitive," "closer" to "the id," with its "uncivilized, highly unspecific basic drives" (p. 96). It is no wonder, then, that this counter-ego-nucleus is delusive. And if avowing our engagements is a necessary condition of moral action, but the Ego does not avow engagements initiated by the delusive counter-ego-nucleus, then it is no wonder that unlawful and immoral actions may follow.

Social Constructionist Theory

Social constructionist theory (e.g., Harré, 1998; Harré & Gillett, 1994; Harré & van Langenhove, 1999; Sabat, 2001) adds nuance to this picture. That theory speaks of Self 1, Self 2, and Self 3, and to distinguish these, we turn to Sabat (2001):

> *Self 1* is the self of personal identity which is experienced as the continuity of one's own singular point of view from which one perceives, and acts in, the world. . . . In principle, one could be amnesic with regard to one's name and yet still demonstrate an intact Self 1 by saying such things as, "I wish I could recall my name." (p. 17)

Regarding Self 2, Sabat stated that "each of us has a unique set of mental and physical attributes [along with beliefs about those attributes] that render us different to some extent from any other person. Some of those attributes may be relatively stable or constant over time, others may change" (p. 17). Self 3 is the most plural and interpersonal of the three, for

> one and the same person can be a loving parent, a demanding professor, a helpful neighbor, a delightfully humorous friend, a devoted, romantic, loving spouse, to name but a few. . . . [But to maintain each persona] the cooperation of others in the social world is required. . . . [and thus] they can be especially vulnerable. (p. 18)

What sort of disavowed thoughts are likely to develop into a delusion within that counter-ego-nucleus? Some classic psychiatric writings by patients able to describe their delusional worlds provide the illustrations. Daniel Paul Schreber's *Memoirs of My Nervous Illness* (1903/1988) was "the most influential account of a psychotic disorder ever produced by a psychiatric patient," wrote Sass (1992, pp. 242–243), and Freud made it the subject of his case history on paranoia. Schreber, a presiding judge (*Senatspräsident*) in the Superior Court in Dresden, was hospitalized for his illness, which featured hallucinations and somatic delusions involving penetrating rays that were changing his nerves and handling his body in revolting ways. Schreber also manifested delusions of persecution (i.e., that God was tormenting him, in Freud's account), and later in the course of his illness, grandiose delusions (i.e., that in his transformation into a woman, he was to be the wife of God who bears God's offspring, in Freud's account).

We can imagine, for this judge, that being a hospitalized mental patient, having wild swings of emotions, hearing voices, and having delusions of rays entering one's body and transforming one's nerves into those of a woman was difficult to assimilate and reconcile with the abilities and capabilities of his former Self 2. Moreover, if others who knew him as *Senatspräsident* learned about his emotional state and his delusional ideation, it would be difficult for Schreber to maintain Self 3. And in the latter stages of his delusion, when he believed he was the bride of God destined to give birth to a new race of beings, it would be difficult to maintain his personal identity, Self 1. In *A Mind That Found Itself*, Clifford Beers (1935) penned an autobiography that included a biography of a delusional self who took over this Yale man:

> In telling the story of my life, I must relate the history of another self—a self which was dominant from my twenty-fourth to my twenty-sixth year. . . . An Army of Unreason, composed of the cunning and treacherous thoughts of an unfair foe, attacked my bewildered consciousness with cruel persistency, and would have destroyed me, had not a triumphant Reason finally interposed a superior strategy that saved me from my unnatural self. (p. 1)

Beers's metaphorical "Army of Unreason" is similar to Erskine's "distraction," though a notable difference is that Beers's "Reason" comes to his rescue, whereas Erskine's "reason" never rescues Hadfield.

As Beers's (1935) story unfolds, he begins having somatic sensations and the "mad belief" that he is suffering from epilepsy, like his older and physically healthier brother, and his fear and delusion become a conviction, the "half-resolve, made before my mind was actually impaired, namely, that I would kill myself rather than live the life I dreaded" (p. 14). His attempted suicide fails, and when he wakes up in Grace Hospital he has a new delusion. He believes not only that he will be prosecuted for the crime of attempted suicide but also that all the doctors and nurses are really detectives out to obtain evidence to convict him; what is more, he believes that his family members are not really his family members, but exact duplicates working with the police. While he is recovering in the hospital, thousands of Yale alumni, who had come to New Haven for a baseball game between Yale and Harvard, march with brass bands past Grace Hospital, and in Beers's *ideas of reference* delusion (i.e., attributing a personal meaning to an impersonal event) he is convinced that these Yale men loathe him for disgracing his alma mater, and he concludes that they intend to take him from his bed and tear him limb from limb. Again, with just these facts, we can predict which thoughts and emotions are likely disavowed to the counter-ego-nucleus and how they may rent Selves 3, 2, and 1.

Although these two cases illustrate how the psychic disconnect and delusions come to be, neither Beers nor Schreber commits an act that leads to a not guilty by reason of insanity (NGRI) verdict. Our next case does lead to an NGRI verdict. Simon Winchester (1998) told the story of *The Professor and the Madman: A Tale of Murder, Insanity, and the Making of the Oxford English Dictionary*. In 1897, Dr. James Murray of the London Philological

Society left the Scriptorium at Oxford and traveled 50 miles by train to the village of Crowthorne to finally meet the bashful American surgeon Dr. W. C. Minor (also a Yale man). Murray was the editor of the *Oxford English Dictionary*; Minor was the most prolific of the volunteer contributors, who regularly sent Murray his meticulous cards containing word origins, meanings, and examples of first usages yet declined all invitations to come to Oxford. When Murray finally met Minor and the two sat down for tea surrounded by Minor's extensive library of books, they were sitting in Minor's cell at the Broadmoor Criminal Lunatic Asylum, where Minor had been committed in 1872, having been found NGRI for killing George Merritt.

One of Minor's delusions developed from his service as a Union surgeon during the Civil War, when this sensitive young man had to brand the faces of Union deserters (who were predominantly Irish) with the letter *D*, for deserter. After the war, Minor used his family's wealth and left for England, where he lived in a rundown section of London frequented by prostitutes and developed a delusion of persecution—that the Irish were out to kill him. Early one morning when it was still dark, as the innocent George Merritt was going to work, Minor shot and killed him, believing that this man was an Irishman out to kill him.

Another of Minor's delusions began much earlier, when his Congregationalist missionary parents were in Ceylon with the 13-year-old Minor. He was sure that indelible memories of the "young, chocolate-skinned, ever-giggling naked girls with sleek wet bodies . . . had unknowingly set him on the spiral path to his eventually insatiable lust, to his incurable madness, and to his final perdition" (Winchester, 1998, p. 44). These images would nightly torment the man, who would line the floor of his asylum cell with metal sheets so these succubi could not attack him. But he was able to neither quell his emotions and dreams, nor stop his lifelong masturbating, until this bookish surgeon put an end to his demons by tying a string to the base of his penis and surgically cutting it off.

Minor's last delusional act clearly passes "the craziness test" for most people, and a jury earlier judged his delusional murder of George Merritt as insane. Nonetheless, Minor fits within Erskine's "partial insanity," for he functioned normally most of the time, and thus his delusions coexisted with his reasonable and normal self. But when he was in the delusional self, disconnected from reality and the shared background nexus, he neither saw reality clearly nor understood his thoughts, emotions, and acts for what they were, and therein he would take the life of Merritt and make "the unkindest cut" (Winchester, 1998, p. 189).

"INCAPACITY" AND A DEEPER "DEFECT OF REASON"

This disconnect within the psyche and between psyche and reality, we believe, was what Isaac Ray (1838/1983) had in mind when he said that in "madmen" their "abstract conceptions of crime" are not "perverted by the influence of disease," but the *particular* criminal act, however, becomes divorced in their minds from its relations to crime in the *abstract*" (pp. 33–34). There is a disconnect, then, between the morality and the legality of criminal acts.

Isaac Ray's *A Treatise on the Medical Jurisprudence of Insanity* (1838/1983) was highly influential on the justices who formulated the M'Naghten Rules (*M'Naghten's Case*, 1843) 5 years later, as the justices highlighted Ray's *defect of reason* phrase (N. Walker, 1968). This defect of reason is the disconnect and essence of insanity, Fingarette and Hasse (1979) argued, for it connotes the splitting of the ego, disavowing of the counter-ego-nucleus, and developing of a delusion unchecked, which leaves the individual with a "lack of capacity for rational conduct in regard to the criminal significance of the conduct," such that the person is not "response-able" (p. 218). This "is central to what we wish to express when we speak of someone as 'out of his mind,' 'out of touch with reality,' 'mentally incompetent,' 'crazy,' or 'mad'" (Fingarette & Hasse, 1979, p. 218). When we understand nonculpability this way, the person who is insane is not someone whose *mens rea* is simply negated, for if that were the case, a delusional individual such as Hadfield would be found guilty, because he knew that what he was doing was legally wrong; rather, the defect of reason points to a defect in the *mens*, revealing a more fundamental incapacity (Fingarette, 1972).

A Commonsense Justice Perspective

The various voices we have been hearing, citing, and following so far—philosophic, psychological, and medical–jurisprudential—all point to a fundamental incapacity. However, we have yet to hear the voice and perspective of commonsense justice (CSJ). When a Senate subcommittee (Subcommittee on Criminal Law, 1983) did hear the voices and complaints of some *Hinckley* (*United States v. Hinckley*, 1981; Hans & Slater, 1983) jurors—about the constraints of having but two choices in traditional insanity tests—Congress did not redress their concerns. Rather, Congress's "reform" turned out to be a retreat, a reissue of old wine in a new bottle, for once Congress amputated the volitional prong of the American Law Institute's (ALI) test, the Insanity Defense Reform Act (IDRA) test of 1984 turned out to be the 1843 M'Naghten test under a new label, though the old wine hadn't improved with age (Finkel, 1989).

Back in 1843, as members of the House of Lords were congratulating themselves at having solved the insanity problem with the M'Naghten Rules, Lord Cooper (who seems to have been something of a killjoy) maintained that jurors simply retire and ask themselves, "Is this man mad or is he not?" no matter what instructions the judge provided (Moran, 1981). Lord Cooper was prophetic, for empirical research (e.g., Finkel, 1988a, 1988b, 1995b) has shown that different tests of insanity, worded in their particular legalese, produce no significant differences on the verdicts citizens render. Yet, by enacting the IDRA's construct, the Law chose the "knowledge of right from wrong" test from the past for its future, ignoring both the CSJ perspective and the empirical evidence that strongly suggested that this test would fail.

Still, a few legal scholars (e.g., M. S. Moore, 1984; Morse, 1984, 1985) urged a very different direction, suggesting that insanity be put in its proper moral context, which meant removing pseudomedicalizations and legal semantics and creating a test that conformed to the intuitive constructs of jurors. As M. S. Moore (1984, p. 244) put it,

> If the issue is a moral one . . . then the legal definition of the phrase [mental illness] should embody those moral principles that underlie the intuitive judgment that mentally ill human beings are not responsible. . . . What is thus needed is an analysis of that popular moral notion of mental illness. What have people meant by mental illness such that, both on and off juries, they have for centuries excused the otherwise wrongful acts of mentally ill persons?

But to do what Moore suggests we must empirically know what citizens' determinative constructs turn out to be. Along similar lines, Morse (1984, p. 390) proposed a craziness test that asked what Lord Cooper claimed jurors were asking themselves anyway. But even if Morse's test had been enacted and even if it worked better than did previous tests, we would still like to know what constructs citizens were using to discriminate *insane* (i.e., *crazy*) from *sane*.

From empirical research with mock jurors, we know that legal tests (i.e., from the wild-beast test of 1723 to the IDRA test of 1984) that span 250 years of insanity jurisprudence do not produce significantly different verdicts on the same cases, though we know that mock jurors' verdicts vary significantly among cases (e.g., Finkel, 1989; Finkel & Handel, 1989; Finkel, Shaw, Bercaw, & Koch, 1985). In other words, jurors make discriminations, but the tests' constructs of insanity are not the reasons for these discriminations. R. M. James's (1959) early findings suggest that mock jurors reconstrue the instructions to fit with their intuitive notions of *sane* and *insane*, but the question remains: "What are those intuitive notions?"

To try to pin down those notions, Finkel and Handel (1989) asked mock jurors to write out their determinative reasons for their verdicts, and then they categorized those reasons. Citizens invoked approximately three constructs per case, more than the number embedded in the legal tests they received, and they cited most frequently the capacity–incapacity construct and the nonculpable–culpable actions construct (i.e., Were the defendants culpable for bringing about their disability of mind [DOM]?). Those mock jurors who rendered an NGRI verdict saw the defendant as having an incapacity for responsible conduct and as being nonculpable for bringing about the DOM, whereas those rendering a guilty verdict saw the defendant as either having the capacity for responsible conduct or being culpable for bringing about the DOM. The capacity–incapacity construct converges with the essence of insanity we identified previously. The culpable construct, which tracks the second type of culpability we discussed in chapter 8 (this volume), is what Fingarette and Hasse (1979) termed *culpability for bringing about one's disability of mind*, what P. H. Robinson (1985) referred to "as causing the conditions of one's own defense" (p. 2), and what E. W. Mitchell (2003) referred to as *meta-responsibility*; this construct appears particularly important for the jurors voting guilty (e.g., Finkel, 1989, 1991; Finkel & Slobogin, 1995).

A Convergence of Consonant Perspectives, With a Few Dissonant Notes

Although CSJ findings converge with the previous philosophical and psychological theories, we must note the existence of some dissonant notes, lest we conclude, prematurely, that all is harmonious. For example, in the studies we cited earlier, mock jurors put aside their simplistic prototypes of insanity (e.g., Finkel & Groscup, 1997a) and invoked complex determinative reasons for their verdicts (i.e., reasons that were highly nuanced and tied to the case facts)—rather than staying with prototypes, preconceptions, or prejudices. However, the task instructions asked them to focus on the facts of those cases, and perhaps this *demand characteristic*, as it is called, artificially produced a better, more sophisticated picture than what citizens actually do at trial. But in defense of our methodology, a trial judge asks jurors to do just that as well, as the judge instructs jurors to put aside their preconceptions and focus on the evidence. Still, the question remains, will jurors put aside their prototypes at trial as they do in the construct research?

We raise this question because more recent prototype research on insanity (e.g., Skeem & Golding, 2001, p. 580) has shown that insanity prototypes of "idealized individuals" are often biased against insanity defendants, highly resistant to change, and highly influential on jurors' verdicts, and cannot be reduced to legal or psychiatric constructs. The Skeem and Golding findings introduce a dissonant note, whereas the perspectival voices we have followed appear to be singing a consonant song, all tying incapacity to nonculpability at the level of *mens*, seeing individuals who are insane as unable to be response-able actors, because they are unable to connect the moral, legal, and psychological significance of their acts to the shared background nexus.

We find more dissonant notes when we turn to the Law. First, the Law has yet to embrace this theory that lies at the deeper level of *mens*; in fact, the current insanity tests enacted by Congress and the states appear to be going in the opposite direction, toward the surface. The states seem to be like ships fleeing from the *Hinckley* storm, scattering in all directions: a dozen or so have followed Michigan's lead and added the guilty but mentally ill (GBMI) verdict option; a few have abolished the insanity defense, leaving *mens rea* as the battleground; some have reverted to various versions of M'Naghten; some stayed the course with the Model Penal Code's (American Law Institute, 1962) ALI test, and some adopted the IDRA (Finkel, 1988a). Second, when we examine this scatteration, these courses cleave to the surface, not guided by theory at all, being propelled by expedient, pragmatic, or politic quick-fix concerns. As we see it, no jurisdiction gets to the essence of insanity, and when these course changes are taken together, they reveal an underlying scattiness that does not seriously grapple with the problem. And third, no state has created a schema that truly tracked jurors' judgments of types of culpability or their gradations, though such a schema has been created, experimentally tested, and shown to track mock jurors' culpability judgments more faithfully and reduce NGRI verdicts more than do traditional tests (Finkel, 1988a, 1991; Finkel & Slobogin, 1995).

So dissonant notes and disconnects still abound when it comes to the Law's theory of nonculpability for insanity, and we shall hear another dissonant note in a case that resurrects "the Hadfield problem" in a different gender, with a different crime, and with different particulars—but is the same problem nonetheless. We present this case to show how bad law, bad science, and bad prototypes can turn what many thought an easy case into a hard case, and to show that we are still a long way from resolving insanity's challenges.

ANDREA PIA YATES: "A POSTER GIRL FOR THE INSANITY PLEA"

Andrea Yates (*Yates v. the State of Texas*, 2005) was a National Honor Society member, her high school's valedictorian, and captain of the swim team, and after graduation she was a registered nurse; her accomplishments, skills, and abilities are the stuff of a robust Self 2. After a 4-year courtship, she married Rusty, and the two announced to their wedding guests that "they wanted as many children as nature would provide" (Denno, 2003, p. 8). Regarding her personal identity, Self 1 was intact, for Yates was clear about who she was and what she wanted.

She wanted to be a good wife and good mother; she wanted to homeschool her children and be a good teacher; as a former nurse, and with her father having Alzheimer's disease, she wanted to be a good daughter and caretaker; and she wanted to be a good Christian. Social roles—good wife, mother, teacher, daughter, caretaker, Christian—are part of Self 3, and as such, they are dependent on the perceptions of others. Looking at "good Christian" specifically, Denno stated that Yates's beliefs in this matter were heavily influenced by Rusty's spiritual mentor, Michael Woroniecki, a traveling evangelist:

> Woroniecki's "repent-or-burn zeal" captivated her and she corresponded with Woroniecki and his wife for years after she and Rusty bought their bus. Indeed, at times, the Yates family seemed to imitate the Woronieckis—a bus-living, home-schooling, Bible-reading brood relishing the isolation of itinerancy. According to Woroniecki, "the role of woman is derived . . . from the sin of Eve." Likewise, he thought that "bad mothers" create "bad children." There came a time when Woroniecki's "hell burning" influence on Andrea was so great, it distressed both her parents and even Rusty. (pp. 31–32)

On June 16, 1999, approximately 2 years before the day (June 20, 2001) she would drown her five children, Andrea called Rusty at work and asked him to come home, where he found her shaking, crying, and biting her fingers; the next day she attempted suicide and was rushed to the hospital and diagnosed with major depressive disorder (there was a family history of bipolar disorder). A 2-year period of hospitalizations began, and different diagnoses, medications, and treatments failed to put an end to her suicide attempts and self-mutilations, or eliminate her hallucinatory voices and visions; and she was still not caring for herself or feeding her children. She rejected electroconvulsive therapy on two occasions, and refused to take her medication on various occasions, because it made her feel like a weak person. She rejected the doctor's advice not to have more children (i.e., because the doctor said it would all but guarantee a future psychotic depression), became pregnant again, and had a postpartum psychosis. Her father died, and she stopped talking; she was almost catatonic. She filled a bathtub with water, but refused to explain why. The fabric of Self 2 was renting.

Her delusions increased: she believed that cameras in the ceilings were watching her; that an injection given to her was a "truth serum" that would lead her to lose self-control in a way "she abhorred" (Denno, 2003, p. 31); and that she was possessed by the devil. Worse, she saw her children being "sassy" and not succeeding at their schooling, unlike her neighbor's children, and she interpreted this as their "stumbling toward Satan." She wanted to save her children from being "tormented by Satan," as she was (p. 31). The fabric of Self 3 was renting. The worst of it was that her personal identity, Self 1, was renting: the psyche split was widening and the counter-ego-nucleus was growing. She felt that Satan was inside her, believed she was becoming Satan, and saw herself inflicting Satan on her children.

A rescue delusion grew. She believed she must end the harm she was inflicting on her children and must punish the Satan-within-herself for her failures. She must save her children by sending them to God, for each day they spend with her they stumble further into Satan's clutch. So this former swimming champion gave her children a baptismal "send-off" and wanted the law to punish her with death for her sins and failings.

Many citizens, reading news stories about this woman's tribulations and delusions, saw Andrea Yates as a poster girl for the insanity plea (O'Malley, 2004). But many others reached the opposite conclusion: they saw this mother committing the ultimate sin, and to them, she epitomized evil. This case divided the nation, and, as it played out at trial, the defense and prosecution stories were polarized—mad versus bad—with no in-between (Colb, 2003). How polarized they were became evident when Harris County prosecutors announced that they would seek the death penalty for Yates, a move that astounded Yates's sympathizers. Yet, from an objective perspective, the deliberate way she planned the killings so as not to be stopped, and her telephoning the police right after, could easily be construed as proof that she knew that what she had done was legally wrong.

The prosecutors of Harris County (i.e., a county that had sent more people to death row than any county in the nation) were seen as overly zealous by the Yates sympathizers, who pinned their hopes on the independent jurors to set this matter right; many of the Yates sympathizers were astonished that the jury found her guilty, despite the testimony of 11 defense expert witnesses who took the jurors into Yates's disorders, delusion, and psychosis—presenting a picture of Yates consonant with how the astonished citizens viewed her. This case should have been an easy one for insanity, these citizens thought, and they believed that a wrongful verdict resulted.

However, the rightfulness or wrongfulness of that verdict cannot be determined, for the question is a transcendent one, and as "God seldom answers a *subpoena duces tecum* to tell us what really happened and why" (Finkel, 2000b, p. 598), only earthly speculations remain. But reasonable speculations, when tied to facts that are considered from an objective perspective, suggest that the guilty verdict was neither astonishing nor unpredictable.

Texas's Insanity Law Constricts

As prelude to understanding Texas's insanity law, which was changed after *Hinckley*, we make a few historic notes about delusions under the original M'Naghten Rules. Those 1843 Rules spoke of delusions this way:

> Where a person labors under partial delusions only and is not in other respects insane, and commits an offense in consequence thereof, he must be considered in the same situation as to responsibility as if the facts with respect to which the delusion exists were real. (*United States v. Currens*, 1961, n5)

The 15 justices who fashioned the Rules qualified this answer, saying that "the answer must of course depend on the nature of the delusion" (N. Walker, 1968, p. 99), and they gave this differential example:

> If under the influence of his delusion he supposes another man to be in the act of attempting to take away his life, and he kills that man, as he

supposes, in self-defence, he would be exempt from punishment. If his delusion was that the deceased had inflicted a serious injury to his character and fortune, and he killed him in revenge for such supposed injury, he would be liable to punishment. (p. 99)

This Rule and qualification asks jurors to take both a subjective and an objective vantage point toward the delusion: first, to understand "the facts" from the subjective vantage point of the person with the delusion, as if those facts were true; then, the jurors must shift to an objective perspective and judge whether, even if those facts were true, they would amount to an excusing self-defense claim. Under this subjective and objective test, could Yates's delusional motive be seen as a defense of others—an altruistic killing of her children to save them? But if we understand the delusion subjectively, and understand the nature and the quality of the act and its rightness or wrongness in a higher moral sense, then how would we judge a defendant who believes, like Abraham, that he must sacrifice his son Isaac for the higher moral good, for it is God's wish?

Texas narrowed M'Naghten severely, in the objective direction. The typical M'Naghten standard referred to a defendant's ability to know (a) the "nature and quality of the act committed" or (b) whether the act was "right or wrong" (Denno, 2003, p. 16); the Texas standard eliminated a, leaving only b, the right versus wrong standard, with no reference to the delusional part and the necessity on the part of the jurors to take the subjective vantage point. This more restrictive and objective standard worked against Yates. In addition, Texas's new law failed to clarify the ambiguity as to whether knowledge of right versus wrong meant knowledge in the narrow legal sense or in the wider moral sense. This ambiguity also worked against Yates, as the prosecution interpreted this standard for the jurors in the legal sense, and kept hammering away at it. If the jurors were interpreting Yates's deliberate, planful behavior at the moment of the act and her telephone call to the police after the act as knowing that what she was doing was legally wrong, then she had the *mens rea* for guilt. And these particular death-qualified (DQ) jurors were more likely than ordinary jurors to follow the prosecution's interpretation of the law and take the objective perspective.

On the Alleged Crimes and the Alleged Criminal

Yates's alleged murders were a mix of one infanticide and four filicides, and some limited empirical work indicates that infanticide cases do not fit comfortably within insanity's orbit (e.g., Finkel, Burke, & Chavez, 2000). In Hoffer and Hull's (1984) archival analysis, *Murdering Mothers: Infanticide in England and New England, 1558–1803*, they showed that community sentiment changed across that span, moving from a lenient-to-moderate period to a severe period, then changing back to a very lenient period. However, in Dobson and Sales's (2000) review of the past 250 years, they showed that sentiment swung back in the more severe direction, particularly as reflected in American law, which became harsher and overly restrictive when compared with British law. When we examined particular cases, the leniency effect was found generally for very young, unmarried defendants, who, in denial, shame, or panic, abandoned their newborns (neonaticides) or claimed that they were stillborns, whereas sentiment was typically harsher for older, married women, where planfulness was more evident. Moreover, the sentiment was harsher when the manner of death was more violent, when the mother left no chance that the baby might be rescued (Finkel et al., 2000).

Now, let us adopt the likely perspective of most citizens, particularly those serving on the Yates jury, which means dropping certain legal niceties, such as the word *alleged*: citizens see horrific crimes here, five killings of innocent children by a mother, crimes that go against Mother Nature, for which she is raising the insanity defense. Under the insanity defense, it should not matter if one or five children were killed, but we suspect it does matter to citizens (as we believe it mattered in the Malvo case), and we further suspect that citizens raise their threshold for granting an NGRI verdict when there are many victims. If we are correct in our surmise, then one way that jurors may raise their threshold is to invoke their extreme prototype, the wild beast, and want to see someone who is totally out of control. If this is so, then Yates's actions (e.g., her planfulness before and during the act, and telephoning the police after), from an objective perspective, are not those of a person totally out of control.

Jurors judge not only alleged crimes but also the defendant, and Andrea Yates did not help her case. In fact, throughout the trial she maintained that she deserved to be punished, indeed wanted to be punished, and her stance supported the prosecution's case. However, if we look subjectively, through her delusion, her actions and stance can be seen as a continuing part of her delusion, though this was not the likely viewpoint taken by these DQ jurors.

Expert Testimony

In Denno's (2003) analysis, she pointed out that more might have been less, for the 11 defense experts gave different accounts, "presumably in part because she had been treated or assessed by a number of them during different stages of her illness" (p. 22). Taken together, these multiple narratives may have appeared muddled, contrasted with "the more uniform 'factual' narrative presented" (p. 22) by the prosecution's Park Dietz, the only expert who testified that Yates knew that what she did was wrong. However, five experts testified that Yates "did not know right from wrong, was incapable of knowing that what she did was wrong, or believed that her acts were right" (*Yates v. the State of Texas*, 2005, p. 5), according to the Court of Appeals for the First District of Texas, which reversed her conviction on January 6, 2005.

The reason for the reversal involved a factual error made by Dietz, who, as a consultant on the television program known as *Law & Order*, gave the following answer on the witness stand about whether there was a TV episode that dealt with postpartum depression: "As a matter of fact, there was a show of a woman with postpartum depression who drowned her children in the bathtub and was found insane and it was aired shortly before the crime occurred" (p. 6). This was a factual mistake (i.e., there was no such episode, according to Executive Producer Dick Wolf), though the Appellate Court did not find that the mistake was intentional. Yet, it was what the prosecutor did with that mistake in his questioning of another expert and in his final argument that mattered: he stated that "maybe even we heard some evidence that she saw some show on TV and knew she could drown her children and get away with it" (p. 7), thereby suggesting that Yates's delusion was fabricated. The Appellate Court rejected the state's contention that the false information was not material—hence the reversal.

Though this informational error was unfortunate, mistakes of this sort can and do occur. Our graver concerns regarding expert testimony in general, and about Dietz's testimony in particular, are about errors that involved adopting an objective perspective and rational analysis regarding Yates's delusion, and about making inferences that were not scientific inferences, but religious, moral ones. In his interviews with Yates and in his testimony, Dietz clearly adopted the outsider's objective viewpoint, and attempted a rational analysis of her irrational delusion:

> [Dietz claimed that] Andrea Yates failed to act in a way a loving mother would if she really thought she was saving her children from hell by killing them. As Dietz stated, "I would expect her to comfort the children, telling them they are going to be with Jesus or be with God, but she does not offer words of comfort to the children." . . . [but] as one legal critic asked in response to Dietz's comments, "Is one to infer that it is somehow more loving to invoke the name of Jesus while you drown your children than to drown them without any religious commentary?" (Denno, 2003, p. 20)

Dietz's inference was not a scientific inference at all, for he was stressing religion (aligned with Southern Bible Belt culture), not facts. This expert was going way beyond what the facts and the science permit, delivering his own sermon from the stand. But in his sermon, Dietz failed to reference Genesis 22: 4, for when Abraham and Isaac get to Moriah, Abraham says not a word to Isaac, as "Abraham built an altar there, and arranged the wood, and bound his son Isaac, and laid him on the altar, on top of the wood. And Abraham reached out and picked up the knife to slaughter his son" (S. Mitchell, 1996). Yet Dietz's casting of Yates may have fit with these jurors' predilections and prototypes (Finkel, 2003).

Prototypes Revisited, in the Light of Death-Qualified Jurors

Skeem and Golding (2001) have done a series of studies aimed at elucidating jurors' personal conceptions of insanity (i.e., their prototypes), using methodologies that significantly improve on that used by Finkel and Groscup (1997a). Though Skeem and Golding (2001) began by looking at individuals' prototypes and reminded readers that "prototypes of insanity may be as numerous as individuals" (p. 580), they did, however, aggregate (through factor and cluster analyses) to find three prototypes that they called *idealized individuals*: severely mentally disabled (SMD), morally insane (MI), and mental state-centered (MSC). All three prototypes share the following common features of "psychosis (e.g., delusional, has schizophrenia, acts on voices)": an "inability to discern right from wrong, understand the harmful consequences of one's actions, and control one's thoughts, emotions and actions" at the time of the act, and a "lack of awareness about what one is doing" (p. 590). In conveying Skeem and Golding's SMD, MI, and MSC differences, we will relate how each fits, or fails to fit, Yates.

As Skeem and Golding (2001) wrote, "Nearly half (47%) of the jurors were best represented by an idealized individual with an SMD prototype," which corresponds most closely with the wild-beast test, as this prototype emphasizes total debilitation that is "longstanding and resistant to treatment," "that cannot be controlled with treatment," "where the illness is likely to have a physical basis," and where the defendants "did not bring about their impaired state at the time of the offense and made every attempt to control it" (pp. 590–591; Finkel, 1989, 1995b; Finkel & Handel, 1989). "In summary, the SMD prototype is afflicted by a brutal, externally imposed illness that he or she has been unable to contain even by seeking professional help" (Skeem & Golding, 2001, p. 591). In light of the fact that (a) most people misunderstand postpartum depression and psychosis (Dobson & Sales, 2000), believing that this illness is not physical and that the person can control it, coupled with (b) the number of times Andrea Yates threw away her medication, didn't take her medication, and refused certain treatments, and (c) the fact that her impairment did not appear to be a total debilitation, this SMD prototype shows many points of mismatch with the Yates fact pattern.

Their MI prototype, representing 33% of the jurors, is something of a contradiction, for though it emphasizes the psychopathic traits of having no conscience, unfeeling and manipulative, and violent and hostile (most of which do not fit Yates), it also includes psychosis and the elements of distorted vision of reality and being irrational (which would fit Yates). Thus, this prototype brings together "a decidedly unlikely combination" in reality of the "psychotic psychopath" (Wahl, 1995, pp. 19–20), but a Hollywood staple nonetheless, and one of the prototypes that recurs in Finkel and Groscup's (1997a) findings, yet one that does not map well onto Yates.

Finally, the MSC prototype represents only 21% of the jurors. These individuals, claim Skeem and Golding (2001), most strongly support the insanity defense, and they offer two points to support their claim.

> First, the MSC's characteristics are linked by the premise that mental illness is associated with reduced capacity for forming intent, making rational decisions, and controlling one's behavior. Second, . . . there was a trend in this study for those with MSC prototypes to endorse the basic logic of the insanity defense more strongly than the other two groups. Those with MSC-like prototypes tended to believe that when mental illness is associated with reduced capacity, it negates blameworthiness. (p. 595)

This prototype aligns with the incapacity construct of insanity we have been developing as the essence of insanity, and it is the prototype most likely to embrace Yates.

However, the jurors in Yates's case are not representative of citizens at large. Because the prosecution sought the death penalty (i.e., as they did in the Virginia cases of Muhammad and Malvo), only DQ jurors could serve on the Yates jury, and as research (e.g., Ellsworth, Bukaty, Cowan, & Thompson, 1984) has shown, DQ jurors (in comparison to non-DQ jurors) are less likely to accept an insanity defense when the cause is nonphysical. Moreover, DQ jurors tend to favor the prosecution, and are oriented more toward crime control than toward the niceties of due process. These DQ jurors probably endorse more strongly a "strict liability" orientation, which C. F. Roberts and Golding (1991) found in 7% of the population and which holds that everyone is responsible for their actions no matter what their mental condition, an orientation quite hostile to the insanity defense. Thus, the DQ jurors are likely to be more receptive to the prosecution's case and the prosecution's expert witnesses than the defense, are more likely to follow the letter of the law and the legal sense of right and wrong, and are more likely to cleave to objective reality than switch perspectives and see things through the subjective delusions of the defendant. Moreover, their prototypes are more likely to be skewed in the direction of SMD and MI, rather than MSC, which would make an NGRI verdict quite unlikely, if jurors could not or would not set aside their prototypes and take the subjective vantage point.

BLAME AND BLAMELESSNESS

Since *Hinckley*, many studies (e.g., Hans, 1986; Hans & Slater, 1983) have documented citizens' negative attitudes toward the insanity defense. Many believe this defense to be a loophole that allows the guilty to escape blame (e.g., Perlin, 1989–1990, 1994). By contrast, we do not hear those negatives regarding the not guilty by reason of self-defense verdict (our next topic, as that justification verdict seems acceptable, whereas the excusing condition is not).

Why not? This is a complex question, and we offer only a short answer, one that relates to three disconnects. The first disconnect is between Law's underlying theory of not punishing when we cannot impose blame and the feelings of many citizens that the insanity defendant is to blame. The second disconnect is within the Law itself, between its underlying theory and the law as it is codified; this disconnect involves the long-standing objectivity versus subjectivity debate, and resolving this disconnect involves a challenge for the Law. The third disconnect occurs within citizens, between their prototypes and deeper CSJ constructs; this disconnect involves objectivity versus subjectivity of a different sort, and resolving this disconnect involves a challenge as well.

The Disconnect Between Law and Citizens

The Law's underlying theory is that the act is not blameworthy and punishable unless it was committed by a person who had the capacity to understand that the act was wrong, and who voluntarily chose to do the act. This is an old and revered ideal, yet one not easily embraced in reality. For example, what many citizens saw was Yates "killing" her five children, blameless victims who in no way deserved to die. Human beings have a strong emotional and judgmental reaction to blame. This reaction was evident even among Yates's supporters, many of whom wanted to blame someone (Colb, 2003) and pointed fingers toward the husband, family, spiritual advisor, and the many doctors, hospitals, and insurance providers that failed her. Yet the Law's theory seems to be saying to the citizenry, "Let go of your desire to blame, for this defendant is blameless." Letting go of blame is a twofold emotional challenge, for it seems to abandon the victims, while letting the defendant off the hook.

With the Law's NGRI verdict, the problem is the "not guilty" part, for the "not guilty" rubs wrong. This "not guilty" problem arises because under the law the *actus reus* and *mens rea* must conjoin for guilt, and if the *mens rea* is lacking, the Law holds the defendant blameless. Yet this conclusion seems to deny the wrongfulness of the *actus reus*, and the public may want more in the way of a legal acknowledgment that a wrongful act has occurred before it is more willing to accept the basic premise that an incapacity of the *mens* leaves the defendant nonculpable.

The Law's Disconnect With Itself

Insanity law following *Hinckley* has been legislatively driven, and, in the main, it has moved toward the objective surface—in just the opposite direction of this chapter, where we have ventured deep into the subjective to pin the Proteus. Put another way, that legislatively driven law moved further from explicating its underlying premise of why some are held blameless, and seemed to be giving in to the worst of sentiments—just limiting the insanity defense, theory be damned.

Insanity's theory must go further in the subjective direction than any other area, we submit, and this proposition is frightening and challenging. The Law's retreat to the apparent safety of objectivity leaves the theoretical irony that manslaughter's extreme emotional disturbance ends up being more subjective than most insanity tests, a result that is neither coherent nor consistent. The challenge that insanity poses for theory is solving "the Hadfield problem," and the Law has yet to face up squarely to the fact that *mens rea* cannot carry the freight when it comes to "delusion." To resolve the problem requires codifying that fundamental incapacity that lies at the level of *mens*.

The Disconnect Within the Citizenry

Surveys consistently tell us that most citizens hold quite negative opinions about the insanity defense. Moreover, researchers investigating the particular features of insanity prototypes have found that these prototypes do not fit with existing law and with what experts believe about madness, often being unrealistic, stereotypic, and even contradictory (Finkel, 1997). Yet when we take these citizens and give them specific cases to analyze, they are able to set aside their prototypes and engage in a sophisticated analysis of the case facts, in which they balance subjective and objective considerations, and end up finding the "incapacity" and "culpability for bringing about the disability of mind" constructs. Their challenge occurs at trial, where they are faced with horrific crimes and real victims to grieve for, and a delusional defendant whose psychic world and personal identity are far from their own. Will they resist the urge to hold to the simplistic objective vantage point—which, after all, provides an emotional detachment and distance from the defendant's delusional world—and will they resist applying their prototypical shortcuts that reduce a complex case to a stereotype to see the facts through the delusion of the defendant, and find a deeper subjectivity tempered with a clearer objectivity about the facts and the law?

LOOKING BACK, AND LOOKING FORWARD

In the scatteration following *Hinckley*, the dominant motives driving the scatter did not include sound evidence or coherent theory. Legislators were carefully reading the polling numbers, realizing that their voting constituencies wanted the insanity defense tightened, and the policy direction was evident in the title the Senate Subcommittee on Criminal Law (1983) put on its hearings: "Limiting the Insanity Defense." Insanity was clearly on trial after *Hinckley* (Finkel, 1988a), but it turned out to be a Wonderland trial, with sentence (i.e., the issue of disposition) seemingly first in the minds of legislators, and culpability (and a fitting theory of it) second. The alleged culprits—the ALI's volitional prong, the prosecution's burden, and the experts' ultimate opinion—were amputated, relieved, and revised.

The legislators barely had time to congratulate themselves before empirical evidence on the likely effects of their efforts began to accumulate. Finkel's (1989) experiment showed that the IDRA test produced no significant verdict differences when compared with the ALI test across cases, and the mock jurors did not use any different constructs in deciding these cases with either test; Ogloff's (1991) results showed that shifting the burden of proof produced no significant differences; and Fulero and Finkel's (1991) results showed that barring ultimate opinion testimony made no significant difference. All of these results led Finkel and Fulero (1992) to conclude that the IDRA was a case of "making law in the absence of evidence" (p. 383). Moreover, as the Yates and Malvo cases illustrate, there seems to be neither a shortage of experts testifying nor any tempering of the certainty of their inferences, an issue still troubling to many scientific and legal scholars (e.g., Sales & Shuman, 2005; Shuman & Sales, 1998), and one that has troubled judges for the past 2 centuries (e.g., Bazelon, 1982, 1988; R. Smith, 1981). In addition, the results from Michigan's use of the GBMI verdict in addition to NGRI and guilty yielded no reduction in NGRI verdicts, as the GBMI option was apparently given to defendants who might otherwise have been found guilty (Finkel & Duff, 1989).

The flurry of Congressional committees following *Hinckley* paralleled the summoning of the 15 justices before the House of Lords to answer questions following *M'Naghten*, for in both instances, an apparent wrongful verdict triggered the revisions of the law. Though no one could have known the true verdict, it seems that only wrongful NGRI verdicts kick-start legislative action, whereas wrongful guilty verdicts (i.e., in which a truly insane person is found guilty) produce no action; this fact makes political sense (though not theoretical sense), because no politician ever lost an election because he or she lost "the mentally ill" vote, for individuals with mental illness are the most disenfranchised (e.g., Perlin, 2000; Stefan, 2001).

The sad irony is that 160 years after *M'Naghten* no further advances have been made, and some jurisdictions have regressed to the beast, or tried to wipe insanity's madness from the legal landscape entirely. None of these moves honestly or honorably solve the Hadfield problem. This is where we began this chapter, picking up from where Erskine left off, trying to give an adequate account of the split within the psyche to pin the Proteus and elucidate the essence of insanity.

Using multiple sources and perspectives—philosophical, psychological, literary, medico-jurisprudential, and commonsensical—we unpacked the meaning of *defect of reason* and found a disconnect within the psyche, such that the individual had an incapacity to connect his or her thoughts, feelings, beliefs, motives, and actions with the shared background nexus. At the psychological level, this is a theory neither of particular symptoms nor of any psychic part acting in isolation; rather, in this counter-ego-nucleus that creates a delusion the elements of thinking, emotions, and motives operate together. In other words, we maintain that this theory is psychological rather than emotional. At the legal level, this defect and disconnect occur at a subjective level deeper than *mens rea*, at the level of *mens*, such that this actor is not response-able. The "insane actor" is not a legal actor at all, and that is why the insanity end point of this continuum is different not just in degree but in kind from where we have been in our preceding chapters, and from where we are going—to self-defense—for within that justification defense there is no claim that the defendant is not a responsible actor.

Self-defense provides an interesting contrast to the insanity defense, for it arouses no public and political hostility to limit that defense, whereas the resistance to the insanity defense is vocal and visceral. Embracing the blamelessness of insanity is difficult, yet embracing full blame appears difficult as well, as these cases challenge the beliefs and prototypes of citizens like no other. But insanity poses a challenge to the Law that is not being met. The unseemly hodgepodge of current laws, driven by political expediency—backward in time toward tests that have failed the test of time—is diagnostic of "a sore distraction" that reflects a kind of madness. But unlike Hamlet, the Law is not overhearing itself these days, for it does not seem to be seeking coherence or underlying empirical support when it comes to insanity. This *status quo ante* is likely to remain, we believe, until a future group of legal scholars undertakes a revision of the criminal law wherein insanity is reworked, for that is the group that has an investment in producing theoretical coherence as well as looking seriously at how empirical data may inform the endeavor.

10

WHERE SELF-DEFENSE'S JUSTIFICATION BLURS INTO EXCUSE: A DEFENSIBLE THEORY, WITH FITTING VERDICTS, FOR MISTAKEN SELF-DEFENSE

In chapters 8 and 9 (this volume), we presented facts and theory to show that the Law's culpability theory lacks depth, coherence, and validity. Our negative assessment could have applied at almost any point in the 300 years of insanity jurisprudence, though it is particularly apropos now, given the scatteration that followed *Hinckley* (*United States v. Hinckley*, 1981). By contrast, our initial assessment of the Law's self-defense theory is far more positive. Modern self-defense theory—which arose from the two roots of felony prevention (justification defense) and chance medley–*se defendendo* (excusing defense) that were subsequently folded into one justification defense (R. Singer, 1987)—is supported by credible theories, respected philosophical and legal writings, and centuries of case law (Dressler, 2001; Fletcher, 1978). In addition, these sources identify its requisite elements, which have been in place for over a century. Moreover, empirical evidence shows little disagreement between commonsense justice (CSJ) and black-letter law (BLL) over the prototypical self-defense case when we examine liability and punishment judgments (e.g., Finkel, Maloney, Valbuena, & Groscup, 1995; P. H. Robinson & Darley, 1995). And unlike insanity, where the emotions that propel the action can be quite varied, fear is the typical emotion for prototypical self-defense cases. But this is an initial assessment.

In shifting from insanity to self-defense, we move from an excusing to a justifying defense, or so legal texts proclaim. Self-defense is differentiated from insanity in terms of (a) the nature of the act, (b) a focus on the act rather than the actor, and (c) a greater weighting of objective over subjective factors. So if the victim (V) comes at the defendant (D) with a lethal weapon in hand, with the clear and immediate intent to kill or inflict serious bodily injury, and D cannot retreat, then if D kills V under these objective circumstances, then the homicide is justified (Dressler, 2001, p. 202). By contrast, the focus of an excusing defense is on the actor's subjectivity, and the claim is that the actor is not culpable for the wrongful act. For a justified act, we can look at the outcome, *ex post*, and decide that a good resulted, rather than considering the act *ex ante*, as to what the actor may have subjectively perceived or intended.

Two prototypical examples illustrate. The first case, fitting the felony-prevention root, unfolds this way. A stranger (V) approaches a man (D) sitting on a subway car and stands over him, pulls a gun, demands his money, and says he will kill him if he refuses to hand over the money. Fearing for his life, seeing no way of escaping, and believing that V will kill him even if he hands over his money, D reaches for his gun and quickly fires, killing V. D claims his act was self-defense. Our second case, fitting the chance medley–*se defendendo* root, involves intimates, a husband and wife; the latter has been repeatedly battered by the former over many years, having suffered serious injuries as a result. Now, another confrontation begins, with the husband (V) beating his wife (D) with his fists. She races from the room in fear of her life but is cornered in a bedroom. V approaches with a knife in his hand, but D reaches for a gun and fires, killing V. D claims that her act was self-defense.

FROM THE PROTOTYPICAL TO THE PROBLEMATIC: PASSIONS, AND PSYCHOLOGY, ON THE RISE

To see our reasons for calling these cases *prototypical*, insert an invisible observer into these fact patterns, an "objective reasonable person" who represents the "average person"; this legal figment is an ideal, for it represents no one person in reality, and it views the action with detachment, objectively and reasonably. Now, if we ask this exemplar to infer the dominant emotion felt by the two Ds from their facial expressions and body language, this outsider would have little trouble designating fear as the dominant emotion. In addition, this outsider would see a *serious threat*, one likely to produce severe if not fatal injuries, and would see the threat as *imminent*, with *no possibility of escape*, and thus would evaluate the responses of the two Ds as *proportionate* as well as *necessary*. And regarding the intentions of the two Ds, the observer would probably say the two reasonably believed that they were about to die and *just wanted to end the threat to their lives*. The observer, then, would find that all of the requisite elements have been met (Fletcher, 1988, p. 19), which would match the judgments of the Ds (Dressler, 2001, p. 222).

This objective–subjective agreement is why we call these cases prototypical, and why they are easy cases, for which BLL and CSJ judgments generally agree (e.g., P. H. Robinson & Darley, 1995). As these run-of-the-mill justification cases seem settled *within* the Law and *between* Law and CSJ, they hold little interest for us in this chapter, save as a baseline comparison with those cases that do pique our interest. The two specific areas we focus on are mistaken self-defense cases and cases in which a battered woman kills her spouse in nonconfrontational situations but still claims self-defense, for these variations create complications that turn the prototypical cases into problematic ones—such that the line between justification and excuse begins to blur, if not disappear. To introduce our problematic cases, we return to our prototypical examples, having made some significant alterations.

A Mistaken Self-Defense Example?

George Fletcher (1988) began his book, *A Crime of Self-Defense: Bernhard Goetz and the Law on Trial*, with an account of what happened after 37-year-old Bernhard Goetz (*People v. Goetz*, 1986) entered a subway car on December 22, 1984, and chose to sit close to four Black youths who were "noisy and boisterous," despite the fact that other passengers had moved away (p. 1). One of the youths asks Goetz, "How are ya?" and then he and one of the other youths approach and ask for $5. After Goetz asks what he wants, the request appears to become a demand as the youth says, "Give me $5." Goetz quickly fires shots at each of the four. In Goetz's later confession, he states that he paused and then said to one of the youths, "You seem to be [doing] all right; here's another," as Goetz fired a fifth shot, with that bullet severing the spinal cord of the youth.

Goetz would claim self-defense for the four shootings, and the jurors would agree. But was this self-defense as we normally think of it, or was Goetz a "subway vigilante" (as the press quickly dubbed him), with passions antithetical to fear, seeking revenge for himself and others, even provoking the four teens by choosing to sit down among them? It would be particularly hard to claim self-defense for the fifth shot, fired into an already wounded youth, who was no threat at that moment. When viewed through a revenge hypothesis, Goetz's act is not felony prevention but a planned, premeditated murder waiting to happen—waiting for just the right Vs and circumstances to present themselves; moreover, for jurors to acquit Goetz they would have to nullify the law, because the requisite self-defense elements are not met. If this is what they did, then the jurors would have likely cast Rorschach-like projections of "villains" and "hero" on the Vs and Goetz, respectively, and let their punitive passions loose on the former, justifying their verdict with "they got what they deserved," which, as Fletcher (1988, p. 19) wrote, was the refrain heard throughout the trial.

But let us consider an alternative to revenge and true self-defense: Could this be a case of mistaken (putative) self-defense? For example, was there an actual threat likely to cause him serious harm or possibly death—or did Goetz mistakenly believe there was one? Was the serious threat imminent—or was he mistaken in his belief that he had to use deadly force at that moment? Did Goetz have other options (e.g., retreating to the safer part of the subway car, warning the youths to back off, or backing up his warning by showing his gun)—or did he believe, mistakenly, that he had no other options but to fire at the youths? Was Goetz's response proportionate to the threat—or was he mistaken about that too? And was Goetz trying to end the threat out of fear—or was he intending, with his shots (and particularly with that fifth shot), to hurt or kill the Vs? And when we consider that Goetz had been mugged in 1981 (suffering physical injuries to his knees and the loss of his electronic equipment on the subway), and that he subsequently experienced frustrating encounters with the police trying to obtain a pistol permit, might those prior experiences have overly sensitized him, such that he felt like a cornered "rat," who "turns viciously on you and just becomes a vicious killer," which were Goetz's own words (Fletcher, 1988, p. 13)?

If we are to find Goetz not guilty under this mistaken self-defense hypothesis, the focus cannot be exclusively on the objective circumstances or on the objective act (as opposed to the actor), nor can objective factors predominate over subjective factors, as a justification defense requires; rather, we would be steeped in Goetz's subjectivity and psychology—which is where an "excusing defense," such as insanity, leads us. For an acquittal to result under mistaken self-defense, our objective reasonable person must undergo a subjectivizing transformation, understanding the subjective fears of those passengers huddled at the far end of that subway car, and how the previous mugging psychologically distorted what Goetz perceived and construed. And in mistaken self-defense cases, unlike prototypical cases, the Law and its citizens must judge emotions other than fear, which are embedded in more complex stories.

When a Battered Woman Kills Her Spouse in a Nonconfrontational Situation

In our second example, the husband breaks off his physical attack but threatens to hurt her worse after he gets up from his nap, whereupon the wife gets a gun and kills him while he sleeps, but still claims self-defense. First, by way of background, in battering relationships that end in a killing, only a minority of those cases feature the battered woman doing the killing (e.g., Barnard, Vera, Vera, & Newman, 1982; Wolfgang, 1958); and of that minority, approximately 21% (Ewing, 1987) are nonconfrontational killings, where the batterer is asleep or watching television. These nonconfrontational killings pose the toughest challenge for self-defense, as jurors are likely to doubt whether there was a *serious, imminent threat* at that moment which made deadly force *necessary* and *proportionate*, when the *escape* option seems available. Moreover, her *intention* and motives are more likely to be suspect under these conditions. In actual trials, it is the judge who controls the verdict options jurors receive, and some judges may never let jurors consider self-defense under the conditions we described, whereas prosecutors are more likely to bring the harshest charges (e.g., first- or second-degree murder) under these conditions, for such killings under these circumstances appear premeditated, if not deliberate.

A number of feminist jurisprudes (e.g., Gillespie, 1989) have argued that the law of self-defense (i.e., which evolved from fights between men, who were typically strangers) is biased against women who kill their partners, for this law ignores the relationship lives of battered women and the facts of battered-woman syndrome; some critics also claim that citizens share this ignorance and bias, pointing to the fact that when women kill their mates they receive harsher verdicts than when husbands kill their spouses (Gillespie, 1989). Critics (e.g., Schneider, 1980, 1986; Schneider & Jordan, 1978) have also argued that if citizens have any sympathy toward women who kill, they are more likely to see the D as not guilty by reason of insanity (NGRI) rather than as not guilty by reason of self-defense (NGRSD). In support of self-defense and against these alleged biases, advocates have fought successfully for the admission of expert testimony on battered-woman syndrome—to help educate jurors on the facts of battering and the life of the battered woman, particularly as to its causes and the psychological effects that result (e.g., depression and learned helplessness)—and how these may affect how the battered woman sees the situation. This testimony provides a subjective account of how the D can believe that there is a serious threat, that it was immediately necessary to act, and that there was no escape; given these beliefs, she intended to end the threat.

Like mistaken self-defense, this testimony speaks to the psychology of the actor and replaces the objective reasonable person with a subjective exemplar who considers not only gender, size, and power differentials but also her development, socialization, marital history, and syndrome or disorder, and how all of this may color her perceptions and beliefs. This plunge into subjectivity and syndrome testimony leads not to the promised land of justification, but into the disordered realm of an insanity excuse. But if this is neither insanity nor a truly justified self-defense, then it seems to be an excusing case of mistaken self-defense.

MISTAKEN SELF-DEFENSE:
NORMATIVE AND EMPIRICAL LINE-DRAWING

If these are mistaken self-defense cases, then what perspective does the law take to them, what theories govern the law's evaluation of them, and what are their possible outcomes? As Finkel (2003) has written,

> If the law falls back on its "mistake of fact" jurisprudence, outcomes are likely to vary. If the mistake is reasonable, NGRSD may still result. If the mistake is honest but unreasonable, however, the outcome is in greater doubt: we do not know with certainty whether such a mistake will still exculpate, or whether it will only mitigate, or whether it will remit nothing. . . . There is still another possibility: if the mistake is grand enough—being an outright delusion—it might exculpate through an insanity (NGRI) verdict, which is an excusing condition. With mistake of fact, then, all bets are off as to predicting the verdict and its underlying rationale, for verdicts may run the culpability table, from full culpability to mitigation to exculpation, and, under the latter, either the justifying or the excusing rationale may carry the day. (pp. 187–188)

Depending on the type of mistake, how reasonable or unreasonable that mistake appears, and whether the mistake is judged as dishonest rather than honest, the mistaken self-defense judgment may fall at many different points along a juror's culpability scale. Whereas culpability and verdict are legal questions, the jurors' evaluations of mistakes are psychological judgments first, and normative judgments second. Moreover, jurors taking an objective perspective on mistakes of fact are likely to reach different judgments as to where "reasonable" ends and "unreasonable" begins than are those taking a subjective perspective.

This variance is mirrored in the long history of court decisions and legal commentary regarding mistaken self-defense cases, where subjectivity first dominated, then objectivity came to ascendancy, then the objective reasonable person began to undergo resubjectivization. The Model Penal Code (American Law Institute, 1962) brought a resurgence of *mens rea* and the subjective perspective to the fore, though many jurisdictions rejected this approach, leaving the field divided and confused (R. Singer, 1987). To add to the confusion, the drafters of the Code were unsure that defensible lines *could* be drawn between the two types of mistakes or between justification and excuse, and even if defensible lines could be drawn, there was the question of whether they *should* be drawn, if doing so increased the complexity of the statutory system, and this negative outweighed the benefits of line drawing (Dressler, 2001, pp. 216–217).

Contrary to the Model Penal Code's (American Law Institute, 1962) drafters, Dressler (2001) and other legal scholars (e.g., Fletcher, 1978; Greenawalt, 1986; P. H. Robinson, 1975) take the position that the distinction is important for the Law, conceptually and normatively, for it sends a clear moral message. We endorse this position as well. Dressler argued that the Law wants individuals to take justifiable rather than excusable paths, and the law ought to guide citizens, rather than expressing "a moral falsity by characterizing improper-but-excusable conduct as proper" (p. 217).

Still, deciding on normative grounds that the justification–excuse distinction is worth preserving leaves open the practical question as to where to draw the line. We argue that a line can be drawn. But we also argue that a defensible line cannot be drawn dividing *objective* from *subjective* or *act* from *actor*, and that the *ex ante* versus *ex post* division will not work either. The answer we offer is based, in part, on empirical evidence regarding distinctions between reasonable and unreasonable mistakes. Our answer is also based on what is revealed when we parse the phrase *honest but reasonable (or unreasonable) mistakes*. We find two different judgments (which have been conflated), one relating to the accuracy of the D's perceptions or beliefs, and one relating to the moral worthiness of the D's motive or intent (i.e., such that there can be dishonest but reasonable mistakes and dishonest but unreasonable mistakes as well). To develop our argument, we must first examine the self-defense requirements under mistake-of-fact conditions.

THE REQUIREMENTS OF SELF-DEFENSE UNDER MISTAKE-OF-FACT CONDITIONS

A confrontation between two men frequently occurs in both felony-prevention and *se defendendo* root-line cases, but in felony prevention the aggressor or wrongdoer and the innocent V are clearly differentiable. In felony prevention, the wrongdoer approaches the V with a knife and demands the V's money; the D, seeking to prevent the felony and acting like a surrogate of the law, slays the wrongdoer with his knife, having justifiably done what is right, and under this root-line the D need not retreat.

In applying this pre-19th century understanding of felony prevention to *Goetz*, we immediately run into trouble: for though "give me $5" may be a frightening or bothersome hassle, without the show of a weapon this is not an armed robbery for which deadly force is a proportionate response. Applying this felony-prevention understanding to the battered woman who kills her sleeping husband runs into even greater difficulties: his pre-nap threat may have been just bluster, but even if it was a real threat at the time he uttered it, he might have forgotten his threat—if he had awoken. In the eyes of an objective observer, there is no imminent threat of a felony when she killed, so her deadly act can appear as a premeditated preemptive strike.

The Retreat Requirement's Retreat

In our chapter on manslaughter (chap. 7, this volume) we raised the question as to why deadly actions resulting from the heat of passion and loss of control to provocations in chance-medley quarrels led only to mitigation and not to exculpation. The answer hinges on distinguishing *se defendendo* cases from chance-medley quarrels that escalate, in which one or both sides reaches for deadly force, and in which the killing is on the spot: when an on-the-spot killing occurs, it is manslaughter (a homicide chance medley), but if one party retreats before actually slaying until his or her back is literally against the wall, then this is homicide *se defendendo*, which results in no conviction "but only forfeiture of goods" (R. Singer, 1987, p. 472).

But there are notable differences between felony prevention and *se defendendo*. For one, both parties in *se defendendo* participated in the quarrel, and therefore the D is not totally innocent. For another, the *se defendendo* D was not performing a social good through killing such an assailant, because this D was merely saving his own skin. In pre-19th-century law, the excusing defense was regarded as less worthy than a justifying defense, for a penalty, a forfeiture of goods, attached to the former; though forfeiture was formally abolished by English courts in 1828, ambiguity remained as to whether this defense was justification or excuse, as some courts and writers used the terms interchangeably, until justification came to dominate (R. Singer, 1987, p. 473).

The essential requirement for this *se defendendo* excuse was retreat. Retreating gave the D time and opportunity to assess the intent of the aggressor, whether the threat coming at him or her was indeed serious and imminent, and if escape options were available—all of which leads to greater clarity and a lower likelihood of mistaken perceptions as to whether deadly force was proportionate and necessary. Retreat, then, connects to the other requirements through the interpersonal, psychological context.

This pre-19th-century requirement of "retreating to the wall" made good sense—in that era—when aggressors were coming at Ds with knives or swords. But when times changed and aggressors began pulling guns, a slow retreat often meant a quick death. In the "time of the gun," the fact that someone pulls a gun is all that most frightened Vs need to quickly draw the conclusion that he who hesitates is lost, for a more careful appraisal of intent, necessity, and proportionality may not be completed in the V's lifetime. If exceptions to the retreat rule were being made in gun cases, or in cases in which the V may have been going for a gun, or the D thought the V was going for a weapon, then the law was willing to countenance more mistake cases—reasonable and unreasonable. But this broadening allows for claims of a dishonest but reasonable mistake and a dishonest but unreasonable mistake, which were staples on old western movies and television shows. In these instances, the "bad guy" (typically dressed in black to eliminate moral ambiguity) either provokes some hapless innocent to make a sudden move and then shoots him, or shoots when the sweaty V reaches for his handkerchief; the bad guy uses "the reach" as pretext for his claim of reasonable or unreasonable mistake, which hides his dishonesty. Was this what Goetz was doing, minus the black outfit?

If the retreat requirement was yielding in gun cases, the retreat rule was waived entirely when the confrontation occurred in a man's home (i.e., the castle exception), for if there was any place a man should feel safe and not have to retreat it was in his own home; however, this exception would be problematic in battering relationships, because the castle belongs to both the husband and the wife. A "true man" exception was also proposed, though it was not accepted; but the argument for it—"Why should a good and true man have to turn tail and give ground when an aggressor is coming at him?"— did have its supporters, and still does.

Today, the retreat requirement has undergone retreat in some jurisdictional statutes while being required in others. This is one requirement for which empirical testing has revealed discrepancies between community sentiment and the Model Penal Code (American Law Institute, 1962). P. H. Robinson and Darley (1995) tested three retreat variations off a basic self-defense case: in one variation the D could retreat but did not, in another the D could retreat safely from his home but did not, and in the third variation the D mistakenly believed he could not retreat. Regarding their "retreat" conditions, Robinson and Darley wrote,

> Americans, stereotypically, "stand their ground," and our subjects seem to want them to even when legal codes say they should not. That is, when one's use of deadly force is unnecessary because that person could safely retreat . . . our subjects mitigate liability while the Code does not. [When] subjects agree that the person could retreat, . . . the liability mean . . . reflects a considerably less severe sentence than the liability for murder that the current legal doctrine imposes. Apparently, some of our subjects are unsure about whether retreat should be required at all. (p. 60)

The P. H. Robinson and Darley (1995) results seem directly applicable to *Goetz*. Citizens may be less concerned than the Model Penal Code (American Law Institute, 1962) that Goetz did not retreat, or that he mistakenly believed that retreat was not possible. But the rejoinder to Goetz's not retreating before firing is, where was the serious threat in "give me $5"? An answer to this rejoinder is found in the P. H. Robinson and Darley data (p. 55). Of the nine conditions they tested, two were control conditions, used to set upper and lower boundaries: one was a "true self-defense case," which produced a mean liability rating (on a 0–10 scale) of almost nil (0.14), which was expected, and the other was a killing in which there was no self-defense at all (i.e., a beggar approaches a person and asks for money and the person shoots him), for which the researchers expected a liability rating close to 10, but got only 7.97, with punishment set at approximately 15 years, which surprised them.

In reexamining their beggar scenario, they came up with a possible interpretation about why subjects may have mitigated the liability:

Apparently, what to us seemed a trivial annoyance (being pestered by a beggar who persists in requesting money after he is initially turned down) led the subjects to see the pestered person as less blameworthy than the typical murderer . . . with the intention to kill. There is, unfortunately, the possibility that the respondents "read into" the case some degree of threat in the beggar's behavior or believed that the person who shot the beggar felt such a threat. (p. 57)

If we extrapolate this to *Goetz*, the jurors could easily "read *threat* into" the situation of four "noisy and boisterous" teenagers, their demand for money, and 15 to 20 frightened passengers huddled at the far end of the subway car (Fletcher, 1988, p. 1). If so, then the jurors might have mitigated to the point of exculpation if Goetz was mistaken about the imminence of the threat and the retreat possibility.

The retreat issue is highly pertinent, particularly when battered women kill their sleeping partners. The most frequently asked question about the killing (and the relationship) is, But why didn't she just leave? Though P. H. Robinson and Darley (1995) did not test this situation, they did find a sizable mitigation of liability when the D could retreat safely from his or her own home or was mistaken about whether he or she could retreat.

Mistakes About the Seriousness and Imminence of the Threat

In *Grainger v. State* (1830), the D was described as "a timid, cowardly man," who killed "a reckless bully" named Broach, believing that Broach was going to kill him; however, the court concluded that it "is equally certain to our minds that Broach only designed to commit trespass and battery to the body of Grainger, without intending to kill him" (R. Singer, 1987, pp. 461–462). In an "objective reality" view, Grainger was not facing a serious, imminent threat to his life, and therefore his self-defense claim should fail. But the court ruled for him, holding that Grainger's belief must be viewed subjectively, showing that even an unreasonable belief of danger can sustain a self-defense claim.

In *Grainger*, objective and subjective perspectives collided, and subjectivity won. The *Grainger* court seemed to be upholding Blackstone's subjective position in his *Commentaries* (1765–1769/1779) that "mistake" was a "defect of will," and that wherever there was a mistake, "the deed and the will acting separately, there is not that conjunction between them, which is necessary to form a criminal act" (p. 27). Blackstone was restating Sir Matthew Hale's (1678/1972) earlier formulation that an act done in ignorance or mistake of the true facts was morally involuntary, which would excuse all mistakes, reasonable and unreasonable.

The *Grainger* case foreshadowed troubles yet to come. If the D's subjectivity is the sole determiner of the requisites of a self-defense claim, then all self-defense claims ought to succeed no matter how unreasonable (or even delusional) the mistake may be. If we carry this subjectivity to its extreme, there would be no difference between mistaken self-defense and insanity, save for how the exoneration gets labeled. *Grainger* also prefigured the transformations that the "objective average reasonable man" would be subjected to: although later courts would take size, power, and gender differences between V and D into account when it came to judging the seriousness of the threat, *Grainger* infused the exemplar with character traits that are far from exemplary or average, such as cowardice, timidity, or a particularly traumatic history. Such an exemplar is not just subjectively transformed, it is transmogrified.

Something like that seems to have happened in the Georgia case of *Monroe v. State* (1848), in which "the defendant, having been threatened and beaten by the victim at an earlier time, simply lay in wait for the victim" (R. Singer, 1987, p. 480) and preemptively struck; the court, adopting a subjective test, "held, nevertheless, that this could be self defense," though the "serious threat" and "imminence" requirements could be satisfied only if the "objective, average, reasonable person" (p. 480) had been infused with the history and passions of Monroe, thereby becoming atypical and unreasonable. *Monroe* foreshadowed a problem that arose later in cases in which a battered woman kills her sleeping batterer—where the emotion may be anger and the motive may be revenge, and where a focus on the reasonableness or unreasonableness of the mistake may misdirect the law from examining the honesty (or dishonesty) of the intent driving the act.

The objective backlash had to come, and in *Shorter v. People* (1849), the New York Court of Appeals excoriated *Grainger's* subjective approach. Perhaps the Law feared that jurors would yield too readily to subjectivity and would fail to make distinctions they should make, acquitting one and all. With *Shorter*, objective reality was back, and so was the "reasonable versus unreasonable" mistakes distinction, wherein the former exonerated but the latter did not. The problems with this distinction were with drawing a defensible line between the two types of mistakes and with treating the unreasonably mistaken actor as a murderer.

When we examine the empirical evidence on threats, community sentiment makes graded discriminations. According to P. H. Robinson and Darley (1995), as the unarmed attacker's threat becomes less serious and more trivial, liability increases, whereas the "legal doctrine adopts a simple cutoff," such that if "the approacher threatens serious bodily injury, the attacked person is granted a complete defense. If less than serious bodily injury is threatened, murder liability is imposed" (p. 58). Finkel et al. (1995) empirically tested "mistaken self-defense cases," in which the "mistake" went from "reasonable" to "dubious" to "unreasonable" to "delusional." They created a highly simplified version of *People v. Goetz* (1986), in which one teenager stands over a Mr. Jones, pulls a gun and points it at Mr. Jones's head, and demands $5; Mr. Jones reaches into his jacket, pulls his gun, fires, and kills the youth.

This was Finkel et al.'s so-called true self-defense condition, which served as a baseline, though only 62.5% of their mock jurors gave an NGRSD verdict; the 37.5% who gave a guilty verdict did not see the killing meeting the necessary requirement, citing the fact that other options short of deadly force could have been tried, such as showing his gun, or firing a warning shot.

Their "reasonable mistake" condition was the same as their true self-defense condition, except the police discover that the teenager's pistol was a plastic toy gun. Thus, what subjectively appeared, *ex ante*, as a real threat justifying the deadly response, turns out, in hindsight (*ex post*), not to be a serious threat in the objective sense. But if subjectivity is what matters, and this D honestly and reasonably believed he was facing a serious and imminent threat, then the NGRSD percentage should be the same as in the true self-defense condition. It is curious that the NGRSD percentage here (78.6%) was higher than it was in the true self-defense condition. A sympathy–leniency effect was found, as many respondents wrote that this man will have to live with his guilt the rest of his life, and that he has been "punished enough."

In the "dubious mistake" condition, the teenager asks for $5, but has no weapon in his hand,

> although he seems to be reaching into his pocket; Mr. Jones fires and kills, and tells the police he thought the kid was going for a gun. Hindsight reveals that the teenager had no weapon, only some note cards saying, "Thank you for giving to a homeless person." In this version, subjectivity is increased because the perceived threat lies further in Mr. Jones' mind, as the objective tie to a gun, even a toy gun, is eliminated. (Finkel et al., 1995, pp. 603–604)

The NGRSD percentage drops to 25% for this condition.

In the "unreasonable mistake" condition, the teenager asks for $5 but makes no move; Jones kills, claiming that he thought the kid was going to kill him, though no weapon is found. Here, the threat lies even further back in Jones's mind, as objective indicia of threat are almost completely removed, and the NGRSD percentage drops to 4%. Finally, in the "delusional mistake" condition, the teenager is sitting across from Jones doing a crossword puzzle, now and again stabbing his pencil into his newspaper, and occasionally making eye contact with Mr. Jones, who fires and kills, telling police he believed the boy was planning to kill him, and the looks and pencil stabs were a warning sign that the end was near, so he fired to save himself. This D's claim is rejected completely, with the NGRSD percentage at 0%.

In this experiment, mock jurors were given no history on Mr. Jones, which contrasts with what the jurors received in regard to Bernhard Goetz. Without such sensitizing, these mock jurors seemed to require clear, objective, and reasonable signs of threat. Moreover, they drew distinctions among types of mistakes, and even in our baseline condition they saw alternatives to the necessity to act. In other words, they showed no strong predilection to plunge unrestrained into subjectivity; rather, they seemed anchored in the objective reality.

However, our reasonable mistake condition results suggest that we could have created even harder reasonable mistake variants, not just situations in which many or even most would have made the mistake, but situations in which almost every reasonable person would have made the mistake: for example, consider a variation in which the teenager had a real gun and was starting to squeeze the trigger when Mr. Jones quickly reached for his gun and fired, but as it turned out there were no bullets in the teenager's gun, or the firing mechanism was not working, such that Mr. Jones could not have been killed (i.e., "an impossible act" case). If Mr. Jones had been a police officer in this variation, this shooting would have been judged to be justifiable, so why not if Mr. Jones was a private citizen carrying a licensed firearm? What we are driving at is that both a true self-defense case and a mistaken self-defense case *that every reasonable person would make* must involve the subjective factors of perception and judgment. Hence the *ex ante* versus *ex post* distinction of calling the former *justification* and the latter *excuse* makes no sense, from a psychological perspective, because the seriousness and imminence of the threat, psychologically, are identical in both conditions.

Mistakes About Proportionate Responding

When batterers start to strangle their wives with their hands, or begin beating them with their fists or kicking them with their feet, courts in decades past did not view hands, fists, or feet as serious threats, and therefore if battered women picked up a knife or a gun and killed their spouses, their self-defense claim would likely fail because their deadly response was seen as disproportionate. To those who claimed that the law was biased against women who kill their mates, these legal rulings confirmed their assertion. But so did criminological evidence (Wolfgang, 1958), which showed that most women who got killed in battering relationships died from hands, fists, and feet.

The landmark case of *State v. Wanrow* (1977) gave recognition to the psychological fact that a woman was not likely to "duke it out" with a man who came at her with fists raised; rather, as the *Wanrow* court held, women were not acculturated to physically fight when threatened, but rather were socially trained to either submit to the beating or resort to deadly force. This case seemed to throw out the "proportionate responding" requirement by subjectivizing the reasonable person standard to take into account not only gender, size, and power differentials (i.e., Wanrow, a small woman on crutches because of a broken foot, shot a much larger man whom she believed was about to sexually molest her children) but also the way most women are socialized in terms of physical violence.

The actual case facts, however, suggest that unwholesome motives may have been operating. It seems Wanrow had invited the V to her house early one morning, and had two male friends ready in her driveway to "straighten him out." But she chose to let him into her house at 5 a.m., leaving the male friends outside; the children and another woman friend were inside with Wanrow who was armed with a small pistol. Furthermore, it was not clear that the V made any move toward the children or toward her when she shot him. These facts leave open the possibility that this was a setup, and a preemptive strike.

Still, an empirical question remains as to whether citizens countenance disproportionate force. P. H. Robinson and Darley (1995), whose experiment had respondents rate the maximum force that was permissible for each scenario, wrote,

> These ratings of the maximum force allowable are consistent with the subjects' judgments of liability and (we would suggest) probably provide the basis for those judgments. . . . This suggests that the respondents are arriving at some global judgment—based on the set of facts they read—about what would constitute a reasonable action in the case, comparing the person's action and judging liability from the degree of discrepancy between the person's action and the "reasonable" action. Again, this view contrasts with the simple cutoff approach of current codes. Under the Model Penal Code, for example, only a threat of serious bodily injury or greater justifies the use of deadly force; a lesser threat justifies only the use of force short of deadly force. (pp. 59–60)

These results suggest a global and psychological reading of the situation and a greater leeway regarding deadly force. However, the findings of Finkel, Meister, and Lightfoot (1991) are directly on point when it comes to the disproportionate deadly force question. In their experiment, they had three confrontation killing conditions, in which the battered woman is cornered by the batterer, and in each condition she kills with a gun, but in the first condition he comes at her with a gun (thus, she responds with equal force), whereas in the second and third conditions he comes at her with a knife and his fists, respectively, and thus these are disproportionate response conditions. Her NGRSD percentages in the three conditions were 80%, 78%, and 71%, and the differences were not significant; thus it did not matter to respondents whether her deadly force response was exactly equal. Respondents saw his fists and the knife as deadly threats, more or less equivalent to her gun, contrary to what earlier court rulings held.

THE REASONABLE PERSON ACTING UNREASONABLY BECAUSE OF A PSYCHIATRIC SYNDROME

As we claimed earlier, when *Grainger* (1830) took the D's mental state into account, this highly subjective approach foreshadowed psycholegal developments to come. We now consider such a development: What happens when the objective reasonable person is subjectivized in ways that affect each requirement of self-defense, and the exemplar now has a psychiatric syndrome that affects the entire context of events? The particular syndrome in focus is battered woman syndrome (BWS). BWS evidence has been admitted in many cases for more than 2 decades (Schuller, 2003), and a significant amount of empirical research on this syndrome and on how mock jurors respond to this testimony has been done. But though our focal question concerns whether BWS testimony helps to sustain a justification claim for nonconfrontational killings, as advocates hope, or whether this is an excuse claim masquerading as justification, as we believe, we wish to note that syndrome testimony per se is not gender specific. For example, a clever attorney could attempt to enter syndrome evidence in a Goetz-type case, arguing that the D had posttraumatic stress disorder, that having been mugged produced symptoms (e.g., chronic anxiety, fears, and obsessions over being mugged in the future) that colored the D's perceptions and judgments of the events, and his reactions to them.

Battered Woman Syndrome Testimony:
A Justification Strategy Contradictorily Pulling Toward Excuse

Lenore Walker (1979, 1984), who coined the term *battered woman syndrome*, used the term not just to describe the pattern of violence battered women experience, but in a clinical way, as a syndrome, a subcategory of posttraumatic stress disorder. Walker used *cycle of violence* and *learned helplessness* as theoretical constructs to explain the woman's psychological paralysis, passivity, and depression, and why she believes that leaving will not work. Many advocates for battered women pleading self-defense in nonconfrontational killings initially greeted the admissibility of BWS testimony with jubilation, seeing this "as a landmark victory for battered women" (Schuller, 2003, p. 226). However, some feminist scholars began to worry because BWS testimony accented women's victimization instead of showing how their actions could be a "normal" response to the situation (e.g., Schneider, 1986), whereas other feminists saw this "excuse" as stigmatizing, demeaning, and promoting a "misogynist defense" (Coughlin, 1994, p. 70). Although the intent of BWS testimony is to contextualize and normalize her psyche and behavior, many feel that it ends up pathologizing it, for it offers not an explanation of why she acted reasonably in the circumstances—but of why she acted unreasonably.

Finkel (2003) argued that BWS is not a *justification* defense, but an *excuse* defense wrapped in the guise of a justification defense. The mistake-of-fact defense is more similar to insanity than to justification, for the focus in justification is on the reasonableness of those mistakes, given the objective circumstances; in this instance, to the contrary, the expert claims that the D's mistaken perceptions and beliefs are not what they would be for non-BWS individuals. The "reasonable person" standard is thus inapt, for this person is not reasonable. As Schulhofer (1990) has noted, some claim that what she is, and what the standard ought to be, is the "reasonable battered woman." But what would such a new and different norm and standard convey? Would it mean that her killing, when evaluated against the reference subgroup of battered women, is reasonable? This interpretation is demonstrably false, for studies of battered women (e.g., Browne, 1987) show that most do not kill their batterers. And the dictionary meaning of *reasonable* certainly contradicts what we have here. So in what sense can this nonconfrontational killing by a woman with BWS be said to be reasonable?

Empirical Evidence on the Effects of Expert Testimony and on Battered Woman Syndrome

From the late 1980s to the present, empirical researchers have done a number of mock juror and mock jury experiments in which they have manipulated cases, expert testimony, and verdict options while controlling extraneous variance, so that causal effects could be assessed. These findings, overall, have refuted notions that jurors are biased against women who killed their spouses, biased against giving such Ds a self-defense verdict, or predisposed toward the insanity verdict (e.g., Follingstad et al., 1989; Greenwald, Tomkins, Kenning, & Zavodny, 1990; Finkel et al., 1991). When comparing BWS cases with insanity cases, there is much more support for battered women who kill, even when they kill in nonconfrontational situations. For example, in Finkel et al. (1991), although in their two nonconfrontational conditions (called "sleep" and "awake") the NGRSD verdicts dropped to 45% and 42%, respectively (compared with 80% in "gun," 78% in "knife," and 71% in "fists," their confrontational killing conditions), these NGRSD percentages were still the highest among all of their verdict options. However, the first-degree murder (FDM) and second-degree murder (SDM) verdict percentages did not rise, as might be expected; rather, voluntary manslaughter (VM) rose, which was surprising, given that this mitigating and lenient verdict did not fit the facts of the case, and the two "mentally ill" verdicts, guilty but mentally ill (GBMI) and NGRI, also rose. Punitive sentiments (e.g., FDM and SDM) did not show; rather, mitigating (e.g., VM and GBMI) and exculpating sentiments showed (NGRI and NGRSD), even if some of these verdicts (e.g., VM and NGRSD) did not fit the legal requirements for those verdicts.

But the expert testimony conditions did not have a significant effect on verdict in either Follingstad et al. (1989) or Finkel et al.'s (1991) experiments, although in the latter experiment, the researchers demonstrated that expert opinion did affect mock jurors' views of the D: they saw her as more distorted in her thinking, less capable of making responsible choices, and less culpable for her actions—findings that suggest that the expert testimony may "shift mock jurors' perceptions closer to the diminished capacity and insane portraits" (Finkel et al., 1991, p. 598). This finding recurred in the experimental work of Kasian, Spanos, Terrance, and Peebles (1993), and these researchers concluded that such testimony "is likely to be useful only under circumstances where the sanity of the defendant is called into question" (p. 309). Schuller's (1992) research found a verdict effect for expert testimony, toward greater leniency, and in subsequent work, Schuller (2003) stated that "there were also indications in the data that the presence of the testimony may foster interpretations of psychological instability" (p. 239). Finally, the empirical evidence shows that only when a nullification instruction was given (e.g., Schuller & Hastings, 1996; Schuller & Rzepa, 2002) or when an instruction allowed jurors to consider a psychological self-defense (e.g., Greenwald et al., 1990)—instructions that no court would endorse— do we find expert testimony moving verdicts toward self-defense. Still, these effects are more consistent with a "sympathy" interpretation for the plight of the battered woman and less so with a "justification" interpretation.

A growing amount of research about the BWS construct also raises some troubling questions. In a review of Lenore Walker's (1979) interviews with battered women, Schopp, Sturgis, and Sullivan (1994) found that the majority of women said to have BWS experienced neither the "cycle of violence" nor low self-esteem, nor did they hold the traditional attitudes about marriage and divorce that these syndrome women were said to hold; to the contrary, many saw themselves stronger and more independent, and their values were found to be less traditional than those of nonbattered women (Faigman, 1986). In terms of the alleged symptoms of passivity and depression, the inability to plan, and the belief that they could not control their batterers, Follingstad, Hause, Rutledge, and Polek (1992) found that most battered women who were still in long-term or short-term battering relationships, or those who got out, started to make plans to leave when the earliest of batterings began, and most believed that they could control, to some degree, the batterer's violence, and these women did not describe themselves as passive or depressed. Finally, the "learned helplessness" construct did not appear to fit the majority of these women either (Schopp et al., 1994). In sum, the BWS construct may be badly flawed or, at best, may fit only a small minority of battered women.

These findings raise scientific and legal questions regarding the BWS construct—as to whether the construct is flawed, and whether it has been accepted by courts prematurely. Second, as a matter of applicability, this syndrome appears to fit only a small minority of battered women. Third, from mock juror experiments, there is no evidence that BWS testimony moves jurors toward the NGRSD verdict under nonnullification instructions, but much more evidence that it gets jurors to see "diminished capacity." Fourth, there are strategic questions as to whether this defense is contradicting and undercutting itself, trying to promote a reasonable justification defense but presenting a pathologizing excuse defense. And fifth, there are theoretical reasons for why trying to expand the contours of self-defense justification in this direction "is mostly wrong-headed," wrote Dressler (2002, p. 261). Still, the empirical evidence from mock juror experiments consistently shows sympathy for these Ds. It is time to look more closely at emotions, and the desire behind exculpation.

SYMPATHY FOR THE "VICTIM," RAGE AT THE "MORAL MONSTER," AND EXCULPATING SENTIMENTS

One of the themes running through this work is "variance," and this chapter is no exception. Even hard cases, in which a woman kills her batterer in a nonconfrontational setting, generate more sympathy and a higher percentage of NGRSD verdicts in mock juror experiments than do the less sympathetic insanity cases. We also find variance when it comes to the propensity to violence, for battered women who kill, in contrast to insanity acquittees, turn out to be some of the least violent offenders in terms of either their past history of violence or their likelihood of committing future violent acts (e.g., Browne, 1987). And variance extends to emotions, as we have noted, for whereas insanity Ds are often propelled by a variety of emotions that are often difficult to comprehend, fear is what we generally cite in self-defense cases, and when we learn about the battered woman's life with "that monster," we understand her fear.

Finally, we have noted great variance among battered women in their psychological state, as not all battered women, not even a majority, had BWS. And there is considerable variance in the way battered women kill. According to Ewing's (1987) data, approximately 33% of battered women kill in confrontational settings, where BWS testimony would not be needed because these are straightforward justification claims. On the least sympathetic extreme, accounting for approximately 6% of the killings, are battered women who hire someone to kill their batterers; in these cases prosecutors typically bring first-degree murder charges. Then in approximately 40% of the killings the battered woman is not passive but quite active: she files for divorce, moves out, and gets an order of protection, but she is repeatedly pursued and beaten by her spouse, and ultimately kills him in desperation. And then there are the 21% who kill while the batterer is asleep or watching television, but even within this group there is variance, for here the emotions may range far beyond fear.

Moral Forfeiture for a Moral Monster?

Among self-defense lines, there is variance between the cases of battered women who kill and the historic lines of felony prevention and chance medley–*se defendendo*, which are typically stranger confrontations between men. The battered woman who kills stands in contrast, for she kills within a relationship, with a history, and from a context deeper and longer than the moment of the act. Moreover, the testimony at trial is likely to arouse strong feelings: the deceased is easily cast as the villain while the D gets the role of V, and jurors may believe that the V got what he deserved. This construction, along with the emotions that follow, probably account for mock jurors' sympathetic NGRSD verdicts in nonconfrontational killings, even when those conditions would not warrant that justification verdict.

Dressler (2002) wrote about "an implicit acceptance of the moral theory of forfeiture, namely, that a person by his wilful, egregious conduct may forfeit his right to life; therefore, termination of his life constitutes no socially recognized harm to society" (p. 270). But as Dressler noted, an individual has no right under Anglo-American law to decide that someone has forfeited the right to live and can therefore be squashed like a bug; nor should jurors decide on this basis, because the law holds that each of us, the saint and the sinner, has an equal claim to the preservation of life "simply because life itself is an irreducible value" (p. 271). Moral forfeiture suggests the contrary:

> that human life is expendable. . . . The logic of an unvarnished version of the forfeiture principle is that a battered woman has a moral claim against her abuser, *in infinitum*. She—or others at her behest—may kill him at any time. Consider a battered woman who hires a contract killer to take her husband's life, and then asserts self-defence. No court has allowed such a claim to go to the jury, but the logic of forfeiture suggests otherwise. (p. 271)

In a battering relationship case, jurors may not be restricting either their context to just the events surrounding the moment of the act or their culpability analysis to just whether her actions meet the requisite elements of justification. Our hunch, here, is drawn from Finkel et al.'s (1991) finding that a significant predictor of mock jurors' verdicts was their rating on a construct variable identified as "other," where respondents were weighing the V's culpability along with the D's—which is not what ought to be done under black-letter law. This finding raises a possibility different from moral forfeiture: it suggests that respondents see this "criminal case" more like a civil or tort case, with "plaintiff" and "tortfeasor," weighing culpability of two individuals against one another. If this is what some jurors are doing, then the batterer's considerable culpability, particularly in a wider context, surely mitigates her culpability. Still, with our focus narrowed to battered women who kill under nonconfrontational conditions, the question remains, "Can a reasonable justification claim be put forth?"

Can a "Reasonable" Justification Claim Be Made?

In our opinion, the best attempt at a justification defense for nonconfrontational killings has been made by Schopp et al. (1994), who make no use of BWS testimony at all. Instead, they rely on ordinary witnesses to present factual testimony regarding the battered woman's persistent efforts to seek protection and escape from the documented horrors of her batterer. If it could be shown that her repeated calls for help to the police went for naught, that her efforts to obtain restraining orders were thwarted, and that her efforts to find a safe harbor secured none (i.e., that alternatives were not available to her), then Schopp et al. claimed that if it could also be shown that it was immediately necessary for her to use deadly force when she did, then a justification claim could fit for those particular battered women.

This justification claim is not without problems, though. For one, the burden of proving that persistent efforts were made to find alternatives and that alternatives were either unavailable or unresponsive in the objective reality is unlikely to be met, in most cases. A second problem is that Schopp et al.'s (1994) justification argument does not eliminate the subjective. And a third problem is that it relies on psychological predictions that are speculative, for humans "sometimes defy predictions" (Dressler, 2002, p. 275). As Finkel (2003) explained, Schopp et al.'s

> justification defense . . . involves a reasonable belief that no alternatives existed, at the time when another reasonable belief was formed and acted upon that there was a necessity to use deadly force. These two "reasonable beliefs" in the sentence must involve the defendant's subjectivity and the objective facts, [being] . . . a quasi-objective, quasi-subjective judgment, as all judgments must be. (p. 206)

On the basis of her past experiences, the D makes a prediction that another call to the police would be futile, but this prediction may be an underestimation, whereas her prediction that her husband will beat her severely or even kill her when he wakes up may be an overestimation. Yet Schopp et al. (1994) argued that, in light of what has been documented in the past, these predictions are reasonable and not unduly subjectively distorted. But there is no getting around the fact that these are still predictions (guesses), and reasonable outside evaluators may disagree with the D's conclusions; some may regard them as honest but reasonable mistakes or even as honest but unreasonable mistakes.

But in trying to base their justification defense on objective facts that make the conduct "acceptable under the circumstances" (1994, p. 106), Schopp et al. presented the following example, which we find objectionable, because it raises the possibility of a "*dishonest* but reasonable mistake of fact":

> Suppose, for example, Jones accurately believes that her batterer will beat her severely, as he has previously, when he awakens from his drunken stupor. Jones attempts to call the police, but discovers that the January blizzard preventing her from leaving her isolated farmhouse has also blown down the telephone lines, preventing her from securing legal assistance. Jones responds to this discovery with malevolent glee, realizing that these

circumstances create actual necessity because the forthcoming beating is virtually certain, she will be unable to defend herself at that time, and legal assistance is not available. She plunges a kitchen knife into her batterer's chest, delighted by the opportunity to exploit the justificatory circumstances. (pp. 105–106)

Though Schopp et al. may believe this self-defense claim is valid, Fletcher (1988) would disagree, we believe, because he listed as a requirement that "the defender must act with the *intention* not of hurting the V per se, but of thwarting the attack" (p. 19). From our vantage point, Jones could have plunged the knife into her batterer's leg and then tied him up, thereby thwarting her own demise without killing him. She had options, in other words, contrary to what Schopp et al. maintained, and she had time to think of other options. But her "malevolent glee" to do him in reveals a calculated, deliberate, and dishonest intent to take advantage of the situation. Schopp et al. may believe that she gets a justificatory free ride based on the fortuitous appearance of most (but not all) of self-defense's requirements, but we do not.

FASHIONING AN EXCUSING DEFENSE, AND DEFAULT OPTIONS

If the D found no safe harbors and the law repeatedly failed to protect her safety, and she also came to believe that it was immediately necessary to kill the sleeping batterer when she did, we believe that these conditions and subjective conclusions best fit an excusing defense, not one of justification. Professor Joshua Dressler (2002) also saw this as an excusing or partially excusing defense, and he has analogized the battered woman under like circumstances to someone under duress, who may have a "no-fair-opportunity" (p. 277) to exhibit free choice. Finkel (2003) also saw these facts as amounting to an excusing defense, but he based his conclusion, in part, on psychological findings that have been recognized by a few courts (e.g., *State v. Kelly*, 1984; *People v. Torres*, 1985) regarding some battered women's keen abilities to recognize when violence is likely to escalate from small subtle changes in tone of voice or facial expression.

Finkel (2003) then analogized the battered woman's predictions to psychologists' predictions of risk assessment. For example, if the D's prediction of serious danger turns out to be an honest overestimation, and if her prediction of escape options turns out to be an honest underestimation, she is nonetheless making the sort of honest mistakes that the best psychologists sometimes make when performing risk assessments that are routinely accepted by courts, even though the experts do not have the extensive first-hand experiences in making their predictions that the D does. If we are willing to excuse the experts' honest efforts, why not the D's? But *excuse* is the key word. We would not applaud her act, as felony prevention was once applauded, and we would not see her act as doing the right thing. This type of excusing defense would be very different from insanity, for there is no insinuation that she is mad or is incapable of making response-able choices.

The Need for Default Options

The need for default options becomes apparent through the following question: if the jurors believe that her mistakes were honest but unreasonable, or worse, careless or reckless, would she lose everything and be treated as a first-degree murderer, a verdict that does not appear to fit her *mens rea* and culpability? However, R. Singer (1987), a subjectivist, argued that honest but unreasonable mistakes ought to excuse, because the D is caught in the maelstrom of circumstance, seeking "merely to achieve in whatever way possible the termination of the threat." To say that she "'intends' or 'purposes' death would be a fiction, for she did not intend (purpose) a killing" (p. 515).

But Fletcher (1988) rejected Singer's approach, claiming that subjectivists are confused about "the nature of blameworthiness," seeming "to think that guilt and blame must be mirrored in the offender's thoughts" (p. 61). Fletcher argued that the "basis for all blaming is not the offender's thoughts, but our judgment about whether he could and should have acted otherwise under the circumstances" (Fletcher, 1988, p. 61). With a sleeping V, she is not caught in the maelstrom of a confrontational killing, for now she has time to think and consider other options, and has the capacity to do so. Fletcher, in our opinion, has the better of the argument, and CSJ seems to agree (e.g., Finkel et al., 1995): mock jurors rejected a completely subjective approach to mistakes, as they gave significant weight to the objective facts and the type of mistake made.

One of the earliest suggestions of a mitigating verdict appeared in East's (1803) *Pleas of the Crown*, in which he stated that if the D did not have "reasonable grounds for believing that the person slain had a felonious design against him" (p. 273), this should be treated as manslaughter, but R. Singer (1987) noted that East's citations for this position were "not persuasive" (p. 475). In the 20th century, the mitigating category of "imperfect" or "putative self-defense" arose, and under the Model Penal Code's (American Law Institute, 1962) provisions, "if the defendant has been reckless or negligent in reaching a conclusion about a set of facts, the defendant can be prosecuted for either reckless or negligent homicide" (R. Singer, 1987, p. 504); the former equates with manslaughter, but the latter is punished less severely. But for Ds such as the hypothetical Jones, jurors may want to slide all the way to a murder verdict, because she deliberately intended to kill her sleeping husband and used the mistake of "no other options" as a justificatory pretext for murder.

When jurors cannot find among a restricted array of verdicts the one that accurately reflects their culpability judgment for the D, their choice is not likely to do justice for the D *and* the Law. For example, when they do not have an appropriate excusing condition option, jurors may reconstrue the justification defense (i.e., NGRSD) out of sympathy for the D, or may pick that other excusing option (i.e., NGRI), if it is available, though neither option fits the facts. And if they do not have an appropriate partial excusing default option, they may be forced to render a murder verdict, though this is not likely to fit. Self-defense law has yet to accommodate, in theory or with appropriate options, a third line of relationship cases involving "mistakes," as we still have "poorly tailored crimes" with "ill-fitting verdicts," a legal wardrobe "too bare to clothe all the sizes and situations that appear in court" (Finkel, 2003, p. 208).

LOOKING BACK, AND LOOKING FORWARD

We began considering self-defense's "justification" with prototypical cases, and found clarity in the Law's theory and a consistency between BLL and CSJ. But once we introduced "mistake" into these cases, the line between justification and excuse began to blur, and disparities between BLL and CSJ reemerged. Mistakes expose a fault line (and false hope) within the Law: that we can neatly separate justification and excuse defenses because the former focus on the objective act and its *ex post* "good outcome," whereas the latter focus on the subjectivity of the actor and the *ex ante* intent. This is a mistake, as this fault line cracks.

Alleged self-defense cases, whether they be true self-defense or putative self-defense cases, must involve Ds subjectively perceiving and interpreting objective events within a context. As this process is psychological, it involves both objective and subjective factors. In making our point, we created a thought experiment involving a mistaken self-defense case in which every person would make the mistake, and in which this *ex ante* mistake variation could not be discriminated from the true self-defense case (*ex post*) based on the objective facts. If this mistake case is regarded as an excuse while the true self-defense case is deemed a justification—on grounds that only the Divine could have realized—then the distinction fails.

The psychology of perception and apperception, as Kant well knew (T. M. Greene, 1957), conjoins the subjective and objective, though the weighting of the two can surely shift for different Ds, and the balance point can thus slide for the jurors. When the Law examines a particular case, it breaks it down to specific elements. In self-defense, those elements concern whether the threat was serious and imminent, whether retreat was possible, whether deadly force was necessary and proportionate, and whether the intent was to end the threat. But empirical evidence strongly suggests that CSJ looks at a self-defense situation by making a more global judgment (P. H. Robinson & Darley, 1995) rather than considering specific requisite elements and definitive cutoffs. Still, this global judgment is not some gestalt that cannot be further reduced, for we find that it has its own elements and factors. For example, when it comes to battered women who kill a sleeping batterer, mock jurors see the situation more subjectively and contextually, opening up the time frame to consider her history with the batterer and with the law, and they may weigh his culpability along with hers in reaching their ultimate determination (Finkel, 1995b).

But CSJ does not yield to an unrestrained subjectivity. To the contrary, CSJ makes fine objective discriminations beyond the Law's crude "reasonable versus unreasonable" mistake distinction, with many gradations along a mistake continuum. Not only is mistake more finely graded but the type of mistake and the moral intent behind the mistake are weighed, as CSJ will question whether a mistake was an honest or dishonest one.

Some of these CSJ distinctions appear theoretically worthy of inclusion in self-defense law, though unwholesome sentiments, such as moral forfeiture, ought not to be. This is not just a matter of reconciling the disparity between BLL and CSJ, but of achieving coherence among the Law's culpability theories, a matter we shall examine in our next chapter. But beyond theory, the Law has a pragmatic interest in preventing nullifications or having legal instructions reconstrued beyond their meaning. Yet those may be the unenviable results when jurors do not have the verdict options they seek— such as a true excusing defense and appropriate default options. The Law, we argue, needs to alter its poorly tailored crimes and its ill-fitting verdict options for the line of cases in which neither justification nor murder seem fitting.

III

CONCLUDING THOUGHTS: PSYCHOLOGY'S INFORMING FUNCTION

11

MOVING THE LAW TOWARD A COHERENT EMOTION AND CULPABILITY STORY

In a galaxy far away from Psychology and Law, theoretical physicists ponder interrelated questions about the nature of this space the universe inflates in—once Time began—and what the universe's smallest fundamental elements are (B. Greene, 2004). Physicists looking at the vast expansiveness of this universe theorize about the very fabric of spacetime, which provides their in-the-beginning story with background context, gravity's woof and warp, and a direction to time's arrow; physicists looking to the smallest units of matter theorize about vibrating string patterns, which bring their in-the-beginning story to life. Yet the theories of the infinite and the infinitesimal do not cohere. That is why physicists seek a grand unifying theory, laws that govern strings and stars, gravitons and galaxies, and incorporate the very fabric of spacetime. This passionate search for theoretical coherence within physics contrasts with what we find within the Law, which lets stand contradictory theories of emotion and culpability.

227

THREE MAJOR THEMES

In this chapter, we strive toward a coherent story of emotion and culpability, borrowing some notions from physics to use analogously. The particular notions, as we label them, are *psychological spacetime*, *determinative elements*, and *relativistic perspective*. In regard to *psychological spacetime*, we draw the following conclusions: first, the Law's culpability stories (i.e., for its different crimes, defenses, and doctrines) are, at times, inconsistent and contradictory, revealing a lack of a coherent, unifying theory of emotions. Second, these inconsistent emotion theories appear to rest on an underlying psychological theory that has been characterized (Haney, 2002) as "psychological individualism" (p. 5), which was rooted in 19th-century notions that are "markedly at odds with the approach of contemporary psychology" (p. 7), which "now embraces a largely social contextual model of human nature" (p. 4). And third, the Law's theories foreshorten psychological spacetime.

Our prior analyses of the Law's treatment of time (e.g., in murder, manslaughter, insanity, and self-defense) have shown that these stories typically narrow culpability considerations down to the moment of the act, which freezes time in a still-life snapshot. This narrowing has a distorting effect on a story, for it reduces a moving full-length drama to the last scene of Act V and reduces subjectivity's complexity to triviality. The criminal law's treatment of space, be it interpersonal or intrapsychic, is similarly limited. As a result, a number of relevant factors that may appear in background scenes, in the culpable actions of others, or in the defendant's emotions, motives, morals, fateful decisions, and deeper capacity are generally not given consideration, or, if considered, not given proper weight.

By contrast, the dimensional threads of space and time interweave for physicists and psychologists, as they do in the stories of citizen–jurors, novelists, and dramatists. But these interwoven threads of space and time unravel in the Law's stories, and each dimension is foreshortened to a minimalist tale. These stories, we maintain, fail to validly represent the complexity of reality and human nature.

In regard to our second notion, the determinative elements, the criminal law's "periodic table" has traditionally had but two elements, *actus reus* and *mens rea*, the first reflecting the objective criminal act, the second reflecting the subjective intent. Moreover, both must conjoin for guilt, or so the euphemism proclaims. The conclusion we draw from our analyses of the subjective element is that neither *mens rea* nor the Model Penal Code's (American Law Institute, 1962) *intent* can adequately carry the freight, albeit for somewhat different reasons. Intent, in our opinion, is the weaker and more superficial of the two subjective concepts, for it fails to reflect the full array of determinative elements that constitute our complex psychological nature, failing, for example, to integrate emotions within its theoretical ambit. This failure creates problems when the Code is forced to consider emotions in manslaughter cases under its extreme emotional disturbance formulation, for here emotions are left as dangling, disembodied psychic entities, unrelated to intentions in the interior psyche or to provocations in the objective reality. In broader terms, *intent* gives nary a hint of the motives that initiate and drive the act and give it moral meaning, a failure we shall soon illustrate.

Although the older and deeper *mens rea* concept does a better job than *intent* in terms of emotions, motives, and morals, it still lacks the depth to resolve the *Hadfield* (*Hadfield's Case*, 1800) problem that lies at the core of insanity, for Hadfield had *mens rea*, in the simplistic sense of knowing that killing and treason were legally wrong, but what he lacked was the capacity to connect those intentions, emotions, and motives with the shared background nexus; in regard to this problem, an intent analysis fails here as well. Thus, on theoretical and conceptual grounds, the Law's key subjective element fails, and on applied grounds, neither a *mens rea* nor an intent analysis matches well with the complex determinative elements we find in a commonsense justice (CSJ) analysis.

Before we turn to specifics, we return to physics for one more comparison to complete this overview of our three major themes. Just as Einstein's general theory of relativity provides the basis for our psychological spacetime analogue, now we invoke his special theory of relativity to make a more complex point. In his special theory of relativity, Einstein realized that two individuals (e.g., the actor and the observer) from different reference frames— one moving, which we shall call the *subjective perspective*, the other stationary, which we shall call the *objective perspective*—will not see the same event as simultaneous, though this effect (in the physical world) is dramatic only when the velocity of the moving actor approaches light speed. In the Einsteinian relativistic worldview, the answers the two actors give to measurements of time will vary, as will their perceptions of the event, and both accounts will be accurate and true from their respective, relative (subjective and objective) points of view. This analogous view seems to hold, at times, in the psychological and legal worlds, where actors and observers perceive, construe, and judge the same actions (e.g., manslaughter, insanity, self-defense, and mistake) differently—from their respective vantage points.

But as we said, when we move from the physical to the psychological– legal world, things get more uncertain and complex, for the normative side of the Law cannot be content with the physicist's relativistic position—in which a defendant is innocent from his or her perspective, but guilty from the objective perspective—for if both perspectives are equally valid, as the physicist claims, then all defendants would walk free. Such a position is intolerable for the Law, as there would be no point to trials, charges, or even a criminal law at all in such a relativistic universe. Under the Law, where a normative culpability judgment is rendered, objective and subjective perspectives must somehow be unified in a psychologically sane and normatively sound way. Yet it is our conclusion that such a grand unified theory of objectivity and subjectivity is nowhere in sight. Rather, what we find is a hodgepodge: either objectivity or subjectivity may dominate in different crimes, defenses, and doctrines, but the situation may flip-flop in the next century, or in a neighboring jurisdiction.

These three broad themes—regarding the story's psychological spacetime fabric, its fundamental elements, and how the perspectives of objectivity and subjectivity must unify—guide us as we seek to integrate our threads into a coherent culpability story. We begin this quest with a concrete, specific, and relativistic question left hanging from our discussion of insanity (see chap. 8, this volume): Why did a Virginia jury not give Malvo the death sentence, when another Virginia jury gave Muhammad the death sentence?

WHERE THE FUNDAMENTAL ELEMENT OF *INTENT* FAILS TO DISCRIMINATE

In *Malvo* (*Commonwealth of Virginia v. Lee Boyd Malvo*, 2003), the jurors rejected the defense's insanity claim, agreeing with the prosecution that Malvo was guilty for the crimes of murder and terrorism; but in the capital sentencing phase, that jury rejected the prosecution's argument for the death sentence. Now, perform the following thought experiment: imagine a hypothetical case with no Muhammad and in which Malvo acted alone, but like the original *Malvo*, this hypothetical also proffers an insanity defense, which the jury rejects. Having removed Muhammad from the picture, we believe that this hypothetical Malvo would get the death sentence, for if any 17-year-old deserves the death sentence, it is this defendant. The aggravating factors include the following: his crimes were motivated by hate and pecuniary gain; they were wanton and heinous; they spread terror throughout the region; and he is a future risk to the community if he should somehow get out of prison. If our speculation sounds about right for what another Virginia jury might consider, weigh, and do with this hypothetical Malvo, then the primary factor that spares the original Malvo the death sentence is not likely the juvenile factor, but more likely "the Muhammad factor": this "Other" (e.g., Muhammad), who was not objectively present but was psychologically present in *Malvo*, is the determinative factor, then, in the jury's psychological spacetime context. We shall explore what this factor means in a moment, but first a bit of background.

When the Law Sanctions a Wider Context—for the Last Judgment

We ordinarily think of the guilt determination as *the* culpability judgment, but when jurors make sentencing decisions a second culpability judgment occurs, and the death penalty decision is paradigmatic: in death-versus-life-imprisonment decisions, jurors must discriminate the most blameworthy (i.e., who warrant death) from those less so (i.e., who do not). In the guilt phase, the culpability context is narrowed tightly, as jurors are instructed to consider only the specific elements of the charges and whether the burden of proof has been met; in the death penalty phase, by contrast, the context is thrown wide open. For example, the tight moment-of-the-act focus broadens in both past and future directions, as the defendant's past priors and the future danger he poses may be weighed. In addition, certain motives may act as aggravating factors, whereas any and all aspects of his history or psyche may act as mitigating factors, and the weight and balance jurors give to aggravating and mitigating factors is left to their discretion.

Focusing on purposeful intent (i.e., the highest level of intent under the Model Penal Code [American Law Institute, 1962]), both Malvo and Muhammad purposefully intended to kill and terrorize, and this fundamental element does not discriminate the two. In light of this "equality," why didn't the *Malvo* jury follow the equalist position and give the same sentence as Muhammad? We suggest that certain CSJ distinctions involving first-degree, felony, and accessory-felony murderers, and between perpetrator-by-means and accessories, can shed light on the question. In mock juror research on felony murder (e.g., Finkel, 1990a; Finkel & Duff, 1991; Finkel & Smith, 1993; Finkel et al., 1997), the primary reason for the higher percentages of first-degree murder convictions and death sentences for the felony-murder triggerman than for the accessories was because the triggerman planned the crime, not because he pulled the trigger, for in some versions tested no trigger was pulled (e.g., a storekeeper dies of a heart attack at the sight of a gun): it was the triggerman's evil design, his instigation of the crime, and his manipulation of the others into the conspiracy that set in motion acts that led to a wrongful death, and which account for his greater punishment. And when we added the premeditated murderer for comparison, the percentages of convictions and death sentences jumped significantly higher, for this defendant's evil motive was clearly more culpable than the felony-murder triggerman's. Thus, if Muhammad was "psychologically present" in the jurors' minds, and if jurors were using CSJ and drawing such culpability distinctions, then it is easy to cast Muhammad as the planner and major perpetrator of these crimes, which leaves Malvo cast as the accessory, drawn into the conspiracy by Muhammad.

Another legal casting, "perpetrator by means," also fits, for Muhammad can be viewed as the main perpetrator who induces his puppet-like son Malvo to fire the shots. Still, whether we invoke the perpetrator-by-means versus the accessory analogue, or the premeditated murderer (or felony-murder triggerman) versus accessory analogue, the Other's culpability comes powerfully and comparatively into psychological spacetime (e.g., Finkel, Maloney, Valbuena, & Groscup, 1996), and thus into the set of determinative elements.

Once we admit Muhammad into psychological spacetime and into the story, Malvo assumes the accessory role, being different from either the hypothetical Malvo who acted alone and was the planner of the acts, or

Muhammad, the planner and major perpetrator. What is more, when Malvo is cast as the accessory–puppet, the 17-year-old factor and his vulnerability (short of insanity) are in play as well—for both Malvo's youth and his mental vulnerabilities are likely to play a mitigating part.

The differentiations between Muhammad and Malvo continue to grow when we consider their respective "emotions," which are likely to work in opposite aggravating and mitigating directions in the capital sentencing phase. For the perpetrator Muhammad, his "adult" emotions of hate and rage—at society and the shared background nexus of legal and moral notions and norms that the citizenry holds—likely add to our sense of his moral evil. In contrast, Malvo displays "juvenile" emotions, with their characteristic impetuosity and lack of foresight for the consequences, as this dependent foundling clings to the ideals of his "father." These juvenile emotions may engender mitigating pity. Thus, in our comparative story—with discriminable differences between Muhammad and Malvo as to who plans the evil and who is the underling, about who is the adult and who is the juvenile, about whose mental faculties are clear and whose are clouded, and about whose emotions are propelled by hate and rage and whose are mixed with love and devotion—it is not surprising that equalism is set aside in favor of proportional justice, where Malvo's blameworthiness is different from what "purposeful intent" predicts.

As our theory of emotion and culpability emerges, it is clear that we have added another fundamental element to the periodic table: the culpability of the Other. But we have also argued that the Model Penal Code's (American Law Institute, 1962) element of intent actually blurs appropriate distinctions between Muhammad and Malvo—in terms of the motives that drove the respective actors. In our theory, *motive* returns to the periodic table as a fundamental element, as Pillsbury (1998) recommended.

At this point, those in the Law would be quick to point out that the sentencing phase permits a far more expansive consideration of factors than does the guilt phase. This is true. Still, we have started with these expansive, sentencing considerations because these are often in jurors' minds during the narrower guilt phase, though such considerations in the guilt phase often have no legitimating outlet. We illustrate our proposition in the next subsection, where we return to the guilt phase to find a defendant who has rendered a last judgment, and where mock jurors pass judgment on what seems to be a very clear case of first-degree murder—but where the verdict, for most, is not first-degree murder.

Judging the Last Judgment—Euthanasia Cases at the Boundary of the Law

In experimental tests of right-to-die and euthanasia cases, Finkel, Hurabiell, and Hughes (1993a, 1993b) set up the following scenario, with multiple variations. A man carrying a duffel bag enters a hospital room where his wife is being kept alive by feeding tubes and machines—against her alleged wishes. In these scenarios, her mental competence varies, for she has either amyotrophic lateral sclerosis, lymph cancer, or Alzheimer's disease or is comatose, conditions that affect her mentation, consciousness, and competence differently, though in all cases the condition is chronic and irreversible. The husband has deliberated and premeditated for a week about what he is about to do, ever since a court turned down his request to have the feeding tubes removed so his wife could die (we also tested a condition in which he did not go to court). The hospital had opposed his wife's claim (or the husband's assertion of his wife's claim) of a right to die, and refused her wish that she be removed from tubes and machines (a wish that she had expressed either in a living will and verbally to two individuals including her doctor, or just verbally to two individuals including her doctor, or a wish she expressed to no one, though the husband claimed that he knew her wishes). We tested all of these variations. In the basic vignette, once the husband entered his wife's hospital room, he barred the door, took out a gun from his duffel bag, and purposefully shot and killed his wife. We set up these cases so that all the elements for a first-degree murder conviction seemed satisfied. To make the case even more damning for the defendant, we have him admit that he purposefully intended to take his wife's life and that he deliberated and premeditated the act.

Mock jurors rendered verdicts and gave their reasons. It is surprising that only 35.9% of the verdicts across all the variations were first-degree murder, whereas 25.4% were not guilty verdicts, with the remaining 38.7% being lesser offenses, which included second-degree murder, voluntary manslaughter, and involuntary manslaughter, with the majority of verdicts being voluntary manslaughter. These results strongly suggest that most mock jurors were either nullifying or partially nullifying the law, an interpretation that was confirmed when we examined their reasons for their verdicts. Some of the mock jurors saw the action as no crime at all, viewing this, rather, as a private matter falling outside the bounds of law, into which the law should not intrude. Others, at a slightly lesser extreme, acknowledged that the law had a place in this life-and-death matter, yet they thought the law was wrong and ought to be changed. Others saw the actor not as an actor, but merely as an extension of his wife, doing what she was physically unable to do for herself. Still others looked at the motivation for the act and saw a loving act, a merciful killing that ended her physical pain and psychological anguish. And even some whose verdict was first-degree murder wrote that they disagreed with the law but were following their oath to obey the law, yet they hoped the judge would show mercy in sentencing, even giving no sentence.

We highlight these results for a number of reasons. First, in contrast to the sanctioned death penalty phase of Malvo and Muhammad, these results occur in the narrow guilty phase, yet clearly the mock jurors' reasons convey that many factors beyond the sanctioned ones are determinative of their verdicts. Second, in these case variations, the husband's motives and emotions are perceived as antithetical to Muhammad's hate and rage, as many see the husband motivated by love and caring, which makes a huge difference, even an exculpatory difference to 25% of the participants. Our third point is that once again an Other (the wife) features prominently in the case: though the husband is the defendant being tried for first-degree murder, the wife's intentions and wishes become prime factors for many mock jurors, transforming the defendant into a "nonactor," akin to robotic arms and legs that simply bring about the death she wants but cannot physically effect herself. And fourth, once again we see that motive is a determinative factor, for a strict intent analysis or *mens rea* analysis fails to grasp the psychological complexities of culpability, as many citizens see it.

MAKING THE STORY PSYCHOLOGICAL

In the manslaughter chapter (see chap. 7, this volume), we detailed the *Gounagias* (*State v. Gounagias*, 1915) case, along with mock juror findings on variations of that case. *Gounagias* was a "rekindling case," in which the defendant stabbed his tormenting assailant to death 3 weeks after the assailant had sodomized him and then repeatedly taunted him in the intervening period. The court, however, ruled that the killing could not have been heat-of-passion manslaughter because the sodomy occurred too far in the past, and because the just-preceding taunt was an inadequate provocation under the law. We now summarize the court's holding in terms of psychological spacetime, foundational elements, and perspectives of objectivity and subjectivity.

In contrast to the mock jurors' CSJ reasons for their verdicts, the *Gounagias* court dramatically foreshortened spacetime, eliminating the main provocation (the sodomy), which thereby eliminated the Other's crime and culpability for what followed. As a result, the court's story had no beginning and development, only denouement. In addition, the court's story had no psychology to it, for it failed to recognize that the sodomy was neither past history nor "dead," but was subjectively alive and simmering, and probably brought to an emotional boil by the repeated taunts of the assailant. The likely emotions these taunts engendered (e.g., anger, rage, humiliation, and fear of another attack) or reawakened may have summed or even multiplied, but a good guess is that Gounagias's passions raged red-hot at that moment of the act. These emotions, like a gravitational pull, may have warped Gounagias's psychological spacetime, such that his sense of threat was magnified and his ability to see less-deadly options was minimized, though we cannot say with certainty what Gounagias sensed and saw. What we do know for sure is that the law would not enter his subjectivity to find out. The court's foreshortened analysis—which removed the origin of the story, the emotional cauldron boiling and bubbling within, and the psychological connection of the present spark igniting time past into time present—necessarily distorted the story of why the killing happened. In light of all these differences between the court's analysis and CSJ's analysis, it makes little sense to refer to the court's *psychological* spacetime context within its story, for the court did not proffer a "story," and there is nothing psychological in its analysis.

In chapters 8 and 9 (this volume), on insanity, we made the point that to distinguish whether a killing was murder or madness the analysis had to get to the deeper *mens* level of capacity, for if it stayed strictly at the *mens rea* level, then most delusional defendants would be found guilty because most generally know right from wrong in the abstract. The *mens* element thus needs to be added to the periodic table. But in regard to this *mens* element, we saw that jurors wanted psychological spacetime to widen to incorporate the origins of the insanity story, as a way of authenticating that the alleged insanity was true, rather than being merely a fiction spun by a clever attorney. In addition, mock jurors wanted to assess yet another fundamental element (that needs to be added to our periodic table and culpability story): whether the defendant was culpable, to some degree, for bringing about his or her disorder.

In chapter 10 (this volume), on self-defense and mistaken self-defense, we featured the subway shootings by Bernhard Goetz (*People v. Goetz*, 1986) and variations of cases in which a battered woman kills her sleeping batterer, believing he would kill her when he wakes. When these cases are viewed in psychological spacetime, we understand that these stories began long before Goetz was approached by one of the youths on the subway, and long before the husband made his last threat before taking his nap. These cases have objective and subjective histories to them, involving prior traumas, along with emotions and beliefs that were part of the defendants' psychological context. As with Gounagias, past traumas can oversensitize an individual to the likelihood of a threat. Past emotions, now coloring the present, may warp what a person may see and interpret, such that he or she may be mistaken about the seriousness of the threat. Intense emotions such as fear may so focus one's attention on one course of action that people fail to see escape alternatives, and may distort their sense of time, whereby they may mistakenly believe that they need to act right now. Emotions, then, may saturate so-called objective perceptions with a distorting subjectivity that leads to tragic mistakes, and a theory of culpability will need to account for mistakes—a topic we will address later.

Widening the Context, Adding Elements, and Bringing Subjectivity and Objectivity Into Balance

How, then, do we make the story more psychological? To summarize, we have argued that the psychological spacetime context must widen from the narrow moment-of-the-act, that neither *intent* nor *mens rea* adequately represent the fundamental subjective element, and that other elements need to be taken into account. However, the examples offered implicitly point to problems regarding the perspectives of objectivity versus subjectivity—and a black-letter law (BLL)–CSJ divide—where CSJ appears to take a more subjective, psychological perspective to context, acts, intentions, emotions, and motives than does BLL. We take up this problem explicitly, beginning with the less controversial element of *actus reus*.

Being visible, the *actus reus* requires less of a subjective leap than does inferring intentions, motives, and emotions. But being visible does not mean that determining whether an act occurred is free of contention. As we saw in regard to insanity (see chap. 8, this volume), even a sequence of seemingly purposeful behaviors might not be considered an act, if they were done in a somnambulistic (sleepwalking) state, as in the Griggs case, for these automatism cases (Finkel, 1988a) challenge the prosecution's *actus reus* claim. But we do not have to go to the extreme of insanity to find contentions with determining whether something is or is not a criminal act, for attempt crimes (Fletcher, 1978) bring the problems to the fore. This is our starting point for an examination of that long-standing perspectival divide of objectivity versus subjectivity, to see how these opposed perspectives can be reconciled in some sound way.

SUBJECTIVITY AND OBJECTIVITY: PERSPECTIVAL CONJOININGS AND CONFUSIONS

Consider the following legal conundrums, called *impossible act* cases, which law school students typically confront in a first-year course on criminal law. In each of the following cases we tested, the subjective element is known, for the case states that the actor intended to kill a victim. In each case the question is this: Is the actor guilty of attempted murder? In the first case, called *dead body*, the actor desires to kill his neighbor, and sneaks up to his neighbor's window where he sees his neighbor apparently sleeping, and then fires several bullets into his body. But unbeknownst to the actor, the victim died in his sleep just moments before the shooting. Can the actor be guilty of attempted murder (or murder) for firing bullets into an already dead body? This is an "impossible act" under the law, which could not have produced the offense-in-chief, murder, for if act and intent must conjoin for guilt, we do not have the conjoining. Thus, under law, it seems that no crime (e.g., attempted murder) has occurred, because no murder could have occurred.

In *no bullets*, a man plans to kill his wife. He drives her to a deserted area, invites her to step out of the car to enjoy the scenic view, pulls out his gun, points it at her head, and fires. But to her surprise—and, particularly, to his—nothing happens. He forgot to load the gun. Again, this is an impossible act case, because one cannot murder by firing an unloaded pistol. In *sugar cubes*, the wife seeks to return the favor and plans to dump arsenic-laced sugar cubes in his morning tea. But she, like he, makes a mistake, for instead of reaching for the arsenic-laced sugar cubes she deposits a real sugar cube in his tea. Is she guilty of attempted murder? Again, murder by a sugar cube is impossible, extreme hypoglycemia notwithstanding, hence this is neither a murderous act nor a crime. For these three impossible act cases, the legal answer appears to be no, for though the subjective "intent" element is there, the objective "criminal act" element is not satisfied.

Where CSJ and BLL Part Company

"Not guilty" may be BLL's answer, but it was not CSJ's answer: the mock jurors' guilty percentages for *dead body*, *no bullets*, and *sugar cubes* were 86%, 100%, and 100%, respectively, as the "subjective intent" element clearly predominated in their reasons for their verdicts (Finkel, Maloney, Valbuena, & Groscup, 1995). If we think in terms of motive, plan, weapon, victim, and opportunity, the actors in *no bullets* and *sugar cubes* had motive, plan, victim, and opportunity, and although they potentially had a lethal weapon at the ready, their mistake was failing to load the lethal weapon or reach for it correctly; in *dead body*, there was motive, plan, and weapon, but fortuity intervenes, as the actor just misses his opportunity, with the victim expiring moments before. The broad principle that seems to govern is this: mock jurors do not believe these actors should profit from either fortuity (in *dead body*) or their ineptness (in *no bullets* and *sugar cubes*).

In terms of the Law's conjoining of the objective *actus reus* and the subjective *mens rea* for guilt, one way of interpreting these results is as an exception to the usual findings: instead of CSJ taking a wider view of culpability than does BLL, it may appear that CSJ is taking a narrower view, demanding less for culpability than a full-fledged possible criminal act when the subjective intent is clearly murderous. In other words, does CSJ weigh the subjectivity factor so heavily that it will ignore the fact that the objective act could not result in murder?

Though this narrower interpretation remains a possible explanation for the CSJ findings, we suggest that a better interpretation is that CSJ actually takes a more expansive view of the *actus reus* than does BLL, deciding (in all three cases) that these attempted acts had gone far enough to be considered as legitimate attempts, for all were likely to produce death, had not fortuity or blunder intervened. In this view, the legitimacy of the attempt is *not* nullified by blunder or fortuity—which legally and technically saves the actor from an attempted murder charge under BLL's impossible act analysis. In our interpretation, mock jurors, no doubt swayed by the clarity of the actor's subjective intent to kill, interpret the objective *actus reus* through the subjective intent. In other words, objective and subjective conjoin for CSJ, but in a different way than under BLL: instead of two separate and distinct elements needing to co-occur, as under BLL's euphemism, we propose that for CSJ the objective (*actus reus*) and subjective (intent) interweave in a union.

The Demands of Objectivity, and Woe to Subjectivity for Culpable Mistakes

Finkel et al. (1995) ran two more impossible act cases, *effigy* and *tree stump*, in which the subjective intent to murder was also clear, but the verdict results were different, which adds complexity to the picture. In *effigy*, imagine a student who is angry about his grades in Professor Finkel's undergraduate Psychology and Law course, believing that his chances of getting into law school are going down the toilet, and thus decides that desperate times call for desperate measures: he brings to class a Finkel effigy doll into which he sticks pins, planning his professor's demise in this manner. In this case, only 17% of the mock jurors find him guilty of attempted murder, and most cite objective factors as reasons: though he has motive, opportunity, and victim close at hand, so to speak, his plan and weapon seem ludicrous if not delusional, in the objective sense, and thus his mistake is in his belief (i.e., that his plan could actually cause a death). In addition, there is also the objective factor of the risk or immediacy of the danger, had the mistake been recognized. For instance, had *no bullets* caught his mistake before he got into his car (and ran back into the house for the bullets), or had the wife caught her mistake at the breakfast table (and then reached for the arsenic-laced cubes), death would surely have resulted, but for *effigy*, had the student eventually realized his error (after his effigy doll had been pinpricked to smithereens while his professor still stood firm), he would need to fashion a new plan, as the danger to the professor would not be immediate.

In *tree stump*, a man believes he is aiming his rifle at his sworn enemy and fires, but when he approaches he realizes that what he had aimed at and hit was a tree stump. He had the intent to kill, but his mistake was one of perception. This case divided the jurors, as 53% find him guilty of attempted murder. He had motive, weapon, and plan, but, as it turned out, he had no victim, and hence no opportunity. Had he realized his mistake before he fired, he would have had to undertake a search for his intended victim, so the immediate danger of death for the victim is not as great as with *dead body*, *no bullets*, and *sugar cubes*, though probably greater than in *effigy*. Moreover, the key differentiation between *effigy* and *tree stump* is that the latter's plan is judged to be objectively sound and capable of producing a lethal result.

Summarizing across these five impossible act cases, we see that objective factors matter, in several ways. First, there must be some overt act that starts the culpability inquiry, rather than simply a subjective intent without any action at all. For example, had *no bullets* and *sugar cubes* merely thought about how each would kill the other—but had taken no action whatsoever in that direction—the likely culpability judgment would be "none," we believe. If our surmise is correct, then some objective act is critical. Furthermore, the objective act (and the subjective plan that propels the act) must be realistic: that is, able to objectively cause the death. And finally, as the objective probability that the act would have produced a death had not the actor made a mistake or fortuity not intervened increases, subjectivity predominates over the impossibility of the objective act. Put another way, mock jurors do not let these actors off the culpability hook for their mistakes or their luck.

In all of the impossible act cases tested, subjective intent was held constant, at the highest level (i.e., the actor purposefully intends to kill), although mistakes varied among these cases, coming in a variety of forms: through misperception, misjudgment, false belief, and fortuity. Perhaps our interpretation can be extended by linking the impossible act results to those cases involving a man on a subway car claiming mistaken self-defense, where the subjective intent level of the actor was lower. In the variations we tested, the actor never purposefully intends to take a life, for he claims he was merely trying to save his own life, though we manipulated different types of mistakes the actor made (e.g., reasonable mistakes, dubious mistakes, unreasonable mistakes, and delusional mistakes). In this experiment, the results strongly suggest that objectivity matters greatly when judging culpability. If we then put the results of the two experiments together, mock jurors seem quick to put defendants "on the culpability hook" (i.e., in the "impossible act" experiment) when the actor's subjective intent was to purposefully kill, when the plan was realistic, and when the objective act had gone far enough to be judged legitimate, but mock jurors were slow to remove an actor from the culpability hook (i.e., in the "mistaken act" experiment) for subjective mistakes unless those mistakes were objectively grounded and judged reasonable.

This interpretation of the objective–subjective interplay highlights what Immanuel Kant (Greene, 1957) would have been quick to point out: that we do not take in the objective world directly; rather, we subjectively perceive, construe, and interpret it, so that what we call *objective* is already tainted with our subjectivity. Thus, when the Law separates and sees *actus reus* and *mens rea* as two independent elements, the former cast as objective and the latter as subjective, this independence is something of a fiction, for the two are more closely entwined. The psychological acts of perceiving and interpreting objective acts necessarily bring subjectivity to external events. But there is the other side of the coin for Kant, who tells us that experiences, the starting source of our knowledge, come from the external world, rather than germinating as a solipsistic product divorced from objective reality. Jurors seem to endorse this Kantian claim as well, as it relates to a defendant's subjective intent claim that his or her act was justified or warrants a mitigating excuse, for jurors are willing to grant the defendant's claim when the actor's subjectivity is grounded in objective reality.

When Subjectivity and Mistake Are Manipulated, Dishonestly

Artificially separating objectivity and subjectivity into two distinct elements (when they are entwined) creates problems. But we also saw in our analysis of accessory felony murder (see chap. 6, this volume) that entwining and fusing different defendants' actions, motives, intentions, and *mens rea* under an "equalist" theory, rather than treating each defendant separately, creates a legal incoherence that CSJ has little trouble parsing. We now take this latter confusion even further, with the scandalous British case of *Regina v. Morgan* (1975), a case that may have set a new low in marital relations (at that time). Morgan (whom we shall refer to as the perpetrator-by-means) convinced three men (whom we shall refer to as the accessories) to rape his wife—by telling them that it was not a rape at all, but part of her rape fantasy that she wanted fulfilled in reality, and that she wished to be overpowered and "forced" to submit to gain some "perverse satisfaction"; furthermore, he told them she would fake resistance to heighten her pleasure.

When the three accessories were tried for rape (Morgan was tried and convicted for aiding and abetting a rape) the "trial judge instructed the jury that not only did the defendants have to 'really believe' that the victim consented, but that the belief had to be reasonable" (Fletcher, 1978, p. 699). But on appeal (*Director of Public Prosecutions v. Morgan*, 1976), the appellate court changed the standard from a "reasonable mistake" to "an honest, although unreasonable, mistake of fact as to the female's consent." Thus, if the men honestly though mistakenly thought she was consenting, then this "could negate a conviction for rape" (R. Singer, 1987, p. 460).

Contemplate the following possibility, and then a question. Let us say that under this new standard, the jury at the retrial believes that it was an honest though unreasonable mistake, and thereby acquits the defendants. Question: Must an appellate court then overturn Morgan's conviction for aiding and abetting a rape—if no rape has occurred? Under the theory of accessorial liability, which links the triggerman and the accessories in felony-murder situations, Morgan might have a case for overturning his conviction. But the perpetrator-by-means theory unlinks the behind-the-scenes manipulator from the pawns up front and holds the former culpable. In an experimental test of these different theories and what CSJ endorses, Finkel et al. (1996) first presented the case to mock jurors and asked them to make verdict decisions for either the accessories or Morgan: 89% found the accessories guilty of rape (i.e., the overwhelming majority did not believe that it was an honest but unreasonable mistake of fact) and 94% found Morgan guilty of aiding and abetting, though the verdict difference between the two types of defendants was not significant. But because the guilty verdict percentages were so high for both types of defendants, a ceiling effect may have obscured true differences, which is why the researchers ran a "sentencing" condition, in which other participants played the part of mock judges, being told that the two juries had found the accessories and Morgan guilty of their respective crimes and they had to give a sentence for each type of defendant. The average sentence for the accessories was 191 months, whereas it was 449 months for Morgan, a significant difference, and the mock judges' reasons for their decisions indicated that they saw these actors quite differently.

The researchers ran three more conditions, in which a new group of participants acted as appellate justices, having to make a "let stand" or "reverse and remand" decision on Morgan's appeal after the accessories had been freed. In the first of these appellate cases (accessorial), Morgan makes the familiar argument that he is the accessory, and if the three principals have now been found not guilty, then he cannot be guilty (Finkel et al., 1996); the participants overwhelmingly rejected his argument, as 82.4% let his conviction stand. In the second version (perpetrator), the Crown counters Morgan's accessorial claim, arguing that he "was not just an accessory, but the principal actor, manipulating the three men from behind" (p. 484), and in this version the let-stand percentage (73.3%) was not significantly different from that in the first version. In the final version (no dominance), Morgan counters the perpetrator-by-means argument, claiming that it requires the principal to dominate the other actors, and he did not dominate, did not threaten the three men, and thus did not cause or control the act (p. 484); our justices rejected his claim, letting his verdict stand 90% of the time, though this was not significantly different from the other versions. But when the appellate and sentencing results are taken together, the perpetrator-by-means is viewed differently, and his culpability is assessed independently of the accessories.

With the previous empirical evidence as backdrop, we shall now recast the *Morgan* case through the perspectives of objectivity and subjectivity. From the victim's vantage point, she knows that she is not giving consent, and that what is happening to her is rape. An invisible observer, watching and listening to this scene, would also be convinced that this is a rape, we believe, and not a dissimulation (the men pulled Morgan's wife out of bed, where she was asleep beside her 11-year-old son, whereupon she screamed for her son to call the police). We will call this vantage point (e.g., the victim's and invisible observer's) the objective perspective. The vantage point of the three assailants claiming "honest but unreasonable mistake" we call the subjective perspective, and we know that their mistaken beliefs were a direct result of Morgan's dishonest manipulation.

Our main point concerns Morgan's perspective. With regard to Sartre's (1974) differentiation between the liar and the self-deceiver, Morgan is clearly the liar, for he knows the truth in order to fashion the lie, which he "sells" to the accessories. When we consider Morgan as the defendant, he is not mistaken at all about the truth, which is the objective truth of his wife's perspective, for he knows that a rape is taking place. Like Iago weaving and selling Othello (Shakespeare, 1938) a story of Desdemona's infidelity and betrayal, Morgan sells these three dupes a fantasy too tempting for them to pass up or seriously question, perhaps because they wanted to believe it. But there is no doubt about what Morgan believed and intended: his subjectivity—motivation, cruelty, planfulness, and dishonesty—is evident and can be normatively evaluated independent of the accessories. In judging Morgan, we need not be confused by what the duped middlemen mistakenly thought, as that mistake was the direct result of this defendant's malevolence. Thus, to let Morgan off the culpability hook because of a mistake he engineered, or through a legal legerdemain of objective versus subjective perspectives, would be to miss this key point. And CSJ does not choose to miss the key point.

ARE WE RESPONSIBLE FOR OUR NEGLIGENT MISTAKES?

"Mistakes happen" may be the prosaic excuse of our time; but in a more poetic time, 1709, when Alexander Pope (1962) penned his "Essay on Criticism," he said that "to err is human." When it comes to the Law, or to interpersonal judgments, for that matter, we do not divinely or supinely forgive mistakes (Finkel & Groscup, 1997b; Murphy, 2003). As law professor George Fletcher (1978) wrote, "The most difficult problems in criminal theory are generated by dissonance between reality and belief, between the objective facts and the actor's subjective impressions of the facts" (p. 683), and mistakes occur in subjectivity. On this point we quote a passage from Fletcher, in which he differentiates *accident* from *mistake*, a distinction we use shortly:

> The place to begin is with a clarification of the distinction between accidents and mistakes. To paraphrase J. L. Austin's example, if I shoot at a tree stump and the bullet ricochets and hits a man standing nearby, my hitting him is an accident; but if I shoot at what I take to be a tree stump and it turns out to be a man, my hitting him is the consequence of a mistake. Accidents occur in the realm of causation. Mistakes occur in the realm of perception. (p. 487)

Subjective Mistakes Changing Psychological Spacetime and the Fundamental Elements

Fletcher oversimplifies when he says that mistakes occur in the realm of perception, for we know that mistakes can occur higher up in psychological processing, in thinking, interpreting, and judging. Still, at whatever stage in the psychological processing mistakes occur, mistakes may tilt the subjective–objective balance toward the former, such that perceptions and beliefs may become misperceptions and erroneous. Second, subjective mistakes may alter one's perceptions and judgments of the psychological context, as in cases of manslaughter, insanity, and putative self-defense. And third, mistakes may significantly alter the fundamental elements of culpability. The question for the criminal law has been, what do we do in terms of culpability when mistake of fact arises, and why?

The Law's early answer, endorsed by Aristotle, Hale, and Blackstone, was that all mistake of fact excuses (i.e., because it negates the volitional will), but this subjective answer is generous to a fault, because it ignores fault or negligence for mistakes. As the criminal law evolved, the Law would draw a new line between honest but reasonable mistakes and honest but unreasonable mistakes, a line that would blur in many cases, with the *Director of Public Prosecutions v. Morgan* (1976) being illustrative. Still, the confusion over whether mistakes exculpate, mitigate, or lead to full culpability continues to plague the Law. This confusion is certainly complicated by legal differences among offenses, as Dressler (1995) noted, for there is one rule for specific intent offenses, another for strict liability offenses, and yet another for general intent offenses, such that the same mistake could result in exculpation, mitigation, or full culpability.

Turning back to Fletcher's distinction between *accident* and *mistake*, we begin with an example of what appears to be an accident, which was experimentally tested by Finkel and Groscup (1997b): a man is taking target practice with a licensed rifle at the center of his own property, but a bullet ricochets off a tree, hitting and killing a trespasser, who ignored the "no trespassing" signs and came on the man's private property from the adjacent common land to pick wildflowers. We can say, as Fletcher does, that the accident results in the realm of causation; we could also say that the death resulted because of the victim's (V) mistake, for which V, according to mock jurors, bears some culpability. As for the shooter, whom we shall call the defendant (D), he, under these conditions, is typically found to have no culpability, as most see this as a tragic accident, particularly given V's culpability for trespassing. But when Finkel and Groscup tested variations of this case, mock jurors questioned whether there was some negligence on D's part, particularly if D, in some variations, was shooting not in the center of his property, but at the property's edge, adjacent to the common land, where others might be put in danger from a stray or ricocheting shot. D's negligence and culpability increased further in variations in which he had not clearly marked the boundary of his property with "no trespassing" signs: in these variations, mock jurors were considering mistakes of thoughtlessness or negligence on the part of D, and D's culpability is weighed against V's culpability in determining the ultimate culpability of D.

But now, in a new variation, we replace the accident (i.e., the ricochet) with a mistake, having D's bullet miss his intended tree target and hit V. If V happens to be a deer hunter hunting during deer season, and D has not posted "no trespassing" signs, the question of negligence rises higher. But if the deer hunter is hunting without a license, and not during deer hunting season, then V's culpability rises higher. And if D had a grudge against deer hunters for coming on his land, some mock jurors will then question whether D's miss of the tree was really a mistake at all, or an act motivated by more sinister reasons, for which D's culpability rises. Finkel and Groscup (1997b) stated,

> The main effect for Other's culpability and the interaction effect of Defendant's Intent x Other's Culpability strongly indicate that participants are viewing these mistake stories as an interpersonal story—where the *actus reus* and *mens rea* to be evaluated do not arise solely from the isolated depths of the main actor/defendant alone. D's act and intent, and thus his culpability, arise in a context, where more than one player may play a culpable and conjoining part. . . . They find Other's culpability along with the defendant's intent, and weigh them in interactive and mitigable ways to reach an overall culpability judgment of D. In the way criminal law and commonsense justice go about reaching a culpability judgment in these mistake cases, we see disparity. (pp. 100–101)

We have brought these accident–mistake variation results to light because they reveal that in the messy realm of juror decision making, Fletcher's neat and tidy conceptual distinction between accidents and mistakes (i.e., the former occurring in the objective realm "of causation," whereas the latter occurs in the subjectivity "of perception") begins to blur. But our most important reason for citing these results is that they provide some support for a point Fletcher makes about shifting the very basis of culpability—from the question of the thoughts and intentions in D's mind to the question of whether D could have, and should have, acted otherwise than he did.

CULPABILITY BASED ON THE FAILURE TO THINK AND EXERCISE SELF-CONTROL

George Fletcher (1988) took the subjectivists to task for being

> confused about the nature of blameworthiness in the criminal law. They seem to think that guilt and blame must be mirrored in the offender's thoughts. If he is not thinking guilty thoughts, if his mind is pure, they can find no way to blame him for his actions. (p. 61)

But this subjectivist position, said Fletcher,

> misconstrues the foundation of criminal responsibility. The basis for all blaming is not the offender's thoughts, but our judgment about whether he could and should have acted otherwise under the circumstances. This judgment about "could" and "should" applies to cases in which offenders have wicked thoughts as well as cases of innocent mistake. If the actor cannot control his actions, we cannot blame him for his wicked thoughts.

But if he could have been more attentive to his situation and avoided a mistake that resulted in harm to others, we can blame him for not having tried harder. (p. 61)

We endorse Fletcher's view that when an actor does not think about his or her situation or others who might be involved as a consequence of his actions, and fails to exert self-control when he or she has the capacity to do so, that such factors ought to be weighed as fundamental elements in culpability. A number of mock juror studies offer empirical support for this proposition. For example, mock jurors in Finkel and Groscup's (1997b) experiment increase their culpability ratings when they perceived negligence on D's part for failing to think about others when he should have, and a majority of mock jurors in Finkel's (1995a) experimental variations of the Bedder (*Director of Public Prosecutions v. Bedder*, 1954) case find Bedder guilty of second-degree murder rather than manslaughter because he put himself and others in danger when he knew (or should have known) that he might not be able to control his emotions and actions if he failed to perform the sexual act. As Fletcher stated,

> There is no difficulty perceiving fault in failing to meet the common standards of human interdependence. We make these expectations of each other every day, and there is no reason why the criminal law should not enforce conventional expectations of reasonable behavior. (p. 61)

Finding (or increasing) culpability for failure to exert self-control also shows in experimental results in insanity cases, when defendants contribute to bringing about their disability of mind when they had the capacity to do otherwise (see chap. 8, this volume), and failure to exert self-control is judged culpable by many in nonconfrontational self-defense claims, and, of course, in many manslaughter claims.

Still, if Fletcher is really shifting the entire basis of culpability to self-control and away from the subjectivists' traditional focus on the offender's guilty thoughts in mind, then this position appears to abandon the fundamental element of intent, and, presumably, an analysis of motive as well, when the latter, particularly, discriminates the worst of crimes (e.g., Pillsbury, 1998). This shift seems to us to be too drastic, for though it adds an important element, it would drop other important elements. A better alternative is to add *self-control* to our growing list of fundamental elements. Moreover, some points about Fletcher's proposition remain unclear. For example, what, specifically, are we responsible for under self-control, where do the emotions fit in, and what limits to thinking and control would Fletcher recognize? Surely Fletcher expects individuals to control their acts such that they do not become criminal and believes we ought to be responsible for thinking about others and the situational context in which interactions and acts arise. This "person in context" view that Fletcher subscribes to is also the view that most contemporary psychologists subscribe to, but psychological research shows that this widened psychological spacetime context is highly complex, with many causal and correlative factors associated with criminogenic situations (Haney, 2002), which may modify "our understanding of the nature of choice and autonomy" and "how we can and should view criminal responsibility, blameworthiness, and the fairness of various legal punishments" (p. 34).

We are left with unanswered questions about what we are responsible for, and what we are expected to control. A comprehensive and coherent culpability scheme rests on clarifying these points. But before we get to these questions, we turn, as a final example, to someone who thinks as deeply as any about himself and whose awareness and consciousness expands and expands—yet whom we see as responsible and culpable.

ARE WE RESPONSIBLE FOR KEEPING OTHERS IN MIND? HAMLET REVISITED

In *Hamlet: Poem Unlimited*, Bloom (2003) advised the reader

> to confront both the play and the prince with awe and wonder, because they know more than we do. I have been willing to call such a stance Bardolatry, which seems to me only another name for authentic response to Shakespeare. (p. 7)

Bloom's Bardolatry is rooted, in part, in Shakespeare's study and Hamlet's (Shakespeare, 1938) focus on the "consciousness of his own consciousness, unlimited yet at war with itself" (p. 88). Remarking further on this consciousness, Bloom told us that the aim and end of all of this expanding of consciousness is that "Hamlet discovers that his life has been a quest with no object except his own endlessly burgeoning subjectivity" (p. 98), for "what matters most about Hamlet is his genius, which is for consciousness itself. He is aware that his inner self perpetually augments, and that he must go on overhearing an ever-burgeoning self-consciousness" (p. 120).

Setting Bardolatry Aside, and Seeing Hamlet as Social, Civic, and Legal Being

For our purposes, which are psycholegal rather than literary, we put aside the stance of Bardolatry to ask pointed questions about Hamlet's consciousness and culpability, as we forward the general issue of responsibility. In this regard, we shall view Hamlet within the context of a social, civic, and legal being and begin by asking, what sort of "ever-burgeoning self-consciousness" or "endlessly burgeoning subjectivity" is this?

Hamlet's consciousness is certainly not burgeoning in the interpersonal direction, for he has no genuine caring for any other living being in the drama, as he shows no empathy for the feelings of others. Hamlet's one moment of genuine caring is at the graveyard scene, over the skull of poor Yorick, the court jester to King Hamlet who has been dead for 23 years. Yorick, a playmate to Hamlet, carried the Prince on his back a thousand times and kissed him frequently; he was more father to the Prince than King Hamlet, that "uxorious killing machine with whom the great soliloquist has absolutely nothing in common" (Bloom, 2003, p. 132).

Hamlet's burgeoning subjectivity certainly contains a rather huge blind spot when it comes to his feelings for his mother Gertrude, who, as Bloom (2003) noted, "had much to endure, and little to enjoy, in her brilliant son" (p. 60). Hamlet rages at her in the closet scene (as she fears he might kill her in his fury)—and for what? The son chastises his mother for enjoying a happy marriage of love and sex "at your age . . . O shame, where is thy blush?" (III, iv, 68, 81). The text offers nothing to indicate that she knew that Claudius had poisoned King Hamlet, so if Hamlet holds her guilty of something, it might be for taking up an adulterous relationship with Claudius while his father was alive, though Shakespeare is purposefully vague about when that relationship began. Still, if she did seek comfort in the arms of Claudius while her killing machine husband was away doing battle, Hamlet might have been the first to understand: King Hamlet showed no empathy for Hamlet even as a Ghost, caring not a whit for the Prince's feelings, only that the boy do the revenge. The King was probably as lousy a husband as he was a father, and if Hamlet had a shred of empathy, he might have commiserated with his mother about her plight rather than deliver his self-righteous and wrongheaded stabbing thrusts, which are then displaced into a literal and lethal stab that kills Polonius. Not even at the end of the play, with his subjective self-consciousness at its fullest, can Hamlet overcome his blind spot for his mother, for "After Gertrude dies, calling out, 'O my dear Hamlet!' her son delivers the extraordinary line 'I am dead, Horatio. Wretched Queen, adieu.'" (Bloom, 2003, p. 60). Though Bloom rejects "the urgings of Freud" to see any traces of the incestuous, Oedipal drama in Hamlet, we see a psychological and emotional blind spot that remains from beginning to end, quite apart from Bloom's preferred hypothesis that this is just theatrical.

Hamlet shows no feelings of remorse for his manslaughter of Polonius, and he shows no feelings of remorse for his premeditated murders of his old school chums Rosencrantz and Guildenstern, who seem to have merely gotten in the Prince's way. Whatever Hamlet personally thinks of Polonius, Rosencrantz, and Guildenstern—and he may well have regarded them as fools, dupes, and lightweights in the service of Claudius—in the context of what a modern civic-minded and legal-minded man ought to think, they nonetheless have the same rights to life, liberty, and the pursuit of happiness as Hamlet. Hamlet, then, is not a Rawlsian (Rawls, 1971): he does not recognize that if he claims certain rights then others have the same rights, and that he has a duty to respect those rights if he wishes others to respect his.

Moreover, there is no sense of "justice as fairness" for Hamlet. Poor Ophelia bears the brunt of his unfairness, as he pushes her to madness and suicide through undeserved cruelty. As Bloom (2003) stated,

> Despite his passion in the graveyard, we have every reason to doubt his capacity to love anyone, even Ophelia.... Shakespeare's wisdom avoided the only fate for Ophelia that would have been more plangent than her death-in-water: marriage to Hamlet the Dane. (p. 44)

At the end of the play, as Hamlet dies, his sycophantic friend Horatio says, "Now cracks a noble heart. Good night, sweet prince/And flights of angels sing thee to thy rest!" (V, ii, 348–350). But what has the "noble" Hamlet wrought? Eight dead, including himself, litter the stage, many of them needless victims of Hamlet's burgeoning self-consciousness. On the civic and legal side of things, he has elevated neither the law nor the morality of Denmark, which now falls under the rule of another killing machine, the younger Fortinbras, who earlier in the drama "marches off to Poland 'to gain a little patch of ground' not large enough to bury those who will die disputing it" (Bloom, 2003, p. 108). Now, Denmark is to be ruled by Norway and another headbasher, which may not be Denmark's gain.

Hamlet has pursued his own subjectivity to its limits, but he has not in any sense explored the subjectivity of others, or even considered it in his own decision making. Others are there merely as pieces on the chess board—for him to move, manipulate, and sacrifice, if necessary, in the service of his expanding self-consciousness. But this consciousness is missing a social, civic, and legal conscience. Were he a modern defendant dragged into a modern courtroom, few would be singing praises to his noble heart. As a social, civic, and legal actor, Hamlet appears culpable for not controlling his feelings when he could and should have, for not thinking about others when he could and should have, and for not considering other options when he could and should have.

RESPONSIBILITY FOR SELF-CONTROL: DOES PSYCHOLOGY UNDERMINE OR SUPPORT THIS NOTION?

We now resume with our questions regarding Fletcher's (1988) proposal for a significantly different basis for blameworthiness: guilt based on a failure of self-control, based on "individuals' having the capacity to act other than they have acted" (p. 61). If this is to be either the new basis of culpability, as Fletcher seems to suggest, or a new aspect of culpability that ought to be considered (as we favor), then is there a determinative element within the criminal law's existing culpability schema that could account for this factor? The obvious candidate, under the Model Penal Code (American Law Institute, 1962), is intent, and specifically, negligence. Yet, in regard to mistake, R. Singer (1987) wrote,

Section 2.04 provides that "ignorance or mistake as to a matter of fact . . . is a defense if: (a) the ignorance or mistake negatives the purpose, knowledge, belief, recklessness or negligence required to establish a material element of the offense." In a word, even an honestly held mistake is a defense to a crime which requires purpose, knowledge, or recklessness; the "unreasonable," that is, negligent, mistake is no defense only where the crime charged can be committed "negligently." The MPC's [Model Penal Code's] general reluctance to establish either negligent or strict liability crimes make the apparent compromise rather meaningless; for all practical purposes, an honestly but unreasonably mistaken actor is to be exculpated from all criminal liability. (pp. 502–503)

If R. Singer is right about the Model Penal Code's (American Law Institute, 1962) reluctance to establish negligence crimes, which makes exculpation the likely outcome for mistaken and negligent actors, then this is not the outcome either Fletcher (1988) or Finkel and Parrott desire. Our question, then, is worth repeating: What element in the criminal law's culpability schema accounts for this factor? It seems that we have to broaden the "intent" element by adding a negligence factor within its ambit, add another element that specifically addresses this point, or radically redo the criminal law's culpability basis entirely; resistance to these propositions, which is most likely to be found within the Law itself, is likely to be loudest regarding the radical proposition that Fletcher apparently favored.

But Fletcher (1988) went on to identify other sources of resistance, for he asserted not only that society has "lost confidence in the very notion of guilt based on self-control" but that "this confusion exists in the academy as well" (p. 61) and here he singled out the discipline of Psychology specifically. Instead of recognizing "individuals' capacity to act other than they have acted," said Fletcher (p. 61), "there lurks the suspicion that humans have no more control of their actions than do animals driven by instinct and reflex. And if that is what we are, there is no room left in moral discourse for guilt, blaming, and condemnation." In returning to the view that he is critical of, Fletcher stated,

> If fault consists in a state of mind, then there is no need to speculate about counterfactual conditional situations, about what would have happened had the actor desired to do otherwise. In an age in which psychology has nearly replaced moral philosophy, this is a tempting way out. It fills the old moral vessels of guilt and blameworthiness with psychological surrogates. (p. 62)

Setting Straw Men and Caricatures Aside

The problem we have with Fletcher's (1988) characterization of modern psychology is similar to the one we had with Pillsbury's (1998) characterization: it is simply not an accurate portrayal of where modern psychology currently stands, for the views Fletcher cites, which arose more than a half-century ago, have faded from predominance; thus, Fletcher's etch-a-sketch of psychology is a dated caricature, which creates a straw-man argument. In contrast to what Fletcher puts forth, the predominant view in academic psychology is the evaluative view of emotions, which demonstrates that normal adults have the capacity to make judgments, appraisals, inferences, and attributions, which includes the capacity to reappraise the situation, one's feelings, and one's options; this capacity provides the psychological requisites for self-control—and the wherewithal "to do otherwise." Thus, had Fletcher seen psychology more accurately, he might have found support for his position, rather than a foil.

For instance, when it comes to emotions, most psychologists today do not ascribe to the mechanistic stimulus–response view (i.e., according to which emotions are triggered reflexively and operate unconsciously, without cognitive input). Yet, if such a view was alleged to be the cause of an irresistible criminal act (such as in *Hadfield*), then psychologists would expect solid scientific evidence for this causal claim. But as we noted, causal proof for the missing links within the chain of Erskine's motives irresistible argument for Hadfield was not offered to the jury then, nor could it be offered now, for that matter.

Perhaps Fletcher (1988) was alluding to Freudians, neuropsychologists, and behaviorists when he claimed that psychology held that "humans have no more control of their actions than do animals driven by instinct and reflex" and concluded that psychology would leave no room "in moral discourse for guilt, blaming, and condemnation" (p. 61)—for those psychologists who treat or do research under those orientations stress the unconscious, the brain, or prior conditioning as the underlying source of behavior. Yet we would argue that these orientations and practitioners recognize individual variability in their empirical research data and in their clinical therapeutic results. For example, Freudians recognize that where id was ego can be, an acknowledgment that humans can achieve insights into their feelings and motives, and through insights achieve greater control; neuropsychologists believe that even with damage localized to certain areas of the brain, most of the time individuals can use still-functioning parts of their brains to learn new adaptive skills to achieve some control; and a tenet of behavior therapy has held that one can unlearn faulty behavior patterns, learn new patterns, and change, achieving greater control. Contrary to what Fletcher stated, modern academic psychology's findings turn out to be good news for Fletcher's "self-control" ("free will") view, for the main conclusion seems to be that under most situations and circumstances people are not prisoners of past traumas, brain damage, conditioning, or their emotions.

The CSJ understandings seem to accord at many places with this "responsibility for self-control" position. That is why a majority of mock jurors held the young Bedder guilty of second-degree murder: Bedder knew he was impotent, and should have known that if he put himself in a situation where embarrassment, humiliation, and anger were likely to arise, then he might not be able to control his feelings and actions at that point, yet he chose to do so anyway, disregarding the consequences to others. And this is why a minority of mock jurors held Gounagias guilty of second-degree murder: although he knew, or should have known, that seeing the man who had sodomized him and would likely taunt him again would likely set off feelings and actions that he might not be able to control, he chose not to leave the restaurant and come back for his paycheck at a safer time, when his assailant was not there.

Throughout this work, we have been advocating and illustrating the evaluative view of emotions, a more psychological view, in contrast to the mechanistic view. This view can inform the Law about how subjectively construed current and past events, along with one's beliefs, feelings, motives, and capacity, may affect what emotions come to be experienced, and with what degree of intensity, and how these emotions may play a part in mistakes of perception, thinking, and judgment. Complex actions are likely the result of a complex confluence of factors, and Psychology may be able to better inform the Law and its theories as to how these factors may play a part in culpability determinations. But this informing function does not usurp or preclude normative, moral judgments, contrary to what Fletcher fears.

A RECAPITULATION

Fletcher's (1988) fears and erroneous view of modern academic psychology do not come out of nowhere, we believe. Many lawyers and judges (e.g., Bazelon, 1988) have witnessed psychological experts entering the courtroom to offer their clinical and forensic testimony wherein "psychological surrogates" have been proffered that seem to excuse defendants from criminal responsibility. This situation occurs in trials where mental disorders are alleged, with insanity cases being the most accessible heuristic, and if experts ascribe to a disease model, then the defendant may be portrayed as a passive victim of the disease (Seligman, 1998).

But as we saw in our last chapter on self-defense and mistaken self-defense, disorders have been asserted here as well. For example, let us assume that a hypothetical expert claimed at trial that Bernhard Goetz (the trial of whom Fletcher [1988] sat through) had posttraumatic stress disorder (PTSD). However, from the psychological position from which we are arguing, Goetz should have been aware of his sensitization from his past mugging, for he was aware enough to pack a gun. That he chose to sit next to the four Black youths when he entered the subway car was "his right," as Fletcher noted, but it was a poor and provocative choice, given his history and current emotional state and the lethal weapon he was packing. He could have been held responsible for failing to take the options he still had—before he fired shots into the four youths—for there is no causal inevitability that can be concluded from a PTSD diagnosis.

But what if the hypothetical expert gets on the witness stand and weaves a story of Goetz's "victimology," saying that the disorder (PTSD) and not the moral chooser triggered the action? This expert's story would reflect an older view in psychology, which is just the view that Fletcher is highly critical of, because it removes responsibility from the person and attaches it to a psychological surrogate of disorder that lies outside of self-control, which renders those moral concepts of will, choice, and culpability inapt. But also critical of this victimology view is Martin Seligman (1998), past president of the American Psychological Association, who wrote in his "President's Column" that this disease model view, theoretically,

> has been a victimology in which human beings are viewed as passive, "responding" to external stimuli, or as consumed with unresolved conflicts dictated by childhood trauma, or as acting from tissue needs, drives, and instincts, or as the helpless victims of oppressive cultural and economic forces. (p. 2)

This victimology view, unfortunately, still rears its head in the courtroom, chiefly because the testimony of clinicians and forensic experts has been held to less rigorous standards (Sales & Shuman, 2005) than has scientific evidence, despite *Daubert* (*Daubert v. Merrell Dow Pharmaceuticals*, 1993), though it is our view the "victim position" cannot withstand scientific scrutiny under most conditions.

Are humans culpable, then, for letting their emotions—be it in the present moment, or when emotions from time past affect time present—come to distort what they see, construe, and conclude, but most of all, get murderously out of hand? Culpability is a normative issue, in part, and the Law sets its normative expectations through its criminal law statutes. But laws, we have also argued, must be grounded on the empirical nature of human nature, and this is where the science of psychology has something of significance to say. From the empirical evidence on emotions, we see no reason why the Law cannot set a general expectation that individuals ought to be mindful about their emotions and keep them under sufficient control, such that they do not result in harm to others. As a further qualifier, the Law can set an expectation that if people are especially sensitive because of a known condition or syndrome, they have a special onus to take extra care that they do not distort, mistakenly jump to conclusions, act rashly, or negligently put themselves in dangerous situations that are likely to imperil others.

Yet these expectations run into obvious objections and exceptions. They assume that everyone has the capacity to act otherwise, which is not always the case, as we discussed in chapter 2 (this volume). But it seems to us, two psychologists, that the science of Psychology does not bar the door to empirical and normative considerations of these issues that affect culpability judgments. Quite the contrary. Science has not served up facts and theories that foreclose the moral question. Rather, the Law's contradictory mix of folk theories of emotion and human nature stand in contradiction to many of the facts and theories of Psychology, creating stories of culpability far less real than the fictional accounts flowing from our best dramatists and literary minds. This factual and theoretical gap between the disciplines of Law and Psychology has become more pronounced, and problematic, in our time (Haney, 2002). Still, these discredited folk theories remain the bedrock of the Law's normative culpability schema, raising troubling questions about the validity of some of the Law's normative conclusions, and whether the citizens' CSJ will embrace or even abide these laws—when citizens enter the courtroom, hear the story, and make their "to be or not to be" culpability decisions of defendants.

12

A REFORMULATION, AND CONCLUDING RECOMMENDATIONS

As an entrée to this work, we discussed the "first murder" in Genesis, where Cain's emotions were in some way connected to his thoughts, motive, and act, and were in some way relevant in the Lord's culpability judgment that followed. But the central questions relating to how and why a defendant's emotions affect culpability were unanswered, in the biblical story. We then turned to the Law, and to its theories of emotions as they relate to culpability, where answers are offered. We highlighted emotions because in this area we found consistent inconsistencies, if not outright contradictions, among the criminal law's theories, which we found embedded within the Law's statutes, case decisions, and dicta. These embedded folk theories did link emotion (more so than emotions) to culpability—although the *how*, *when*, *why*, and *under what conditions* of that linkage, and *why certain emotions* sometimes aggravated, mitigated, or exculpated culpability, were seldom answered with clear and convincing reasons, let alone reasons that cohered across crimes, defenses, and doctrines.

For example, when the common law generated objective rules in its manslaughter doctrine about how provocations and cooling-off time related to emotion, the killing act, and culpability, these rules paradoxically removed

(a) individual variability and (b) the defendant's psyche and subjectivity from its culpability analysis. These objective rules rest on theories, all seeming to reflect a one-size-fits-all stimulus–response folk-psychology. These theories, however, did not mesh with how humans actually evaluate and react to provocations in their contexts, and they did not address (through individualized assessments) the thoughts, emotions, malice, and degree of control that defendants had at the time of the killing. As these rules fail to address and assess these key intrapsychic aspects in a sound way, those theories never went to the next level—exploring the complex interrelationship of thinking, feeling, and acting. It was not surprising, then, that many of these legal notions turned out to be invalid, in light of the fact that they were drawn from the folk fancies and fictions of judges and treatise writers rather than from the scant empirical facts available at that time.

But insufficient psychological evidence was not the case in the early 1960s, when academic Psychology flowered and the Model Penal Code's (American Law Institute, 1962) extreme emotional disturbance (EED) theory replaced the objective rules with an unrestrained subjectivity, and turned out to be no theory at all. In its EED doctrine and in the case law that followed, the Law seemed to throw up its hands and throw in the towel on the twin problems of linking emotions to (a) interpersonal events in the objective world and (b) cognitions, motives, and volition within the subjective world. The EED theory turns out to be the antithesis of the theoretical perspective that predominates in modern academic psychology, that of person-in-context (or emotion-in-context), for in the Law's EED theory no interpersonal–social context and no intrapsychic context is in sight. This is most curious, given that the theories address the crime of manslaughter, which is psychologically driven.

Yet it gets "curiouser and curiouser," as Alice in Wonderland (Carroll, 1978) noted, for the Law's theories of emotion are psychological theories in that they attempt to describe and explain the psychological nature of our human nature, however poorly they do so. From its folk-psychological theories, the Law clearly makes inferences regarding the defendant's capacity, thinking, feeling, intentions, motives, and actions, and then uses these suspect inferences to make normative judgments about whether the defendant should have done otherwise than what he or she did, given the defendant's particular situation and circumstances.

When the proverbial dust settles, we are left with three troubling disconnects. The first, within the Law, is between its unsupportable faux facts and folk theories of emotion, and its normative culpability theories that follow: to embrace its normative fictions one must first suspend disbelief about the Law's false facts and regard them as true—which is akin to the process delusional defendants engage in.

This first disconnect leads to our second—between the psychological folk theories of the Law and the theories and empirical facts generated by research psychologists. This disconnect, in the opinion of some (e.g., Haney, 2002), appears to be widening, particularly over what Psychology sees as (a) the centrality of *context* (the psychological spacetime context) that gives meaning to facts; (b) the multiple number of determinative elements that affect emotions, thoughts, motives, and alleged criminal acts; and (c) the perspective people use to understand facts and relationships.

The third disconnect appears from mounting psychological research of the lay theories jurors invoke, the complex story construction they do, and the varied prototypes they bring and use when making culpability judgments. These empirical findings reveal numerous disconnects between black-letter law (BLL) and commonsense justice (CSJ) in regard to notions of justice (Finkel, 1995b), fairness (Finkel, 2001), rights, and duties (Finkel & Moghaddam, 2005)—disconnects that bode ill for jurors complying with legal instructions, and for citizens respecting the law.

Our purpose in writing this book on the criminal law's story of emotion and culpability was to do neither a pure critique nor an impure jeremiad. We believe that the rule of law is vital in maintaining (a) personal conduct; (b) domestic tranquility in our interpersonal, societal, and civic life (Spragens, 1999, 2004); and (c) international tranquility, or the law of peoples, as John Rawls (1999) called it. Our aim, rather, was to evaluate the Law's psychological theories in the light of modern psychological knowledge and CSJ findings—to inform the Law, so that the Law could make "better law," to paraphrase George Fletcher (1988, p. 154). We have come quite far in this direction, but here we must stop, for it would be presumptuous for two psychologists to attempt to rewrite the laws, defenses, and doctrines based on this review and analysis; that is the job for legal scholars far more competent in their field than we. As the title of chapter 11 (this volume) states, our objective is to move the Law toward a coherent emotion and culpability story, not develop its final form. Still, on the basis of the lessons we have abstracted from our admittedly limited survey of crimes, defenses, and doctrines, we put forth some broad suggestions for the Law toward that end.

OUR THREE BROAD RECOMMENDATIONS

Our first suggestion is to better frame stories and theories of emotions and culpability. This recommendation involves altering the psychological spacetime fabric: this fabric needs to be contextual, stretched in space and time, to bring an interpersonally and intrapsychically richer story to the jurors, one that resonates as a dramatic human story rather than as an artificially fragmented snapshot from a story.

Our second suggestion involves the traditional fundamental elements that the Law uses to determine culpability, *actus reus* and *mens rea*–intent, which we have found insufficient for the task. For instance, we find that the *mens rea*–intent element gets neither at motives nor to incapacity at the level of *mens*, nor to an inquiry into the origins of that incapacity, nor to an assessment of culpability for bringing about one's incapacity. As for mistakes, the Law's focus has been on distinguishing honest and reasonable mistakes from honest but unreasonable mistakes, but dishonest mistakes and culpability for mistakes or accidents generally are inadequately considered. In a similar manner, the Other's culpability and how this interacts with the defendant's culpability are seldom adequately considered. And there is the added question of "What thoughts and intentions were not in the defendant's mind but should have been?" which would lead to culpability judgments of negligence (or worse), and to the issues of self-control and responsibility for thinking about others, which need to be included and integrated into the Law's fundamental elements.

Our third suggestion involves unifying the perspectives of objectivity and subjectivity, for this long-standing division divides jurisdictions over certain crimes, defenses, and doctrines and adds to the theoretical inconsistency and incoherence. Regarding this issue, there appears to be a basic confusion about objectivity itself that appears to overlook or deny that people subjectively perceive, construe, and interpret reality, rather than taking in the objective truth directly. Similarly, there is confusion about subjectivity as well, which is never applied as the Law depicts it, unconstrained by objective reality. For example, when subjective mistakes are said to occur, we find that whether D is excused or held culpable for the mistake turns on how objectively reasonable the mistake was. Our evidence suggests that far from being separate and distinct, both the act and the intent, when mock jurors evaluate them, turn out to be an admixture of both objectivity and subjectivity.

This disjunct was dramatic in "impossible act" cases. Here, the Law begins its analysis by conceiving *actus reus* and *mens rea* as two independent elements, the former objective, the latter subjective, with both needing to conjoin for guilt: so if the act could not objectively produce a murder, even when the subjective intent (*mens rea*) to kill was clear, the person is judged not guilty of attempted murder. But when mock jurors subjectively judge this *actus reus* as a legitimate attempt in the light of a clear subjective intent, then this subjectively judged objective act and their subjective intent judged to be objectively realizable conjoin. For CSJ, this is a very different type of conjoining than under BLL, as each of these elements conjoins objectivity and subjectivity.

The simplistic view, that something is either objective or subjective, leads to confusion when it comes to emotions (see chap. 4, this volume). Folk theories place an exaggerated emphasis on the subjective nature of emotions, and this focus has led the Law to ignore emotions out of fear that they might trump objective evidence in court. For example, when a person makes the claim that he or she was subjectively angry, that claim seems to end (before it begins) any debate that an outsider might raise about the validity of the angry feeling. The claimant's trump card would be "My feeling is my feeling, and that's that." But, as researchers such as Averill (1982) have demonstrated, there is an objective side to emotions, for there are objective rules concerning the conditions under which one is entitled to be angry. When viewing emotions in this objective way, the outsider can indeed question the rightness of the feeling and make a culpability judgment on actions that follow from objective consideration of that feeling.

THE POST-*HAMLET* WORLD OF MODERNIST STORIES

We do not claim that our suggestions solve the knotty problems of emotions and culpability, let alone provide a detailed road map for how such a culpability schema would look across all areas of the criminal law, many of which we have not even taken up in this volume. In regard to the "still to be solved," consider our proposal that the Law reenter the problem of motive, as the legal scholar Pillsbury (1998) proposed in his normative approach, although we propose adding this factor (along with others) to the fundamental elements rather than using it exclusively as the moral basis of culpability, as Pillsbury recommended. Our proposal adds (rather than subtracts) problems, for we recommend pursuing motive in wider ways than did Pillsbury, whose subtitle of "Rethinking the Law of Murder and Manslaughter" reflected his limited scope. We believe that *motive*, far more than mere *mens rea*–intent, provides for the richer understanding of the story of alleged criminal actions not only at one end of the continuum but at the other end as well: this factor not only helps citizens separate the "death-worthy" murderers from those warranting only life imprisonment but it also helps citizens understand, at the *mens* level, why some delusional defendants kill and warrant an NGRI verdict, whereas others do not. Jurors, like those who read mysteries and detective fiction, want to know what motive drove the actor, as Bennett and Feldman (1981) documented in their *Reconstructing Reality in the Courtroom: Justice and Judgment in American Culture*.

But here we reencountered our "first psychologist," the genius of William Shakespeare, who, as Stephen Greenblatt (2004) told us, radically transformed Saxo the Grammarian's account of the medieval telling of the Hamlet saga (i.e., wherein the Prince was too young and not a threat, then, to avenge his father's murder, which accounts for why the Prince needed the antic disposition to play for time; Shakespeare, 1938). Shakespeare also radically flipped the lost version of *Hamlet* (which many attribute to Thomas Kyd, and which Shakespeare no doubt saw) from an outward revenge tragedy into the modern interior psychological story—in which the mystery of what is in Hamlet's mind (beneath his antic disposition and his actions) becomes the focus for the audience, and for the play's characters. In Shakespeare's version, with a grown-up Hamlet and with the murderer having "no reason to suspect that Hamlet has or can ever acquire any inkling of his crime," the "feigned madness is no longer coherently tactical" and "the play should be over by the end of the first act" (Greenblatt, p. 305). And if a theater audience "is not particularly tolerant of long gestation periods" (p. 304)—"the long interval between the first motion—the initial impulse or design—and the acting of the dreadful thing" (p. 303)—then Shakespeare's *Hamlet* should have been an interminable nightmare and a box-office disaster, yet "out of the wreckage he constructed what most modern audiences would regard as the best play he had ever written" (p. 305).

Shakespeare had been gradually developing and subtly refining "a particular set of representational techniques" (e.g., using soliloquies, creating "opacity" as to motive), such that he now "had perfected the means to represent inwardness" and "make the epochal breakthrough" (p. 299). But Shakespeare gives us more than just the first modern drama, or even the ways and means to write a modern novel; in fact, he shows us through his *Hamlet*, and the dramas that immediately followed it (e.g., *Othello, King Lear*, and *Macbeth* [Shakespeare, 1938]), that reality is messy and opaque when it comes to pinning down the motive, despite people wanting it. For example, in regard to the ending of *Othello*, Greenblatt (2004) wrote,

> When Othello has finally understood that he has been tricked into believing that his wife was unfaithful, that he has murdered the innocent woman who loved him, and that his reputation and whole life has been destroyed, he turns to Iago and demands an explanation. Exposed as a moral monster, caught and pinioned, Iago's terrible reply—his last utterance in the play—is a blank refusal to supply the missing motive: "Demand me nothing. What you know, you know./From this time forth I never will speak word." (V, ii, 309–310; Greenblatt, 2004, pp. 326–327)

The words are specific to *Othello* and to the fathomless cruelty of its villain, but the opacity extends to crucial elements in each of Shakespeare's great tragedies.

Opacity draws people to pursue its opposite, clarity: it draws the audience into the character's psychic interior of emotions, thoughts, and motives—wherein they use their imagination, empathy, intuitions, and projections to conjure the motive. But requiring a prosecutor to prove a particular motive (i.e., Is it motive *a* or motive *b*?)—beyond reasonable doubt, no less—may bar the prosecution and conviction for the most disturbing defendants (e.g., the murderer and the "madman"); Greenblatt's citation of Coleridge's memorable phrase, "the motive-hunting of motiveless malignity" (p. 326), is the point we are underscoring. "Motive" may not be simple; it may not even be a question of *a* or *b*. For example, what if Hamlet has turned his famous *or* question—"To be or not to be?"—into a paradoxical *a and b* answer?

For example, why is Hamlet, now in Act V (following his sea change and return), ready to step into an obvious death trap set by Claudius and

Laertes? If he is doing so to finally finish this revenge business (to be), why now? Is it just that (a) Hamlet knows that Claudius knows that Hamlet knows and (b) Hamlet knows that Claudius will not rest until Hamlet is dead, so therefore he does it to end this charade and do the deed his father's Ghost commanded him to do? In short, is he now ready "to be"? But might there be another reason and motive, even one antithetical to the first? For example, if Bloom is correct in his surmise—that Hamlet is now ready to leave this world because his study of his self-consciousness has gone as far as it can take him—then his "not to be" motive is operational. If Hamlet is now enacting a paradoxical answer—"to be" *and* "not to be"—then we may never have proof beyond a reasonable doubt about which of the two motives drives his act, for both answer the question.

This doubt may have been one of the reasons the Law eschewed the deep motive in favor of the shallower intent, for whereas the latter offers an incomplete story rather than the whole story, people's consciences, legal and moral, may be able to rest more comfortably with the lower-level inferences (and fewer errors that result?) regarding intent, as opposed to enduring the slings and arrows of greater uncertainty and greater likelihood of errors with motive. But significant losses result from removing motive. For one, without this fundamental element, the Law loses the moral meaning of the act and the reason someone is held culpable and worthy of punishment, and for another, jurors lose that critical motive insight that connects and explicates their reasons for their culpability judgment with, and of, the defendant's act.

Yet the Law's pendulum has swung back to motive in recent times, for consider new laws making some crimes "hate crimes." This was one of the issues in the Supreme Court's decision in *Apprendi v. New Jersey* (2000), a case that dealt with a weapons offense, in which the judge "found" racial animus present, which elevated the crime to a hate crime, and that aggravating factor was the reason the judge used to increase the penalty. But note that finding racial animus, like finding the generic "hate," requires making significant inferences from observable acts into the emotions and motives that drive the actor. This can lead to a situation in which there are two identical objective acts, where the subjective intent is also identical (e.g., to kill), but where the crimes and punishments are different. What makes differential judgments defensible are the different motives in the two cases.

But what makes *Apprendi* and subsequent Supreme Court rulings in *Ring v. Arizona* (2002) and *Blakely v. Washington* (2004) more noteworthy for us is the fact that the Supreme Court ruled that the racial animus found in *Apprendi* was not an aggravating factor but a specific element of the offense. As a specific element, it needed to be proved beyond a reasonable doubt by the jury (under the Sixth Amendment), rather than being claimed by the judge after all of the evidence at trial was presented. So motive was not only in the culpability matrix, according to the Supreme Court, but its assessment was relocated—removed from the judge's purview and given to the jurors'—to be situated within their culpability judgment, and to be found (or not) by using their discretion, insights, and inferences. We do not know whether these rulings will increase verdict variance and the likelihood of wrongful verdicts, for to know that would require an empirical assessment, which has not been done. What is clear, however, is that the Supreme Court made a normative assessment that justice and fairness required the element, and the Justices placed faith in the jurors to do the job. We hold to that belief and faith as well.

AND A FUTURE WORLD OF TWO DISCIPLINES, PLUS COMMONSENSE JUSTICE

Our final remarks go to a lingering confusion and miscasting of Psychology, which we have cited at several places in this work. Assertions have been put forth, by respected law professors, whose writings we cite and whose thinking we respect, wherein an old bugbear resurfaces that the science of psychology will somehow undermine the moral, normative nature of culpability with its psychological surrogates, or with mechanistic, causal, and deterministic claims, that will eliminate free will, choice, and the moral chooser all at once.

In contrast with this dire, undermining view, the general, modern, and mainstream view Psychology puts forth regarding emotions stresses the central role of evaluation in judging emotions and the actions that may follow. In the chapters on murder or manslaughter, for example, there was not a single instance of putting forth any psychological claim, founded on empirical evidence, for a mechanistic, causal, or deterministic explanation that would preclude a normative evaluation. In the insanity chapter (see chap. 8, this volume), the contrary was evident, for there we made a sharp critique of a mechanistic, causal, deterministic claim that was offered by the lawyer Erskine for his client Hadfield (*Hadfield's Case*, 1800). Moreover, we noted that if causal claims are made regarding brain-to-mind-to-behavior connections, as they might be, say in cases of epilepsy causing loss of consciousness where involuntary contractions might cause the squeezing of a trigger which might, in some unlikely circumstance, send a bullet into a person causing death, a hypothetical case that Finkel and colleagues have tested and written about (Finkel, 1988a; Finkel & Sabat, 1984), then the onus is on the expert to make the scientific case for such a claim. Still, even when that claim seems scientifically valid, jurors may yet find such defendants guilty for bringing about their epileptic seizure, if it can be shown that they were negligent in stopping their medication without consulting their doctor, for example.

But in returning to our main point, once the bugbears and straw men are seen for what they are and cleared from the Law's vision, the normative Law has little to fear from the discipline of Psychology. To the contrary, we believe it has much to gain. Psychology's substantive knowledge, where facts are found through research and where theories are tested empirically, can help put the Law's emotion theories on firmer ground, such that they accord with the nature of human nature, or with "men [and women] being taken as they are and laws as they might be," as stated by Rousseau at the beginning of *The Social Contract* (1762/1950, p. 3).

Still, the Law ought to be vigilant, and we acknowledge the policing function that the Law rightly exercises, now mandated in the Supreme Court's *Daubert* decision (1993) and its progeny. That decision places the judge in the role of gatekeeper who must evaluate experts and their to-be-proffered testimony using certain "scientific" criteria to keep junk science out of the courtroom. These criteria are what the discipline of Psychology applies when editors and reviewers judge the credibility and relevance of its own "science." In this light, it is fair game for those in the discipline of Law to apply these standards, as well as its own legal and normative standards, in judging this work, and critique where it is warranted.

Psychologists must also police themselves, through training, standards, and ethical precepts, and even by blowing the whistle through amicus briefs, when their "more than kin but less than kind" brethren admit psychological surrogates masquerading as science into testimony, in violation of scientific criteria. In this light, it is fair game for those in Psychology to apply its standards in judging this work, and critique, where warranted.

Finally, we offer this book to both disciplines and ordinary citizens, believing that empirical facts and findings, and the psychological insights that follow, can help inform the Law—to improve the law. Improvement is admittedly a more modest goal than Fletcher's (1988) "perfecting the law," but reaching perfection, like eliminating variance and wrongful verdicts, is quite beyond human means. In looking back to the story with which we started this book, we realize that it has been a long time since the Lord spoke to Cain, or chose to enter a courtroom to deliver the Final Word on culpability; improvement, then, is the best we can hope for. We offer and highlight, in brief summary form, these three recommendations: (a) to bring the perspectives of objectivity and subjectivity together more closely, sometimes conjoining in a different way around emotions and emotion theories; (b) to expand the fundamental elements to make the story psychologically more real; and (c) to present those elements in a complex context, stretched out in psychological spacetime, as biblical, archetypal, ancient, and modern real-life human dramas of culpability—with all their uncertainty and opacity—tend to be.

REFERENCES

Abramson, J. (2004). Death-is-different jurisprudence and the role of the capital jury. *Ohio State Journal of Criminal Law, 2,* 117–164.

Alter, R. (2004). *The five books of Moses: A translation with commentary.* New York: Norton.

American Law Institute. (1962). *Model penal code* [Proposed official draft]. Philadephia: Author.

American Psychiatric Association. (1987). *Diagnostic and statistical manual of mental disorders* (3rd ed., rev.). Washington, DC: Author.

American Psychiatric Association. (1994). *Diagnostic and statistical manual of mental disorders* (4th ed.). Washington, DC: Author.

Amsterdam, A. G., & Bruner, J. (2000). *Minding the law.* Cambridge, MA: Harvard University Press.

Anderson, R. L. (1966). *Elizabethan psychology and Shakespeare's plays.* New York: Russell & Russell. (Original work published 1927)

Apprendi v. New Jersey, 430 U.S. 466 (2000).

Aristotle. (1984). *Nicomachean ethics* (W. D. Ross, Trans.). In J. Barnes (Ed.), *The complete works of Aristotle* (Vol. 2, pp. 1729–1867). Princeton, NJ: Rutgers University Press.

Austin, J. L. (1885). *Lectures on jurisprudence or the philosophy of positive law* (5th ed., rev. by R. Campbell). London: John Murray.

Averill, J. R. (1974). An analysis of psychophysiological symbolism and its influence on theories of emotion. *Journal for the Theory of Social Behaviour, 4,* 147–190.

Averill, J. R. (1982). *Anger and aggression: An essay on emotion.* New York: Springer-Verlag.

Averill, J. R. (1990). Inner feelings, works of the flesh, the beast within, diseases of the mind, driving force, and putting on a show: Six metaphors of emotion and their theoretical extensions. In D. E. Leary (Ed.), *Metaphors in the history of psychology* (pp. 104–132). Cambridge, England: Cambridge University Press.

Bandes, S. A. (Ed.). (1999). *The passions of law.* New York: New York University Press.

Barnard, G. W., Vera, H., Vera, M. I., & Newman, G. (1982). Till death do us part: A study of spouse murder. *Bulletin of the American Association of Psychiatry and Law, 10,* 271–280.

Bazelon, D. L. (1982). Veils, values, and social responsibility. *American Psychologist, 37,* 115–121.

Bazelon, D. L. (1988). *Questioning authority: Justice and criminal law.* New York: Knopf.

Beers, C. W. (1935). *A mind that found itself.* Garden City, NY: Doubleday.

Bennett, W. L., & Feldman, M. S. (1981). *Reconstructing reality in the courtroom: Justice and judgment in American culture.* New Brunswick, NJ: Rutgers University Press.

Berkowitz, L. (1993). Towards a general theory of anger and emotional aggression: Implications of the cognitive–neoassociationistic perspective for the analysis of anger and other emotions. In R. S. Wyer Jr. & T. K. Srull (Eds.), *Perspectives on anger and emotion: Advances in social cognition* (Vol. VI, pp. 1–46). Hillsdale, NJ: Erlbaum.

Blackstone, W. (1779). *Commentaries on the laws of England* (Vol. 4). Chicago: University of Chicago Press. (Original work published 1765–1769)

Blakely v. Washington, No. 02-1632 (2004, slip opinion).

Bloom, H. (2002). *Genius: A mosiac of one hundred exemplary creative minds.* New York: Warner Books.

Bloom, H. (2003). *Hamlet: Poem unlimited.* New York: Riverhead Books.

Booth v. Maryland, 482 U.S. 496 (1987).

Bowers, F. T. (1940). *Elizabethan revenge tragedy 1587–1642.* Princeton, NJ: Princeton University Press.

Breuer, J., & Freud, S. (1982). *Studies on hysteria* (J. Strachey, Trans.). New York: Basic Books. (Original work published 1893)

Brooks, P., & Gewirtz, P. (1996). *Law's stories: Narrative and rhetoric in the law.* New Haven, CT: Yale University Press.

Browne, A. (1987). *When battered women kill.* New York: Free Press.

Bruner, J. (1986). *Actual minds, possible worlds.* Cambridge, MA: Harvard University Press.

Carroll, L. (1978). *Alice's adventures in wonderland and through the looking glass* (With ninety-two illustrations by John Tenniel). Suffolk, England: Puffin Books.

Casado Lumbreras, C. (2003). *La concepción de la emoción desde una perspectiva intercultural: El concepto de emocionado en varios idiomas y culturas* [Conceptions of emotion from a cross-cultural perspective: The concept of *emocionado* in various languages and cultures]. Unpublished doctoral dissertation, Universidad Autónoma de Madrid, Spain.

Ceci, S. J. (2003). Cast in six ponds and you'll reel in something: Looking back on 25 years of research. *American Psychologist, 58,* 855–864.

Ceci, S. J., & Bruck, M. (1995). *Jeopardy in the courtroom: A scientific analysis of children's testimony.* Washington, DC: American Psychological Association.

Cohen, D., & Nisbett, R. E. (1994). Self-protection and the culture of honor: Explaining southern violence. *Personality and Social Psychology Bulletin, 20,* 551–567.

Coke, E. (1979). *The first part of the Institutes of the laws of England.* New York: Garland Publishing. (Original work published 1628)

Colb, S. F. (2003). The conviction of Andrea Yates: A narrative of denial. *Duke Journal of Gender Law & Policy, 10,* 141–147.

Commonwealth of Virginia v. Lee Boyd Malvo, a/k/a John Lee Malvo, Case No. K102888 (2003).

Coughlin, A. M. (1994). Excusing women. *California Law Review, 82,* 1–93.

Crump, D., & Crump, S. W. (1985). In defense of the felony murder doctrine. *Harvard Journal of Law & Public Policy, 8,* 359–398.

Daly, M., Wilson, M., & Weghorst, S. J. (1982). Male sexual jealousy. *Ethology and Sociobiology, 3,* 11–27.

Danziger, K. (1997). *Naming the mind: How psychology found its language.* London: Sage.

Darwin, C. (1872). *The expression of the emotions in man and animals.* London: Murray.

Daubert v. Merrell Dow Pharmaceuticals, 509 U.S. 579 (1993).

Davidson, R. J., Scherer, K. R., & Goldsmith, H. H. (Eds.). (2003). *Handbook of affective sciences.* Oxford, England: Oxford University Press.

Denno, D. W. (2003). Who is Andrea Yates? A short story about insanity. *Duke Journal of Gender Law & Policy, 10,* 1–139.

Director of Public Prosecutions v. Bedder, 1 W.L.R. 1119 (1954).

Director of Public Prosecutions v. Morgan, A.C. 182 (1976).

Dixon, T. (2001). The psychology of the emotions in Britain and America in the nineteenth century: The role of religious and antireligious commitments. *Osiris, 16,* 288–320.

Dixon, T. (2003). *From passions to emotions: The creation of a secular psychological category.* Cambridge, England: Cambridge University Press.

Dobson, V., & Sales, B. (2000). The science of infanticide and mental illness. *Psychology, Public Policy, and Law, 6,* 1098–1112.

Dressler, J. (1979). The jurisprudence of death by another: Accessories and capital punishment. *University of Colorado Law Review, 51,* 17–75.

Dressler, J. (1995). *Understanding criminal law* (2nd ed.). New York: Bender.

Dressler, J. (2001). *Understanding criminal law* (3rd ed.). Danvers, MA: Bender.

Dressler, J. (2002). Battered women who kill their sleeping tormenters: Reflections on maintaining respect for human life while killing moral monsters. In S. Shute & A. P. Simester (Eds.), *Criminal law theory: Doctrines of the general part* (pp. 259–282). Oxford, England: Oxford University Press.

Dworkin, R. (1986). *Law's empire.* Cambridge, MA: Harvard University Press.

East, E. (1803). *Pleas of the Crown* (Vol. I). London: A. Strahen for J. Butterworth & J. Cooke.

Eigen, J. P. (1995). *Witnessing insanity: Madness and mad-doctors in the English court.* New Haven, CT: Yale University Press.

Ekman, P. (1985). *Telling lies.* New York: Norton.

Ekman, P., & O'Sullivan, M. (1991). Who can catch a liar? *American Psychologist, 46,* 899–912.

Eliot, T. S. (1932). Shakespeare and the stoicism of Seneca. In *Selected essays* (pp. 107–120). New York: Harcourt.

Eliot, T. S. (1934). *The waste land and other poems.* New York: Harcourt.

Ellsworth, P. C., Bukaty, R. M., Cowan, C. L., & Thompson, W. C. (1984). The death-qualified jury and the defense of insanity. *Law and Human Behavior, 8,* 45–54.

Ellsworth, P. C., & Scherer, K. R. (2003). Appraisal processes in emotion. In R. J. Davidson, K. R. Scherer, & H. H. Goldsmith (Eds.), *Handbook of affective sciences* (pp. 572–595). Oxford, England: Oxford University Press.

Elwork, A., Sales, B. D., & Alfini, J. J. (1977). Juridic decisions: In ignorance of the law or in light of it? *Law and Human Behavior, 1,* 163–189.

Elwork, A., Sales, B. D., & Alfini, J. J. (1982). *Making jury instructions understandable.* Charlottesville, VA: Michie.

English, P. W., & Sales, B. D. (1997). A ceiling or consistency effect for the comprehension of jury instructions. *Psychology, Public Policy, and Law, 3,* 381–401.

Enmund v. Florida, 458 U.S. 782 (1982).

Ewing, C. P. (1987). *Battered women who kill.* Lexington, MA: Lexington Books.

Faigman, D. L. (1986). Note, The battered woman syndrome and self-defense: A legal and empirical dissent. *Virginia Law Review, 72,* 619.

Fingarette, H. (1972). *The meaning of criminal insanity.* Berkeley: University of California Press.

Fingarette, H. (1974). Self-deception and the "splitting of the ego." In R. Wollheim (Ed.), *Freud: A collection of critical essays* (pp. 80–96). Garden City, NY: Anchor Press.

Fingarette, H., & Hasse, A. F. (1979). *Mental disabilities and criminal responsibility.* Berkeley: University of California Press.

Finkel, N. J. (1988a). *Insanity on trial.* New York: Plenum Press.

Finkel, N. J. (1988b). Maligning and misconstruing jurors' insanity verdicts: A rebuttal. *Forensic Reports, 1,* 97–124.

Finkel, N. J. (1989). The Insanity Defense Reform Act of 1984: Much ado about nothing. *Behavioral Sciences and the Law, 7,* 403–419.

Finkel, N. J. (1990a). Capital felony-murder, objective indicia, and community sentiment. *Arizona Law Review, 32,* 819–913.

Finkel, N. J. (1990b). De facto departures from insanity instructions: Toward the remaking of common law. *Law and Human Behavior, 14,* 105–122.

Finkel, N. J. (1991). The insanity defense: A comparison of verdict schemas. *Law and Human Behavior, 15,* 533–555.

Finkel, N. J. (1995a). Achilles fuming, Odysseus stewing, and Hamlet brooding: On the story of the murder/manslaughter distinction. *University of Nebraska Law Review, 74,* 201–262.

Finkel, N. J. (1995b). *Commonsense justice: Jurors' notions of the law.* Cambridge, MA: Harvard University Press.

Finkel, N. J. (1996). Culpability and commonsense justice: Lessons learned betwixt murder and madness. *Notre Dame Journal of Law Ethics and Public Policy, 10,* 101–154.

Finkel, N. J. (1997). Commonsense justice, psychology, and the law: Prototypes common, senseful, and not. *Psychology, Public Policy, and Law, 3*, 2–3, 461–489.

Finkel, N. J. (2000a). But it's not fair! Commonsense notions of unfairness. *Psychology, Public Policy, and Law, 6*, 898–952.

Finkel, N. J. (2000b). Commonsense justice and jury instructions: Instructive and reciprocating connections. *Psychology, Public Policy, and Law, 6*, 591–628.

Finkel, N. J. (2001). *Not fair! The typology of commonsense unfairness.* Washington, DC: American Psychological Association.

Finkel, N. J. (2003). Haute couture, poorly tailored crimes, and ill-fitting verdicts. *Duke Journal of Gender Law & Policy, 10*, 173–223.

Finkel, N. J., Burke, J. E., & Chavez, L. J. (2000). Commonsense judgments of infanticide: Murder, manslaughter, madness, or miscellaneous? *Psychology, Public Policy, and Law, 6*, 1113–1137.

Finkel, N. J., & Duff, K. B. (1989). The insanity defense: Giving jurors a third option. *Forensic Reports, 2*, 235–263.

Finkel, N. J., & Duff, K. B. (1991). Felony-murder and community sentiment: Testing the Supreme Court's assertions. *Law and Human Behavior, 15*, 405–429.

Finkel, N. J., & Fulero, S. M. (1992). Insanity: Making law in the absence of evidence. *International Journal of Medicine and Law, 11*, 383–404.

Finkel, N. J., & Groscup, J. L. (1997a). Crime prototypes, objective vs. subjective culpability, and a commonsense balance. *Law and Human Behavior, 21*, 209–230.

Finkel, N. J., & Groscup, J. L. (1997b). When mistakes happen: Commonsense rules of culpability. *Psychology, Public Policy, and Law, 3*, 65–125.

Finkel, N. J., & Handel, S. F. (1989). How jurors construe "insanity." *Law and Human Behavior, 13*, 41–59.

Finkel, N. J., Hurabiell, M., & Hughes, K. (1993a). Competency, and other constructs, in right to die cases. *Behavioral Sciences & the Law, 11*, 135–150.

Finkel, N. J., Hurabiell, M., & Hughes, K. (1993b). Right to die and euthanasia: Crossing the public/private boundary. *Law and Human Behavior, 17*, 487–506.

Finkel, N. J., Liss, M. B., & Moran, V. R. (1997). Equal or proportional justice for accessories? Children's pearls of proportionate wisdom. *Journal of Applied Child Development, 18*, 229–244.

Finkel, N. J., Maloney, S. T., Valbuena, M. Z., & Groscup, J. L. (1995). Lay perspectives on legal conundrums: Impossible and mistaken act cases. *Law and Human Behavior, 19*, 593–608.

Finkel, N. J., Maloney, S. T., Valbuena, M. Z., & Groscup, J. L. (1996). Recidivism, proportionalism, and individualized punishment. *American Behavioral Scientist, 39*, 474–487.

Finkel, N. J., Meister, K. H., & Lightfoot, D. M. (1991). The self-defense defense and community sentiment. *Law and Human Behavior, 15*, 585–602.

Finkel, N. J., & Moghaddam, F. M. (Eds.). (2005). *The psychology of rights and duties: Empirical contributions and normative commentaries*. Washington, DC: American Psychological Association.

Finkel, N. J., & Sabat, S. R. (1984). Split-brain madness: An insanity defense waiting to happen. *Law and Human Behavior, 3–4*, 225–252.

Finkel, N. J., Shaw, R., Bercaw, S., & Koch, J. (1985). Insanity defenses: From the jurors' perspective. *Law and Psychology Review, 9*, 77–92.

Finkel, N. J., & Slobogin, C. (1995). Insanity, justification, and culpability: Toward a unifying schema. *Law and Human Behavior, 19*, 447–464.

Finkel, N. J., & Smith, S. F. (1993). Principals and accessories in capital felony-murder: The proportionality principle reigns supreme. *Law & Society Review, 27*, 129–156.

Fletcher, G. P. (1978). *Rethinking criminal law*. Boston: Little, Brown.

Fletcher, G. P. (1988). *A crime of self-defense: Bernhard Goetz and the law on trial*. Chicago: University of Chicago Press.

Fletcher, G. P. (2001). *Our secret constitution: How Lincoln redefined American democracy*. Oxford, England: Oxford University Press.

Follingstad, D. R., Hause, E. S., Rutledge, L. L., & Polek, D. S. (1992). Effects of battered women's early responses on later abuse patterns. *Violence and Victims, 7*, 109–128.

Follingstad, D. R., Polek, D. S., Hause, E. S., Deaton, L. H., Bulger, M. W., & Conway, E. D. (1989). Factors predicting verdicts in cases where battered women kill their husbands. *Law and Human Behavior, 13*, 253–269.

Forgas, J. P. (1995). Mood and judgement: The affect infusion model (AIM). *Psychological Bulletin, 117*, 39–66.

Fortenbaugh, W. (1975). *Aristotle on emotion*. London: Duckworth.

Frank, J. (1932). Mr. Justice Holmes and non-euclidean legal thinking. *Cornell Law Quarterly, 17*, 568.

Fridlund, A. J., & Duchaine, B. (1996). "Facial expressions of emotion" and the delusion of the hermetic self. In R. Harré & W. G. Parrott (Eds.), *The emotions: Social, cultural and biological dimensions* (pp. 259–284). London: Sage.

Frijda, N. H. (1986). *The emotions*. Cambridge, England: Cambridge University Press.

Frijda, N. H., Mesquita, B., Sonnemans, J., & Van Goozen, S. (1991). The duration of affective phenomena or emotions, sentiments, and passions. *International Review of Studies on Emotion, 1*, 187–225.

Fulero, S. M., & Finkel, N. J. (1991). Barring ultimate issue testimony: An insane rule? *Law and Human Behavior, 15*, 495–507.

Galen. (1984). *On the doctrines of Hippocrates and Plato* (P. De Lacy, Trans.) Berlin, Germany: Akademie-Verlag.

Gardiner, H. M., Metcalf, R. C., & Beebe-Center, J. G. (1937). *Feeling and emotion: A history of theories*. New York: American Book Company.

Gerber, R. J. (1984). *The insanity defense*. Port Washington, NY: Associated Faculty Press.

Gibson, J. L., & Caldeira, G. A. (1996). The legal cultures of Europe. *Law & Society Review, 30*, 55–85.

Gillespie, C. K. (1989). *Justifiable homicide: Battered women, self-defense, and the law.* Columbus: Ohio State University Press.

Grainger v. State, 13 Tenn. 459 (1830).

Green, T. A. (1985). *Verdict according to conscience: Perspectives on the English criminal trial jury, 1200–1800.* Chicago: University of Chicago Press.

Greenawalt, K. (1986). Distinguishing justifications from excuses. *Law & Contemporary Problems, 49*, 89–108.

Greenblatt, S. (2004). *Will in the world: How Shakespeare became Shakespeare.* New York: Norton.

Greene, B. (2004). *The fabric of the cosmos: Space, time, and the texture of reality.* New York: Knopf.

Greene, T. M. (Ed.). (1957). *Kant selections.* New York: Scribner.

Greenwald, J. P., Tomkins, A. J., Kenning, M., & Zavodny, D. (1990). Psychological self-defense jury instructions: Influence on verdicts for battered women defendants. *Behavioral Sciences & the Law, 8*, 171–180.

Gross, J. J., & Levenson, R. W. (1993). Emotional suppression: Physiology, self-report, and expressive behavior. *Journal of Personality and Social Psychology, 64*, 970–986.

Gurney, E. (1884). What is an emotion? *Mind, 9*, 421–426.

Hadfield's Case, 27 Howell's State Trials 1281 (1800).

Haidt, J. (2001). The emotional dog and its rational tail: A social intuitionist approach to moral judgment. *Psychological Review, 108*, 814–834.

Hale, M. (1972). *Historia plasitorum coronae* [The pleas of the Crown]. London: Professional Books. (Original work published 1678)

Hallett, C. A., & Hallett, E. S. (1980). *The revenger's madness: A study of revenge tragedy motifs.* Lincoln: University of Nebraska Press.

Hamilton, A., Madison, J., & Jay, J. (1961). *The federalist papers.* New York: A Mentor Book. (Original work published 1787)

Hamilton, V. L., & Hagiwara, S. (1992). Roles, responsibility, and accounts across cultures. *International Journal of Psychology, 27*, 157–179.

Hamilton, V. L., & Sanders, J. (1992). *Everyday justice: Responsibility and the individual in Japan and the United States.* New Haven, CT: Yale University Press.

Haney, C. (2002). Making law modern: Toward a contextual model of justice. *Psychology, Public Policy, and Law, 8*, 3–63.

Hans, V. P. (1986). An analysis of public attitudes toward the insanity defense. *Criminology, 24*, 393–414.

Hans, V. P. (1990). Law and the media: An overview and introduction. *Law and Human Behavior, 14*, 399–407.

Hans, V. P., & Slater, D. (1983). John Hinckley, Jr., and the insanity defense: The public's verdict. *Public Opinion Quarterly, 47*, 202–212.

Hans, V. P., & Vidmar, N. (1986). *Judging the jury.* New York: Plenum Press.

Harré, R. (1972). The analysis of episodes. In J. Israel & H. Tajfel (Eds.), *The context of social psychology: A critical assessment*. New York: Academic Press.

Harré, R. (Ed.). (1986). *The social construction of emotions*. Oxford, England: Basil Blackwell.

Harré, R. (1998). *The singular self: An introduction to the psychology of personhood*. London: Sage.

Harré, R., & Gillett, G. (1994). *The discursive mind*. London: Sage.

Harré, R., & van Langenhove, L. (Eds.). (1999). *Positioning theory: Moral contexts of intentional action*. Malden, MA: Blackwell.

Hart, H. L. A. (1968). *Punishment and responsibility: Essays in the philosophy of law*. New York: Oxford University Press.

Hastie, R., Penrod, S. D., & Pennington, N. (1983). *Inside the jury*. Cambridge, MA: Harvard University Press.

Hatfield, E., Cacioppo, J. T., & Rapson, R. L. (1994). *Emotional contagion*. Cambridge, England: Cambridge University Press.

Hermann, D. H. (1983). *The insanity defense: Philosophical, historical and legal perspectives*. Springfield, IL: Charles C Thomas.

Hochschild, A. R. (1983). *The managed heart: Commercialization of human feeling*. Berkeley: University of California Press.

Hoffer, P. C., & Hull, N. E. H. (1984). *Murdering mothers: Infanticide in England and New England, 1558–1803*. New York: New York University Press.

Holmes, O. W. (1963). *The common law* (M. D. Howe, Ed.). Cambridge, MA: Harvard University Press. (Original work published 1881)

Homer. (1950). *The Iliad* (A. H. Chase & W. G. Perry Jr., Trans.). New York: Bantam Books.

Horowitz, I. A. (1997). Reasonable doubt instructions: Commonsense justice and standard of proof. *Psychology, Public Policy, and Law, 3*, 285–302.

Hume, D. (2000). *A treatise of human nature* (D. F. Norton & M. J. Norton, Eds.). Oxford, England: Oxford University Press.

Hunter, E. (1951). *Brain-washing in Red China*. New York: Vanguard Press.

Hupka, R. B. (1991). The motive for the arousal of romantic jealousy: Its cultural origin. In P. Salovey (Ed.), *The psychology of jealousy and envy* (pp. 252–270). New York: Guilford Press.

Insanity Defense Reform Act of 1984, Pub. L. No. 98-473, secs. 401, 402, 20 (1984).

Jackman, T. (2003a, December 10). Malvo killed to please Muhammad, court told. *The Washington Post*, pp. B1, B4.

Jackman, T. (2003b, December 16). Prosecution psychologists say Malvo was not insane. *The Washington Post*, pp. B1, B4.

Jackman, T. (2003c, December 11). 2 psychiatrists testify that Malvo was insane. *The Washington Post*, pp. B1, B8.

Jackman, T. (2004, July 21). Muhammad team makes appeal to high court in Va. *The Washington Post*, pp. B1, B5.

Jackson v. Indiana, 406 U.S. 715 (1972).

Jacoby, S. (1983). *Wild justice: The evolution of revenge.* New York: HarperCollins.

James, W. (1884). What is an emotion? *Mind, 9,* 188–205.

James (Simon), R. M. (1959). Jurors' assessment of criminal responsibility. *Social Problems, 7,* 58–67.

Jamison, K. R. (2004). *Exuberance: The passion for life.* New York: Knopf.

Kahan, D. M. (1997). Social influence, social meaning, and deterrence. *Virginia Law Review, 83,* 349–395.

Kahan, D. M., & Nussbaum, M. C. (1996). Two conceptions of emotion in criminal law. *Columbia Law Review, 96,* 269–374.

Kahneman, D. (1994). New challenges to the rationality assumption. *Journal of Institutional and Theoretical Economics, 150,* 18–36.

Kahneman, D. (2003). A perspective on judgment and choice: Mapping bounded rationality. *American Psychologist, 58,* 697–720.

Kahneman, D., & Tversky, A. (1982). On the study of statistical intuitions. In D. Kahneman, P. Slovic, & A. Tversky (Eds.), *Judgment under uncertainty: Heuristics and biases* (pp. 493–508). New York: Cambridge University Press.

Kalven, H. H., Jr., & Zeisel, H. H. (1971). *The American jury.* Chicago: University of Chicago Press.

Kasian, M., Spanos, N. P., Terrance, C. A., & Peebles, S. (1993). Battered women who kill: Jury simulation and legal defenses. *Law and Human Behavior, 17,* 289–312.

Kassin, S. M., Goldstein, C. C., & Savitsky, K. (2003). Behavioral confirmation in the interrogation room: On the dangers of presuming guilt. *Law and Human Behavior, 27,* 187–203.

Kassin, S. M., & Kiechel, K. L. (1996). The social psychology of false confessions: Compliance, internalization, and confabulation. *Psychological Science, 7,* 125–128.

Keltner, D., & Haidt, J. (1999). Social functions of emotions at four levels of analysis. *Cognition and Emotion, 13,* 505–521.

Kirschner, S. M., Litwack, T. R., & Galperin, G. J. (2004). The defense of extreme emotional disturbance: A qualitative analysis of cases in New York County. *Psychology, Public Policy, and Law, 10,* 102–133.

Kövecses, Z. (1995). Metaphor and the folk understanding of anger. In J. A. Russell, J.-M. Fernández-Dols, A. S. R. Manstead, & J. C. Wellenkamp (Eds.), *Everyday conceptions of emotions: An introduction to the psychology, anthropology and linguistics of emotion* (pp. 49–71). Dordrecht, the Netherlands: Kluwer Academic.

Kövecses, Z. (2000). *Metaphor and emotion: Language, culture, and body in human feeling.* Cambridge, England: Cambridge University Press.

Kyd, T. (1966). *The Spanish tragedie.* Leeds, England: Scolar Press. (Original work published 1592)

Lakoff, G., & Johnson, M. (1980). *Metaphors we live by.* Chicago: University of Chicago Press.

Lazarus, R. S. (1966). *Psychological stress and the coping process.* New York: McGraw-Hill.

Lazarus, R. S. (1982). Thoughts on the relations between emotion and cognition. *American Psychologist, 37,* 1019–1024.

Lazarus, R. S. (1984). On the primacy of cognition. *American Psychologist, 39,* 124–129.

Lazarus, R. S. (1991). *Emotion and adaptation.* New York: Oxford University Press.

LeDoux, J. E. (1994). The degree of emotional control depends on the kind of response system involved. In P. Ekman & R. J. Davidson (Eds.), *The nature of emotion: Fundamental questions* (pp. 270–272). New York: Oxford University Press.

LeDoux, J. E. (1996). *The emotional brain: The mysterious underpinnings of emotional life.* New York: Touchstone.

Levesque, R. J. R. (2001). *Culture and family violence: Fostering change through human rights law.* Washington, DC: American Psychological Association.

Lewis, D. O. (1998). *Guilty by reason of insanity.* New York: Fawcett Columbine.

Lewis, M., & Haviland-Jones, J. M. (Eds.). (2000). *Handbook of emotions* (2nd ed.). New York: Guilford Press.

Lieberman, J. D., & Sales, B. D. (1997). What social science teaches us about the jury instruction process. *Psychology, Public Policy, and Law, 3,* 589–644.

Lieberman, J. D., & Sales, B. D. (2000). Jury instructions: Past, present, and future. *Psychology, Public Policy, and Law, 6,* 587–590.

Lifton, R. J. (1963). *Thought reform and the psychology of totalism: A study of "brainwashing" in China.* New York: Norton.

Llewellyn, K. N. (1931). Some realism about realism: Responding to Dean Pound. *Harvard Law Review, 44,* 1222–1264.

London, P. (1964). *The modes and morals of psychotherapy.* New York: Holt, Rinehart & Winston.

Lutz, C. A. (1988). *Unnatural emotions: Everyday sentiments on a Micronesian atoll and their challenge to Western theory.* Chicago: University of Chicago Press.

Lykken, D. T. (1985). The probity of the polygraph. In S. M. Kassin & L. S. Wrightsman (Eds.), *The psychology of evidence and trial procedure* (pp. 95–123). Newbury Park, CA: Sage.

MacLean, P. D. (1949). Psychosomatic disease and the "visceral brain": Recent developments bearing on the Papez theory of emotion. *Psychosomatic Medicine, 11,* 338–353.

MacPherson, P. (1994, May 24). Injuries on the track. *The Washington Post,* pp. WH10–WH12.

Maher v. People, 10 Mich. 212 (1863).

Mark, V. H., & Ervin, F. R. (1970). *Violence and the brain.* New York: HarperCollins.

McGregor, I., & Holmes, J. G. (1999). How storytelling shapes memory and impressions of relationship events over time. *Journal of Personality and Social Psychology, 76,* 403–419.

Melville, H. (1986). *Billy Budd and other stories*. New York: Penguin. (Original work published 1924)

Merriam-Webster's New Collegiate Dictionary (7th ed.). (1966). Springfield, MA: G. & C. Merriam.

Merry, S. E. (1990). *Getting justice and getting even: Legal consciousness among working-class Americans*. Chicago: University of Chicago Press.

Miller, J. G., & Bersoff, D. M. (1992). Culture and moral judgement: How are conflicts between justice and friendship resolved? *Journal of Personality and Social Psychology, 62*, 541–554.

Mitchell, E. W. (2003). *Self-made madness: Rethinking illness and criminal responsibility*. Aldershot, England: Ashgate Publishing.

Mitchell, S. (1996). *Genesis: A new translation of the classic biblical stories*. New York: Harper Collins.

M'Naghten's Case, 10 Cl. & Fin. 200, 8 Eng. Rep. 718 (1843).

Mogg, K., & Bradley, B. P. (1999). Selective attention and anxiety: A cognitive–motivational perspective. In T. Dalgleish & M. Power (Eds.), *Handbook of cognition and emotion* (pp. 145–170). Chichester, England: Wiley.

Moghaddam, F. M. (1998). *Social psychology: Exploring universals across cultures*. San Francisco: Freeman.

Monroe v. State, 5 Ga. 85 (1848).

Moore, M. S. (1984). *Law and psychiatry: Rethinking the relationship*. Cambridge, England: Cambridge University Press.

Moore, T. (1992). *Care of the soul: A guide for cultivating depth and sacredness in everyday life*. New York: HarperCollins.

Moran, R. (1981). *Knowing right from wrong: The insanity defense of Daniel McNaughtan*. New York: Free Press.

Morris, N. (1982). *Madness and the criminal law*. Chicago: The University of Chicago Press.

Morse, S. J. (1984). Statement on behalf of the Association for the Advancement of Psychology and the American Psychological Association. Hearings before the Subcommittee on Criminal Justice of the Committee on the Judiciary, House of Representatives. *Reform of the federal insanity defense* (Serial No. 21, pp. 311–402). Washington, DC: U.S. Government Printing Office.

Morse, S. J. (1985). Excusing the crazy: The insanity defense reconsidered. *Southern California Law Review, 58*, 780–836.

Murphy, J. G. (2003). *Getting even: Forgiveness and its limits*. New York: Oxford University Press.

Neu, J. (1977). *Emotion, thought, and therapy*. Berkeley: University of California Press.

Nussbaum, M. C. (1994). *The therapy of desire: Theory and practice in Hellenistic ethics*. Princeton, NJ: Princeton University Press.

Oakley, J. (1992). *Morality and the emotions*. London: Routledge.

Oatley, K. (1992). *Best laid schemes: The psychology of emotions*. Cambridge, England: Cambridge University Press.

Oatley, K. (2000). *Shakespeare's invention of theatre as simulation that runs on minds.* Paper presented at the Artificial Intelligence & Simulation of Behaviour meeting, Birmingham, England.

Ogloff, J. R. P. (1991). A comparison of insanity defense standards on juror decision making. *Law and Human Behavior, 15,* 509–531.

Öhman, A. (2000). Fear and anxiety: Evolutionary, cognitive, and clinical perspectives. In M. Lewish & J. M. Haviland-Jones (Eds.), *Handbook of emotions* (2nd ed., pp. 573–593). New York: Guilford Press.

Oldenburg, D. (2003, November 21). Stressed to kill: The defense of brainwashing. *The Washington Post,* pp. C1, C2.

O'Malley, S. (2004). *Are you there alone? The unspeakable crime of Andrea Yates.* New York: Simon & Schuster.

Orth, U. (2003). Punishment goals of crime victims. *Law and Human Behavior, 27,* 173–186.

Ortony, A., Clore, G. L., & Collins, A. (1988). *The cognitive structure of emotions.* Cambridge, England: Cambridge University Press.

Oxford English Dictionary. (2002). Oxford, England: Oxford University Press.

Panksepp, J. (1998). *Affective neuroscience: The foundations of human and animal emotions.* Oxford, England: Oxford University Press.

Papez, J. W. (1937). A proposed mechanism of emotion. *Archives of Neurology and Psychiatry, 38,* 725–743.

Parkinson, B., Fischer, A. H., & Manstead, A. S. R. (2005). *Emotion in social relations.* New York: Psychology Press.

Parrott, W. G. (1991). The emotional experiences of envy and jealousy. In P. Salovey (Ed.), *The psychology of jealousy and envy* (pp. 3–33). New York: Guilford Press.

Parrott, W. G. (1993a). Beyond hedonism: Motives for inhibiting good moods and for maintaining bad moods. In D. M. Wegner & J. W. Pennebaker (Eds.), *Handbook of mental control* (pp. 278–305). Englewood Cliffs, NJ: Prentice-Hall.

Parrott, W. G. (1993b). On the scientific study of angry organisms. In R. S. Wyer Jr. & T. K. Srull (Eds.), *Perspectives on anger and emotion: Advances in social cognition* (Vol. VI, pp. 167–177). Hillsdale, NJ: Erlbaum.

Parrott, W. G. (1995). The heart and the head: Everyday conceptions of being emotional. In J. A. Russell, J.-M. Fernández-Dols, A. S. R. Manstead, & J. C. Wellenkamp (Eds.), *Everyday conceptions of emotions: An introduction to the psychology, anthropology and linguistics of emotion* (pp. 73–84). Dordrecht, the Netherlands: Kluwer Academic.

Parrott, W. G. (2000). The psychologist of Avon: Emotion in Elizabethan psychology and the plays of Shakespeare. In B. Landau, J. Sabini, J. Jonides, & E. Newport (Eds.), *Perception, cognition, and language: Essays in honor of Henry and Lila Gleitman* (pp. 231–243). Cambridge, MA: MIT Press.

Parrott, W. G. (2001). Implications of dysfunctional emotions for understanding how emotions function. *Review of General Psychology, 5,* 180–186.

Parrott, W. G. (2002). The functional utility of negative emotions. In L. F. Barrett & P. Salovey (Eds.), *The wisdom in feeling: Psychological processes in emotional intelligence* (pp. 341–359). New York: Guilford Press.

Parrott, W. G. (2003). Positioning and the emotions. In R. Harré & F. Moghaddam (Eds.), *The self and others: Positioning individuals and groups in personal, political, and cultural contexts* (pp. 29–43). Westport, CT: Praeger Publishers.

Parrott, W. G., & Sabini, J. (1989). On the "emotional" qualities of certain types of cognition: A reply to arguments for the independence of cognition and affect. *Cognitive Therapy and Research, 13,* 49–65.

Parrott, W. G., & Schulkin, J. (1993). Psychophysiology and the cognitive nature of the emotions. *Cognition and Emotion, 7,* 43–59.

Parrott, W. G., & Smith, R. H. (1993). Distinguishing the experiences of envy and jealousy. *Journal of Personality and Social Psychology, 64,* 906–920.

Pauline v. State, 21 Tex. Crim. 436, 1 S.W. 453 (1886).

Payne v. Tennessee, 501 U.S. 808 (1991).

Pennington, N., & Hastie, R. (1986). Evidence evaluation in complex decision making. *Journal of Personality and Social Psychology, 51,* 242–258.

Pennington, N., & Hastie, R. (1990). Practical implications of psychological research on juror and jury decision making. *Personality and Social Psychology Bulletin, 16,* 90–105.

Pennington, N., & Hastie, R. (1992). Explaining the evidence: Tests of the story model for juror decision making. *Journal of Personality and Social Psychology, 62,* 189–206.

Penry v. Johnson, 532 U.S. 916 (1999).

People v. Goetz, 506 N.Y.S.2d 18 (N.Y. 1986).

People v. Stamp, 2 Cal.App.3d 203, 82 Cal.Rptr. 598 (1969).

People v. Torres, 488 N.Y.S.2d 358 (N.Y. Sup. Ct. 1985).

People v. Washington, 402 P.2d 130, 133 (Cal. 1965).

Perkins, R. M., & Boyce, R. N. (1982). *Criminal law.* Mineola, NY: Foundation Press.

Perlin, M. L. (1989–1990). Unpacking the myths: The symbolism mythology of insanity defense jurisprudence. *Case Western Reserve Law Review, 40,* 599–731.

Perlin, M. L. (1990). Psychodynamics and the insanity defense: "Ordinary common sense" and heuristic reasoning. *Nebraska Law Review, 69,* 3–70.

Perlin, M. L. (1994). *The jurisprudence of the insanity defense.* Durham, NC: Carolina Academic Press.

Perlin, M. L. (2000). *The hidden prejudice: Mental disability on trial.* Washington, DC: American Psychological Association.

Peters, R. S. (1970). The education of emotions. In M. B. Arnold (Ed.), *Feelings and emotions: The Loyola symposium.* New York: Academic Press.

Pillsbury, S. H. (1998). *Judging evil: Rethinking the law of murder and manslaughter.* New York: New York University Press.

Pincus, J. H. (2001). *Base instincts: What makes killers kill?* New York: Norton.

Planalp, S. (1999). *Communicating emotion: Social, moral, and cultural processes.* Cambridge, England: Cambridge University Press.

Pollock, F., & Maitland, F. W. (1968). *The history of English law before the time of Edward I.* Boston: Little, Brown.

Pope, A. (1962). Essay on criticism. In R. M. Schmitz (Ed.), *A study of Bodleian manuscript text with facsimiles, transcripts, and variants.* St. Louis, MO: Washington University Press. (Original work published 1709)

Posner, R. A. (1985). An economic theory of the criminal law. *Columbia Law Review, 85,* 1222–1223.

Posner, R. A. (1988). *Law and literature: A misunderstood relation.* Cambridge, MA: Harvard University Press.

Posner, R. A. (1990). *The problems of jurisprudence.* Cambridge, MA: Harvard University Press.

Pound, R. (1907). The need of a sociological jurisprudence. *Green Bag, 19,* 607–615.

Pratto, F. (1994). Consciousness and automatic evaluation. In P. M. Niedenthal & S. Kitayama (Eds.), *The heart's eye: Emotional influences in perception and attention* (pp. 115–143). San Diego, CA: Academic Press.

Rawls, J. (1971). *A theory of justice:* Cambridge, MA: Harvard University Press.

Rawls, J. (1999). *The law of peoples.* Cambridge, MA: Harvard University Press.

Ray, I. (1983). *A treatise on the medical jurisprudence of insanity.* New York: Da Capo Press. (Original work published 1838)

Regina v. Fisher, 8 Car. & P 182, 173 Eng. Rep. 452 (1837).

Regina v. Morgan, 2 W.L.R. 923 (1975).

Regina v. Smith, 4 Post & F 1066 (1866), 176 Eng. Rep. 910.

Rex v. Arnold, 16 Howell's State Trials, 684 (1723).

Rights and wrongs for victims. (2003, April 23). *The Washington Post,* p. A34.

Ring v. Arizona, 536 U.S. 584 (2002).

Roberts, C. F., & Golding, S. L. (1991). The social construction of criminal responsibility and insanity. *Law and Human Behavior, 15,* 349–376.

Roberts, J. V., & Doob, A. N. (1990). News media influences on public views of sentencing. *Law and Human Behavior, 14,* 451–468.

Robinson, D. N. (1980). *Psychology and law: Can justice survive the social sciences?* New York: Oxford University Press.

Robinson, D. N. (1996). *Wild beasts & idle humours: The insanity defense from antiquity to the present.* Cambridge, MA: Harvard University Press.

Robinson, P. H. (1975). A theory of justification: Societal harm as a prerequisite for criminal liability. *UCLA Law Review, 23,* 266.

Robinson, P. H. (1985). Causing the conditions of one's own defense: A study in the limits of theory in criminal law doctrine. *Virginia Law Review, 71,* 1–63.

Robinson, P. H., & Darley, J. M. (1995). *Justice, liability and blame: Community views and the criminal law.* Boulder, CO: Westview Press.

Roper v. Simmons, No. 03-633 (slip opinion, March 1, 2005).

Roseman, I. J., & Smith, C. A. (2001). Appraisal theory: Overview, assumptions, varieties, controversies. In K. R. Scherer, A. Schorr, & T. Johnstone (Eds.), *Appraisal processes in emotion: Theory, methods, research* (pp. 3–19). Oxford, England: Oxford University Press.

Rosenhan, D. L. (1973). On being sane in insane places. *Science, 179,* 250–258.

Roth, N. E., & Sundby, S. E. (1985). The felony-murder rule: A doctrine at constitutional crossroads. *Cornell Law Review, 70,* 446–492.

Rousseau, J. J. (1950). *The social contract and discourses* (G. D. N. Cole, Trans.). New York: Dutton. (Original work published 1762)

Royley's Case, Cro. Jac. 296, 79 Eng. Rep. 254 (England 1666).

Sabat, S. R. (2001). *The experience of Alzheimer's disease: Life through a tangled veil.* Oxford, England: Blackwell Publishers.

Sabini, J., & Silver, M. (1982). *Moralities of everyday life.* New York: Oxford University Press.

Sales, B. D., & Shuman, D. W. (2005). *Experts in court: Reconciling law, science, and professional knowledge.* Washington, DC: American Psychological Association.

Sartre, J. P. (1974). *Mauvaise foi* and the unconscious. In R. Wollheim (Ed.), *Freud: A collection of critical essays* (pp. 70–79). Garden City, NY: Anchor Books.

Sass, L. A. (1992). *Madness and modernism: Insanity in the light of modern art, literature, and thought.* New York: Basic Books.

Saxe, L. (1991). Lying: Thoughts on an applied social psychologist. *American Psychologist, 46,* 409–415.

Saxe, L., Dougherty, D., & Cross, T. (1985). The validity of polygraph testing: Scientific analysis and public controversy. *American Psychologist, 40,* 355–366.

Schank, R., & Abelson, R. (1977). *Scripts, plans, goals, and understanding.* Hillsdale, NJ: Erlbaum.

Schein, E. H., Schneier, I., & Barker, C. H. (1961). *A socio-psychological analysis of the "brainwashing" of American civilian prisoners by the Chinese Communists.* New York: Norton.

Schklar, J., & Diamond, S. S. (1999). Juror reaction to DNA evidence: Errors and expectancies. *Law and Human Behavior, 23,* 159–184.

Schneider, E. M. (1980). Equal rights to trial for women: Sex bias and the law of self-defense. *Harvard Civil Rights Law Review, 15,* 623–647.

Schneider, E. M. (1986). Describing and changing: Women's self-defense work and the problem of expert testimony on battering. *Women's Rights Law Reporter, 9,* 195–222.

Schneider, E. M., & Jordan, S. B. (1978). Representation of women who defend themselves in response to physical or sexual assault. *Women's Rights Law Reporter, 4,* 149–163.

Schoeck, H. (1969). *Envy: A theory of social behaviour* (M. Glenny & B. Ross, Trans.). Indianapolis, IN: Liberty Press. (Original work published 1966)

Schopp, R. F., Sturgis, B. J., & Sullivan, M. (1994). Battered woman syndrome, expert testimony, and the distinction between justification and excuse. *University of Illinois Law Review, 1994*, 45–113.

Schreber, D. P. (1988). *Memoirs of my nervous illness* (I. Macalpine & R. A. Hunter, Trans.). Cambridge, MA: Harvard University Press. (Original work published 1903)

Schulhofer, S. J. (1990). The gender question in criminal law. *Social Philosophy & Policy, 7*, 105–137.

Schuller, R. A. (1992). The impact of battered woman syndrome evidence on jury decision processes. *Law and Human Behavior, 16*, 597–620.

Schuller, R. A. (2003). Expert evidence and its impact on jurors' decisions in homicide trials involving battered women. *Duke Journal of Gender Law & Policy, 10*, 225–246.

Schuller, R. A., & Hastings, P. A. (1996). Trials of battered women who kill: The impact of alternative forms of expert testimony. *Law and Human Behavior, 20*, 167–188.

Schuller, R. A., & Rzepa, S. (2002). Expert testimony pertaining to battered woman syndrome: Its impact on jurors' decisions. *Law and Human Behavior, 26*, 655–673.

Seligman, M. E. P. (1998). Positive social science. *Monitor on Psychology, 29*(4), p. 2.

Shakespeare, W. (1938). *The works of William Shakespeare, gathered in one volume* (prepared by Arthur Henry Bullen), The Shakespeare Head Edition. Oxford: Oxford University Press. Works cited: *King Richard the Third* (pp. 98–138); *King John* (pp. 302–328); *The Merchant of Venice* (pp. 388–415); *King Henry the Fifth* (pp. 485–519); *Julius Caesar* (pp. 582–610); *Hamlet, Prince of Denmark* (pp. 670–713); *Troilus and Cressida* (pp. 714–752); *Measure for Measure* (pp. 786–817); *Othello, The Moor of Venice* (pp. 818–857); *Macbeth* (pp. 858–884).

Sharpsteen, D. J. (1991). The organization of jealousy knowledge: Romantic jealousy as a blended emotion. In P. Salovey (Ed.), *The psychology of jealousy and envy* (pp. 31–51). New York: Guilford Press.

Shaver, K. G. (1985). *The attribution of blame: Causality, responsibility, and blameworthiness.* New York: Springer-Verlag.

Shaver, P., Schwartz, J., Kirson, D., & O'Connor, C. (1987). Emotion knowledge: Further exploration of a prototype approach. *Journal of Personality and Social Psychology, 52*, 1061–1086.

Sherman, N. (1989). *The fabric of character.* Oxford, England: Clarendon Press.

Shields, S. (2002). *Speaking from the heart: Gender and the social meaning of emotion.* Cambridge, England: Cambridge University Press.

Shorter v. People, 2 N.Y. 193 (1849).

Shuman, D. W., & Sales, B. D. (1998). The admissibility of expert testimony based upon clinical judgment and scientific research. *Psychology, Public Policy, and Law, 4*, 1226–1252.

Singer, M. T., & Lalich, J. (1995). *Cults in our midst*. San Francisco: Jossey-Bass.

Singer, R. (1986). The resurgence of mens rea: I. Provocation, emotional disturbance, and the model penal code. *Boston College Law Review, 27*, 243–322.

Singer, R. (1987). The resurgence of mens rea: II. Honest but unreasonable mistake of fact in self defense. *Boston College Law Review, 28*, 459–519.

Skeem, J. L., & Golding, S. L. (2001). Describing jurors' personal conceptions of insanity and their relationship to case judgments. *Psychology, Public Policy, and Law, 7*, 561–621.

Smith, R. (1981). *Trial by medicine: Insanity and responsibility in Victorian trials*. Edinburgh, Scotland: Edinburgh University Press.

Smith, R. H. (2004). Envy and its transmutations. In L. Z. Tiedens & C. W. Leach (Eds.), *The social life of emotions* (pp. 43–63). Cambridge, England: Cambridge University Press.

Smith, V. L. (1991). Prototypes in the courtroom: Lay representations of legal concepts. *Journal of Personality and Social Psychology, 61*, 857–872.

Smith, V. L. (1993). When prior knowledge and law collide: Helping jurors use the law. *Law and Human Behavior, 17*, 507–536.

Smith, V. L., & Studebaker, C. A. (1996). What do you expect? The influence of people's prior knowledge of crime categories on fact-finding. *Law and Human Behavior, 20*, 517–532.

Solomon, R. C. (1976). *The passions*. Garden City, NY: Anchor Press.

Solomon, R. C. (1980). Emotions and choice. In A. O. Rorty (Ed.), *Explaining emotions* (pp. 251–281). Berkeley: University of California Press.

Sorabji, R. (2000). *Emotion and peace of mind: From Stoic agitation to Christian temptation*. Oxford, England: Oxford University Press.

South Carolina v. Gathers, 490 U.S. 805 (1989).

Spackman, M. P. (1998). *Folk theories of attribution of responsibility for emotions*. Unpublished doctoral dissertation, Georgetown University, Washington, DC.

Spackman, M. P., Belcher, J. C., Calapp, J. W., & Taylor, A. (2002). An analysis of subjective and objective instruction forms on mock-juries' murder/manslaughter distinctions. *Law and Human Behavior, 26*, 605–623.

Spackman, M. P., Belcher, J. C., & Hanson, A. S. (2002). Effects perceived emotional intensity on mock jurors' murder/manslaughter distinctions. *Journal of Applied Social Psychology: Biobehavioral Research, 7*, 87–113.

Spackman, M. P., & Parrott, W. G. (2001). Emotionology in prose: A study of descriptions of emotions from three literary periods. *Cognition and Emotion, 15*, 553–573.

Spragens, T. A., Jr. (1999). *Civic liberalism: Reflections on our democratic ideals*. Lanham, MD: Rowman & Littlefield.

Spragens, T. A., Jr. (2004). Theories of justice, rights, and duties: Negotiating the interface between normative and empirical inquiry. In N. J. Finkel & F. M. Moghaddam (Eds.), *The psychology of rights and duties: Empirical contributions and normative commentaries* (pp. 253–270). Washington, DC: American Psychological Association.

Stalans, L. (1993). Citizen's crime stereotypes, biased recall, and punishment preferences in abstract cases: The educative role of interpersonal sources. *Law and Human Behavior, 17,* 451–470.

Stalans, L. J., & Diamond, S. S. (1990). Formation and change in lay evaluations of criminal sentencing: Misperception and discontent. *Law and Human Behavior, 14,* 199–214.

Stanford v. Kentucky, 492 U.S. 361 (1989).

State v. Bianci, No. 79-10116 (Wash. Sup. Ct., October 19, 1979).

State v. Elliot, 177 Conn. 1, 411 A.2d 3 (1979).

State v. Gounagias, 153 P. 9 (Wash. 1915).

State v. John, 30 N.C. (8 Ired.) 330 (1848).

State v. Kelly, 685 P.2d 564, 570 (Wash. 1984).

State v. Wanrow, 88 Wash. 2d 221, 559 P. 2d 548 (1977).

State v. Zdanis, 182 Conn. 388, 438 A.2d 696 (1980).

Stearns, C. Z., & Stearns, P. N. (1986). *Anger: The struggle for emotional control in America's history.* Chicago: University of Chicago Press.

Stearns, P. N. (1989). *Jealousy: The evolution of an emotion in American history.* New York: New York University Press.

Stefan, S. (2001). *Unequal rights: Discrimination against people with mental disabilities and the Americans With Disabilities Act.* Washington, DC: American Psychological Association.

Stephen, J. F. (1883). *History of the criminal law of England.* London: Macmillan.

Subcommittee on Criminal Law of the Committee of the Judiciary, United States Senate. (1983). *Limiting the insanity defense* (Serial No. J-97-122). Washington, DC: U.S. Government Printing Office.

Tavris, C. (1989). *Anger: The misunderstood emotion* (Rev. ed.). New York: Touchstone.

Thompson v. Oklahoma, 487 U.S. 815 (1988).

Tiedens, L. Z., & Leach, C. W. (Eds.). (2004). *The social life of emotions.* Cambridge, England: Cambridge University Press.

Tison v. Arizona, 481 U.S. 137 (1987).

Toulmin, S. E. (1990). *Cosmopolis: The hidden agenda of modernity.* New York: Free Press.

Tourneur, C. (1966). *The revenger's tragedy.* Cambridge, MA: Harvard University Press. (Original work published 1607)

Tugade, M. M., & Fredrickson, B. L. (2002). Positive emotions and emotional intelligence. In L. F. Barrett & P. Salovey (Eds.), *The wisdom in feeling: Psychological processes in emotional intelligence* (pp. 319–340). New York: Guilford Press.

Tversky, A., & Kahneman, D. (1974). Judgment under uncertainty: Heuristics and biases. *Science, 185,* 1124–1131.

Tyler, T. R. (1994). Governing amid diversity: The effect of fair decisionmaking procedures on the legitimacy of government. *Law & Society Review, 28,* 809–831.

United States v. Currens, 290 F2d (3d Cir. 1961).

United States v. Hinckley, 525 F. Supp. 1342 (D.C. 1981).

Wahl, O. (1995). *Media madness: Public images of mental illness.* New Brunswick, NJ: Rutgers University Press.

Walker, L. E. (1979). *The battered woman.* New York: HarperCollins.

Walker, L. E. (1984). *The battered woman syndrome.* New York: Springer.

Walker, N. (1968). *Crime and insanity in England. Vol. I: The historical perspective.* Edinburgh, Scotland: Edinburgh University Press.

Watkins, J. G. (1984). The Bianchi (L. A. Hillside Strangler) Case: Sociopath or multiple personality? *The International Journal of Clinical and Experimental Hypnosis, 32,* 67–101.

Weems v. United States, 217 U.S. 349 (1910).

Weisberg, R. H. (1984). *The failure of the word: Protagonist as lawyer in modern fiction.* New Haven, CT: Yale University Press.

Westermann, C. (1984). *Genesis 1–11: A commentary* (J. J. Scullion, S.J., Trans.). Minneapolis, MN: Augsburg Publishing.

Wexler, D. (1972). Review of "Violence and the brain." *Harvard Law Review, 85,* 1489–1498.

White, G. M. (2000). Representing emotional meaning: Category, metaphor, schema, discourse. In M. Lewis & J. M. Haviland-Jones (Eds.), *Handbook of emotions* (2nd ed., pp. 30–44). New York: Guilford Press.

Wierzbicka, A. (1999). *Emotions across languages and cultures.* Cambridge, England: Cambridge University Press.

Winchester, S. (1998). *The professor and the madman: A tale of murder, insanity, and the making of the Oxford English Dictionary.* New York: HarperCollins.

Wittgenstein, L. (1958). *Philosophical investigations* (3rd ed., G. E. M. Anscombe, Trans.). New York: MacMillan.

Wolfgang, M. E. (1958). *Patterns in criminal homicide.* Philadelphia: University of Pennsylvania Press.

Wootton, B. (1959). *Social science and social pathology.* London: George Allen & Unwin.

Wrightsman, L. S., Greene, E., Nietzel, M. T., & Fortune, W. H. (2002). *Psychology and the legal system* (5th ed.). Belmont, CA: Wadsworth.

Wrightsman, L. S., & Kassin, S. M. (1993). *Confessions in the courtroom.* Newbury Park, CA: Sage.

Yates v. the State of Texas, Court of Appeals, First District of Texas (2005).

Zajonc, R. B. (1980). Feeling and thinking: Preferences need no inferences. *American Psychologist, 35,* 151–175.

Zajonc, R. B. (1984). On the primacy of affect. *American Psychologist, 39*, 117–123.

Zajonc, R. B. (2000). Feeling and thinking: Closing the debate over the independence of affect. In J. P. Forgas (Ed.), *Feeling and thinking: The role of affect in social cognition* (pp. 31–58). New York: Cambridge University Press.

Zillmann, D. (1979). *Hostility and aggression.* Hillsdale, NJ: Erlbaum.

TABLE OF AUTHORITIES

AUTHOR INDEX

SUBJECT INDEX

and murder, 117, 118, 121, 129, 131, 136

Common Law, The (Holmes), 31–32

Commonsense justice (CSJ), *xiv–xv*, 7–8, 129

    and black-letter law, 257

        and "impossible act" cases, 237–238, 258

        and objective vs. subjectivity, 236

    and degrees of culpability for homicides, 231

    determinative elements in, 229

    and "equalist" theory, 240

    on felony murder, 126

    in insanity cases, 167, 169, 174, 185–187, 196

    and Law's culpability schema, 253

    vs. Law's theories, 115

    and manslaughter, 132, 143–146

    on responsibility for self-control, 250–251

    on self-defense theory, 201–202, 203, 222, 223–224

    and victim relief, 114–115

    and "wild justice," 112

    See also Juries

Conclusive presumption, 126

Confessio Amantis (Gower), 119

Conspiratorial liability, 123

Constructive malice, and felony-murder doctrine, 124

Constructivist thesis, 87–88

Control

    and EED vs. insanity, 148

    of emotions, 76–78

        and evaluative process, 12

    and manslaughter, 151

    and time between provocation and killing, 135–136

    See also Self-control

Cook, Keenya, 168

Cooling (cooling-off) time, 81, 83, 86, 136

    and manslaughter, 133, 136–137

        and irresistible impulse, 151

    and Model Penal Code, 147

    and subjectivizing of time, 140, 141, 144

    in subjectivizing of provocation, 138

Cooper, Lord, 185, 186

"Cost" of crime, 87

Counter-ego-nucleus, 181–182, 199

    and defect of reason, 185

    examples of, 182–184

and social constructionist theory, 182

Counterfactual conditional situations, 249

Creighton, Dr. (Hadfield case witness), 161, 162, 163

Crimes

    vs. harms, 115

    hate crimes, 261

    as personal feuds, 111

Crime of Self-Defense, A: Bernhard Goetz and the Law on Trial (Fletcher), 203–204

Crimes of envy, 100–101

Crimes of passion, 150

    and manslaughter, 151

    provocations for, 103

Criminal act, deed–will conjunction necessary for (Blackstone), 210

Criminal law, 29, 30–31

    contradictions in, 255

    history of

        distinctions established, 120–122

        and felony murder, 122–125, 126–128, 129

        and malice, 116–120

        in 18th century, 125–126

        in "wild justice," 111–116

    lack of progress in, 22

    and space, 228

Critique of Pure Reason, The (Kant), 29. *See also* Kant, Immanuel

Cruel and unusual punishment, and social science analysis, 36

CSJ. *See* Commonsense justice

Culpability, 24, 252

    actus reus plus *mens rea* needed for, *xiii*

    for bringing about one's disability of mind, 168–169, 187, 197, 262

    and Cain vs. Abel, 4, 115, 255, 263

    coherent story of needed, 230

    contradictory bases of, 253

    and death penalty decision, 230–231

    degrees and types of (insanity defense), 167–168, 188

    and emotions, *xiii*, 5, 6, 21, 64, 228, 257

        and anger vs. fear, 11

        and Cain vs. Abel, 3–5

        chaotic theories of, *xiii–xiv*, 21–23

        and common law on manslaughter, 255–256

        and context (organizing stories), 104–107

        and folk conception, 64, 73, 255

        and madness, 15–21

Envy, 99–101
Epilepsy
    and mechanical causation, 262
    and violence, 74
Erskine (Hadfield's attorney), 19, 156, 198
    arguments of, 19–21, 163–166, 174,
        175–176, 178, 250, 262
        and delusions, 19–20, 163, 163–166,
            172, 175
        and "partial insanity," 158, 184
        and prototypes, 159
        and reason in questioning delusions,
            180
"Essay on Criticism" (Pope), 242
Euthanasia cases, 232
Evaluative view of emotions, 12, 81, 250–
    251, 262
Excuse
    emotions as bringing about, 65
    and justification, 206, 207, 208, 213
    psychologists' proffering of, 251
    and self-defense theory, 201, 222, 223
        for battered woman, 215, 221
        mistaken self-defense, 204
    and subjectivity, 202
Expert testimony
    on battered woman syndrome, 205, 215,
        216–217
    vs. junk science, 263
    and Pillsbury on capacity defenses, 38
    in Andrea Yates case, 192–193
Extreme emotional disturbance (EED) doc-
    trine, xiv, 11, 104, 117–118, 132,
        146–148, 151, 229, 256
    jurors' use of, 148–149, 151
    as subjective, 197

Faking, 169–171
    and Malvo, 172, 178
False-belief–delusion, 171
Fear, 53, 103–104
    and anger, 11, 53, 104
    as basic category, 92
    and EED defense, 149
    and mock manslaughter jury, 144
    in self-defense cases, 202, 218, 235
        Goetz case, 204
Federalist Papers, The, 31, 82
Feeling and Emotion: A History of Theories
    (Gardiner, Metcalf, and Beebe-Cen-
    ter), 49
Felony-murder, 122–125, 126, 129

    and "malice," 118
    mock jury trial on, 126–128
    in Pennsylvania law, 120
    Pillsbury on, 36–37
Felony prevention cases, 207, 208, 218–219
    vs. excuse for battered woman, 221
    self-defense as, 202
Female emotionality, folk conceptions of,
    63–64
Fernández Dols, José Miguel, 50
Fingarette, Herbert, 176, 177, 181, 185
Finkel, N. J.
    on battered women, 221
    on culpability in mistake cases, 244,
        245
    on expert testimony, 216
    and felony murder, 37, 128
    and insanity mock jury, 186, 198
    and insanity prototypes, 157, 159–160,
        194
    on justification, 220
    and manslaughter, 145
    and mechanistic hypothetical, 262
    on mistake vs. accident, 243
    on mistaken self-defense, 206, 211
    and negligence, 249
    on proportionate response, 214
    on right-to-die/euthanasia cases, 232
First movements, Stoics on, 77
Fisher (homicide defendant), 139–140
Five Books of Moses: A Translation With
    Commentary (Alter), 3
Fletcher, George, 45
    on Bedder case, 143
    and folk conceptions of emotion, 48
    on Goetz case, 203, 204, 251–252
    on improving law, xv, 9, 29, 257, 263
    and negligent mistakes, 242
    on objective basis of blameworthiness,
        222
    on psychology, 27–28, 45, 249–250,
        251, 252
    on self-control, 248
    on self-defense, 221
    on subjectivists, 222, 244–245
Folk psychology. See Psychology, folk
Folk theories, 253, 255
    on subjective nature of emotions, 258
    thinking vs. emotion in, 117
    and "wild justice," 112
Force metaphor for emotions, 57
Forfeiture, moral theory of, 219, 224

Free choice, and scientific explanation, 74
Free will, 37, 73
Freud, Sigmund, and Freudianism, 10, 57–58, 175, 176, 250
   and Hamlet, 247
   and Schreber, 182
   and Shakespeare, 178
Functionalism, and emotions, 93–95
Furiousus, 158

GBMI (Guilty but mentally ill) verdict, 188, 198
Gender
   and anger, 99
   and emotionality, 63
Genesis: A New Translation of the Classic Biblical Stories (Mitchell), 3
Genesis 1-11: A Commentary (Westermann), 3
Genetic abnormalities, 73–74
Genetic basis, for jealous violence, 102
Genius: A Mosaic of One Hundred Exemplary Creative Minds (Bloom), 178
George III (king of England), 159, 164
Getting Even: Forgiveness and its Limits (Murphy), 114
Gettysburg Address, 30
Gillespie, C. K., 205
Goetz, Bernhard, 203–204, 207, 208, 209, 210, 211, 212, 215, 235, 251–252
Golding, S. L., 187, 194
Gounagias (homicide defendant), 142, 143, 144–145, 234, 251
Gower, John, 119
Greenblatt, Stephen, 259, 260
Griggs, Esther, 173, 236
Groscup, Jennifer, 60, 157, 159–160, 194, 243, 244, 245
Gross, J. J., 77–78
Guilt
   act and intent conjoined for, 236
   as *actus reus* and *mens rea*, 228
   as extra-legal punishment (in mistaken self-defense), 212
   for failure of self-control, 248–249
   of Malvo, 168
Guilty but mentally ill (GBMI) verdict, 188, 198
Gurney, Edmund, 69

Hadfield, James, 19–21, 156–157, 158, 160–161, 162–163, 173–174, 197, 198

   and delusions, 19–20, 163–166, 172, 197
   and dispositional issue, 166–167
   and Malvo, 163, 172
   and *mens rea*, 229
   and reason, 180
   See also Erskine
Hale, Sir Matthew, 210, 243
Hallett, C. A., 180
Hallett, E. S., 180
Hamilton, Alexander, 31
Hamlet (Shakespeare), 246–248, 259–261
   Bloom on, 178, 181, 246, 248, 261
   and cause of disorder, 161
   and context, 137, 246
   distraction of, 22, 178–181
   and Hamlet as brooder, 11
   and malice of Claudius, 120
   and "overhearing," 159, 178, 199
   and revenge as duty, 125
   and self-deception, 177, 180–181
Handel, S. F., 186
Happiness, as basic category, 92
Harms, vs. crimes, 115
Hart, H. L. A., 115
Hasse, A. F., 185
Hastie, R., 105
Hate crimes, 261
Head–heart distinction, 59–62, 82
Hearst, Patricia, 154
Heat of passion, 10–11, 54, 81, 86, 132–133
   in manslaughter, *xiv*, 6, 11, 47, 132–133
      and irresistible impulse, 151–152
      and Pillsbury on emotion, 41
   as metaphor, 57
   and relative valuations, 85
Henry V (Shakespeare), 56
Hinckley case foreperson, 167
Holmes, J. G., 105
Holmes, Oliver Wendell, Jr., 31–32
Home, and retreat rule in self-defense, 209
Homer, 133, 136. *See also* Achilles
Homicide, reckless or negligent, 222
Honest and reasonable mistakes, 207, 243, 258
Honest but unreasonable mistake, 207, 222, 240, 243, 258
Hughes, K., 232
Hume, David
   and "emotion," 51–52
   on reason and passion, 60

Hunter, Edward, 154
Hurabiell, M., 232
Hysteria, hydraulic model of, 58

Idealized individuals, 194
Ideas of reference delusion, 183
Idiothetic viewpoint, 12, 136, 141
IDRA (Insanity Defense Reform Act)
    (1984), 185, 186, 188, 198
Ignorance, Model Penal Code on, 249
Iliad (Homer), 133, 134, 158, 159. *See also*
    Achilles
Impaired capacity defenses, and Pillsbury, 38–
    40
Imperfect self-defense, 222
Impossible act cases, 236–239, 258
Individual variability, as psychological re-
    search finding, 250
Infanticide, 191–192
Informational words exception, 138–139
Information processing, cognition as, 79, 80
"Insane actor," 199
Insanity defense, 6, 17–18, 122, 152, 155–
    156, 173–174, 178
    and blameworthiness, 195–197
    brainwashing as, 154–155, 156
        Malvo's claim of, 153
        success rate for, 172
    commonsense justice perspective on,
        167, 169, 174, 185–187, 196
    and confounding factors, 166
        "after issue" (dispositional issue) of
            results of verdict, 166–167
        and culpability for submitting to de-
            terioration, 168–169, 187
        degree or types of culpability, 167–
            168
        faking as possibility, 169–171, 172
        false-belief–delusion, 171
    Congressional endeavors on, 197–198
    and counter-ego-nucleus, 181–184
    and "defect of reason" (Ray), 184–185,
        198–199
    and disease model, 251
    and dissociative disorders, 172–173
    dissonant views on, 187–188
    and distraction, 178–181
    Erskine's theory on, 19–21, 163–166,
        174, 175–176, 178, 250, 262
        and delusions, 19–20, 163, 163–166,
            172, 175
        and "partial insanity," 158, 184

and reason in questioning delusions,
    180
as excusing defense, 202, 204
and failure to exercise self-control, 245
and "insane actor," 199
and irresistible impulse, 47
jurors not predisposed toward, 216
lack of progress on, 198, 201
for Malvo, 153, 174, 230, 230 (*see also*
    Malvo, Lee Boyd)
and manslaughter, 134, 137, 152
and *mens rea*, 229
need to rework. 199
and Othello, 15
past history vs. moment of act in, 160–
    163
and Pillsbury, 39
and prototypes of insanity, 157–160
    and fakers, 169, 172
and psychological spacetime, 235
questions on, 156–157
and self-deception, 176–177
and self-defense, 199, 202, 211, 218, 222
    and battered women, 205, 215, 216
and subjective mistakes, 242–243
wild-beast test in, 6, 18–19, 39, 47–48,
    157, 158, 159, 186, 192, 194
and Andrea Yates case, 188–195
    citizens' response to, 196
    and expert witnesses, 198
Insanity Defense Reform Act (IDRA)
    (1984), 185, 186, 188, 198
Intellect
    vs. passions, 51, 53–55, 59
    See also Cognition; Reason
Intent(s), 228–229
    as absent in stressful situations (Singer),
        150
    and distinction between Muhammad
        and Malvo, 232
    and failure of self-control, 248, 249
    general, 23
    in "impossible act" cases, 236, 237, 239
    vs. motive, 261
    purposeful (Model Penal Code), 231,
        232
    recommendations on, 257–258
    in self-defense cases, 221
    specific, 23
    subjective element inadequate in, 236
    See also Mens rea; Motives and motiva-
        tion

Intentionality, cognitive, 23
Interpersonal cases, 83
Irrationality
    and belief in emotions, 80
    and emotionality, 62–63
"Irresistible impulse," 6, 47
    and heat of passion, 151–152
"Irresistible motive"
    in *Hadfield's Case*, 20–21, 163, 165–166, 250
Is–ought divide, *xv*, 9, 24
    and Pillsbury on the Law, 33
    and psychology, 28, 37
    and realist movement, 32

James, William, 68–69, 93
Jay, John, 31
Jealousy, 101–103
    and EED defense, 149
    and envy, 99–100, 101–102
    and Othello, *xiv*, 13–15, 22, 85
Jefferson, Thomas, 29
Jones, Jim, 155
Jordan, S. B., 205
Judging Evil: Rethinking the Law of Murder and Manslaughter (Pillsbury), 28
Judgment, and emotion, 82
Julius Caesar (Shakespeare), 100
Juries
    and commonsense justice, 7–8
    culpability calculus of, 17
    death-qualified, 126, 191, 195
    decision-making process of, 30
    defendants judged by as well as actions, 192
    and disconnect between black-letter law and commonsense justice, 257
    and folk conceptions of emotion, 48
    historical advent of, 115
    in insanity cases, 160, 161–162, 174
        constrained choices for, 167, 185
        and judges' instructions, 185–186, 187
        prototype bias of, 187
        and types or gradations of culpability, 188
    and mistaken self-defense, 206
    mock juries on felony murder, 126–128, 231
    mock juries in "impossible act" cases, 237, 238, 239, 258
    mock juries on insanity defense, 235

mock juries on manslaughter, 143–146, 250–251
mock juries on mercy killing, 233–234
mock juries on negligence cases, 243
mock juries on rape case, 240–241
mock juries on self-control, 245
mock juries on self-defense claims, 224
    and battered woman syndrome, 215, 216–217, 218
    mistaken self-defense, 211–213, 214
    and subjective vs. objective approaches, 222
    and victim's culpability in battered-woman cases, 219
and motive, 261
narrative organization imposed by, 105
nullification by, 8, 22, 31
    Law's interest in preventing, 224
    in mock trial for felony murder, 127, 128
    in mock trial on mercy killing, 233
objective–subjective balance of (extreme emotional disturbance), 149
and racial animus as element, 261–262
subjective vantage point of, 141
See also Commonsense justice
Jury instructions, 31
Justification defense
    and excuse, 206, 207, 208, 213
    objective factors primary in, 202
    and self-defense theory, 201
        and battered women, 219–221

Kahan, D. M., 12, 81, 85, 86, 87, 88, 89
Kant, Immanuel
    on perception and apperception, 223, 239
    and Pillsbury, 34
    on punishment, 33
    on "radical evil," 44
    on thought and content, 29
Kenyon, Judge, 166–167
King John (Shakespeare), 55
King Lear (Shakespeare), 260
King Richard The Third (Shakespeare), 116, 119, 125
King's Peace, 113, 116
Kirson, D., 92
Kövecses, Zoltan, 57, 58–59
Kyd, Thomas, 179, 259

Language, confusion in interpreting of, 31

Mens rea, xiii, 9, 22, 23, 117, 125, 129, 161, 228, 229
   actus reus in absence of, 196
   actus reus entwined with, 239
   in 18th-century law, 121
   and emotions, 48
   in "impossible act" cases, 258
   in insanity cases, 160
   and mock jurors on sensitivity, 146
   and Model Penal Code on murder, 132
   and motives, 40, 42–43, 44
   and Othello, 17
   recommendations on, 257–258
   subjective analysis of, 134, 135
      in manslaughter, 150
   subjective element inadequate in, 236
Mentally retarded individuals, and Pillsbury, 39
Mental state-centered (MSC) prototype, 194, 195
Merchant of Venice, The (Shakespeare), 55
Merry, Sally Engle, 82–83
Metaphor, in folk psychology of emotions, 57–59, 81
   of emotions as bodily, 81
Meta-responsibility, 187
Mind (journal), 69
Mindszenty, Cardinal, 154
Mind That Found Itself, A (Beers), 183
Minor, W. C., 184
Mistake(s), 242–243
   vs. accident, 242, 243–244
   delusional, 212 (see also Delusions)
   dishonest, 258
   dishonest but reasonable, 220
   dubious, 212
   honest and reasonable, 207, 243, 258
   honest but unreasonable, 207, 222, 240, 243, 258
   Model Penal Code on, 248–249
   negligent, 242–244
   reasonable, 212, 240
   unreasonable, 212
Mistaken self-defense, 206–207, 213
   and battered women, 205
   and Goetz, 203–204, 251–252
   and justification vs. excuse, 223
   requirements of, 207–214
Mitchell, Stephen, 3
M'Naghten's Rules, 17–18, 185, 188, 190–191, 198
Mock juries. See under Juries

Model Penal Code
   cognition emphasized in, 125–126
   on divisions of criminal homicide, 120
   on extreme emotional disturbance, xiv, 11, 117–118, 256 (see also Extreme emotional disturbance doctrine)
   and felony murder, 122, 129
   on hierarchy of culpability, 42
   insanity test of (ALI), 185, 188, 198
   and intent or intentionality, 23, 228, 231, 232
   and malice, 118–119, 119–120
   on manslaughter, xiv, 132, 146, 147, 151
   and mens rea, 23
   on mistake, 248–249
   on murder, 117, 118, 129, 132
      and evolution of first-degree murder, 121
   on murder and manslaughter, 81
   on reckless or negligent homicide, 222
   and retreat requirement in self-defense cases, 209
   on self-defense, 206, 214
Muhammad, John Allen, 52, 153, 155, 157, 168, 173, 230, 231, 232, 234
Moore, M. S., 186
Moral choice, vs. moral capacity, 37–40
Moral commitment, 114
Moral forfeiture, 219, 224
Morality
   and counter-ego-nucleus, 182
   vs. law (Hamlet), 179
   and law (Pillsbury), 42
   and psychology (Fletcher), 27–28
   vs. scientific method, 24
   See also Value(s)
Moral judgment, and emotions, 40
Morally insane (MI) prototype, 194
Moral meaning or significance
   of emotions, 107
   and motive, 261
Morgan (rape defendant), 240
Motives and motivation, 20, 232, 259–260
   in death penalty phase, 231
   of hate crimes, 261–262
   of husband in hypothetical mercy killing, 234
   vs. intent, 229, 261
   irresistible (Hadfield's Case), 20, 163, 165–166, 250
   of Leopold and Loeb, 38

and Pillsbury, 40, 41, 42–43, 259
results of removal of, 261
and Shakespeare, 260
of Hamlet, 260–261
Movie westerns, and "reach" as pretext for
shooting, 208
MSC (mental state-centered) prototype, 194,
195
Multiple personality disorder, and Malvo,
173
Murder
common law on, 117, 118, 121, 129,
131, 136
of envy, 101
history of
distinctions established, 120–122
and felony murder, 122–125, 126–
128, 129
and malice, 116–120
in 18th century, 125–126
in "wild justice," 111–116
Model Penal Code on, 117, 118, 129,
132
and evolution of first-degree murder,
121
vs. voluntary manslaughter, 80–81
Murder, first-degree, 129
and cool deliberation vs. hot emotions,
122
and emotions, 6, 118
Murder, second-degree
depraved-heart, 47, 117, 121–122, 123
emotions in, 6
and Othello, 14
*Murdering Mothers: Infanticide in England and
New England, 1558–1803* (Hoffer
and Hull), 191
Murdrum, 112–113
Murphy, Jeffrie, 114
Murray, James, 183–184
Myths, of insanity, 158

Narrative mode of thinking, 106
Narrative structure
of emotions, 96–97, 104–107
in insanity cases, 163
by mock manslaughter jury, 144–145
Negligence, 258
and failure of self-control, 248–249
and sensitivity to/from provocation, 144
Negligent mistakes, responsibility for, 242–
244

New York Court of appeals, and mistaken
self-defense case, 211
NGRI (not guilty by reason of insanity), 15,
196
as excusing condition, 16
and GBMI verdict, 198
for Hadfield, 156
and mistaken self-defense, 206
and motive, 259
and true vs. fake cases, 160
and types or gradations of judgments,
188
and women who kill, 205
NGRSD (not guilty by reason of self-defense), 206
and women who kill, 205
Nietzsche, Friedrich, 4
19th-century four, 103
Nisbett, R. E., 99
No bullets case, 236, 238, 238–239
Nomothetic theory or viewpoint, 12, 14, 134,
136, 150
Nonculpable–culpable actions construct,
186–187
Normative realm, and Law vs. psychology, 9
Normative view of law, 27–28
and criminal law, 29, 30
and national values, 29–30
and Pillsbury's theory of deserved punishment, 33–34, 44–45
on emotions and motives, 40–44
and moral choice vs. moral capacity, 37–40
and values, 34–37
psychology in, 28, 29
and Pillsbury, 33–34, 40, 43–44, 86
and realist movement, 32
See also Is–ought divide
Norms. *See* Cultural or social norms
Not guilty by reason of insanity verdict. *See*
NGRI
Not guilty by reason of self-defense verdict.
See NGRSD
Nussbaum, Martha, 12, 49, 50, 81, 85, 86,
88, 89

Oakley, Justin, 107
Oatley, Keith, 72
Objective reasonable person, 202
Objectivity and objective perspective
and *actus reus*, xiii
and anger, 86

in common law on manslaughter, 132–138, 255–256
and delusions, 191
in emotions, 11, 101, 258–259
of expert witness in Andrea Yates trial, 193
and extreme emotional disturbance, 149
and insanity defense, 197
and judgments of "reasonable," 206
and justifying defense, 202
and mechanistic view, 12, 83
and mistaken self-defense, 204
in perpetrator-by-means rape case (Morgan), 241–242
in self-defense cases, 210, 223
  and mock jury, 212–213, 222
and subjectivity, 82–84, 196, 229
  and battle over legal rules, 22
  conjoining of recommended, 263
  in "impossible act" cases, 236–239
  and mistakes, 242
  need for unification of, 229–230, 258
  and passage of time, 140, 141, 144–145
  as simplistic, *xiv*
O'Connor, C., 92
Offenders Bill (1800), 167
Organic brain disorder, 162–163, 165
Othello, *xiii*, *xiv*, 13–15, 16–17, 21, 22, 43, 85, 169, 242, 260
Other(s)
  culpability of, 232, 258
    in negligence case, 244
  lack of regard for (Hamlet), 246–48
  and Muhammad's relation to Malvo, 230, 231
  wife killed in mercy killing as, 234
"Overhearing," 159, 178, 199

Papez, J. W., 93
Paradigmatic mode of thinking, 106
Parrott, W. G., 62, 75, 96, 249
Passion(s)
  and cognition, 53–55
    and as bodily, 80
  crimes of, 103, 150, 151
  and desires or motives, 49
  and emotions, 50–52
  vs. intellect, 51, 53–55, 59
  moralizing of (Pillsbury), 40
  origin of word, 51

and *pathē*, 49, 53
and reason (Hume), 60
and scientific research on emotions, 68
violence as, 88
See also Emotion(s); Heat of passion
Pathē, 49, 53
Pennington, N., 105
Pennsylvania, divisions of murder in, 120, 125
Perelman, S. J., 114
Perpetrator-by-means, 231, 240, 241
  Iago as, 17, 169
"Person in context" view, 245–246, 256
Personhood, and insanity, 152
Physics, search for coherence in contrasted with Law, 227
Pillsbury, Samuel, 24, 28, 33, 48, 232, 249
Pillsbury's normative theory of deserved punishment, 33–34, 44–45
  on emotions, 40–44
  and moral choice vs. moral capacity, 37–40
  on motives, 40, 41, 42–43, 259
  and psychology, 40, 43–44, 67, 86
  and values, 34–37
Planfulness, 17, 19, 159
  and insanity claim, 170
  of Andrea Yates, 190, 191, 192
  and judgment on infanticides, 192
  of Morgan, 242
Plato
  on emotions, 53
  and lawmaking, 30
  and passions, 51
  on reason as charioteer, 54
Pleas of the Crown (East), 222
Poetry, Eliot on, 60
Polygraphs, 170
Pope, Alexander, 242
Posidonius, 54
Posner, R. A., Judge, 36
Posttraumatic stress disorder, 104
  battered woman syndrome as, 215
  and Goetz hypothetical, 251–252
Pound, Roscoe, 32
Pragmatics, of the word *emotion*, 66
Premeditation, 121
  and "aforethought," 118
  and emotions of serial killers, 6
  and murder–manslaughter contradiction, 136
  See also Cooling time; Deliberation

Psychopaths, and Pillsbury, 38
Punishment
    and anger, 98
    Kant on, 33
    Pillsbury's normative theory of, 33–45
Putative self-defense, 222

Racial animus, 261
Rape law, 35–36
Rawls, John, *xv*, 9, 247, 257
Ray, Isaac, 184–185
Realist movement, 32
Reason (rationality)
    defect of, 184–185, 198–199
    and distraction, 181
    vs. emotion, 53–55
    and emotional control (Stoics), 77
    and Erskine on delusion, 165, 175
    in evaluative process, 12
    and gender, 63
    and Hamlet's madness, 180
    and manslaughter, 150, 151–152
    and passions (Hume) 60
    and time between provocation and kill-
        ing, 135–136
    See also Cognition(s); Intellect
Reasonable behavior, conventional expecta-
        tions of, 245
"Reasonable mistake" condition, 212
    and Morgan case, 240
Reasonable person standard, 202, 211
    and battered woman syndrome, 215–
        216
    subjective and objective interpretations
        of, 206
    subjectivizing of (battered women), 213,
        214
Recklessness, and sensitivity to/from provo-
        cation, 144
Recommendations for the Law, 257–258, 263
*Reconstructing Reality in the Courtroom: Jus-
        tice and Judgment in American Cul-
        ture* (Bennett and Feldman), 259
Rekindlers or rekindling, 137–138, 140, 146
    and *Gounagias* case, 144, 234
    and past provocations, 142
Relativistic perspective, 228, 229, 230
    in *Gounagias* case, 234
Religion, in "expert testimony" on Andrea
        Yates, 193
Responsibility
    diminished, 122

and emotions, 73–76
    cognitive nature of, 81–82
    as folk-psychology concern, 48
    and scientific explanation, 74
    See also Culpability; Guilt
Ressentiment, 4
Retreat, in self-defense cases, 208–210
Revenge killing
    and battered woman cases, 211
    and EED defense, 149
    and Goetz, 203
    and Hamlet, 22, 125, 177, 259, 261
    and *Hamlet*'s audience, 179
Revenger's Tragedy, The (Tourneur), 179
Revision of law, along commonsense lines,
        8. *See also* Recommendations for the
        Law
Right-to-die cases, 232
Roberts, C. F., 195
Robinson, D. N., 158, 164
Robinson, Paul, 169, 187, 209, 211, 214
Romantic movement, 53
Rousseau, Jean-Jacques, *xv*, 9, 263
Royley, John, 138–139, 151
Rule of law, 257

Sabat, S. R., 182
Sadness, as basic category, 92
Sartre, Jean-Paul, 176–177, 241
Saxo the Grammarian, 259
Schadenfreude, 100
Schneider, E. M., 205
Schoeck, Helmut, 100–101
Schopp, R. F., 219–221
Schreber, Paul, 182–183
Schuller, R. A., 217
Schwartz, J., 92
Science, and the normative, 68
Scientific method, vs. morality, 24
Se defendendo cases, 201, 202, 207, 208, 218–
        219
Self-control, 258
    culpable failure of, 244–246, 248, 249,
        252–253
    as fundamental element, 245
    psychology on responsibility for, 248–
        251
    and victimology view, 252
    See also Control
Self-deception, 175, 176, 181
    and Erskine's theory of insanity, 176
    and Hamlet, 177, 180–181

Self-defense, 6, 16, 201–202
 by battered women, 202, 204–205, 207
  as excuse not justification, 221–222
  and moral forfeiture, 219, 224
  motives of, 211, 220–221, 222
  and proportionate response, 213–214
  as reasonable choice among alternatives, 219–221
  and retreat issue, 210
  variance among, 218–219
 and citizens' attitudes, 195
 commonsense justice on, 201–202, 203, 222, 223–224
 elements of, 202–203, 223
 and failure to exercise self-control, 245
 and fear, 104
 felony prevention as, 202, 207
 and "impossible act" cases, 239
 and insanity defense, 199, 202, 211, 222
  and battered woman syndrome, 205, 215, 216
 mistaken, 206–207
  and battered women, 205
  and Goetz, 203–204, 251–252
  and justification vs. excuse, 223
  requirements of, 207–214
  and need for intermediate mitigating verdict option, 222–223, 224
  and psychiatric syndrome, 214–215
  battered woman syndrome, 215–218
 putative, 222
 and subjective mistakes, 242–243
Self 1, Self 2, Self 3, 182
 in Andrea Yates, 188, 189
Self-overhearing, 178. See also "Overhearing"
Self-regulation, of emotion, 96
Seligman, Martin, 252
Semantics, of the word emotion, 66
Senate Judiciary Committee, and victims-rights amendment, 112
Senate Subcommittee on Criminal Law of the Committee of the Judiciary, insanity-defense hearings of, 197–198
 foreperson testimony to on constrained choices, 167, 185
Seneca, 54, 77
Serial killers, 6, 73
Severely mentally disabled (SMD) prototype, 194
Shakespeare, William, xiii–xiv, 9–10, 22, 55–56, 82, 89, 106, 119, 125, 129 , 178,

259, 260. See also Hamlet; King John; King Lear; King Richard the Third; Macbeth; Othello
Shaver, P., 92, 95, 102
Shields, Stephanie, 63
Singer, Margaret Thaler, 154
Singer, Richard, 117, 135, 138, 147, 150, 222, 248–249
Skeem, J. L., 187, 194
Smith, S. F., 128
Smith, William (homicide defendant), 139
Sniper murders in DC area, 153. See also Malvo, Lee Boyd; Muhammad, John Allen
Social constructionist theory, 87–88, 182
Social Contract (Rousseau), 263
Social influence, 87
Social meaning, 87
Social (societal) role
 emotion as, 59
  and anger, 84
  and head–heart distinction, 62
Sociological jurisprudence, 32
Sociology, and law, 32
Sorabji, Richard, 49, 50
Spacetime, psychological. See Psychological spacetime
Spackman, Matthew, 75, 145
Spanish Tragedy, The (Kyd), 179
Spencer, Herbert, 68
Stephen, James Fitzjames, 27, 36
Stoics, 41, 49, 51, 54, 77
Storytelling, 105
Straw-man arguments,
 of Fletcher on psychology, 250
 on psychology as mechanistic, 41
Strict liability offense, 115
 and DQ jurors, 195
 felony murder as, 124
Stutz, Michael, 60
Subjectivity and subjective perspective
 and actus reus, 236
 and battered woman self-defense, 205
 and blameworthiness (Fletcher), 222
 and emotions, 11, 101, 258–259
 and evaluative theory, 12
 and excusing defense, 202
 and extreme emotional disturbance, 146–149, 151
 and Hamlet, 246, 248
 and insanity defense, 155, 197, 242–243
  and delusions, 165, 191, 192

ABOUT THE AUTHORS

Norman J. Finkel, PhD, is a professor of psychology at Georgetown University in Washington, DC. He received his PhD in clinical psychology from the University of Rochester in 1971 and has been at Georgetown ever since, where he recently received the Dean's Award for Teaching Excellence (2005–2006). His scholarly interests are in the area of psychology, public policy, and law, looking at ordinary citizens' (jurors') views of justice, fairness, rights, and duties, what he calls "commonsense justice," and how these views compare and contrast with black-letter law. His empirical work has focused on such areas as insanity, infanticide, self-defense, capital felony-murder, the juvenile death penalty, manslaughter, and rights and duties—areas and issues at the empirical–normative nexus. His books include *Insanity on Trial* (1988), *Commonsense Justice: Jurors' Notions of the Law* (1995), and *Not Fair! The Typology of Commonsense Unfairness* (American Psychological Association, 2001), and he has recently published an edited volume (with Fathali Moghaddam), *The Psychology of Rights and Duties: Empirical Contributions and Normative Commentaries* (American Psychological Association, 2005). He is a coeditor of *Law and Public Policy: Psychology and the Social Sciences*, a book series published by the American Psychological Association.

W. Gerrod Parrott, PhD, is a professor of psychology at Georgetown University in Washington, DC. He received his doctorate in psychology from the University of Pennsylvania in 1985. After 2 years of postdoctoral research at the University of Illinois at Urbana–Champaign, he joined the faculty at Georgetown. His scholarly interest is in the nature of human emotion, especially emotion's social foundations, functions, and dysfunctions. These interests have led to research focusing on envy, jealousy, shame, embarrassment, and guilt as well as research on the influence of emotion and emotional self-regulation on thought. He is the author of more than 60 scholarly articles and is editor of two books: *Emotions in Social Psychology: Essential Readings* (2001) and, with Rom Harré, *The Emotions: Social, Cultural and Biological Dimensions* (1996). He served as editor of the journal *Cognition and Emotion* from 1995 through 1999.